IMMIGRANT WOMEN

SUNY Series in Ethnicity and Race in American Life
John Sibley Butler, editor

IMMIGRANT WOMEN

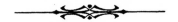

Edited by Maxine Schwartz Seller

REVISED, SECOND EDITION

State University of New York Press

Published by
State University of New York Press, Albany

For information, address State University of New York Press,
State University Plaza, Albany, N.Y., 12246

Production by Cathleen Collins
Marketing by Dana Yanulavich

Library of Congress Cataloging in Publication Data

Immigrant women / edited by Maxine Schwartz Seller.
        p.   cm. — (SUNY series in ethnicity and race in American
   life)
    Includes bibliographical references and index.
    ISBN 0-7914-1903-7. — ISBN 0-7914-1904-5 (pbk.)
    1. Women immigrants—United States—Social conditions.   2. Women
immigrants—United States—History—19th century.   3. Women
immigrants—United States—History—20th century.   4. Women
immigrants—United States—Biography.   I. Seller, Maxine, 1935–   .
II. Series.
HQ1410.I43 1994
305.42—dc20   93–25028
                                                                  CIP

10 9 8 7 6 5 4 3 2 1

*In memory
of my grandmothers,
Lena Wolk
and
Annie Schwartz*

Contents

CONTENTS   ix

CONTENTS

Introduction

Millions of women left their homes in Europe, Asia, and Latin America to immigrate to the United States in the nineteenth and twentieth centuries. Many hoped that life in America would be better, not only for their families but also for themselves as women. Often their hopes were nourished by their initial encounter with America, as is evident in the following passage, written by Slovenian immigrant Marie Prisland:

> A group of Slovenian immigrants, of which this writer was one, arrived in New York from that part of Austria which presently is the territory of Yugoslavia. It was a beautiful morning, in May 1906. After leaving the French ship La Tourairle, we were transported to Ellis Island for landing and inspection. There we were "sorted out" as to the country we came from. . . .
>
> There were at least a hundred Slovenian immigrants. We separated ourselves, as was the custom at home—men on the right and women and children on the left. All of us were waiting to leave for all parts of the United States.
>
> The day was warm and we were very thirsty. An English-speaking immigrant asked the near-by guard where we could get a drink of water. The guard withdrew and returned shortly with a pail of water, which he set before the group of women. Some men stepped forward quickly to have a drink, but the guard pushed them back saying: "Ladies first!" When the women learned what the guard had said, they were dumbfounded, for in Slovenia, as in all Europe, women always were second to men. Someone dramatically explained it this way: "First comes man, then a long time nothing, then comes the woman."
>
> Happy at the sudden turn of events, one elderly lady stepped forward, holding a dipper of water, and proposed this toast:
>
> "Zivijo Amerika, kjer so zenske prve!" (Long live America, where women are first!)[1]

For Prisland, who later founded the Slovenian Women's Union of America and created a woman's magazine, *The Dawn*, the American dream became a reality. Not all immigrant women were so fortunate. For many, life in

1

the United States was bitter and the slogan, "ladies first," cruelly ironic. "Ladies" were first to be underpaid, unemployed, and abused.

Bitterness is the lot of young Jewish immigrant Sara Smolinsky, the central figure in Anzia Yezierska's semiautobiographical novel, *Bread Givers*. Sara lives in near starvation on the meager wages she earns doing "woman's work"—ironing in a commercial laundry. When she accidentally scorches a shirt, her employer deducts three dollars from her wage of five dollars, condemning her to a diet of bread and water for weeks to come.

A terrible hunger rose up in me. . . . The starvation of days and weeks began tearing and dragging down my last strength. Let me at least have one dinner with meat . . . for that last hour of work, I saw before my eyes meat, only meat, great big chunks of it. And I biting into the meat.

Like a wolf with hunger, I ran to the cafeteria. . . .

At last I reached the serving table.

"Stew with a lot of meat in it."

Breathlessly, I watched how far the spoon would go into the pot. A hot sweat broke over my face as I saw the mean hunks of potato and the skinny strings of meat floating in the starched gravy which she [the server] handed me.

"Please, won't you put in one real piece of meat?" and I pushed back the plate for more.

I might as well have talked to the wall. She did not see me or hear me. Her eyes were smiling back to the fat man behind me [in the food line] who grinned knowingly at her.

"Stew," was all he said.

She picked up my plate, pushed the spoon deep down into the pot and brought it up heaping with thick chunks of meat.

"Oh, thank you! Thank you! I'll take it now," I cried, reaching for it with both hands.

"No, you don't." And the man took the plate from the server and set it on his tray.

Speechless, bewildered, I stood there, unable to move. . . .

"But you didn't give me as much as you gave him. Isn't my money as good as his?"

"Don't you know they always give men more?" called a voice from the line. . . .

"But why did she give more to the man just because he was a man. I'm hungry."

All the reply I got was a cold glance. "Please move on or step out of line."

People began to titter and stare at me. . . .

I was too trampled to speak. With tight lips I walked out . . .
boiling with hate for the whole world.
In my room, I found the tail end of a loaf of bread. Each bite
I swallowed was wet with my tears.[2]

The immigrant woman's encounter with America, for better or for worse, was not the same as the immigrant man's. Like the men, the women faced poverty, loneliness, discrimination, and physical danger as they struggled to build new lives in a new land. But their identity as women shaped the roles, opportunities, and experiences available to them in the family, the workplace, the community, and the nation. Much of the voluminous literature on immigration has been male-centered, taking men's experience as the norm and assuming that women's experience was either identical to men's or not important enough to warrant separate and serious attention. Using documents written by immigrant women themselves, or by others who knew them intimately, *Immigrant Women* offers a different perspective, a woman-centered perspective on American immigration history.

Women as Immigrants

Between 1820 and the mid-1970s over 46 million immigrants entered the United States: 35 million from Europe, 8 million from Latin America, Canada, and the Caribbean, 2 million from Asia, and half a million from Africa, Australia, and elsewhere.[3] In the 1980s legal (documented) immigrants, illegal (undocumented) immigrants, and refugees numbered from half a million to a million each year, most of them from Latin America and Asia. Peak immigration periods for men have not always coincided with those for women, however. During the nineteenth and early twentieth centuries, male immigrants outnumbered females by roughly three to two, while among Asian and some eastern European groups the preponderance of men was even greater. By 1920, however, women outnumbered men among West Indians, Bohemians, and Jews, and from World War II into the 1990s, the majority of immigrants were women.[4]

Women outnumbered men among the Irish who came to the United States in the nineteenth century to escape destitution. During the anti-Semitic massacres in the dying years of czarist Russia, almost as many women as men fled for their lives to the United States. On the other hand, in the early twentieth century southern Italian, Polish, and other Slavic male immigrants outnumbered their female counterparts five to one because of the attraction of "male" jobs in mining, construction, and heavy industry. By mid-century, however, many of these jobs had been automated out of existence, and a rising demand for service workers of all kinds created an American labor market more favorable to women. This mid-twentieth-century labor market was especially attractive to Third World women. Many of these women were displaced from their traditional occupations as their countries modernized but were not provided the same job opportunities as men in the new economic order.[5]

Immigration policy, as well as economic development, sometimes affected women differently than men. Reflecting racist views on Asian sexuality, a special act of Congress in 1870 gave immigration officials in California the right to determine whether an incoming woman (but not an incoming man) was "a person of correct habits and good character," an indignity that helped discourage the immigration of Asian women. Discrimination against women was carried further by the Chinese Exclusion Act of 1882, which restricted Chinese immigration to a very small number of students and merchants, effectively shutting women out altogether. In the 1900 Census there was only one Chinese female to every twenty-six Chinese males in the United States; the Chinese community remained heavily male until after World War II.[6] Folksongs express the frustration and sorrow of the many wives left behind:

I am still young, with a husband, yet a widow.
The pillow is cold, so frightening.

O, don't every marry a daughter to a man from Gold Mountain,
Lonely and sad, her only companion is her cooking pot.[7]

The National Origins Quota legislation of the mid-1920s barred all immigration from Asia, preventing Japanese as well as Chinese women from joining their countrymen. Favoring western Europeans over the supposedly inferior eastern Europeans, it also kept southern Italian and Slavic women from immigrating to join male relatives. By mid-century, however, immigration policy was more favorable to women. Special legislation admitted World War II "war brides," many of them Asian, and subsequent laws admitting displaced persons and refugees were gender neutral. New immigration laws passed in 1965 gave preference to relatives of persons already in the United States, regardless of gender or country of birth.

Women came to the United States to escape the economic, political, and religious oppression that all immigrants faced in their native lands. Many also came to escape forms of oppression unique to them as women. For example, some nineteenth-century Scandinavian servant girls fled sexual harassment, others unequal wages and working conditions that were more difficult than those endured by their male counterparts.[8] Marie Zakrzewska, who became a noted physician and medical educator, emigrated from Berlin in 1853 because women could not become physicians there.[9] Future trade-union organizer Rose Pesotta left Russia at seventeen because she could see "no future for myself except to marry some young man returned from his four years of military service and to be a housewife. That is not enough."[10]

A Korean "picture bride" married an unknown man in America to escape the social restrictions of her homeland: "Since I became ten, I've been forbidden to step outside our gates, just like all the rest of the girls of my day. . . . Becoming a picture bride, whatever that was, would be my answer and release."[11]

In the New Land

Women's adjustment to life in the United States, like their immigration, often differed from that of men. Most women were, or soon became, wives and mothers. Housework, pregnancy, childbirth, and childcare gave their lives dimensions of pleasure and pain not shared even by the men closest to them. Sometimes pregnancy was an intolerable burden, to be avoided or terminated regardless of the disapproval of husband, church, or state. More often, children were the welcomed antidote of the loneliness of immigration; "having my own baby, that was heaven," wrote a Bulgarian immigrant.[12] Children were also a link to the new world and an important factor in the Americanization of the immigrant homemaker.

In the workforce as in the family, women usually fared differently than men. Whether they arrived in the nineteenth or the twentieth centuries, from Europe, Asia, or Latin America, most women took jobs in areas related to traditional women's occupations: domestic service or needlework. Like their predecessors, many of the Hispanic and Asian women who immigrated after 1965 became "sewing women," but others moved into newer female occupations. In the late 1980s, 90 percent of the workers in California's Silicon Valley electronics industry were women, about half of them Filipinas, Vietnamese, Koreans, and South Asians.[13]

Though many women needed to earn a living, typically their job opportunities were fewer than men's; between 1845 and 1859 the Boston Society for the Prevention of Pauperism received applications for employment from 14,000 women "foreigners" (mainly Irish) as opposed to 5,034 men.[14] Typically, too, their wages were lower. In the famous 1913 "Protocol in the Dress and Waist Industry" (won largely through the efforts of militant women workers), labor and management reserved the highly skilled job of "cutter," at $27.50 a week, for men only. The jobs of "finisher," "examiner," and "sample maker," at $9.50, $11.50, and $13.00 respectively, were reserved for women.[15] Mostly nonunionized, contemporary Asian women workers in the electronics industry endure forced overtime, work speedups, and health hazards for minimum wages and with little chance for advancement.

The differences between women's and men's roles at home and in the workforce were reinforced by women's differential and inferior access to education. Early twentieth-century Americanization programs for men offered instruction in industrial skills, civics, and English. Parallel programs for women, fewer in number, were usually limited to American-style domestic skills and "pots and pans" English. Robert Woods, an authority in settlement work, spoke for many educators when he suggested in 1903 that the education of immigrant girls in the public schools and settlement houses have a similar domestic focus because "the girls can discuss sewing and cooking with their mothers when they have no language to discuss trade winds and syntax."[16] Time did not necessarily alleviate the problem. In the 1970s and 1980s women refugees from Southeast Asia faced discrimination in government-sponsored language and job training programs. The need to find and pay babysitters further restricted some women's access to education, as did fear of venturing out at night in dangerous neighborhoods.

Even nativist prejudice affected women differently than men. Foreign-born men from many countries of origin have been characterized at different times as drunkards, brutes, criminals, and political radicals. Just as consistently—and with evidence just as scanty—immigrant women have been characterized in equivalent "female" terms: as loose women, poor housekeepers, and bad mothers. During the rapid urbanization of the early twentieth century, eastern European immigrant women were blamed for a real or imagined decline in family life as well as for the rise of juvenile delinquency because "they do not learn English; they do not keep up with other members of the family."[17] Racism reinforced nativism to make prejudice against Third World women even more intense and more lasting. Hispanic and black immigrants, their daughters, and their granddaughters are still frequently relegated to the sidelines of American life, condemned as being sexually immoral, dirty, and maternally inadequate. Asian women have been, and are, stereotyped as exotic and erotic, or passive and docile, or both.

Recovering the Story: The New Ethnicity
and the Women's Movement

Before 1965 most traditional American historians viewed immigrants as "problems" to be solved by assimilation, while liberals emphasized discrimination, the ethnic American as victim. The distinctive experiences of immigrant women were usually subsumed under men's history or given perfunctory or patronizing treatment. In the late 1960s and 1970s, however, the rise of the "new ethnicity" and the revival of the women's movement changed the way many scholars approached the history of immigration in general and the history of immigrant women in particular. The new perspectives offered by these movements have had a major influence on the conceptualization of this book and on the selection and interpretation of the documents in it.

The new ethnicity was an outgrowth of the post-World War II black civil rights movement. In the social ferment of the 1960s, Mexican-

Americans, Asian-Americans, native Americans, and descendants of many European immigrant groups followed the lead of black Americans by organizing to pursue political and economic justice for their communities and by taking increased pride in their ethnic heritages. Ethnic activism increased the number of ethnic officeholders, helped introduce bilingual education and ethnic studies programs, and prompted the removal of some of the most blatantly insulting stereotypes from the media.

The new ethnicity as an organized movement faded away. Immigration continued, however, stimulating new debates about immigration policy and new research about the expanding Asian and Hispanic communities. As the 1990s began, ethnic minorities continued to be an active political force, and pluralism continued to challenge the melting pot as the ideal for American society.

Scholars responded to the new ethnicity by placing new emphasis on the struggle of immigrants to resist oppression and, within the limits imposed upon them, to adjust to America on their own terms. Oscar Handlin's Pulitzer Prize-winning study, *The Uprooted*, published in 1951, focused on the emotional and social disruption caused by immigration. More recent studies by Rudolph Vecoli, Virginia Yans McLaughlin, Donna Gabaccia, and others have stressed the resourcefulness of immigrants in using their ethnic traditions to help adapt successfully to their new life. Similarly, the "Chicago school" of sociologists of the 1920s and 1930s had emphasized assimilation, whereas Nathan Glazer, Rudolph Vecoli, Andrew Greeley, and other scholars of the 1960s and after have stressed the continuing survival of these communities as political and economic interest groups, as focal points for alternative value systems, and as touchstones for social and personal identity.[18]

Immigrant Women does not neglect the traditional concerns of immigration historians. It documents the disorientation and pain that accompanied immigration, and the racism and ethnic and class prejudice that scarred many lives. But its main concerns are those of the newer scholarship. This book sees immigrant women as subjects rather than as objects and ethnic life as an enduring (and valuable), though constantly evolving, feature of the American social landscape. Readings such as Corinne Azen Krause's study of the successful Americanization of Italian, Slavic, and Jewish women in Pittsburgh and Emma Gee's description of Japanese "picture brides" coping with "culture shock" present immigrant women as problem solvers rather than as problems. In similar fashion the selections in Part 7, "Social and Political Activists," illustrate the impact of immigrant women, from nuns to labor leaders, on many areas of American life. The concluding part, "Daughters and Granddaughters," documents not only Americanization, but also the continued survival, often in altered form, of ethnic life-styles, interests, and values. It also documents the complex and evolving meaning of ethnic identity.

While the insights of the new ethnicity apply to all immigrants, those of the women's movement pertain specifically to women. Like the new ethnicity, the revived women's movement grew out of the reform movements of the 1960s, when many women became aware that as women they suffered discrimination similar in some ways to that of ethnic minorities. In a best-selling book, *The Fenimine Mystique*, Betty Friedan described the malaise of homemakers for whom the lonely routines of suburban housewifery did not provide the fulfillment promised by psychologists and the advertising media. Simone de Beauvoir, Kate Millett, Elizabeth Janeway, Juliet Mitchell, and other scholars and theorists investigated the oppression of women by social and political institutions, asking hard questions about the origins of men's power over women, about the use of sex, like race, to perpetuate economic inequality, and about mechanisms for positive change in women's lives.

Like the new ethnicity, the women's movement affected the world of scholarship. By the mid-1970s gender was beginning to take its place alongside ethnicity and class as a category for historical analysis. Alice Kessler-Harris pioneered in the history of the working women. Carl Degler cautioned against the identification of prescriptive sources (what women ought to do) with descriptive sources (what women actually did). Working at the intersection between ethnic and women's history, Virginia Yans McLaughlin, Betty Boyd Caroli, Norma Fain Pratt, Hasia Diner, Sarah Deutch, Judy Yung, and others turned their attention to the recovery of the story of immigrant women.[19] Donna Gabaccia called attention to the fact that research on immigrant women, especially more recent immigrants, was being done by sociologists, anthropologists, psychologists, and literary scholars as well as historians and scholars in women's studies. By the 1980s women's studies (and, to a lesser extent, other disciplines) was beginning to explore the interaction of gender, class, and ethnicity in the lives of their subjects.

In 1975 Gerda Lerner reviewed the various levels on which women's history was being written: first "compensatory history," the recovery of "lost" women; then "contributions" history, women's roles in man-centered historical movements and events; and, finally, woman-centered history and the search for new woman-centered syntheses and conceptual frameworks.[20] *Immigrant Women* addresses its subject at all three levels. It includes "compensatory history," documents by or about "lost" women such as black nationalist Amy Jacques Garvey and labor leader Mother Jones. It also includes "contributions" history, readings describing women's participation in man-centered movements suchas trade unionism and the campaign against child labor.

Immigrant Women does not propose new women-centered syntheses or conceptual frameworks. Rather, it presents women-centered materials from which such syntheses and frameworks can eventually be built. It documents women's work, their participation in their own institutions such as "mothers' clubs" in settlement houses and ethnic women's organizations, and their struggles to gain control over their political and personal lives through movements for women's suffrage and birth control. It explores women's relationships not only with their husbands and their communities but also with one another as mothers, sisters, daughters, lovers, colleagues, and friends. It examines the impact of immigration in women-centered areas of life: women's work in the factory and the home, childbirth on the frontier, women's roles within the family, women giving and receiving help, old age, widowhood, the death of a child.

The selection of materials for a documentary collection on so broad a topic as immigrant women in the United States is highly subjective. Nevertheless, I have used a number of criteria. I have selected materials that address both the classic concerns of immigration history and the issues raised by the new ethnicity and the women's movement. Literary merit has been taken into account. My primary consideration in including a document, however, is its authenticity and effectiveness in conveying the thoughts, feelings, and experiences of immigrant women. Therefore, most of the documents are first-person accounts or materials by relatives or others who knew them well, sympathetic social workers, or researchers in direct contact with their subjects.

The collection focuses on the impact of change—immigration—and how women have coped with that change. It includes women who came to the United States from Europe, Asia, Latin America, and elsewhere from the 1820s to the early 1990s. The 1820s have been taken as a beginning point because the Anglo-Saxon Protestant baseline for American identity had been established by that time, and the government had begun to collect data on immigrants. Indentured servants and slaves who arrived before 1820, therefore, are not included, nor are native American women, whose experience was that of being displaced and colonized in their native land rather than that of immigration. Women from Puerto Rico who came to the mainland are included, although they were citizens of the United States in both locations, because their experience in moving from Hispanic to Anglo-American culture paralleled that of women emigrating from foreign countries.

Immigrant women differed from one another in ethnic background, religion, social class, age, political and sexual orientation, education, personality, and character, as well as in their motivation for coming to the United States. Their life-styles embraced a broad spectrum, from the most traditional to the most unconventional. Although it would be impossible to include materials representing all immigrant women, the readings reflect the diversity of this population.

The readings also reflect the diversity of the available historical materials. Many are drawn from traditional historical sources: the speeches and memoirs of public figures, such as Polish-born suffragist Rose Winslow and Golda Meir, who became prime minister of Israel, and government reports, such as the life stories of industrial workers from a bulletin of the Department of Labor Women's Bureau. Readings from less traditional and less "official" sources include oral histories, poems, short stories, and excerpts from novels by or about immigrant women. Quantitative academic studies have been excluded as inappropriate in tone, but many of these studies are cited in the bibliographic essay.

The opening part of the book documents the reasons women left their homelands. Succeeding parts deal with the immediate problems of survival in the United States, then with work, family, community life, education, and the impact of immigrant women upon "mainstream" American social and political life. The last section documents continuity and change, the relationship between immigrant women and their daughters and granddaughters. An introductory essay opens each part, providing a historical context for the selections that follow. Brief headnotes introduce the individual selections. The book concludes with a bibliographic essay that directs the reader to a wide range of published materials about immigrant women in the United States.

The Revised Edition

This second, revised edition of *Immigrant Women* explores the same themes and uses the same organizational structure as the first edition and the same criteria for the selection of readings. However, in editing the revised edition I have included proportionately more material on the Latina and Asian immigration of the late twentieth century immigration, adding new readings about Korean, Cambodian, Vietnamese, Chinese, Japanese, Pakistani, Mexican, Chilean and Cuban women in the United States. There are also new readings about immigrant women in theater and art and about immigrant lesbians. Finally, the revised edition includes poetry as well prose and has an expanded, updated bibliographical essay. To provide space for these new materials I have eliminated—with great reluctance—a number of the readings that appeared in the original edition.

In conclusion, I would like to thank the generous authors and publishers who gave me permission to use their work. I would also like to thank the editors of the State University of New York Press who made this new edition possible.

Notes

1.   Marie Prisland, *From Slovenia to America: Recollections and Collections* (Chicago: Slovenian Women's Union of America, 1968), p. 19.

2. Anzia Yezierska, *Bread Givers* (1925; reprint, New York: George Braziller, 1975), pp. 166–69.

3. United States Immigration and Naturalization Service, Annual Report, 1973.

4. Walter Wilcox, *International Migration Statistics* (New York: Gordon Breach Science Publishers, 1969), pp. 401–43.

5. For the impact of "development" on Third World women, see Helen Safa and June Nash, *Sex and Class in Latin America* (New York: Praeger, 1976); Ester Boserup, *Woman's Role in Economic Development* (New York: St. Martin's Press, 1970); and Louise Lamphere and Michele Rosaldo, *Women, Culture, and Society* (Stanford: Stanford University Press, 1974).

6. Mary Coolidge, *Chinese Immigration* (1909; reprint, Tapei: Ch'eng Wen 1968), p. 19.

7. Marlon Kau Hom, "Some Cantonese Folksongs on the American Experience," in *Western Folklore* (1983), p. 130, as cited in Asian Women United of California, ed., *Making Waves: An Anthology of Writings by and about Asian American Women* (Boston: Beacon Press, 1989), p. 5.

8. Edith Janson, *The Background of Swedish Immigration, 1840–1930* (Chicago: University of Chicago Press, 1931), pp. 112–13.

9. Marie Zakrzewska, *A Woman's Quest: The Life of Marie Zakrzewska, M.D.*, ed. Agnes C. Vietor (New York: D. Appleton, 1924), p. 67.

10. Rose Pesotta, *Bread upon the Waters*, ed. John Nicholas Biffel (New York: Dodd, Mead, 1944), p. 9.

11. Harold H. Sunoo and Sonia S. Sunoo, "The Heritage of the First Korean Women Immigrants in the United States, 1903–1929," in *Koreans in America* (1976): 149.

12. Corinne Azen Krause, "Urbanization Without Breakdown: Italian, Jewish and Slavic Immigrant Women in Pittsburgh, 1900–1945," *Journal of Urban History* 3 (May 1978): 302.

13. Asian Women United of California, ed., *Making Waves*, p. 19.

14. Maxine Seller, *To Seek America* (Englewood Cliff, N.J.: Jerome S. Ozer, 1977), p. 77.

15. Charlotte Baum, Paula Hyman, and Sonya Michel, *The Jewish Woman in America* (New York: Dial Press, 1976), p. 147.

16. Robert A. Woods, *Americans in Process: A Settlement Study of Residents and Associations of the South End House* (New York: Riverside Press, 1903), pp. 303–4.

17. *Second Annual Report of the Commission of Immigration and Housing of California* (Sacramento: California State Printing Office, 1916), p. 139.

18.   See, for example, Nathan Glazer and Daniel P. Moynihan, *Beyond the Melting Pot: The Negroes, Puerto Ricans, Jews, Italians, and Irish of New York City* (Cambridge, Mass.: MIT Press, 1963); Andrew Greeley, *Why Can't They Be Like Us: America's White Ethnic Groups* (New York: E. P. Dutton, 1971; and idem, *Ethnicity in the United States: A Preliminary Reconnaissance* (New York: Wiley, 1974).

19.   Examples of work by these and other historians of immigrant women are cited in the bibliographic essay.

20.   Gerda Lerner, "Placing Women in History: A 1975 Perspective," *Feminist Studies* 3, nos. 1–2 (1975): 5–15.

PART I

Why They Came

Farewell, my old spinning wheel. How I shall miss you; the
thought of leaving you breaks the heart in my breast.
No more in the evening shall we sit by the fireside, old
friend of mine, and gossip together.
Ah, all that I see has its roots in my heart. And now they
are torn out do you wonder it bleeds?[1]

As is apparent in this Norwegian immigrant woman's song, nineteenth-century women did not find it easy to say goodbye to parents, brothers, sisters, and friends, probably forever, and depart on a long and hazardous journey to an uncertain future in an unknown land. Later immigrants had the advantage of better transportation and information. But even for the most recent, immigration entailed the pain of breaking old ties and the risk of an unpredictable outcome. Part 1 of this book explores why women accepted the pain and took the risk.

Nineteenth- and twentieth-century women came to the United States from diverse backgrounds. Many grew to adulthood in agrarian settings, their lives reflecting the seasonal rhythms of the potato fields of Ireland and Germany, the cane plantations of the Caribbean, or the rice paddies of Southeast Asia. Others emigrated from the great urban centers of the world—Vienna, Warsaw, Budapest, Tokyo, Buenos Aires, Mexico City, Hong Kong, Seoul, Manila, Bangkok.

Cultural identities were as varied as geographic origins. Although Jewish, Polish, and southern Italian women came at about the same time (the late nineteenth and early twentieth centuries) and although the native-born lumped them together as the "new immigration," each had a distinctive lifestyle. Jewish women's lives were molded by a centuries-old legal and moral religious tradition. The parish and the village provided a focal point for the activities of the Polish woman. The energies and loyalties of the southern Italian woman were more likely to be absorbed by the close, virtually self-sufficient extended family. Moreover, within each of these groups there were ideological, class, and regional distinctions. A growing minority of Jewish women had abandoned religious tradition for the secular ideologies and lifestyles of socialism and Zionism. While most Polish immigrants were peasants, some were upper-class urban women of great sophistication. An Italian woman from one province might find the customs, even the language, of her counterpart from another province so different as to be almost incomprehensible. Asian, Latina, and other European women came with a similarly wide range of cultural backgrounds and life-styles.

Flight from Poverty

Despite their differences the societies from which most immigrant women came had one thing in common. They were experiencing far-reaching economic and social changes, changes that set large numbers of people in motion. The most significant change was a sudden and rapid increase in population. This increase, which began in the seventeenth and eighteenth centuries and continues to the present, affected Europe first, then Asia, Latin America, and Africa as well.

As increasing numbers of children survived to adulthood in nineteenth-century Europe, farms were subdivided until they were too small to sustain the families that depended upon them. Though industrialization eased the problem in the long run, its immediate impact was to aggravate the difficulties. Traditional family farms were unable to compete with mechanized agriculture, and urbanization drove taxes and land prices higher. Sons without land and daughters without dowries faced declining social status at best, hunger at worst. To avoid these dismal alternatives for themselves and, more important, for their children, land-owning families like that of Karl Oskar and Kristina Nilsson, described in selection 1, sold their meager holdings to make a new start in the United States.

The flight from poverty was even more urgent for landless single women in agrarian societies who lived by selling their labor. In the nineteenth and early twentieth centuries these "surplus" women had only two occupational choices: farm labor or domestic service. Galician women who worked in the fields were paid twenty-five cents a day by landowners who viewed them as "a different order of human being from themselves."[2] In Paule Marshall's novel *Brown Girl, Brownstones*, an immigrant woman from Barbados describes her childhood as an agricultural laborer: "picking grass in a cane field from the time God sun rise in his heaven til it set. With some woman called a Driver to wash yuh tail in licks if yuh dare look up. . . . Working harder than a man at the age of ten. . . . No, I wun let my mother know peace til she borrow the money and send me here."[3]

Domestic service was scarcely a more inviting prospect, especially in rural areas. Many Irish, Scandinavian, and Slavic women came to the United States to work as maids rather than take service with a farm family near home. The reasons for this choice are evident in the following description of the job that earned a sixteen-year-old Swedish woman $7.50 a year in the nineteenth century: "I had to work like a wolf, go out and spread manure and fertilizer in the summer, and on the worst snowy days in winter carry water to eleven cows. This was besides all the . . . housework. I worked every minute from 6:00 A.M. until 9:00 P.M., Sundays and weekdays just the same."[4] Menial though it was, domestic service in the United States offered greater rewards.

After the abolition of national origins immigration quotas in 1965, Asian and Latina women followed their European predecessors to the United States for the same reason: to escape the poverty that accompanied population increase and economic change. As their "developing" homelands were drawn into an increasingly integrated international economy, rural women were displaced from traditional occupations such as nonmechanized farming, handicrafts, and marketplace trade. Many migrated (or were sent) to increasingly crowded cities to earn the cash to support themselves and their families and to pay taxes and other fees in the "developing" economy. They took jobs as servants, as prostitutes, or as low-paid workers in "sweatshop" clothing, electronics, and other factories along the Pacific Rim or the Mexican border. Many of these factories were "runaway" shops that had moved from the United States to Third World countries to avoid higher labor and safety costs. The second selection describes the plight of impoverished young women in the Philippines, a major source of post-1965 immigration.

For desperately poor Third World women in the mid- and late twentieth century, emigration to the United States seemed a lifesaving alternative. Many learned about economic opportunities in the United States from American business or military personnel in their homeland, from the media, and from relatives and friends already there. Some were recruited by American agencies to become live-in domestics or "mail order" brides for American men seeking loyal, subservient wives. Many made great sacrifices to come, legally or illegally, to the United States.

Mavericks and Unwilling Immigrants

Economic necessity was not the only reason for emigration. Some women left their homelands because they were out of step with the societies in which they lived. A few had problems with the law. A Mexican immigrant confessed that "I came to this country because I broke a woman's head; I almost killed her and got myself put into jail."[5] Often the problems that drove "mavericks" to the United States were related to their status as women. Married women emigrated to escape abusive husbands. Single women emigrated to avoid unwanted marriages or to escape condemnation for sexual activity that would have been condoned in a man. Some women emigrated to break free of restrictive sex roles. One such woman was Prussian-born Marie Zakrzewska, who came to the United States to become a physician. She tells her story in selection 3. Lesbians were sometimes forced to emigrate in order to exercise their sexual preference—or to survive. According to a 1989 National Organization for women (NOW) report,

> Carmen left Ecuador ten years ago because she couldn't live in her country as a lesbian. Amelia, caught holding hands with her lover by her parents, was forced to leave Colombia virtually overnight because she had brought "shame" to her family. Maria Elena had to choose between emigrating to the United States or facing jail in Cuba, even though she had taken an active part in the Cuban Revolution, because homosexuality in Cuba is a crime.[6]

Sometimes the decision to emigrate was made by someone else, a parent or a spouse, and women acquiesced willingly or from a sense of duty. A Puerto Rican woman emigrated to join her husband, who had gone to New York to enter the merchant marine: "He sent for me. I had nobody but him, so I didn't stop to think and set off right away. When one is in love one never thinks."[7] Rosa, the Italian immigrant who tells her story in selection 4, emigrated to join her husband in the United States. She felt that it was her duty to obey him even though she hated him.

The Flight from Oppression

Many women came to the United States as refugees from civil or foreign wars or because of religious and political oppression. In the early twentieth century revolutions in Mexico increased emigration, as did the suppression of ethnic minorities in the Russian, German, Turkish, and Austro-Hungarian empires. Russian Jews were the largest early twentieth-century group driven to the United States by oppression. The tottering Russian Empire restricted its large Jewish population to a limited geographic area, deprived them of most educational and economic opportunities, and kept them impoverished by imposing discriminatory taxes and regulations. In recurrent pogroms (massacres) encouraged by the government and the Church, Russian peasants raped and murdered Jews and pillaged their homes. Two million Jews, almost half of them women, left eastern Europe for the United States between 1880 and 1914. Golda Meir, who became prime minister of Israel, describes her family's flight in the fifth selection.

The pogroms in Russia foreshadowed greater violence elsewhere. The Turks killed a million and a half Armenians in the years following World War I, and the Nazis killed 6 million Jews, as well as millions of Slavs, Gypsies, homosexuals, and others during World War II. Women were among the survivors who trickled into the United States before and after World War II, their numbers constrained by the American government's refusal to alter immigration restrictions.

During the "Cold War" decades following World War II, special legislation permitted hundreds of thousands of women to enter the country as refugees from Communist rule in eastern Europe, Cuba, and Southeast Asia. Soviet Jews emigrated to avoid anti-Semitic social and economic discrimination. Half of Cuba's teachers (most of them women) emigrated to avoid political indoctrination and control of their work.[8]

Some of the most terrifying refugee stories came from Cambodia, where between 1976 and 1979 the Communist Khmer Rouge killed 2 to 4 million people out of a population of 7 million.[9] Eighteen-year-old Ti Ly was sent to a labor camp for political "reeducation" during the rule of Khmer Rouge dictator Pol Pot.

> I worked in the rice field and took care of cows. My husband had to dig ditches. . . . It was very hard work. . . . we were always hungry. I was certain we would die because we had so little food. . . . in that time period he [Pol Pot] killed half of all Cambodian people. Most people died because they had no food or medicine. Most of my relatives died. . . . They were killed like animals. Why? Because they were city people or because they had some education.[10]

Ti Ly escaped but was forced by the Thai government to return to Cambodia. "There were many bombs on the way, ground mines, and a lot of people died."[11] She escaped again and spent two years in refugee camps, where her husband died, before entering the United States.

Refugees from right wing dictatorships found it more difficult to enter the United States than refugees from communism. Women fled right wing dictators, "death squads," and other forms of violence, as well as poverty, in Nicaragua and Haiti. Although some succeeded in remaining in the United States, most were sent home as economic rather than political refugees.

Journey to America

Whenever they came and for whatever reason, women found the journey to America arduous and often dangerous. Months of planning and hard work often separated the decision to leave from the actual departure. As one large nineteenth-century Norwegian family prepared to sail for America in the spring, the women "spun, wove, and sewed throughout the winter, making dresses, suits, underclothing, and other garments. . . . Since there were twelve persons in the family, one can readily understand that the task was no small one, particularly since they also had to prepare food for twelve mouths on what might be a three month journey."[12]

The voyage in a sailing vessel was long, uncomfortable, and sometimes fatal because of shipboard epidemics. Women suffered even more than men from lack of privacy in crowded, vermin-infested quarters and inadequate sanitary facilities. Since advanced pregnancy was not considered sufficient reason to postpone the journey, childbirth was a frequent occurrence on shipboard, and a dangerous one for mother and infant. The replacement of sailing vessels by steamships in the late nineteenth century made the trip shorter and safer. Still, as Golda Meir, who emigrated in 1906, pointed out, "it was not a pleasure trip."[13]

The first glimpse of the United States was a joyous occasion. However, confrontation with immigration officials and health inspectors could be a frightening ordeal. When the health inspectors rejected a child as too sick or weak, the distraught mother was forced to send the little one back alone or abandon her hopes for a better future for the rest of the family. Asian women traveling to join husbands or fiancés were routinely held at Angel Island, within sight of San Francisco, for weeks, even months of questioning. At a time when all Asian immigrants were suspected of being illegal—and, given the stringent immigration restrictions, many were—one mistaken answer, one detail falsely remembered, meant deportation.

By the mid-twentieth century fast, comfortable airplanes had replaced ships as the main means of immigrant travel, and more humane procedures made arrival easier. Still, the trip remained a dangerous, occasionally even fatal, ordeal for refugees and for the many thousands desperate enough to enter illegally. Illegal immigrants paid unscrupulous guides to smuggle them across the Mexican or Canadian border in trucks or on foot. Vietnamese and Cambodian "boat people" faced hunger, pirates, and shipwreck as they took to the open seas in whatever vessels they could find, heading for Thailand, Hong Kong, or Malaysia, and, eventually, the United States (see selection 6). Women left Cuba or Haiti in small, open boats, hoping to avoid storms and Coast Guard patrols long enough to reach Florida. On August 13, 1979, a ship captain, realizing that he had been sighted by the authorities, forced seventeen illegal Haitian immigrants overboard near the coast of southern Florida. Eliane Lorfel and five of her children, ages three to ten, drowned.[14]

Immigration and Traditional Female Roles

Though women who immigrated to the United States were diverse in background and motivation, some generalizations are possible. Most were young and were motivated, at least in part, by the desire to improve their economic situation. Most came as part of family groups or to join a family already here. A sizable minority, however, came alone. In the nineteenth and early twentieth centuries these lone immigrants were generally single, young (often in their teens), and usually from Ireland, Scandinavian countries, or eastern Europe. In the latter half of the twentieth century women immigrating alone were likely to be older. Many were single mothers—divorced, separated, or never married—from Third World countries.

Although their cultures usually insisted on women's subordination to the family, young women often came to the United States on their own initiative, independent of and sometimes in defiance of the wishes of their parents. Some were dutiful daughters, motivated by the desire to send money to needy parents and siblings at home. Others came because they preferred the freedom and independence of even poorly paid work in the United States to the dependence of unpaid work in the home of parents or a future husband. For them, immigration was a rejection, conscious or unconscious, of traditional female roles.

Autobiographies suggest that some of the women who emigrated on their own initiative were less strongly committed than other women to traditional social roles. Many remember atypical childhood activities. Marie Zakrzewska turned her back on the domestic occupations of most young women of her class to accompany her midwife mother on calls throughout the city. Mary Anderson's favorite childhood occupation on a Swedish farm was to ride the horses during the thrashing of grain on bitter winter days. "I did not like anything in the way of housework," she recalled. "I would get the boys to come in and ask if I could go out, so that I could escape the weaving and other household chores."[15] Aristocratic Mexican-born Flores de Andrade had a similarly active, nontraditional childhood: "I would run over the estate and take part in all kinds of boyish games. I rode on a horse bareback and wasn't afraid of anything."[16]

Autobiographies also suggest that many women who emigrated at their own initiative received support from strong mothers at home and from sisters who preceded or accompanied them to the United States. Marie Zakrzewska's mother encouraged her professional ambitions, and her younger sister emigrated with her. Labor leader Rose Pesotta followed an older sister to America, as did Mary Anderson, and in both cases the sisters helped them find employment. When Anderson's father objected to her emigration, her mother intervened. "I think Mother was really a feminist and believed in women doing things they wanted to do, if they could," wrote Anderson.[17]

In the mid- and late twentieth century, women's immigration became even more clearly a collective female enterprise. This was especially true among Latinas and women from the Caribbean. Women friends and relatives already in the United States helped newcomers through the maze of immigration regulations and supplied practical job counseling. Aunts and grandmothers cared for children temporarily left behind. Thus, in the nineteenth and twentieth centuries, networks of women in the homeland and in the United States have joined together to support the immigration of women seeking better lives for themselves and their families.

Notes

1. Immigrant song from Henrik Wergeland's play, *Fjeldstuen*, reproduced in *Norwegian Immigrant Songs and Ballads*, ed. Theodore C. Blegen and Martin B. Ruud (Minneapolis: University of Minnesota Press, 1936), pp. 85–87.

2. Grace Abbott, *The Immigrant and the Community* (New York: Century, 1917), pp. 58–59.

3. Paule Marshall, *Brown Girl, Brownstones* (Catham, N.J.: Chatham Bookseller, 1972), p. 45.

4. Edith Janson, *The Background of Swedish Immigration, 1840–1930* (Chicago: University of Chicago Press, 1931), pp. 112–13.

5. Manual Gamio, *The Mexican Immigrant: His Life Story* (Chicago: University of Chicago Press, 1931), pp. 79–80.

6. Olga E. Vives, "The Hard Reality of Latina Lesbians," *National Times* 22, no. 3 (July/August/ September 1989).

7. Oscar Lewis, *A Study in Slum Culture: Backgrounds for La Vida* (New York: Random House, 1968), p. 136.

8. Eugene F. Provenzo, Jr., and Concepcio Garcia, "Exiled Teachers and the Cuban Revolution," *Cuban Studies/ Estudios Cubanos* 13, no. 1 (Winter 1983): 2.

9. Tricia Knoll, *Becoming American: Asian Sojourners, Immigrants, and Refugees in the Western United States* (Portland, Oreg.: Coast to Coast Books, 1982), pp. 182–83.

10. John Tenhula, *Voices from Southeast Asia: The Refugee Experience in the United States* (New York: Holmes and Meier, 1991), p. 117.

11. Ibid.

12. Theodore Blegan, *The American Transition* (Northfield, Minn.: Norwegian American Historical Society, 1940), p. 7.

13. Golda Meir, *My Life* (New York: Dell, 1976), p. 29.

14. *Daytona Beach Morning Journal*, August 16, 1979, as cited in Jake C. Miller, *The Plight of the Haitian Refugees* (New York: Praeger, 1984), p. 64.

15. Mary Anderson, *Women at Work: The Autobiography of Mary Anderson*, as told to Mary N. Winslow (Minneapolis: University of Minnesota Press, 1951), p. 7.

16. Gamio, *Mexican Immigrant*, p. 29.

17. Anderson, *Women at Work*, p. 9.

1

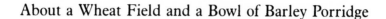

About a Wheat Field and a Bowl of Barley Porridge

Usually the immigration of family units was the result of a joint decision by hus-
band and wife, and the most common reason for such a decision was concern for
the future of the children. The following selection, from Swedish author Vilhelm
Moberg's sensitive and well-researched novel The Emigrants, *describes the long,*
painful process by which a young Swedish couple decide to immigrate to the Min-
nesota frontier in the mid-nineteenth century. As independent farmers, Kristina
and Karl Oskar Nilsson were better off than others who rented land or worked as
day laborers. But their heavily mortgaged, stony farm was too small to support
them and to provide for their growing family. (Kristina was pregnant four times in
four years, and Karl Oskar's elderly parents also lived with them.) A series of bad
harvests and bad luck, culminating in tragedy, convinced first Karl Oskar and
then Kristina that immigration was necessary for the future of their children.
Though the Nilsson family is fictitious, thousands of real families faced similar
problems, shared similar doubts, and made a similar decision.

Karl Oskar Nilsson had seen a picture. He had called one day on the
churchwarden, Per Persson in Akerby, and had borrowed a newspaper;
there he had seen the picture.

It was a field at harvest-time, and the crop was still standing in shocks.
An even field was visible, an endless field without borders or fences. The
wheat field had no end at the horizon, it stretched beyond the place where
sky met the earth. Not a single stone or heap of stones, no hillock or knoll
was visible on this whole wide field of wheat stubble. It lay even and smooth
as the floor boards of his own cottage. And in this field shock stood by shock
so close they almost touched each other. . . . Every head of wheat was like a
mighty blossom, every straw like a sapling, every sheaf like a shrub. . . . It
was the fruit of the earth that he saw here, an unmeasurable quantity of
bread for man: "A Wheat Field in North America."

Source: Vilhelm Moberg, *The Emigrants*, trans. Gustaf Lannestock (New York: Simon
and Schuster, 1951), pp. 13–15, 91–110. Reprinted by permission. Copyright © 1951
by, Vilhelm Moberg. Reprinted by permission of SIMON AND SCHUSTER, a division of Gulf and Western Corporation.

Karl Oskar Nilsson, owner of seven stony acres in stone-country Korpamoen, sat quietly for a long time, his eyes lingering upon the picture. His mind's eye reveled in this grandeur. He held up the paper reverently before him, as if he were sitting on a church bench of a Sunday, following the hymn with the psalmbook in his hand.

It was in the Old World that God once had cursed the soil because of man; in the New World the ground still was blessed. . . .

So far he had shown the picture of the North American wheat field only to Kristina, and she had looked at it casually. She could not know that her husband carried that picture in his mind wherever he went.

Through the long autumn evenings they sat in front of the fire busy with their indoor activities. Karl Oskar whittled ax handles and wooden teeth for the rakes, and Kristina carded wool and spun flax. At last, one evening after the children had gone to sleep and it was quiet in the room, he began to talk. In advance he had thought over what he should say, and in his mind he had fought all the obstacles and excuses his wife might make.

As for himself, he had decided on the move and now he would like to hear what she thought of it.

She asked first: "Are you making fun of me?"

What was she to think? Here he sat and suddenly announced that he intended to sell his farm, and all he owned. Then with his whole family—a wife and three children and a fourth not yet born—he would move away; not to another village or parish, nor to another place in this country, or to any country on this continent. But to a new continent! He might just as well have stretched it a little further, it would have made no difference to her had he announced that he intended to move them all to the moon; he must be jesting with her.

But as he continued to talk, she realized he spoke in earnest. . . . Now Kristina must answer with innermost sincerity and let him know what she felt in her heart. So they talked, and exchanged their opinions, evening after evening, while the crackling fire alone interrupted their conversation and at times was even louder than they.

Why Did Karl Oskar Want to Move?

For four years now they had lived in Korpamoen, and today they were several hundred riksdaler poorer than when they started. Four years they had spilled the strength of their youth here, to no purpose. If they remained they would have to continue struggling and slaving until they could move neither hand nor foot, until they finally sat there, worn out, worked out, limp and broken.

However much they struggled and toiled, they could never improve their situation here in Korpamoen.

He didn't know much about conditions in the United States, but he did know that once there he would be given, for next to nothing, fertile, stone-free soil which was now only waiting for the plowshare. . . . Perhaps they must face as much drudgery as here, but they would do it in another spirit, with another hope, another joy. Because the great difference between the two countries was this: In America they could improve their lot through their own work.

He for his part was weary of the struggle which led nowhere. Nonetheless he could continue his work with a happy heart if he believed he could improve the situation for himself and his. . . . One day their children would be grown and shifting for themselves, and what sort of future awaited them here? One child would inherit the farm, but what about the others? They would have to work as hired farmhands or become squatters. No third choice existed. There were already so many hands that they competed in offering their services to farmers; there were too many cottagers already, soon every opening in the forest would have its rotten, rickety shack with the black earth for floor. The people in these huts seldom had meat with their bread—and many days no bread. Karl Oskar and Kristina did not want their children to become hired farmhands or crofters; but they could do nothing better for them unless they took them from this impoverished place. If they felt responsibility for their children, they must move away.

On one point all information from North America agreed: the people had in every way more liberty in that country. The four classes were long ago abolished there, they had no king who sat on a throne and drew a high salary. . . . And at the community meeting everyone spoke as freely as his neighbor, for all had equal rights.

If he now sold his farm with everything on it, chattels and kine included, Karl Oskar would have enough money to pay the transportation for all of them with some small part left over for the settling in the new country. . . .

Why Kristina Wanted to Remain at Home

Karl Oskar had drawn a beautiful and sanguine picture. If Kristina could believe it all as he painted it for her, she would not for one moment hesitate to follow him.

But she was afraid it might turn out to be a wild-goose chase. Her husband believed all he heard and saw about America. But who could guarantee its truth? What did they have to rely on? Who had promised them tillable soil in the United States? Those who ruled over there had not written him a letter or given him a promise. He had no deed to a piece of land that would await them on arrival. One taking such a journey needed written words and agreements before starting.

They had never met a single person who had been to North America; they knew of no one who had set foot in that country, no one who could tell them what the land was like. If a reliable human being who had seen the country with his own eyes had advised emigration, that would be different. In the printed words of newspapers and books she had no confidence. . . .

He had also forgotten to mention the fact that they must sail on a fragile ship across the ocean; he had said nothing about the dangerous voyage. How often they had heard about ships wrecked and sunk? No one knew if they would ever reach America alive. Even if exposing themselves to all these dangers were advisable, had they the right to venture the lives of their children on a voyage which wasn't necessary, which they weren't forced to undertake? The children were too young to consult, and perhaps they would rather remain at home, even as squatters, than be pulled down into the depth of the ocean; perhaps it were better to earn one's bread as a farmhand, and live, then to be a corpse on the bottom of the sea, eaten by whales and other seafaring monsters.

Karl Oskar wanted to emigrate because he felt responsibility for his children; Kristina wanted to remain at home for the same reason.

And what did he know about the children's lot in the foreign country? Had someone there written him that Anna would become a lady, or that Johan would be a gentleman of leisure?

He hadn't mentioned, either, that they must separate from their parents, brothers and sisters, relatives and friends—in short, all those they knew. Had he realized they would come to places where every human being they met was a stranger? They might have to live in communities where people were ill-natured and cruel; they were to live in a land where they would be unable to speak one word of the language, unable to ask a single soul for a drink of water if they needed it; where they might have to die without their tongues being able to cry for help. In such a land they would wander like changelings, alien and lost. Had he never thought that their life might be lonely and bleak?

If she moved so far away she might never be able to return home; she might never see her nearest and dearest again; never meet parents, brothers and sisters. At once she would lose them all, and even though they lived they would be dead to her; they would be alive and yet dead.

True enough, things had gone backwards for them and they had had bad luck. But it might soon change, they might have a good year, they might have good fortune. At least they had the necessary food each day, and even though—as it looked for the moment—they might have to starve a bit this winter, they would most likely eat so much the better next year. They weren't dressed in silk and satin, of course, but at least they were able to cover their bodies and keep their children warm. Surely they would gain their sufficiency at home in future as they had in the past, as other people did. . . .

Kristina wanted to remain at home.

After the drought and crop failure came winter now, and famine. The summer had been short, had died in its youth; the winter would last so much longer with its starvation.

The sheriff's carriage was seen more often on the roads. His errands concerned the poorest farms, and the carriage remained long at the gates. . . .

Even before the snow had set in, little children could be seen along the roads, pale, with sunken cheeks, their running noses blue. Once arrived at a farm, they didn't go to the main entrance; they went to the refuse pile near the kitchen door, where they remained awhile scratching in the debris, searching. Then they went inside the house but stayed close to the door. The boys bowed, the girls would curtsy. With their forefingers they would try to dry their noses; then they would stand there, in the corner near the door, silent, timid.

They had no errand. They had already brought their message to anyone who looked closely: the mute testimony of hunger.

Parents sent their children begging, ashamed to be seen themselves. To the small ones, begging was no shame. For wretched, starving children begging was a natural occupation, the only one they were able to perform, their only help. . . .

Kristina baked famine bread; when the rye flour did not suffice she added chaff, beechnuts, heather seed, and dried berries of the mountain ash. She also tried to grind acorns and mix them in the dough, but such bread caused constipation and the bowels would not move for many days. She boiled an edible porridge from hazelnut kernels, and used it instead of the clear rye porridge which they had to do without this winter. No real nourishment was found, though, in famine food: sprouts, seeds, nuts, and other products from the wastelands did fill the stomach but gave no lasting satisfaction. One left the table because the meal was over, not because one was satisfied. And however much they stretched and added, all the bins and foodboxes would be empty long before the next crop was ripe.

In the middle of the winter the time was up for Kristina, and she bore a son. . . .

Owing to the meager fare this winter the mother had not sufficient milk for the newborn; her breasts were dry long before he was satisfied, and a suckling could not stand the bitter milk from their starved cows. This was a bad winter for a new arrival into the world. Kristina must now choose the most nourishing pieces for herself, in order to give milk to the little one. But the other children needed food too; she noticed that Anna, the eldest, had fallen off and grown very thin. Kristina felt as if she stole food from three of her children to give to the fourth.

The newborn was to be given the name Anders Harald. . . .

Nor was there much from which to prepare a christening feast this winter. Kristina cooked the christening porridge from some barley grains which she had hidden away in a small sack for this very day, and she had also a little butter and sugar to put into the porringer. Her three children stood around her as she poured out the pot. It was a long time since the little ones had seen such food in the house, food with such odor. Kristina poured the porridge into a large earthen bowl, not to be touched until the godparents returned from church with the newly christened one; she put the bowl in the cellar to cool off. . . .

When the parents came in again they missed Anna. They started to look for her, inside and outside the house, but they were unable to find her. She was four years old, and able to go alone to the neighbors, but she never left the farm without permission.

Karl Oskar was greatly disturbed; what could have happened to the child? She was as dear to him as his own eyes, his constant comrade at work, keeping him company everywhere. Only today he had promised to take her to the shoemaker and have her feet measured for a pair of shoes; her old ones were entirely worn out. This she could not have forgotten; so much the stranger that she had disappeared shortly before they were to leave.

They looked in vain for the child in the wood lot, and the father was about to go to the neighbors to inquire when Kristina came running and said that Anna was in the cellar; she had passed by, had heard a faint crying, and had opened the door.

Anna lay stretched out on the floor of the cellar. She cried as if with pain. Next to her on the floor stood the earthen bowl which Kristina had put there a few hours earlier to cool off; at that time it was filled to the brim with barley porridge, now only about a third was left.

The little girl was carried inside the house and put to bed. Tearfully, she asked her parents' forgiveness for what she had done. She had been unable to forget the bowl of porridge which she had seen and smelled in the kitchen; she was so hungry for the porridge. She had seen her mother put it away in the cellar; she could not resist her desire to steal down there and look at it. At first she had only wished to smell it, then she had wanted to taste it a little— . . . each spoonful tasted better—she could not stop until most of the porridge was gone. Then she became afraid, she dared not go back into the house, she dared not show herself after her disobedience. She remained in the cellar, and after a while she was seized by fierce pain in her stomach.

Anna had eaten herself sick on the barley porridge; it was too strong a fare for her after the famine food of the winter. Her stomach swelled up like a drum, firm and expanded. She let out piercing shrieks as the pain increased.

Berta of Idemo was sent for. She was accustomed to relieve stomachache with the heat from woolen clothes. . . .

But nothing eased the suffering of the child. Berta said the barley grains had swelled in the bowels of the little girl to twice the original size, thus causing something to burst. She could not take responsibility for healing such damage.

Anna cried loudly and asked someone to help as the pain grew agonizing. Again and again she asked her parents' forgiveness for having disobeyed: she had known that no one should touch the porridge before evening when the guests returned.

During the night she became delirious at intervals. Berta said that if she didn't improve before morning, God might fetch the child home; she wanted to prepare the parents to the best of her ability.

Anna heard her words and said she did not wish God to fetch her home; she wanted to remain here. . . . As her suffering increased she called her father to help her; she wanted to get up and go with him to the cobbler for the measurements of the shoes she had been promised. Her cries could be heard out into the byre, where the cows answered with their bellowing, thinking someone was on his way to feed them.

Early in the morning the child died in her agony.

Anyone who spoke to Karl Oskar during the next few days got no answer. Nor did a second or third attempt help much. At length, he might answer with a question, showing that he heard nothing at all.

Anna had died because the earth here was cursed. It must be so; this field where the deadly barley had grown must be stricken by the Lord's word to Adam.

Karl Oskar beheld the pale beggar children wandering about, searching for sustenance in the refuse piles, and he thought: My child found good food, her bowels burst from sugared and buttered barley porridge. Yet she too was a pawn to hunger.

For many weeks after the funeral Kristina was crushed; most of what she did she did wrongly, and other chores stayed undone. A thousand times she reproached herself, asking: Why didn't I hide the bowl of christening porridge where no one could find it? Why didn't I let the children taste it before putting it away? If I had done this, Anna would be alive.

A long time elapsed, and the parents had not mentioned the name of their dead child. They never spoke of the little girl they had lost; their sorrow would have become doubly heavy if it had been brought out into clear daylight, and its power acknowledged. Now they tried to push it away, not let it penetrate beyond thought. As long as words didn't help, why use them? Exchanged between two mourning people, they were only a dissonant sound, disturbing the bitter consolation of silence.

A month had passed since Anna's funeral when Kristina one evening said to Karl Oskar: After what had happened, she had now changed her mind; she was not averse to the emigration to North America. Before, she had thought she would be lacking in responsibility if she endangered the children's lives on the ocean. Now she had learned that God could take her little ones even on dry land, in spite of her great care. She had come to believe that her children would be equally safe on the stormy sea, if she entrusted them to the Highest. Moreover, she would never feel the same in this place again. And so—if he thought it would be best for them and their children to emigrate, she would comply. They could know nothing of what was in store for them in so doing, but she wanted to take part in the emigration, she wished to go away with Karl Osker.

The couple agreed: they would look for passage in the spring of next year.

So the decision had been reached, a decision which determined the course of life for both of them, which determined the fate of their children, the result of which would stretch through time to come to unborn generations—the decision which was to determine the birthplace of their grandchildren, and their grandchildren's children.

2

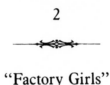

"Factory Girls"

Hunger forced women to leave their homes in the twentieth century as well as the nineteenth. In the late twentieth century, however, these women were leaving Asia and Latin America rather than Europe. In "Factory Girls," author Chea Villanueva, whose father was born in the Philippines, describes the conditions that made the Philippines one of the largest sources of post-1965 immigration to the United States. She blames the "free trade zone" policies of the United States for helping to create and maintain the market for women's labor in factories—and brothels—at wages barely adequate to sustain life. She notes, too, America's former support for the Marcos dictatorship (which has since been overthrown, with American approval).

Like the Philippines, many developing nations in need of capital rely on cheap nonunionized female labor, often recently displaced from traditional occupations, to attract industries (and tourists) from the United States and other developed nations. They have little incentive, therefore, to improve the conditions described in "Factory Girls," and desperate women continue to emigrate.

Source: Chea Villanueva, "Factory Girls," in *Making Waves: An Anthology of Writings by and about Asian American Women,* ed. Asian Women United of California (Boston: Beacon Press, 1989), pp. 295–96.

in the Philippines
women sell their bodies
to buy rice
they live in
factory dormitories
along the "free trade zone."
free
    trade
        zone. . . .
freedom for business
less freedom for women
incarcerated inside the
barbed wire labor camps.
at Mattel toy "motel"
women are told
to lay down or
lay off
free trade
free women's bodies.
at Subic naval base
Filipina flesh is worth
$7 U.S. money
in america they're worth
at least fifty.
on the news today another
woman is kidnapped
via male-order bride
domestic help
secretarial employment.
U.S. fronts for
    sexual slavery
free
    trade
        zone. . . .
in the Philippines
the earth is red
death lurks
in revolution
sisters Alma, Puri, Mia and Lorrie
murdered
by the U.S.-Marcos dictatorship.
the sisters died
with their guns
in hand

murdered
by the
free
trade
zone. . . .

3

———❖———

"My Education and Aspirations Demanded More"

Of Polish ethnic background and Prussian birth, Marie Zakrzewska (1829–1902) rejected the domestic life-style advocated by her father. Influenced by her midwife mother, she studied midwifery and medicine at the Royal Hospital Charite in Berlin, and proved her medical and administrative ability by managing the hospital's obstetrical service. She was denied a permanent appointment there, however—as she had been denied a medical degree—because she was a woman. Hence her decision, described here, to immigrate to the United States in 1853. A maverick in the United States as in Prussia, she earned her medical degree and became an activist in medical and nursing education for women (as a founder of the New York Infirmary for Women and Children and a professor at the New England Female Medical College). She was also active in abolitionism and in the movement for women's rights.

I made my preparations to leave the hospital on the 15th of November, 1852. What was I to do? I was not made to practice quietly, as is commonly done; my education and aspirations demanded more than this. For the time, I could do nothing more than inform my patients that I intended to practice independently.

My father again wished that I should marry, and I began to ask myself whether marriage is an institution to relieve parents from embarrassment. When troubled about the future of a son, parents are ready to give him to the army; when in fears of the destiny of a daughter, they induce her to become the slave of the marriage bond. I never doubted that it was more unendurable and unworthy to be a wife without love than a soldier without a

Souce: Marie Zakrzewska, *A Woman's Quest: The Life of Marie Zakrzewska, M.D.,* ed. Agnes C. Vietor (New York: D. Appleton, 1924), pp. 66–78.

special calling for that profession, and I never could think of marriage as the means to procure a shelter and bread. I had so many schemes in my head that I would not listen to his words. Among these was especially the wish to emigrate to America.

The Pennsylvania Female Medical College had sent its first report to Dr. Schmidt, who had informed me as well as his colleagues of it and had advocated the justice of such a reform. It was in March, 1852, that he spoke of this, saying to those present, "In America, women will now become physicians, like the men; this shows that only in a republic can it be proved that science has no sex."

This fact recurred to my memory, and I decided to go to America to join in a work open to womanhood on a larger scale; and for the next two months, I did nothing but speculate how to carry out my design of emigration. . . .

Little really is known in Berlin about America, and to go there is considered as great an undertaking as to seek the river Styx in order to go to Hades. The remark that I heard from almost every quarter was, "What! you wish to go to the land of barbarism, where they have negro slavery and where they do not know how to appreciate talent and genius?"

But this could not prevent me from realizing my plans. I had idealized the freedom of America and especially the reform of the position of women, to such an extent that I would not listen to their arguments. After having been several years in America, very probably I would think twice before undertaking again to emigrate, for even the idealized freedom has lost a great deal of its charm when I consider how much better it could be.

Having put everything in order, I told my father of my conclusion to leave. He would not give his consent unless my sister Anna accompanied me, thinking her, I suppose, a counterpoise to any rash undertakings in which I might engage in a foreign land. . . .

"Dear Marie, best Marie! make haste to come up on deck to see America! Oh, how pleasant it is to see the green trees again! How brightly the sun is gilding the land you are seeking—the land of freedom!"

With such childlike exclamations of delight, my sister Anna burst into my cabin to hasten my appearance on deck on the morning of the 22d of May, 1853. The beautiful child of nineteen summers was only conscious of a heart overflowing with pleasure at the sight of the charming landscape that opened before her eyes after a tedious voyage of forty-seven days upon the ocean. . . .

A stranger in a strange wide land, not knowing its habits and customs, not understanding its people, nor its workings and aims, yet my mind was not clouded with loneliness. I was happy. Had it not been my own wish that had made me leave the home of a kind father and of a mother beloved beyond all earthly beings. I had succeeded in safely reaching the shores of America. Life was again open before me. . . .

I took my breakfast on deck. No one else seemed to have any appetite, and I felt somewhat reproved when I heard some one near me say, "She seems to have neither head nor heart—see how tranquilly she can eat at such a time as this!" These words were spoken by one of the cabin passengers, a young man who was exceedingly curious to know why I was going to America and had several times tried to make the rest of the passengers believe that it must be in consequence of an unhappy love. The poor simpleton! he thought that women could enter into life only through the tragedy of a broken heart. . . .

I had come here for a purpose—to carry out the plan which a despotic government and its servile agents had prevented me from doing in my native city. I had to show to those men who had opposed me so strongly because I was a woman that, in this land of liberty, equality, and fraternity, I could maintain that position which they would not permit to me at home.

4

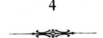

"He Has the Right to Command You"

Rosa, a teen-aged immigrant whose oral history is the source of the following selection, took little part in the decision that brought her from Italy to the United States in the early twentieth century. Although clearly an intelligent, lively, and engaging person, young Rosa had scant opportunity to control her own life. Abandoned as an infant, she was brought up by a foster mother, Mamma Lena, who operated an osteria *(small cafe). When Rosa was barely fourteen years old, Mamma Lena pressured her into marrying a much older man, the brutal Santino. Shortly thereafter she was forced to immigrate to the United States to join her husband, who was working in the iron mines of Missouri. Her foster mother, her lack of alternatives (there were probably none, short of social ostracism and prostitution), and the common wisdom that a husband, however abusive, has the right to command his wife combined to rule out any other possibility.*

As the selection opens, Rosa, married a few months and pregnant (although she does not know it), is being beaten by her husband because she refused to dance with his drunken friends earlier in the evening.

Source: ROSA: THE LIFE OF AN ITALIAN IMMIGRANT, by Marie Hall Ets. Copyright © 1970 by the University of Minnesota. University of Minnesota Press, Minneapolis.

Other nights when Santino was drunk and beating me Mamma Lena had sat up in her bed and watched, but she had said nothing. This night—I guess she could see it that he wanted to kill me for sure—she jumped up and came over and stopped him. She pulled him away so he couldn't reach to kick me. When she did that he started fighting with her. He should have known better than to try to fight Mamma Lena! Mamma Lena was so mad she didn't care what she did. She wasn't afraid of hurting him or anything. And in the end she put him out the door and he went rolling down the steps. "And don't ever come back to this house!" she yelled after him. "Don't ever come back! I never want to see you again!"

Before he married me that man was always talking sweet to Mamma Lena to make her like him. But after the marriage she could see it herself—how bad he was. He was all the time drunk and beating me, and she didn't like him herself.

A few weeks after the fight—Santino was not living in Mamma Lena's—one of those agents from the big bosses in America came to Bugiarno to get men for some iron mines in Missouri. The company paid for the tickets, but the men had to work for about a year to pay them back, and they had to work another year before they could send for their wives and families. So this time when that agent came Santino and some of his friends joined the gang and went off to America. He didn't even come back to the *osteria* to get his clothes.

When I heard that *Santino* was gone, oh, I was happy! I was thinking that probably I would never see that man again. America was a long way off.

Mamma Lena was better to me now and gave me more to eat. And I kept getting bigger and bigger. And then one day I felt kicking inside of me and I knew it was a baby. How that baby got in there I couldn't understand. But the thing that worried me most was how it was going to get out! A baby couldn't make a hole and come out like the moth in a cocoon. Probably the doctor would have to cut me. I didn't want to ask Mamma Lena, but what was I going to do? That baby was kicking to get out—I would have to ask someone. So I told her.

"Well." said Mamma Lena. "You'll have to pray the Madonna. If you pray the Madonna with all your heart maybe the Madonna will make a miracle for you and let the baby come out without the doctor cutting you."

And so I started to pray for that miracle. I prayed to the little statue Madonna over the chicken coop and I prayed to the big Madonna in the church. And every night I gave myself more Ave Marias to say, so that when I woke up in the morning I would find the baby there in bed beside me. But it never was. It was still inside and kicking.

At last there came a day when I had to leave my work and go home. After that I didn't know what happened. I was three days without my senses. Mamma Lena got two doctors—she got the village doctor, then she got the doctor she had to pay. But both doctors said the same. They said the baby could not be born—that they would have to take it in pieces. And they were even scolding her. They said "How can a girl make new bones when her own bones are not finished growing? The girl is too young!" Mamma Lena was in despair. She wanted that baby. So she told the doctors to go and she ran to the church and prayed to the big Madonna. She told the Madonna that if She would let the baby be born alive she would give Her that beautiful shawl that Remo and me won in the dance. . . .

And right then when she was praying, my baby was born—a nice little boy. She came home and she could hear it crying. Think what a miracle! Two doctors said that baby couldn't be born! For a long time she didn't know whether I was going to live or not, but she was so happy to have that baby that she was thanking the Madonna. She took the shawl to the priest the next day. And the shawl made so much money in the raffle that the Madonna got all new paint and a new sky and new stars behind Her.

In the fever that followed the birth of my baby I lost my hair and my voice. Little by little my hair came back, and my voice to speak came back too, but I could never sing like before. And as soon as I could walk again I went back to my work in the mill. They had a special room in the mill just for nursing the babies. So Mamma Lena would bring the baby to me and I would stop work and go in there and nurse him. And I nursed him at lunchtime too. . . .

So I was around fifteen years old and I had to be like an old woman. I was not allowed to walk with the young people when they went to the square on Christmas Eve or dance with the masks when they came to the stables in the time of the carnival. I couldn't even sit with the other young girls at lunchtime at the mill. But as I got strong again I began imitating funny people and telling funny stories again to make the women and girls all laugh. And nighttimes and Sundays I had my baby, my Francesco, to give me joy and make me laugh. And now that I was married Mamma Lena no longer scolded or beat me like before.

"But you did wrong to make that beautiful young girl marry a man like Santino!" Zia Teresa would say.

"Yes, I made a mistake," Mamma Lena would say. "But it was not my fault. I didn't know before how bad he was. And now Rosa is married and has her baby and I don't have to worry anymore."

My Francesco had learned to walk and was learning to talk when here, coming into the *osteria* one Sunday, were some of those men who had gone to America with Santino. I stopped playing with my baby and went and called Mamma Lena from the wine cellar.

"Those men in the iron mines in Missouri need women to do the cooking and washing," said one of them. "Three men have sent back for their wives, and two for some girls to marry. Santino says for you to send Rosa. He sent the money and the ticket." And the man pulled them from an inside pocket and laid them on the table. Then all four sat down and ordered wine and polenta. Mamma Lena took the ticket and the money and put them in the pocket of her underskirt, and without a word started serving them.

When the men were ready to leave the one who had brought the message spoke again. "In two weeks another gang of men from the villages is leaving for the iron mines in Missouri. Your daughter and other wives and girls can go with them." But still Mamma Lena didn't tell him if I was going or not going.

After they were gone I helped her clear the table and wash off the dishes. Then I took Francesco in my arms and waited for her to speak. She took her rag and started to wipe the table, but instead of wiping it she sat down on the bench beside it.

"Yes, Rosa," she said. "You must go. However bad that man is, he is your husband—he has the right to command you. It would be a sin against God not to obey. You must go. But not Francesco. He didn't ask for Francesco and I would be too lonesome without him."

Me, I was even wanting to sin against God and the Madonna before I would leave my baby and go off to Santino in America! But Mamma Lena said I must go. There was nothing I could do. . . .

And so I had to leave Mamma Lena and my baby and go off with that gang of men and one or two women to America. . . .

The day came when we had to go and everyone was in the square saying good-bye. I had Francesco in my arms. I was kissing his lips and kissing his cheeks and kissing his eyes. Maybe I would never see him again! It wasn't fair! He was *my* baby! Why should Mamma Lena keep him? But then Pep was calling and Mamma Lena took Francesco away and Zia Teresa was helping me onto the bus and handing up the bundles.

5

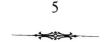

"I Remember How Scared I Was"

In this passage from her autobiography, Golda Meir describes her family's struggle for survival in turn-of-the-century czarist Russia, where economic, educational,

Source: Reprinted by permission of G. P. Putnam's Sons from MY LIFE by Golda Meir. Copyright © 1975 by Golda Meir.

and residential restrictions kept the Jewish masses impoverished and pogroms (government-instigated massacres) made life itself uncertain. While focusing on her own memories, Meir also describes the three women who emigrated with her: her resourceful mother Blume, who kept the family intact during the difficult years between her husband's immigration and her own; her much-admired older sister Sheyna, whose political activity was the immediate cause of the women's flight; and her little sister Zipke, a bewildered participant in events she was too young to understand.

Meir arrived in Milwaukee in 1906, at the age of eight. A Zionist from early childhood, she left the United States for Palestine in 1921, played an important role in the creation of Israel in 1948, and climaxed a lifetime of political activity by serving as prime minister of the new state from 1969 to 1974.

In a way, I suppose that the little I recall of my early childhood in Russia, my first eight years, sums up my beginnings, what now are called the formative years. If so, it is sad that I have very few happy or even pleasant memories of this time. The isolated episodes that have stayed with me throughout the past seventy years have to do mostly with the terrible hardships my family suffered, with poverty, cold, hunger and fear, and I suppose my recollection of being frightened is the clearest of all my memories. I must have been very young, maybe only three and a half or four. We lived then on the first floor of a small house in Kiev, and I can still recall distinctly hearing about a pogrom that was to descend on us. I didn't know then, of course, what a pogrom was, but I knew it had something to do with being Jewish and with the rabble that used to surge through town, brandishing knives and huge sticks, screaming "Christ killers" as they looked for the Jews, and who were now going to do terrible things to me and to my family.

I can remember how I stood on the stairs that led to the second floor, where another Jewish family lived, holding hands with their little daughter and watching our fathers trying to barricade the entrance with boards of wood. That pogrom never materialized, but to this day I remember how scared I was and how angry that all my father could do to protect me was to nail a few planks together while we waited for the hooligans to come. And, above all, I remember being aware that this was happening to me because I was Jewish. . . .

Also, I remember all too clearly how poor we were. There was never enough of anything, not food, not warm clothing, not heat at home. I was always a little too cold outside and a little too empty inside. Even now, from that very distant past, I can summon up with no effort at all, almost intact, the picture of myself sitting in tears in the kitchen, watching my mother feed some of the gruel that rightfully belonged to me to my younger sister, Zipke. Gruel was a great luxury in our home in those days, and I bitterly resented having to share any of it, even with the baby. Years later I was to experience the dread of my own children's hunger and to learn for myself what it is like to have to decide which child is to receive more food, but, of course, in that kitchen in Kiev, I knew only that life was hard and that there was no justice anywhere. I am glad that no one told me then that my older sister, Sheyna, often fainted from hunger in school. . . .

My parents were very different from each other: My father, Moshe Yitzhak Mabovitch, was a slender, delicately featured, fundamentally optimistic man, much given to believing in people—unless and until proved wrong—a trait that, on the whole, was to make his life a failure in worldly terms. In short, he was what you might call an innocent, the kind of man who would probably have been more successful if circumstances had ever been just slightly easier. Blume, my copper-haired mother, was pretty, energetic, bright and far more sophisticated and enterprising than my father, but, like him, a born optimist and very sociable. Despite everything, on Friday nights our house was always full of people, members of the family mostly. I remember swarms of cousins, second cousins, aunts and uncles. None of them was to survive the Holocaust, but they live on in my mind's eye, sitting around our kitchen table, drinking tea out of glasses and, on the Sabbath and holidays, singing for hours—and I remember my parents' sweet voices ringing out above the others. . . .

We lived . . . the way most Jews lived in the towns and villages of Eastern Europe. We went to *shul* (synagogue) on festivals and fast days, we blessed the Sabbath, and we kept two calendars: one Russian, the other relating to that far-off land from which we had been exiled 2,000 years before and whose seasons and ancient customs we still marked in Kiev and Pinsk.

My parents had moved to Kiev when Sheyna (who was nine years my senior) was still very small. My father wanted to better his situation, and although Kiev was beyond the Pale of Settlement and in that part of Russia in which Jews were normally forbidden to live, he was an artisan, and as such, if he could prove that he was a skilled carpenter by passing the necessary examination, he might receive the precious permit to move to Kiev. So he made a perfect chess table, passed the test, packed our bags and left Pinsk, filled with hope. In Kiev Father found work for the government, making furniture for school libraries, and even got an advance. With this money, plus money my parents borrowed, he built a little carpentry shop of his own, and it seemed as though all would be well. But in the end the job fell through. Perhaps, as he said, it was because he was Jewish, and Kiev was noted for its anti-Semitism. At all events, very soon there was no job, no money and debts that had to be paid somehow. It was a crisis that was to recur throughout my childhood. . . .

But my mother had other troubles. Four little boys and a girl all fell ill: Two of them died before they were a year old, two of them went within one month. My mother mourned each one of her babies with a broken heart, but like most Jewish mothers of that generation, she accepted the will of God. . . .

In 1903, when I was about five, we went back to Pinsk. Father, never one to give up, had a new dream now. Never mind the failure of Kiev, he said. He would go to America, to the *goldene medina*—the "land of gold," as the Jews called it—and make his fortune there. Mother, Sheyna, Zipke (the new daughter) and I would wait for him in Pinsk. So he gathered up his few belongings again and left for the unknown continent, and we moved to my grandparents' house. . . .

Anyhow, Father spent three lonely difficult years in America. He had painfully scraped together the money to get there, and like many thousands of the Russian Jews who streamed into the *goldene medina* at the turn of the century, he had thought of America as the one place where he would surely make the fortune that would allow him to return home, to Russia, and to a new life there. Of course, it didn't work out like that—not for him or for the thousands like him—but the idea that he would come back to us made our three years without him easier to bear.

Although the Kiev of my birth is lost to me in the fog of time, I have retained some sort of inner image of Pinsk. I remember mostly the *Pinsker blotte*, as we called them at home, the swamps that seemed to me then like oceans of mud and that we were taught to avoid like the plague. In my memory those swamps are forever linked to my persistent terror of the Cossacks, to a winter night when I played with other children in a narrow lane near the forbidden *blotte* and then suddenly, as though out of nowhere, or maybe out of the swamps themselves, came the Cossacks on their horses, literally galloping over our crouching, shivering bodies. "Well," said my mother later, shivering and crying herself, "what did I tell you?"

Still, not everything could have been so fearful. I was a child, and like all children, I played and sang and made up stories to tell the baby. With Sheyna's help, I learned to read and write and even do a little arithmetic, although I didn't start school in Pinsk, as I should have. "A golden child, they called you," my mother said. "Always busy with something." But what I was really busy doing in Pinsk, I suppose, was learning about life—again, chiefly from Sheyna. . . .

At fourteen, Sheyna was a revolutionary, an earnest, dedicated member of the Socialist-Zionist movement, and as such doubly dangerous in the eyes of police and liable to punishment. Not only were she and her friends "conspiring" to overthrow the all-powerful czar, but they also proclaimed their dream to bring into existence a Jewish socialist state in Palestine. In the Russia of the early twentieth century, even a fourteen- or fifteen-year-old schoolgirl who held such views would be arrested for subversive activity, and I still remember hearing the screams of young men and women being brutally beaten in the police station around the corner from where we lived.

My mother heard those screams, too, and daily begged Sheyna to have nothing to do with the movement; she could endanger herself and us and even Father in America! But Sheyna was very stubborn. It was not enough for her to want changes; she had to participate in bringing them about. Night after night, my mother kept herself awake until Sheyna came home from her mysterious meetings, while I lay in bed, taking it all in silently: Sheyna's devotion to the cause in which she believed so strongly; Mother's overwhelming anxiety; Father's (to me, inexplicable) absence; and the periodic and fearful sound of the hooves of Cossack horses outside.

Although the yearning of the Jews for their own land was not the direct result of pogroms (the idea of the Jewish resettlement of Palestine had been urged by Jews and even some non-Jews long before the word "pogrom" became part of the vocabulary of European Jewry), the Russian pogroms of my childhood gave the idea immediacy, especially when it became clear to the Jews that the Russian government itself was using them as scapegoats of the regime's struggle to put down the revolutionary movement. . . .

On Saturdays, when Mother went off to the synagogue, Sheyna organized meetings at home. Even when Mother found out about them and pleaded with Sheyna not to imperil us, there was nothing she could do about these meetings except nervously walk up and down outside the house when she got back on Saturday morning, patrolling it like a sentry so that when a policeman approached, she could at least warn the young conspirators.

Sometimes, when Sheyna and I got into a fight and I lost my temper, I used to threaten to tell Maxim, the big, red-faced policeman in our neighborhood, all about her political activities. Of course, I never did, and of course, Sheyna knew that my threats were empty; but they worried her all the same. "What will you tell Maxim?" she asked. "I'll tell him that you and all your friends want to do away with the czar," I would shriek.

"Do you know what will happen to me then? I'll be sent away to Siberia, where I'll die of cold and never come back," she'd say. "That's what happens to people who are exiled."

Truth to tell, I was always very careful to keep out of Maxim's way. Whenever I saw him lumbering in my direction, I took to my heels and fled. . . .

It was around this time that Sheyna met Shamai Korngold, her husband-to-be, a strong, clever, gifted boy who had given up the great joy of studying and his burning interest in mathematics in order to join the revolutionary movement. A close-to-wordless romance blossomed between them, and Shamai also became and stayed part of my life. . . . He visited us often, and I can remember his whispered conversations with Sheyna about the increased revolutionary ferment in town and the regiment of Cossacks that were on their way to subdue Pinsk with their flashing swords. It was from these conversations that I gathered that something frightful had happened to the Jews of Kishinev and that in Pinsk the Jews were planning to defend themselves with arms and homemade bombs.

In response to the worsening situation, Sheyna and Shamai did more than merely hold or attend conspiratorial meetings; they did their best to bring other young people into the movement, even, to his horror, the only daughter of our white-bearded *shochet*, the ultra-Orthodox ritual slaughterer from whom we rented the room in which we lived. Eventually, Mother's anxiety for Sheyna and Zipke and me became intolerable, and she began to write frantic letters to my father. It was out of the question, she wrote, for us to stay in Pinsk any longer. We must join him in America.

But like many things in life, this was far easier said than done. My father, who had by now moved from New York to Milwaukee, was barely making a living. He wrote back that he hoped to get a job working on the railway and soon he would have enough money for our tickets. We moved out of the *shochet*'s house to a room in a bagel baker's flat. The bagels were baked at night, so the flat was always hot, and the baker gave my mother a job. Then, late in 1905, a letter came from Milwaukee. My father was working, so we could start getting ready to leave.

The preparations for our journey were long and complicated. It was not a simple matter then for a woman and three girls, two of them still very small, to travel all the way from Pinsk to Milwaukee by themselves. For my mother, relief must have been combined with new anxieties, and for Sheyna leaving Russia meant leaving Shamai and everything for which they had worked so hard and risked so much. I can remember only the hustle and bustle of those last weeks in Pinsk, the farewells from the family, the embraces and the tears. Going to America then was almost like going to the moon. . . . Perhaps if we had known that throughout Europe thousands of families like ours were on the move, headed toward what they, too, firmly believed would be, and was indeed, a better life in the New World, we would have been less frightened. But we knew nothing about the many women and children who were traveling then under similar conditions from countries like Ireland, Italy and Poland to join husbands and fathers in America, and we were very scared. . . .

We had to cross the border into Galicia secretly because, three years earlier, my father had helped a friend reach America by taking that man's wife and daughters with him on his papers and pretending that they were members of his family. So when our turn came to leave, we also had to pretend to be other people. Although we obediently memorized false names and details about our make-believe identities and Sheyna sternly drilled us all until we were letter-perfect—even Zipke—our actual crossing was affected by bribing the police with money Mother had somehow managed to raise. In the confusion most of our "luggage" got lost—or perhaps it was stolen. Anyhow, I remember that early one icy spring morning we finally entered Galicia and the shack in which we waited for the train that would take us to the port. We lived in that unheated shack for two days, sleeping on the unheated floor, and I remember that Zipke cried most of the time until the train finally arrived and distracted her.

It was not a pleasure trip, that fourteen-day journey aboard ship. Crammed into a dark, stuffy cabin with four other people, we spent the nights on sheetless bunks and most of the days standing in line for food that was ladled out to us as though we were cattle. Mother, Sheyna and Zipke were seasick most of the time, but I felt well and can remember staring at the sea for hours, wondering what Milwaukee would be like.

6

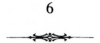

"I Am Alive to Tell You This Story. . ."

Golda Meier's family was not the last to emigrate in fear of their lives. In the second half of the twentieth century hundreds of thousands of women came to the United States as refugees form revolution or war in eastern Europe, Central America, Cuba, and, most numerous of all, Southeast Asia. In this interview a "boat person" describes her escape from Vietnam after the Communist takeover in the mid-1970s. The interview focuses on her perilous boat trip to Malaysia, the first stage of her immigration to the United States. While most of the horrors she describes were shared by women and men, some of the worst experiences—fear of rape and of being sold into prostitution—were unique to women.

Like most "boat people," this woman spent several years in refugee camps in Southeast Asia before she could enter the United States. She was twenty-six years old and living in Pittsburgh at the time of this interview. "I kept thinking how difficult it must be for this woman to talk with me about her escape," recorded the interviewer. "She has beautiful dark eyes and even more beautiful hands. . . . She is busy making tea for me and there is a quiet in the room broken only by her slightly distracting wristwatch noise."

I am alive to tell you this story—at least I am lucky for that. I survived the escape and the Thai pirates. We spent some years in Malaysia and now live in Pittsburgh. It has not been easy to remember these events. If I had been younger or prettier, I, too, would have been taken to Ko Kra [to be sold into prostitution].

Source: John Tenhula, ed., *Voices from Southeast Asia: The Refugee Experience in the United States* (New York: Holmes and Meier, 1991), pp. 67–69.

We left Vietnam on December 15, 1979, from Rach Gia. It was five years since the Communists took power. Things would never again be the same for us. We are really Chinese and our great-grandparents had come south from China. We were businesspeople whose lives were forever changed by the Communists. They took our property and our clothing business and then sent us to a reeducation camp in the west. We survived that. There was no future in Vietnam for us. We paid $5,000 for two places on a boat. It took some months for the plans to materialize, and then our departure was very quick. Our boat was Number SS 060. It was small—only fourteen and a half meters long and there were ninety-one people on board when we left, so you can see how very crowded it must have been. . . .

The first day of the journey was uneventful. The shock of leaving, the size of the boat, and the crowd of people struck me. My husband was very, very quiet the first day; he just sat on our baggage. All of our lives were stored in the baggage we carried. All those memories. It felt so very strange to carry them around. That day, a very old woman was sick all day with the movement of the boat. Her moans kept us all awake. I wanted to move but there was nowhere to go. No space. We had only a little space and if we moved we would lose even that. There were six small babies that cried, cried all the time. One began, they all cried together. We were afraid of being discovered by the Vietnamese border patrol, but after the first day, we didn't need to worry a lot about that.

The second day out, the waters got rougher. Especially in the afternoon, the waters were so high that we were tossed back and forth; back and forth. The drinking water we brought got so hot and it smelled from the heat and other things. More people got sick, and the two medical doctors that were on the boat were being asked many questions and they were busy all of the time. Throughout this difficult period, I held on to my bags very tight. I was watching my husband's bags, too. Two people we knew on the ship had been robbed already. They had been asleep and when they awoke they were missing things—taken from a small bag that one of them was sleeping near, with the straps wrapped around his hands while he slept, but they cut the handles right off. Many people were so close, but no one was caught. Who knows who did it; after a while, everybody looked suspicious, guilty. That evening there was a bad argument over the distribution of drinking water and food. The ship's captain said something about wanting more money, more gold. We never understood what he wanted. Some of the crew were drinking liquor and got very drunk and loud. By the second day, I knew all of the ninety-one faces on board very well, faces I thought I had seen all my life. On the third day of the journey, we encountered three Thai pirate boats.

They were small boats. This is what we all feared, although we had not talked about it. We had all heard stories, and the people that we left behind had told us about the stories. We thought they had warned us in a funny kind of way: they were teasing us with the stories, maybe because they were jealous or they did not want us to leave Vietnam. But you always think that your escape will be different, your example will be different. From now on, the happenings will always be on my mind, engraved on my mind like a carving in a jade stone. Only this was a nightmare carved very, very deep.

We were tied to two of the three boats. There were many protests and screams by all of us, but that was useless, and under the sun, all of this energy was just lost. Some began to cry softly. It was a mixed reaction. The men could do nothing after they had screamed at the pirates. My husband and I stepped very close together; all I can remember is that I could hear his heart beat hard. We were holding each other up for support. An old woman next to me started screaming, so near to my ear; screaming about robbery and rape. She was going crazy. She had a young and pretty daughter under her old cloth that she was trying to protect. At that moment, two of our men fell into the water and the Thai pirates would not let them get back into the boat. They stayed in the water until the pirates left, holding onto the boat.

Some twenty pirates came on board and demanded gold. Gold! Gold! They screamed that they knew we had gold and they did not have time for us. If we did not give them gold, we would die in the water. For the next four hours—but it seemed so much longer—these pirates tore open our bags and our clothes. We tried to hide some rings, but it was not possible. They took our bags and spilled the contents. Our money was kept in a false bottom of the bag that my husband had constructed, but they found it. They knew exactly where to look. All of this at the same time they were teasing the young girls, the pretty girls. They were animals, not people. They were pigs, these pirates!

Two of the young and pretty girls were taken to the front of the boat and raped. Everyone heard everything, all of the screams. That is what I remember, the screams. After a while, the screams stopped, the crying stopped, and there was silence. Everyone on the boat was still, but not for long. The pirates separated twenty women and ordered them off the boat. There were many protests. Nothing helped. People even fell overboard. It was mass confusion, hysteria, and shock. They were the prettiest girls and after they were gone, all we could hear were more cries and muffled protests. They took our girls, water, and food. We were left to die. Five days later, a Norwegian ship picked us up.

The officials said the girls that the pirates stole were taken to Ko Kra island and sold into prostitution. You know it was a nightmare and everyone was part of it. You could not close your eyes. You could not close your ears. I still see the faces and hear the cries. We landed in Lampini camp as a heavy rain began.

PART II

◆━◈━◆

Surviving in a New Land

Though they differed widely in cultural background and in the time and circumstances of their immigration, women entering the United States faced a common set of problems. They had to adjust to an unfamiliar, often hostile physical environment, unfamiliar food and clothing, a new language (in most cases), new customs, perhaps even new values. Women who moved from the traditional, perhaps communal, agricultural villages of the old world to the competitive industrial centers of urban America were entering a society so different from their former homes that it was, literally, a new world. Whatever their point of departure and whatever their destination, most women found their lives so radically changed that their initial years in America were consumed by a struggle for physical and psychological survival. The readings in Part 2 document that struggle and the courage, ingenuity, and determination of the women who waged it.

Culture Shock

Age, personality, and earlier experiences affected the way women coped with the shock of immigration. Adjustment was usually easier for the young, and for the adventurous, the flexible, and the physically and emotionally strong of every age. The move from country to city was easier for women who had lived at least for a short time in a city in their homeland before coming to urban America. By the mid-twentieth century increasing numbers had the advantage of this two-step immigration.

Women who came from a common country of origin at a particular time often shared similar adjustment problems. In the first selection Emma Gee describes the special problems, and strengths for meeting those problems, of early twentieth-century Japanese "picture brides." These women faced not only the cultural shock of moving from a nonwestern to a western society, but, simultaneously, the stress of beginning life with husbands they had married by proxy and had met briefly or not at all. While the situation of the Japanese picture bride was unique, many other women were met upon arrival by fiancés they had known only long ago or, in the case of arranged marriages, never known at all. For young women the cultural shock of immigration often coincided with the sudden (and often difficult) transition from parental care to independence.

For the vast majority of immigrants, earning a living was the most immediate problem. (Part 3 of this book, "Work," tells how women met that need. Part 2 focuses on other problems.) Homesickness was a nearly universal problem. Mexican, Canadian, and Caribbean immigrants were sometimes able to visit their former homes, as were the relatively well-to-do professionals (or wives of professionals) who entered under the new quotas of 1965. Under the family reunification provisions of post-1965 immigration laws, recent immigrants were sometimes able to bring parents and other relatives to the United States. For most women, however, and especially for the earlier immigrants, coming to the United States meant cutting ties with loved ones for many years, often forever. The pain of separation is expressed in the following letter from a Norwegian immigrant to her sisters in 1850:

> It was a bitter cup for me to drink, to leave a dear mother and sisters and to part forever in this life, though living. Only the thought of the coming world . . . [is] my consolation; there I shall see you all. . . . I hope that time will heal the wound, but up to the present I cannot deny that homesickness gnaws at me hard.[1]

For some, the wound never healed.

Loneliness was compounded by the problem of language. While women who were surrounded by friends and relatives from the homeland continued to enjoy companionship in their native language, their more isolated counterparts suffered agonies of loneliness and embarrassment because of an inability to speak English. Many had experiences similar to those of German-born Katharina, the central figure in Hope Williams Sykes' novel, *The Joppa Door*. When an English-speaking neighbor asked to borrow a "pick" to dig with, Katharina showed him her pig pen. The neighbor went away laughing, but Katharina was not amused:

> He is hurrying to tell his familie about the dumb people who live next door. Ach, sure I am shamed inside myself. I did not plan that my children nor myself should live and be foolish and bring much laughter to the neighbors. After this when anyone comes to my door talking American, I shake my head and make no answer.
>
> Better they think I am dumb than a foolish. But a loneliness fills me. . . . In my heart it is barren.[2]

On the Frontier

The women who settled on the frontier during the nineteenth century found adjustment to America a struggle for physical survival. Guri Endreson, the author of the second selection, lost her husband and a son and barely escaped with her own life during one of the mid-nineteenth-century Indian wars. Endreson had no sympathy for the fact that native Americans were resisting white invasion of their ancestral lands. She did have personal courage, however, and a determination to survive and rebuild her home.

For most frontier women the fight for survival was not a battle against other people; it was a battle against the calamities of nature. Women watched helplessly as droughts turned the soil to dust, swarms of locusts devoured their grain, and epidemics decimated and debilitated their families. Hunger and disease were familiar enemies, but the isolation of rural American life was new. Accustomed to the companionship of friends and relatives and the sociability of village life, women on frontier homesteads were dismayed to find themselves many miles from their nearest neighbors. While men were more likely to travel to settlements for supplies, women might go for weeks, even months, seeing no one outside of the immediate family. Isolation could be fatal in times of injury, sickness, or difficult childbirth. The flat, barren landscape of the Great Plains only reinforced the desolation and vulnerability felt by women homesick for the hills, woods, or seas of their birthplace. "This formless prairie had no heart that beat, no waves that sang, no soul that could be touched . . . empty, desolate, endless wastes of green and blue. . . . If life is to thrive and endure, it must at least have something to hide behind."[3]

The struggle for survival on the frontier had a moral as well as a physical dimension. The violent, opportunistic, and fiercely competitive atmosphere of the frontier challenged many of the values women had brought with them from more rigidly structured, traditional societies. While some women adapted quickly, holding their own in cutthroat battles for land and for water and mineral rights, others were dismayed and fearful. "What would become of children who had to grow up in such an atmosphere?"[4]

In the City

The struggle for survival was different in the city, but no less difficult. During the nineteenth and early twentieth centuries, cities were growing so rapidly—some doubling in population every decade, or sooner—that the supply of housing and services never caught up with the need. Poverty and discrimination condemned immigrants to the worst, most crowded housing—in sheds, garrets, and basements as well as in dark and poorly ventilated tenements.

The urban frontier, like the rural frontier, was a dangerous place. In the nineteenth century, sewage disposal and police and fire protection were often left to chance, or taken care of privately by those who had the means. Water supplies became polluted, and epidemics, gang wars, and crime raged unchecked. Saloons, brothels, and gambling houses flourished in ethnic neighborhoods, confined there by authorities who would not tolerate their existence in "better" neighborhoods. Women struggled to rear families safely in this environment.

Though they did not face the isolation experienced by their rural counterparts, urban women learned that one could also be lonely in a crowded city. Adjusting to the demands of the clock, the factory whistle, and the school bell was often difficult for women accustomed to the less rigid rhythm of rural life. There were times when some women regretted having exchanged the quiet meadows and woodlands of former homes for the noise, heat, dirt, and confusion of the American city. A thirteen-year-old Polish girl who came to Chicago at the turn of the century expressed this feeling:

> [In Chicago] the backyards were very small . . . and I didn't see any beautiful gardens, no charming orchards, no flowers that I could pick freely from delightful meadows. . . . My dear little old town was surrounded with those beautiful things—the meadows were so near that we children could play, run, yell whenever we wanted. In America I missed all those lovely things.[5]

Immigrant women coped with the stresses of urban life by drawing on a variety of resources, both within themselves and within the city. In selection 3 Corinne Krause uses oral histories to document ways in which immigrant women in early twentieth-century Pittsburgh used their families, their friends, their neighborhoods, and their churches to help them adjust successfully to their new environment. The same coping mechanisms—family, friends, neighborhoods, religion—were used by rural as well as urban women and by recent immigrants as well as those who came long ago.

Twentieth-century reformers tried to make the cities cleaner and safer, but politicians concentrated these improvements on neighborhoods inhabited by the wealthy rather than on ethnic ghettos. Changes included housing codes, municipal garbage removal and water systems, more schools and playgrounds, the development of police, fire, and welfare departments, and various official "wars" on organized crime and drugs. Still, urban life remained full of hardships and dangers for the nonaffluent women arriving from Mexico, Puerto Rico, China, or elsewhere in the mid- and late twentieth century. Selection 4 describes the struggle of a Puerto Rican immigrant, Innocencia Flores, to survive in one of many "delapidated and deteriorating" housing units in Spanish Harlem.

Late Twentieth-Century Arrivals

Advertising, movies, and newspapers made information about American life more accessible to post-1965 immigrants than to their predecessors. Still, recent immigrants, like their predecessors, faced many problems of adjustment. They had to find a job and a place to live, learn to shop in a supermarket, and master conversational English, an especially difficult task for Asian immigrants whose native languages were so different. Hundreds of thousands of illegal immigrants lived in fear of discovery and deportation. Refugees who had seen loved ones die, or who had been forced to leave them behind, had the burden of learning to live with residual nightmares and the "guilt" of having survived.

Immigrants from preindustrial or "developing" societies had special problems. Women from the "hill country" areas of Southeast Asia were unfamiliar with the technology of everyday life in America—central heating, refrigeration, indoor plumbing. Women from many countries found it difficult to accept "western" style medical care, including examinations by male physicians. Mien women who gave birth to babies in American hospitals might go hungry if doctors did not order the rice, small cubes of chopped chicken, and special broth considered necessary for recovering mothers. Educated as well as uneducated women from more tightly controlled societies were horrified by the crime, drugs, racial conflict, and open displays of sexuality that were part of the fabric of late twentieth-century American life. Like their earlier counterparts, most recent women arrivals made successful adjustments to new customs and values, though not without pain. This is illustrated in selection 5, a short story in which a newly arrived Pakistani widow comes to terms with the life-style and values of her Americanized son.

The Continuing Struggle

Time alleviated most of the problems of initial adjustment. But time also introduced an additional problem—old age in a new land. Women brought up in societies that honored the elderly could find it a painful experience to grow old in the youth-oriented United States. A study of elderly Puerto Rican working-class women in Boston in the mid-1980s found that they maintained a place in the "functional structure" of their families and validated their own importance by providing advice, childcare, food, and other assistance to children and grandchildren who lived nearby.[6] In middle-class, geographically mobile families, however, Puerto Rican and otherwise, close family relationships were more difficult to maintain. Their husbands dead and their children scattered, many women found themselves, like Basha in the final selection, struggling alone to maintain their independence and self-respect.

Not all women who came to America adjusted successfully. Some died of malnutrition, disease, or the complications of pregnancy and childbirth. Overwhelmed by poverty, loneliness, and hopelessness, others lapsed into chronic illness or insanity, or committed suicide. Danish-born journalist Jacob Riis described such cases in an exposé of New York's poor (mostly immigrants) in 1890:

Within a single week I have had this year three cases of insanity provoked directly by poverty and want. One was that of a mother who in the middle of the night got up to murder her child, who was crying for food. . . .

Perhaps this may be put down as an exceptional case, but one that came to my notice some months ago in a Seventh Ward tenement was typical enough to escape that reproach. There were nine in the family . . . honest, hardworking Germans, scrupulously neat, but poor. All nine lived in two rooms. . . . The rent was seven dollars and a half a month, more than a week's wages for the husband . . . the only bread-winner in the family. That day the mother had thrown herself out of the window and was carried up from the street dead. She was "discouraged," said some of the other women from the tenement.[7]

As air travel became safe and more affordable, some women became "binational," shuttling back and forth between the United States and the homeland. As many as a third of the women who immigrated, however, returned home to stay. Some left the United States because they were unhappy; the benefits of immigration seemed too few, the costs too great. Some left for political or ideological reasons, returning to newly liberated homelands after World War I or to the Soviet Union after the Communist Revolution. Some found the United States too materialistic, racist, and uncaring, or too dangerous for the rearing of children. Others left for economic reasons. They had come, alone or with husbands or parents, to make money for the purchase of a farm or a small business in their homeland. Having succeeded—or failed—in this endeavor, they returned home.

Most women stayed because, difficult as life might be, it was better than what they had left behind. A nineteenth-century servant girl who had immigrated from Norway noted her good fortune at having "food and drink in abundance . . . while my dear ones in Bergen . . . lack the necessaries of life."[8] A newcomer to New York City at the turn of the century noted that her tenement lacked running water and indoor toilets, but added that "it seemed quite advanced compared with our home in Khelm."[9] Finally, women stayed because they had hope for a better future—if not for themselves, then for the next generation. They took comfort in the thought that their children would never know the hunger and oppression they had experienced in the old world—or the loneliness they suffered in the new.

Notes

1. Henrietta Jessen to Eleonore and Dorea Williamsin, February 20, 1850, in Theodore Blegen, trans. and ed., "Immigrant Women and the

American Frontier: Three Early 'America Letters,' " *Norwegian American Studies and Record* 5 (1930): 21–22.

2. Hope Williams Sykes, *The Joppa Door* (New York: G. P. Putnam's Sons, 1937), p. 185.

3. O. E. Rolvaag, *Giants in the Earth* (New York: Harper and Brothers, 1927), p. 38.

4. Ibid., p. 153.

5. "Impressions of America by a Polish Trade Unionist," *Life and Labor* 6 (November 1916): 172.

6. Melba Sancchez-Ayendez, "Puerto Rican Elderly Women: Shared Meanings and Informal Supportive Networks," in *All American Women: Lines That Divide, Ties That Bind*, ed. Johnnetta B. Cole (New York and London: Free Press, 1986), pp. 172–86.

7. Jacob Riis, *How the Other Half Lives* (New York: Scribners, 1890), pp. 4–47, 171.

8. Jannicke Saehle to Johannes Saehle, September 28, 1847, in Blegen, "Immigrant Women," p. 21.

9. Rose Schneiderman with Lucy Goldwaite, *All for One* (New York: Paul S. Eriksson, 1967), p. 24.

1

━━◆❖◆━━

Issei Women: "Picture Brides" in America

Although Japanese immigration began in the late 1880s, women arrived in sig-
nificant numbers only after 1900. While married men sent for their wives, single
men either returned to Japan for a bride or, more commonly, arranged a marriage
long distance. These "picture-bride" marriages, in which the couples had seldom
seen each other except by photograph, were negotiated and formalized in confor-
mity with Japanese tradition in which arranged marriages were the rule and the
presence of either or even both parties was not necessary. Already prejudiced
against Asians, many established American citizens declared picture-bride mar-
riages immoral and un-Christian, additional proof that the Japanese would never
assimilate. In response to growing social pressure in the United States, the Japa-
nese government ceased issuing passports to emigrants in 1920, and the American
government barred virtually all immigration from Asia is the 1924 Immigra-
tion Act.

The transition from one culture to another is always difficult, but for
Japanese picture brides the difficulties were multiplied by the American society so
different from and hostile to their own that it did not even recognize the legitimacy
of their marriages. Author Emma Gee notes that sympathetic historians of immi-
gration have been so preoccupied with presenting the Japanese as "objects" of
American discrimination that they have neglected to see them as "subjects," mul-
tidimensional people who acted as well as found themselves acted upon. Here Gee
presents Issei (first-generation Japanese-American) women as subjects, adjusting to
their new lives quietly, as their culture dictated, but with great strength of character.

It is difficult for us today to imagine the experience of the Issei pioneer
woman from the time of her marriage to her arrival and settlement in
America. The following excerpts from accounts written by some of them will
provide, hopefully, some insight into their experience. To begin with, just
how did she feel and think about her marriage and her future in America?
One picture bride comments on her husband:

Source: Emma Gee, "Issei Women," in *Counterpoint: Perspectives on Asian America,*
ed. Emma Gee (Los Angeles, 1976).

I had but remote ties with him. Yet because of the talks between our close parents and my parents' approval and encouragement, I decided upon our picture-bride marriage.

The family in her specific case—indeed, in most marriages—had played the decisive role, and her decision was dependent upon it. But however the decision was arrived at, the prospects of coming to America must have been viewed with mixed emotions. On the one hand, there is the example of a wife whose husband had preceded her to America:

> I was bubbling over with great expectations. My young heart, 19 years and 8 months old, burned, not so much with the prospects of reuniting with my new husband, but with the thought of the New World.

Many women like her placed great store in America, and their glowing images of America accounted for their enthusiasm. This same person continues:

> My husband who had returned to Japan to seek a wife wore a Western style high-collar suit at our *omiai*. He told unusual stories about America which were like dreams to me. Being reared in the countryside, I listened intently with wide-opened eyes. Thus, I thought about how heavenly America was.

Attired in latest Western suits, Japanese males who returned to Japan naturally told tales which, while not necessarily fictional, were probably embroidered to impress prospective brides. After all, they were the "successful" individuals who had the economic means to return to Japan! Other women received similar impressions from letters and photographs from their husbands-to-be in America who were equally anxious to secure wives. An element of vanity no doubt was intermingled, especially with a captive audience eager for news about foreign lands, and the tendency was toward the hyperbole.

Still there were husbands who were candid. "My unknown husband had said," according to another picture bride, " 'If you come with great expectations about living in an immigrant land, you will be disappointed.' I had received letters which said that if I intended to see things through without giving up, then I should come to America." And this particular woman, having this understanding clearly in mind made the following resolution:

> On the way from Kobe to Yokohama, gazing upon the rising majestic Mount Fuji in a cloudless sky aboard the ship, I made a resolve. For a woman who was going to a strange society and relying upon an unknown husband whom she had married through photographs, my heart had to be as beautiful as Mount Fuji. I resolved that the heart of a Japanese woman had to be sublime, like that

soaring majestic figure eternally constant through wind and rain, heat and cold. Thereafter, I never forgot that resolve on the ship, enabling me to overcome sadness and suffering.

The passage across the Pacific was a mixture of sadness at leaving Japan and apprehensions concerning the future. Having left families, relatives, and all that was familiar to them, now the women were actually enroute to meet and live with their husbands in an alien land. In this regard, a picture bride records:

> I left Yokohama on the *Minnesota*. Passengers from Yokohama were placed into rooms partitioned by canvas. Besides myself and two other married women returning to America, there was a couple. The two married women had left their children in Japan and would cry when they talked about them. I, too, broke out in tears when I thought of my father, who had passed away just before my departure.

Yet the passage was tolerable, for in most instances there was the companionship of other women who also were coming to America under similar circumstances, among whom the sadness, excitement, and uneasiness could be shared.

As the ship neared the port of debarkation, the excitement of the future prevailed over the sadness of leaving. Apprehensions also increased as the ship pulled alongside the pier. One of the most typical scenes was the sight of the brides on board and the bridegrooms on the pier both trying to match the photographs in their hands with their respective partners. Since some individuals had forwarded old photographs of themselves, taken as much as ten to fifteen years ago, in such cases both sides had a difficult time of it.

And in other cases the photographs did not match with the actual person—the village "old maid" or the "ugly old man" may have sent someone else's picture out of fear of rejection. . . .

As soon as they were able to debark, it was common for the husbands to whisk off their new brides to a clothing store. The Japanese were well aware that the Chinese had been excluded in 1882. Since the Chinese had not adopted Western-style clothing, according to the common belief among the Japanese, they had provided substance to the charge that they were nonassimilable. To avoid any recurrence of this accusation, Japanese husbands had their new brides fitted in a new set of Western clothing to replace the traditional Japanese kimono in which they had landed. A picture bride describes this event in the following manner:

> I was immediately outfitted with Western clothing at Hara's Clothing Store. . . . At that time a suit of Western clothing cost from $25 to $27–28. Because I had to wear a tight corset around my chest, I

could not bend forward. I had to have my husband tie my shoe laces. There were some women who fainted because it was too tight. There are stories of women being carried to the hotel rooms by their husbands who hurriedly untied the corset strings which were not joking matters. In my case, I wore a large hat, a high-necked blouse, a long skirt, a buckled belt around my waist, high-laced shoes, and, of course, for the first time in my life, a brassiere and hip pads.

For these women unaccustomed to wearing Western-style clothing, their new wardrobe was as strange as it was uncomfortable. This same woman goes on to say:

> What gave me trouble was the underwear. Japanese women used only a *koshimaki* (a sarong-like underskirt). Wearing Western-style underwear for the first time, I would forget to take it down when I went to the toilet. And I frequently committed the blunder.

Once the ordeal of landing and the initial encounter with America were over, their new life with their husbands began, which was anything but easy. For not only did they have to adjust to an alien environment, they also had to establish a new household. On the lack of modern amenities, a woman writes:

> At the farm on Vashon Island to which I went, I had to draw water by bucket from a well. . . . I boiled water and put it into a tub. There was no electricity. I used oil lamps. No matter how backward Japan may have been, this was life in the hinterland. Still I toiled in sweat alongside my husband.

In rural regions, especially in the remote areas to which the Japanese went, the living quarters were primitive:

> I discovered that our house was a house in name only, a shack where hunters had lived located in the middle of the field. There was only one room with beds placed in three corners. My husband was living here with a younger boy and older person. Since he and I had no honeymoon period, a makeshift curtain was created by stretching a rope across the room and hanging clothes from it. It was unsuitable for us newlyweds to say the least! . . . The shack had been fashioned out of boards and leaked. There were no eaves to drain the rain. Sometimes we passed the night with raincoats over our beds.

Small hotel rooms were common quarters for those who settled down in the cities:

Everyone lived in a hotel. We ate beside the beds. And since we had the minimum amount of eating utensils for two persons, if friends came during mealtime, we said 'just one minute please,' washed our bowls, and then had our friends use them. The room was about the size of six tatami with a coal stove which we used for cooking meals. The room had only cold water.

Most Issei women immediately began to work alongside their husbands. Because of the need to eke out a living, they could not afford the luxury of a honeymoon. Besides doing the regular chores of cooking, washing, cleaning, and sewing, they also labored long hours in the fields or shops. A woman recounts her early agricultural work:

At the beginning I worked with my husband picking potatoes or onions and putting them in sacks. Working with rough-and-tumble men, I became weary to the bones; waking up in the mornings I could not bend over the wash basin. Sunlight came out about 4:00 A.M. during the summer in the Yakima Valley. I arose at 4:30. After cooking breakfast, I went out to the fields. There was no electric stove or gas like now. It took over one hour to cook, burning kindling wood. As soon as I came home, I first put on the fire, took off my hat, and then I washed my hands. After cooking breakfast and lunch, I went to the fields.

Work was not less difficult nor shorter in the urban occupations. Take, for example, the case of a woman whose husband operated a laundry. After working the entire day, she records that:

I started at 5:00 P.M. to prepare supper for five to six persons, and then I began my evening work. The difficult ironing remained. Women's blouses in those days were made from silk or lace, with collars, and long sleeves and lots of frills. I could only finish two in one hour, ironing them with great care. Hence, I worked usually until 12:00 to 1:00 A.M. But it was not just me—all women who worked in the laundry business probably did the same thing.

Soon after these experiences with the harsh realities of life in America, Issei women began to bear children. In most rural areas where the Issei settled doctors were not readily available. Even if they were, either the white doctors refused to treat them or the Japanese could not afford their services. Certainly no such institution as a prenatal clinic existed to which the Issei women could turn and prepare themselves for childbirth.

As a general rule, midwives substituted for doctors in the delivery of children. One woman whose inexperienced husband performed the role of midwife for their first child writes about the advice which he received from a friend who had successfully delivered a child. She quotes this friend as stating:

> The cutting of the umbilical cord is what is important. First you must firmly tie the cord near the naval with a string in two places. Then you cut in between the two knots with a scissor.

Following this advice, she reports that she and her husband gave birth to eight children in this manner. . . .

We can safely assume that not all Issei women were as stoic. . . . Think of the young women in remote isolated areas who did not have the benefit of advice and comfort, and who had no one with whom to share their anxieties. What courage it must have taken to bear their children alone! And what happened to the women who developed complications during pregnancy and in the act of giving birth? Until detailed studies are undertaken, we will have to rely upon our imagination to answer this question.

Problems of post-natal care and child-rearing naturally followed successful childbirth. In households where the women also performed crucial economic functions, especially in farming areas, a reasonable period of post-natal recuperation was considered a luxury which could not be afforded. Commenting on her experience, an Issei woman writes:

> Twenty-one days of post-natal rest was common even in Japan. Even busy housewives with household chores to do took this 21-day rest without doing anything. I, however, could not rest for more than three days.

Being a member of a farming household, she had to resume her agricultural work responsibilities after only three days of rest. Most Issei women had to raise their children by themselves because of the sharp sexual division of labor within the home. Even if they worked in the family economic unit, they still had to carry the entire burden of housekeeping and child rearing. An Issei woman reveals:

> My husband was a Meiji man. He did not think of helping in the house or with the children. No matter how busy I may have been, he never changed the baby's diapers. Though it may not be right to say this ourselves, we Issei pioneer women from Japan worked solely for our husband. At mealtime, whenever there was not enough food, we served a lot to our husbands and took very little for ourselves.

Despite long, arduous hours of labor and the innumerable difficulties of childbirth and childrearing, the Issei women persevered.

From the foregoing brief excerpts, it is clear that these were truly remarkable women. From their initial decision to come to America, whether as picture brides or not, through the Trans-Pacific voyage and ordeal of disembarkation, and finally to their adaptation to life in America, they had the physical stamina and moral courage to persist and survive. In spite of the primitive conditions, particularly in the rural areas, they worked unremittingly with a minimum of complaints. They never thought solely of their own welfare. They thought more about giving than taking. They labored beside their husbands and raised their children as best they could within the framework of the beliefs and values they had been taught in late Meiji Japan. Their lives were not sensational. Possessed of an extraordinary strength of character derived from quiet fortitude, the Issei women found life meaningful.

Many Sansei (third-generation Japanese-Americans) today are decrying the image of the "Quiet American" with some measure of justification. Yet amid the clamor for social change, accompanied at times by loud political rhetoric, we should not disparage the quiet fortitude of these Issei women. In America, quietness and modesty tend to be equated with weakness, but with these Issei women, quietness and modesty are sure signs of strength.

2

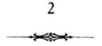

"I Escaped with My Life"

The relentless westward movement of European Americans (old and new) during the nineteenth century resulted in the "Indian Wars," as native Americans fought in vain to protect their lands and preserve their way of life. Guri Endreson describes her experiences during an Indian war in Minnesota in the following letter, written to her parents in Norway in 1860, several years after the tragic events it describes. Despite the destruction of her home and the decimation of her family, Endreson managed to escape and help others, a detail modestly omitted from her letter. Her presence of mind during the attack is equalled by her fortitude in the years that followed. The concluding paragraphs of the letter reveal the widowed Endreson as practical-minded, self-supporting, and so optimistic about the life she has rebuilt that she invites a daughter from Norway to join her.

Source: Guri Endreson to relatives, December 2, 1866, in Theodore Blegen, trans. and ed., "Immigrant Women and the American Frontier: Three Early 'America Letters,' " *Norwegian American Studies and Records* 5 (1930): 26–29.

DEAR DAUGHTER AND YOUR HUSBAND AND CHILDREN, AND MY BELOVED
MOTHER:
I have received your letter of April fourteenth, this year, and I send you
herewith my heartiest thanks for it, for it gives me great happiness to hear
from you and to know that you are alive, well, and in general thriving. I must
also report briefly to you how things have been going with me recently,
though I must ask you to forgive me for not having told you earlier about my
fate. I do not seem to have been able to do so much as to write to you, because
during the time when the savages raged so fearfully here I was not able to
think about anything except being murdered, with my whole family, by these
terrible heathen. But God be praised, I escaped with my life, unharmed by
them, and my four daughters also came through the danger unscathed. Guri
and Britha* were carried off by the wild Indians, but they got a chance the
next day to make their escape; when the savages gave them permission to get
some food, these young girls made use of the opportunity to flee and thus
they got away alive, and on the third day after they had been taken, some
Americans came along who found them on a large plain or prairie. . . . I myself wandered aimlessly around on my land with my youngest daughter and
I had to look on while they shot my precious husband dead, and in my sight
my dear son Ole was shot through the shoulder. But he got well again from
this wound and lived a little more than a year and then was taken sick and
died. We also found my oldest son Endre shot dead, but I did not see the
firing of this death shot. For two days and nights I hovered about here with
my little daughter between fear and hope and almost crazy, before I found
my wounded son and a couple of other persons, unhurt, who helped us to get
away to a place of greater security.

To be an eyewitness to these things and to see many others wounded and
killed was almost too much for a poor woman; but, God be thanked, I kept
my life and my sanity, though all my movable property was torn away and
stolen. But this would have been nothing if only I could have had my loved
husband and children—but what shall I say? God permitted it to happen
thus, and I had to accept my heavy fate and thank Him for having spared my
life and those of some of my dear children.

I must also let you know that my daughter Gjaertru has land, which they
received from the government under a law that has been passed, called in our
language "the Homestead law," and for a quarter section of land they have to
pay sixteen dollars, and after they have lived there five years they receive a
deed and complete possession of the property and can sell it if they want to
or keep it if they want to. She lives abut twenty-four American miles from

---

*Two of the author's daughters.

here and is doing well. My daughter Guri is away in house service for an American about a hundred miles from here; she has been there working for the same man for four years; she is in good health and is doing well; I visited her recently, but for a long time I knew nothing about her, whether she was alive or not.

My other two daughters, Britha and Anna, are at home with me, are in health, and are thriving here. I must also remark that it was four years on the twenty-first of last August since I had to flee from my dear home, and since that time I have not been on my land, as it is only a sad sight because at the spot where I had a happy home, there are now only ruins and remains left as reminders of the terrible Indians. Still I moved up here to the neighborhood again this summer. A number of families have moved back here again so that we hope after a while to make conditions pleasant once more. Yet the atrocities of the Indians are and will be fresh in memory; they have now been driven beyond the boundaries of the state and we hope that they never will be allowed to come here again. I am now staying at the home of Sjur Anderson, two and a half miles from my home.

I must also tell you how much I had before I was ruined in this way. I had seventeen head of cattle, eight sheep, eight pigs, and a number of chickens; now I have six head of cattle, four sheep, one pig; five of my cattle stayed on my land until February, 1863, and lived on some hay and stacks of wheat on the land; and I received compensation from the government for my cattle and other movable property that I lost. Of the six cattle that I now have three are milk cows and of these I have sold butter, the summer's product, a little over two hundred and thirty pounds; I sold this last month and got sixty-six dollars for it. In general I may say that one or another has advised me to sell my land, but I would rather keep it for a time yet, in the hope that some of my people might come and use it; it is difficult to get such good land again, and if you, my dear daughter, would come here, you could buy it and use it and then it would not be necessary to let it fall into the hands of strangers.

And now in closing I must send my very warm greetings to my unforgettable dear mother, my dearest daughter and her husband and children, and in general to all my relatives, acquaintances, and friends. And may the Lord by his grace bend, direct, and govern our hearts so that we sometime with gladness may assemble with God in the eternal mansions where there will be no more partings, no sorrows, no more trials, but everlasting joy and gladness, and contentment in beholding God's face. If this be the goal for all our endeavors through the sorrows and cares of this life, then through his grace we may hope for a blessed life hereafter, for Jesus sake.

Always your devoted
GURI OLSDATTER

Write to me soon.

3

———✦◆✦———

"Urbanization Without Breakdown"

Women who moved from the farms and villages of southern and eastern Europe to the smoke and grime of industrial Pittsburgh in the early twentieth century entered one of the roughest and ugliest environments in urban America. Corinne Azen Krause interviewed forty-five of these women. Like much other recent research, Krause's findings suggest that immigration did not cause severe or permanent pathology in the lives of most people who came from rural Europe to urban America. While Krause gives brief attention to the minority who never adjusted to America at all, what chiefly interests her is the majority, who did adjust successfully. In the following selection, she describes the strength and support these women found in their families, their churches, their neighbors, and their ethnic communities. These resources helped immigrant women in Pittsburgh and throughout urban America not only to survive, but to build satisfying new lives.

Pittsburgh was not an attractive city for women at the turn of the century. While expanding industry sparked demand for all kinds of goods and services that men produced, there was little demand for women in the labor force. In addition, public services and utilities were abysmally inadequate, making living conditions primitive and difficult in poorer neighborhoods. Most immigrants settled in ethnic enclaves in the poorest neighborhoods.

In spite of these difficulties, the evidence points to a successful adjustment for most immigrant women. This article explores the transition of women from southern and eastern Europe who settled in Pittsburgh and surrounding mill towns between 1900 and 1937. Evidence from selected tape-recorded interviews of 45 foreign-born Italian, Jewish, and Slavic women between the ages of sixty-eight and eighty illustrates factors that proved helpful to women in the transition period.

No single factor can be deemed responsible for the adjustment of these immigrant women. Indeed, a wide variety of elements contributed to their adaptation to America, demonstrating that women did find a niche for them-

Source: "Urbanization Without Breakdown: Italian, Jewish and Slavic Immigrant Women in Pittsburgh, 1900–1945" by Corinne Azen Krause is reprinted from JOURNAL OF URBAN HISTORY, vol. 4, no. 3 (May 1978), pp. 291–306 by permision of the Publisher. Sage Publications, Inc.

selves and achieved a degree of self-esteem without transforming themselves into any single "American" model. The varied avenues of adjustment testify to the reality of cultural pluralism.

The data indicate that for the majority of eastern and southern European women in Pittsburgh, informal networks of friends, relatives, neighbors, and their own children were the most significant agents of successful adjustment. In addition, the establishment of ethnic churches and the celebration of religious festivals frequently proved means of forming crucial ties between old and new societies.

The actual process of acquiring citizenship provided a sense of accomplishment and belonging to women from all three immigrant groups. Formal agencies such as the settlement houses and Carnegie Libraries reached relatively few immigrant women. While their children would be active members, immigrant women comprised the group least likely to participate in such activities.

Paid employment also came within the experience of only a small minority of immigrant women in Pittsburgh. Pittsburgh had no textile mills or ladies' garment factories, industries which employed thousands of women in New England and Manhattan. . . .

Even though only a small proportion of immigrant women worked in paying jobs (and most of those were young and single), for those who did, the work experience contributed significantly to the transition to America. Frequently work provided a comfortable social setting with others who spoke the same language; in other cases a job broadened the horizons of immigrants, bringing them into contact with other immigrant groups as well as with native Americans. Perhaps most important, work contributed to a sense of competence that women carried over into other life situations. . . .

Housework, an area almost totally unexplored by historians, broadened the experience and worldliness of peasant women, bringing them into contact with middle class life which they would strive to achieve for their children. As one example, Anna Fovich, said, "I raised my children like rich children. I knew what to do, and I made them go to school. . . ."

For many, the acquisition of citizenship contributed greatly to self-esteem as well as a sense of belonging. This example from Anna Laver's oral history speaks for itself:

I got a letter from United States of America; it's time to go for citizen papers to downtown Pittsburgh. I said to my daughter, "Mary, you have to teach me something." And, she asked me different things. I don't know nothing. Okay, but I had to go get my citizen paper because I got letter. I get two witnesses; two friends from old country went with me. They were already citizens. We wait with lots of people. And then it was my turn. My judge asked me something. I don't know what he said, but I said, "Freedom of speech, freedom of religion, freedom of the press and trial by jury." And, you know what? I'm perfect! We were in a big room, full of people, and the judge looked at me, and he said, "You see this woman? This woman just came from old country but two years, and some of you come twenty years, and you don't know nothing. She pass. Okay, everything correct." I got citizenship papers. Well, everyone look at me—that's true. I was bigger than a prizefighter.

Most women who became citizens had friends to help them. Indeed, friends and relatives were perhaps the most significant agents of adjustment for immigrants. Usually, immigrant women settled in ethnic neighborhoods where neighbors became friends, and frequently earlier immigrants from the same European town helped the newer arrivals find housing and jobs. They acted as matchmakers, and they introduced the immigrants to church, to friends, and to proper American clothes.

In many cases the friends were also relatives. A few women, like Eva Dizenfeld, perceived the Hill District as totally made up of relatives. Mrs. Dizenfeld said:

> We lived in the little Russian town of Pliscov. My mother's parents and my father's parents, and all their brothers and sisters all lived close together. We never met anybody but our own family, and do you know what? It was almost the same thing here in America. We all lived together down in the Hill District and really never mingled with the others. All Father's brothers and sisters came to Pittsburgh and we all lived in the Hill close to each other. . . .

For other women, the neighborhood took the place of family. For Mary Vasil, City Farm Lane in Homestead "was a nice place to live":

> In the evening the ladies would all bring their stools out and sit around and talk about Europe. It was very interesting, even for me, because I remember Europe, and everybody, even the people born in this country, wanted to know. Even now when we ladies meet at church to sew and make quilts, we talk about Europe and what we remember, and how bad it was and it makes us all feel good to be here. My mother never did learn English. The people from Europe—they didn't have anybody to talk to them in English. They talked in Slavish. They had each other, and they felt good to be here because in Europe there was nothing. My mother was happy here. The ladies were all the same; they were like one family.

For single women the neighborhood provided a comfortable social setting where young immigrant men and women could meet. Ruth Hirsh came alone from Russia to live with an aunt in the Hill District. She reported:

All the immigrant boys and girls would meet on Center Avenue and we were friends. I worked sewing pants for a pants factory, and all the girls who worked there were immigrants like me. So, I had friends and we met on the street and we went sometimes to the Irene Kaufmann Center. That's how I met my husband, just on the street where all the immigrant people walked.

The Hill District also played a role in easing the transition of Anna Fodorovich, a young Russian Orthodox woman. She lived with her brother on the South side. She related:

The Russian Church was in the Hill District then. So every Sunday morning my brother would take me and we would walk over the bridge to church. That's where we met people; that's how we socialized, walking back and forth. And, in the Hill District were lots of Jewish people from Russia. And there were all kinds of Russian stores. So, we bought herring and black bread and got together. That's how we met people.

Mrs. Fodorovich mentioned the Russian church. This is only one example pointing to the ethnic church as an agent of adjustment for immigrant women. Several women made such comments as "Church came first," or "Everybody went to church." One said, "I love church; I go every day; a day that I don't go to church is double long. And we ladies bake every week for the church." Among all the Slavic groups, men, women, and children went to church. Among the Jewish immigrants the synagogue was a man's institution, and the role of the woman was limited to visiting in the balcony where some women read the prayers in Yiddish.

During the decade 1900 to 1910, ethnic churches of every denomination were built in the Pittsburgh area, and 11 Jewish synagogues, organized by nationality, were established in the Hill District alone. The establishment of the ethnic church provided what might well have been the single most important source of continuity in a world changed in so many ways. Religion was a basic value in Europe, and the ethnic church represented the continuation of the most important institution in the lives of many poor immigrants. Aside from its religious function, the church played a vital social role. Here was a meeting place and social center where immigrants carried out the traditional observance of holy days and fiestas with festive foods, familiar dances, and meaningful ritual.

Church played a central role in the lives of most Italian women, but many men were ambivalent or even hostile toward organized Catholicism. For Italians, the recreation of the feast day of the patron saint took on even greater importance than it had in Italy. Nicolette DiLucente described an elaborate annual celebration in Braddock. Musicians were hired, a grandstand constructed, and a chapel built. Men carried a statue of the saint through the streets followed by a procession of musicians and excited children. Mrs. DiLucente explained:

All the people were from the same town, San Angelo del Pasco. We decorated the whole street, made special foods, and we celebrated. We did this every year from when I came in 1920 to the 1960s.

Rudolph Vecoli suggests that "The cult of the patron saint was perhaps the strongest emotional bond, outside the family, which tied the Italian immigrants to each other and to the distant past."

Church and religious celebrations were important to both immigrant men and women. For immigrant women, however, the one most emotionally satisfying experience, the one thing in life that could heal the wound of separation from parents and loved ones left behind, was the creation of their very own families.

For some, giving birth to a child brought the first real sense of joy in America. For example, Dianna Jordanoff, an immigrant bride from Bulgaria, expressed her elation at having a child, saying, "My Pat was my rebirth. I felt that I was born again . . . having my own baby, that was heaven. . . ."

Motherhood was (and is) a goal of most women, but for immigrant women, beginning a family carried special significance. . . . For immigrant women separated from their own parental families, children represented the beginning of continuity in America. . . . Among the elements fostering adjustment, motherhood appears to be the one universal factor.

Not every woman was able to make the kind of successful adjustment described in this article. Study of those who could not cope is beyond the scope of this paper, but the incidence must have been significant. In this study, which included 45 immigrant women over age 68, each woman had at least one living child and one adult grandchild, and each was willing to record her life history. These characteristics are in themselves a measure of adjustment; our sample is admittedly skewed toward success. Yet, even in this "successful" sample, women mentioned mothers and friends who did not adjust. One 75 year old Jewish woman described moving back and forth from Philadelphia to Pittsburgh during her childhood because, "My grandmother was, you know, nervous. She never got used to America. Today, you would say she was emotionally disturbed." And a Serbian-American woman reported, "I was born here, but my mother was always sick. She wanted to go back to Yugoslavia. She said she would only get well if she could go home. When I was four years old, Mother took me back to Europe. Daddy came there three times to visit, but Mother never came back to America." Thus, although she was born here, this woman arrived in Pittsburgh at age 25 as an immigrant. One Italian immigrant woman who leads a full and satisfying life here, in spite of poverty, told of her sister-in-law who was killed when she walked in front of a streetcar. "She never got used to things here. She didn't know what she was doing. . . ."

On balance, however, immigrant women did adjust to Pittsburgh's industrial urban environment. Certain factors, true of Pittsburgh, apply equally to most American cities. Improvement in the material conditions of life, the creation of their own families, and close ties maintained with children and other family members aided the positive adjustment of immigrant women throughout the United States. The Pittsburgh environment, however, encouraged the maintenance of a certain amount of traditional culture. Ethnic neighborhoods, ethnic churches, and community celebrations of traditional religious rituals provided the opportunity for association with others of similar background, helping to smooth the transition from European village to this industrial city. These factors overcame the major limiting characteristic of Pittsburgh, an economy based on male-oriented heavy industry. Most Italian, Jewish, and Slavic women did become "at home" in the Pittsburgh area and achieved "urbanization without breakdown."

4

The Diary of a Rent Striker: "Harlem and Hope"

The dangers confronting Puerto Rican immigrant Innocencia Flores—mother of four, separated from her husband, and on relief—in a decaying tenement in East Harlem in 1964 may be less dramatic than those that confronted Guri Endreson a century earlier, but they are no less threatening. Like many other immigrant women in urban America today, Flores wages a courageous though uncelebrated battle against rats, junkies, dirt, and the indifference and hostility of landlords, building inspectors, school authorities, politicians, and police. Like her counterparts in Pittsburgh in an earlier day, and indeed, like Endreson on the frontier, Flores is sustained through her difficulties by the support of her neighbors (the community of tenants in her building), by her religious faith, and by her love and concern for her children. Flores does more than survive (difficult as even that is)—she fights

Source: Frances Sugre, "Diary of a Rent Striker," *New York Herald Tribune*, February 16, 1964, p. 28.

back. At the time this diary was written, February 1964, she and her fellow tenants were staging a rent strike—ultimately successful—to force the landlord to repair their building.

Wednesday, Feb. 5: I got up at 6:45. The first thing to do was light the oven. The boiler was broke so not getting the heat. All the tenants together bought the oil. We give $7.50 for each tenant. But the boiler old and many things we don't know about the pipes, so one of the men next door who used to be superintendent is trying to fix. I make the breakfast for the three children who go to school. I give them orange juice, oatmeal, scrambled eggs, and Ovaltine. They have lunch in school and sometimes they don't like the food and won't eat, so I say you have a good breakfast. Miss Christine Washington stick her head in at 7:30 and say she go to work. I used to live on ground floor and she was all the time trying to get me to move to third floor next door to her because this place vacant and the junkies use it and she scared the junkies break the wall to get into her place and steal everything because she live alone and go to work.

I'm glad I come up here to live because the rats so big downstairs. We all say the "rats is big as cats." I had a baseball bat for the rats. It's lucky me and the children never got bit. The children go to school and I clean the house and empty the pan in the bathroom that catches the water dripping from pipe in the big hole in the ceiling. You have to carry umbrella to the bathroom sometimes. I go to the laundry place this afternoon and I wash again on Saturday because I change my kids clothes every day because I don't want them dirty to attract the rats. . . .

After I go out to a rent strike meeting at night, I come home and the women tell me that five policemen came and broke down the door of the vacant apartment of the ground floor where we have meetings for the tenants in our building. They come looking for something—maybe junkies, but we got nothing in there only paper and some chairs and tables. They knocked them all over. The women heard the policemen laughing. When I came up to my place the children already in bed and I bathe myself and then I go to bed and read the newspaper until 11:30.

Thursday, Feb. 6: I wake up at six o'clock and I went to the kitchen to heat a bottle for my baby. When I put the light on the kitchen I yelled so loud that I don't know if I disturbed the neighbors. There was a big rat coming out from the garbage pail. . . .

Friday, Feb. 7: This morning I woke up a little early. The baby woke up at five o'clock. I went to the kitchen but this time I didn't see the rat.

After the girls left for school I started washing the dishes and cleaning the kitchen. I am thinking about their school. Today they ain't teaching enough. My oldest girl is 5.9 in reading. This is low level in reading. I go to school and English teacher tell me they ain't got enough books to read and that's why my daughter behind. I doesn't care about integration like that. It doesn't bother me. I agree with boycott for some reasons. To get better education and better teachers and better materials in school. I don't like putting them in buses and sending them away. I like to stay here and change the system. Some teachers has to be changed. My girl take Spanish in junior high school, and I said to her, "Tell your teacher I'm going to be in school one day to teach him Spanish because I don't know where he learns to teach Spanish but it ain't Spanish."

I'm pretty good woman. I don't bother anyone. But I got my rights. I fight for them. I don't care about jail. Jail don't scare me. If have to go to jail, I go. I didn't steal. I didn't kill nobody. There's no record for me. But if I have to go, I go.

Saturday, Feb. 8: A tenant called me and asked me what was new in the building because she works daytimes. She wanted to know about the junkies. Have they been on the top floor where the vacant apartment is? That's why I have leaking from the ceiling. The junkies on the top floor break the pipes and take the fixtures and the sink and sell them and that's where the water comes. . . . I'm not ascared of the junkies. I open the door and I see the junkies I tell them to go or I call the police. Many people scared of them, but they scared of my face. I got a baseball bat for the rats and for the junkies. . . . I know my rights and I know my self-respect. After supper I played cards (casino) for two hours with the girls and later I got dressed and I went to a party for the rent strike. This party was to get funds to the cause. I had a good time. . . .

Sunday, Feb. 9: I dressed up in a hurry to go to church. When I go to church I pray for to have better house and have a decent living. I hope He's hearing. But I don't get discouraged on Him. I have faith. I don't care how cold I am I never lose my faith. When I come out of church I was feeling so good.

Monday, Feb. 10: At 9:30 a man came to fix the rat holes. He charged me only $3. Then one of the tenants came to tell me that we only had oil for today and every tenant would have to give $7.50 to send for more oil. I went to see some tenants to tell them there is no more oil. We all have to cooperate with money for the oil. . . .

Tuesday, Feb. 11: This morning was too cold in the house that I had to light the oven and heat hot water. We had no steam, the boiler is not running good. I feel miserable. You know when the house is cold you can't do nothing. When the girls left for school I went back to bed. I just got up at 11:30 and this house is so cold. Living in a cold apartment is terrible. . . .

Wednesday, Feb. 12: I wake up around 5 o'clock and the first thing I did was light the oven and the heater so when the girls wake up is a little warm. I didn't call them to 11 because they didn't have to go to school. It still so cold they trembling. You feel like crying looking your children in this way.

I think if I stay a little longer in this kind of living I'm going to be dead duck. I know that to get into a project [government subsidized housing] you have to have somebody prominent to back you up. Many people got to the projects and they don't even need them. I had been feeling [filling] applications I don't know since when. This year I feel another one. My only weapon is my vote. This year I *don't vote* for nobody. May be my vote don't count, but don't forget if you have fourteen cent you need another penny so you take the bus or the subway. At least I clean my house and you could eat on the floor. The rest of the day I didn't do nothing. I was so mad all day long. I cooked a big pot of soup. I leave it to God to help me. I have faith in Him.

Thursday, Feb. 13: I couldn't get up this morning. The house was so cold that I came out of bed at 7:15. . . . Later on, the inspector came. They were suppose to come to every apartment and look all violations. They knock at the door and asked if anything had been fixed. I think even the inspectors are afraid of this slum conditions thats why they didn't dare to come inside. I don't blame them. They don't want to take a rat or any bug to their houses or get dirty in this filthy houses. My little girl come from school with Valentine she made for me. Very pretty. At 8:30 I went downstairs to a meeting we had. We discuss about why there is no heat. We agreed to give $10 to fix the boiler for the oil. . . .

Friday, Feb. 14: I didn't write this about Friday in my book until this Saturday morning, because Friday night I sick and so cold. . . .

It is really hard to believe that this happens here in New York and richest city in the world. But such is Harlem and hope. Is this the way to live. I rather go to the Moon in the next trip.

5

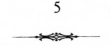

"Paths upon Water"

Most post-1965 immigrants knew a great deal about the United States before they arrived, and many had relatives there. Yet, like their predecessors, they often experienced "culture shock." This short story describes the thoughts and feelings of an educated, middle-aged widow from Pakistan, Sakino Bano, who comes to the

Source: From *The Forbidden Stitch: An Asian American Women's Anthology* edited by Shirley Geok-lin Lim et. al. published by Calyx Books, 1989).

United States to live with her Americanized son. It describes her first trip to the beach or, more accurately, her first encounter with customs and values so alien that she thinks herself to be "among people who had indeed lost their sanity." A devoted mother, she hides her dismay from her son and his friends for fear of being thought impolite or ignorant. However, Sakino Bano is flexible as well as traditional; by the end of the day she begins to see her son—and herself—differently. Although the story is fiction, it speaks to the experience of many women who, like Sakino Bano, must find "paths upon water"—ways to deal with a new physical and social universe. The author of this story, Tahira Naqvi, was born in Pakistan. When the story was published in 1989, she was teaching English at Connecticut State University.

There had been little warning, actually none at all to prepare her for her first encounter with the sea. At breakfast that morning, her son Raza said, "*Ama,* we're going to the seaside today. Jamil and Hameeda are coming with us." She had been turning a *paratha* in the frying pan, an onerous task since she had always fried *parathas* on a flat pan with open sides, and as the familiar aroma of dough cooking in butter filled the air around her, she smiled happily and thought, I've only been here a week and already he wants to show me the sea.

Sakino Bano had never seen the sea. Having lived practically all her life in a town which was a good thousand miles from the nearest shoreline, her experience of the sea was limited to what she had chanced to observe in pictures. One picture, in which greenish-blue waves heaved toward a gray sky, she could recollect clearly; it was from a calendar Raza brought home the year he started college in Lahore. The calendar had hung on a wall of her room for many years only to be removed when the interior of the house was whitewashed for her daughter's wedding, and in the ensuing confusion it was misplaced and never found. The nail on which the calendar hung had stayed in the wall since the painter, too lazy to bother with the detailed preparation, had simply painted around the nail and over it; whenever Sakina Bano happened to glance at the forgotten nail she remembered the picture. Also distinct in her memory was a scene from a silly Urdu film she had seen with her cousin's wife Zohra and her nieces Zenab and Amina during a rare visit to Lahore several years ago. For some reason she hadn't been able to put it out of her mind. On a brown and white beach, the actor Waheed Murad, now dead but then affectedly handsome and boyish, pursued the actress Zeba, who skipped awkwardly before him—it isn't all proper for a woman to be skipping in a public place. Small foam-crested waves lapped up to her, making her *shalwar* stick to her skinny legs, exposing the outline of her thin calves. Why, it was just as bad as baring her legs, for what cover could the wet, gossamer-like fabric of the *shalwar* provide?

The two frolicked by an expanse of water that extended to the horizon and which, even though it was only in a film, had seemed to Sakina Bano frightening in its immensity.

"Will Jamal and his wife have lunch here?" she asked, depositing the dark, glistening *paratha* gently on Raza's plate. She would have to take out a packet of meat from the freezer if she was to give them lunch, she told herself while she poured tea in her son's cup.

"No, I don't think so. I think we'll leave before lunch. We can stop somewhere along the way and have a bite to eat."

"They'll have tea then." She was glad Raza had remembered to pick up a cake at the store the night before (she didn't know why he called it a pound cake), and she would make some rich *kheer*.

If she had anything to do with it, she would avoid long trips and spend most of her time in Raza's apartment cooking his meals and watching him eat. The apartment pleased her. The most she would want to do would be to go out on the lawn once in a while and examine her surroundings. . . .

The apartment building was set against a lawn edged with freshly green, sculptured bushes, evenly thick with grass that looked more like a thick carpet than just grass. Located in a quiet section of town, the apartments overlooked a dark, thickly wooded area, a park, Raza had told her. Although tired and groggy on the evening of her arrival from Pakistan, she had not failed to take note of the surroundings into which she found herself. Her first thought was, 'Where is everybody?' while to her son she said, "How nice everything is."

Looking out the window of his sitting room the next morning, she was gladdened at the thought of her son's good fortune. The morning sky was clear like a pale blue, unwrinkled *dupatta* that has been strung out on a line to dry. Everything looked clean, so clean. Was it not as if an unseen hand had polished the sidewalks and swept the road? They now glistened like new metal. 'Where do people throw their trash?' she wondered when she went down to the lawn again, this time with Raza, and gazed out at the shiny road, the rows and rows of neat houses hedged in by such neat white wooden fences. In hasty answer to her own query, she told herself not to be foolish; this was *Amreeka*. Here trash was in its proper place, hidden from view and no doubt disposed of in an appropriate manner. No blackened banana peels redolent with the odor of neglect here, or rotting orange skins, or worse, excrement and refuse to pollute the surroundings and endanger human habitation.

She had sighed in contentment. Happiness descended upon her tangibly like a heavy blanket affording warmth on a chilly morning. Once again, she thanked her Maker. Was He not good to her son?

"Is the sea far from here?" she asked casually, brushing imaginary crumbs from the edges of her plate. Raza must never feel she didn't value his eagerness to show off his new environment. This was his new world after all. If he wanted to take her to the seaside, then seaside it would be. Certainly she was not to be fussy and upset him.

"No, *Ama*, not too far. An hour-and-a-half's drive, that's all. Do you feel well?" His eyes crinkled in concern as he put aside the newspaper he had been reading to look at her.

She impatiently waved a hand in the air, secretly pleased at his solicitude. "Yes, yes, I'm fine son. Just a little cough, that's all. Now finish your tea and I'll make you another cup." She knew how much he liked tea. Before she came, he must have had to make it for himself. Such a chore for a man if he must make his own tea.

The subject of the sea didn't come up again until Jamil and his new bride arrived. Jamil, an old college friend of Raza's, angular like him, affable and solicitous, was no stranger to Sakina Bano. But she was meeting his wife Hameeda for the first time. Like herself, the girl was also a newcomer to this country.

"*Khalaji*, the sea's so pretty here, the beaches are so-o-o-o large, nothing like the beaches in Karachi," Hameeda informed Sakina Bano over tea, her young, shrill voice rising and falling excitedly, her lips, dark and fleshy with lipstick, wide open in a little girl's grin. There's wanderlust in her eyes already, Sakina Bano mused, trying to guess her age. Twenty-one or twenty-two. She thought of the girl in Sialkot she and her daughter had been considering for Raza. Was there really a resemblance? Perhaps it was only the youth.

"Well child, for me it will be all the same. I've never been to Karachi. Here, have another slice of cake, you too Jamil, and try the *kheer*."

For some reason Sakina Bano couldn't fathom, sitting next to the young girl whose excitement at the prospect of a visit to the seaside was as undisguised as a child's preoccupation with a new toy, she was suddenly reminded of the actress Zeba. The image of waves lapping on her legs and swishing about her nearly bare calves rose in Sakina Bano's mind again. Like the arrival of an unexpected visitor, a strange question crossed her mind: were Hameeda's legs also skinny like Zeba's?

Drowned in the clamor for the *kheer* which had proven to be a great hit and had been consumed with such rapidity she wished she had made more, the question lost itself.

Tea didn't last long. Within an hour they were on their way to the sea, all of them in Raza's car. Jamil sat in the front with his friend, and Sakina Bano and Hameeda sat in the back. . . . Soon she became drowsy and idled into sleep.

To be sure she had heard stories of people who swam in the ocean. She wasn't so foolish as to presume that swimming was undertaken fully clothed. After all, many times as a child she had seen young boys and men from her village swim, dressed in nothing but loincloths as they jumped into the muddy waters of the canal that irrigated their fields. But what was this?

As soon as Raza parked the car in a large, compound-like area fenced in by tall walls of wire mesh, and when her dizziness subsided, Sakina Bano glanced out the window on her left. Her attention was snagged by what she thought was a naked woman. Certain that she was still a little dazed from the long drive, her vision subsequently befogged, Sakina Bano thought nothing of what she had seen. Then the naked figure moved closer. Disbelief gave way to the sudden, awful realization that the figure was indeed real and if not altogether naked, very nearly so.

A thin strip of colored cloth shaped like a flimsy brassiere loosely held the woman's breasts, or rather a part of her breasts; and below, beneath the level of her belly button, no, even lower than that, Sakina Bano observed in horror, was something that reminded her of the loincloths the men and youths in her village wore when they swam or worked on a construction site in the summer.

The girl was pretty, such fine features, hair that shone like a handful of gold thread, and she was young too, not much older than Hameeda perhaps. But the paleness of her skin was marred by irregular red blotches that seemed in dire need of a cooling balm. No one with such redness should be without a covering in the sun, Sakina Bano offered in silent rebuke.

The woman opened the door of her car, which was parked alongside Raza's, and as she leaned over to retrieve something from the interior of her car, Sakina Bano gasped. When the young female lowered her body, her breasts were not only nearly all bared, but stood in imminent danger of spilling out of their meager coverage. O God! Is there no shame here? Sakina Bano's cheeks burned. Hastily she glanced away. In the very next instant she stole a glimpse at her son from the corners of her eyes, anxiously wondering if he too were experiencing something of what she was going through; no, she noted with a mixture of surprise and relief, he and Jamil were taking things out from the trunk of their car. They did not show any signs of discomfort. Did she see a fleeting look of curiosity on Hameeda's face? There was something else, too, she couldn't quite decipher.

Relieved that her male companions were oblivious to the disturbing view of the woman's breasts, Sakina Bano sighed sadly. She shook her head, adjusted her white, chiffon *dupatta* over her head, and slowly eased her person out of her son's car.

The taste of the sea was upon her lips in an instant. Mingled with an occasional but strong whiff of Hameeda's perfume, the smell of fish filled her nostrils and quickly settled in her nose as if to stay there forever.

Milling around were countless groups of scantily clad people, men, women, and children, coming and going in all directions. Is all of *Amreeka* here? she asked herself uneasily. Feeling guilty for having judged Zeba's contrived imprudence on film a little too harshly, she tightened her *dupatta* about her and wondered why her son had chosen to bring her to this place. Did he not know his mother? She was an old woman, and the mother of a son, but she would not surrender to anger or derision and make her son uncomfortable. His poise and confidence were hers too, were they not? Certainly he had brought her to the sea for a purpose. She must not appear ungrateful or intolerant.

While Raza and Jamil walked on casually and without any show of awkwardness, laughing and talking as though they might be in their sitting room rather than a place crowded with people in a state of disconcerting undress, she and Hameeda followed closely behind. Her head swam as she turned her eyes from the glare of the sun and attempted to examine the perturbing nakedness around her.

Sakina Bano's memories of nakedness were short and limited, extending to the time when she bathed her younger brother and sister under the water pump in the courtyard of her father's house, followed by the period in which she bathed her own three children until they were old enough to do it themselves. Of her own nakedness she carried an incomplete image; she had always bathed sitting down, on a low wooden stool.

Once, and that too shortly before his stroke, she came upon her husband getting out of his *dhoti* in their bedroom. Standing absently near the foot of his bed as if waiting for something or someone, the *dhoti* a crumpled heap about his ankles, he lifted his face to look at her blankly when she entered, but made no attempt to move or cover himself. Not only did she have to hand him his pajamas, she also had to assist him as he struggled to pull up first one leg and then the other. A week later he suffered a stroke, in another week he was gone. It had been nearly ten years since he died. But for some reason the image of a naked disoriented man in the middle of a room clung to her mind like permanent discolorations on a well-worn copper pot.

And there was the unforgettable sharp and unsullied picture of her mother's body laid out on a rectangular slab of cracked, yellowed wood for a pre-burial bath, her skin, ash-brown, laced with a thousand wrinkles, soft, like wet, rained-on mud.

But nothing could have prepared her for this. Nakedness, like all things in nature, has a purpose, she firmly told herself as the four of them trudged toward the water.

The July sun on this day was not as hot as the July sun in Sialkot, but a certain oily humidity had begun to attach itself to her face and hands. Lifting a corner of her white *dupatta*, she wiped her face with it. Poor Hameeda, no doubt she too longed to divest herself of the *shalwar* and *qamis* she was wearing and don a swimming suit so she could join the rest of the women on the beach, be more like them. But could she swim?

They continued onward, and after some initial plodding through hot, moist sand, Sakina Bano became sure-footed; instead of having to drag her feet through the weighty volume of over-heated sand, she was now able to tread over it with relative ease. They were receiving stares already, a few vaguely curious, others unguardedly inquisitive.

Where the bodies ended she saw the ocean began, stretching to the horizon in the distance. The picture she had carried in her head of the boyish actor Waheed Murad running after Zeba on a sandy Karachi beach quickly diminished and faded away. The immensity of the sea on film was reduced to a mere blue splash of color, its place usurped by a vastness she could scarce hold within the frame of her vision; a window opened in her head, she drew in the wonder of the sea as it touched the hem of the heavens and, despite the heat, Sakina Bano shivered involuntarily. God's touch is upon the world, she silently whispered to herself.

Again and again, as she had made preparations for the journey across what she liked to refer to as the 'seven seas,' she had been told *Amreeka* was so large that many Pakistans could fit into it. The very idea of Pakistan fitting into anything else was cause for bewilderment, and the analogy left her at once befuddled and awed. But had she expected this?

The bodies sprawled before her on the sand and exposed to the sun's unyielding rays seemed unmindful of what the ocean might have to say about God's touch upon the world. Assuming supine positions, flat either on their backs or their bellies, the people on the beach reminded Sakina Bano of whole red chilies spread on a rag discolored from overuse, and left in the sun to dry and crackle. As sweat began to form in tiny droplets across her forehead and around her mouth, the unhappy thought presented itself to her that she was among people who had indeed lost their sanity.

In summer, one's first thought is to put as much distance as possible between oneself and the sun. Every effort is made to stay indoors; curtains are drawn and jalousies unfurled in order to shut out the fire the sun exudes. In the uneasy silence of a torrid June or July afternoon, even stray dogs seek shade under a tree or behind a bush, curling up into fitful slumber as the sun beats its fervid path across the sky.

Sakina Bano couldn't understand why these men and women wished to scorch their bodies, and why, if they were here by the shore of an ocean which seemed to reach up to God, they didn't at least gaze wide-eyed at the wonder which lay at their feet. Why did they choose instead to shut their eyes and merely wallow in the heat. Their skins had rebelled, the red and darkly-pink blotches spoke for themselves. Perhaps this is a ritual they must, of necessity, follow, she mused. Perhaps they yearn to be brown as we yearn to be white.

She felt an ache insidiously putter behind her eyes. The sun always gave her a headache, even in winter, the only season when sunshine evoked pleasing sensations, when one could look forward to its briskness, its sharp touch. The heat from the sand under the *dari* on which she and Hameeda now sat seeped through the coarse fabric after a while and hugged her thighs; as people in varying shades of pink, white and red skin ran or walked past them, particles of sand flew in the air and landed on her clothes, her hands, her face. Soon she felt sand in her mouth, scraping between her teeth like the remains of *chalia*, heavy on her tongue.

Ignoring the sand in her mouth and the hot-water-bottle effect of the sand beneath her thighs, Sakina Bano shifted her attention first toward a woman on her left, and then to the man on her right whose stomach fell broadly in loose folds (like dough left out overnight); he lay supine and still, his face shielded by a straw hat. Puzzled by the glitter on their nakedness, she peered closely and with intense concentration—she had to observe if she were to learn anything. The truth came to her like a flash of sudden light in a dark room: both the man and the woman had smeared their bodies with some kind of oil! . . .

It's really very simple, Sakina Bano finally decided, sighing again, these people wish to be fried in the sun. But why? Not wishing to appear ignorant, she kept her mouth shut. . . .

Raza and Jamil, both in swimming trunks, appeared totally at ease as they ran to the water and back, occasionally wading in a wave that gently slapped the beach and sometimes disappearing altogether for a second or two under a high wave. Then Sakina Bano couldn't tell where they were. They certainly seemed to be having a good time.

She and Hameeda must be the only women on the beach fully clothed, she reflected, quite a ridiculous sight if one were being viewed from the vantage point of those who were stretched out on the sand. And while Sakina Bano grappled with this disturbing thought, she saw the other woman approaching.

Attired in a *sari* and accompanied by a short, dark man (who had to be her son for he undoubtedly had her nose and her forehead) and an equally short, dark woman, both of whom wore swimming suits (the girl's as brief as that of the woman Sakina Bano had seen earlier in the parking lot), she looked no older than herself. Clutching the front folds of her *sari* as if afraid a sudden wind from the ocean might pull them out unfurling the *sari*, leaving her exposed, she tread upon the sand with a fiercely precarious step, looking only ahead, her eyes shielded with one small, flat palm.

This is how I must appear to others, Sakina Bano ruminated. Suddenly, she felt a great sadness clutching at her chest and rising into her throat like a sigh as she watched the woman in the *sari* begin to make herself comfortable on a large, multi-colored towel thrown on the sand by her son and his wife; those two hurriedly dashed off in the direction of the water. Why are they in such haste? Sakina Bano wondered.

Her knees drawn up, one arm tensely wrapped around them, the woman appeared to be watching her son and her daughter-in-law. . . .

Sakina Bano's attention returned to Hameeda who had not said a word all this time. Like a break-through during muddled thought, it suddenly occured to Sakina Bano that there was a distinct possibility Hameeda would be swimming if it weren't for her. In deference to her older companion she was probably foregoing the chance to swim. Will Raza's wife also wear a scant swimming suit and bare her body in the presence of strange men? The question disturbed her; she tried to shrug it aside. But it wouldn't go away. Stubbornly it returned, not alone this time but accompanied by the picture of a young woman who vaguely resembled the actress Zeba and who was clothed, partially, in a swimming suit much like the ones Sakina Bano saw about her. Running behind her was a man, not Waheed Murad, but alas, her own son, her Raza. Was she dreaming, had the sun weakened her brain? Such foolishness. Sakina Bano saw that Hameeda was staring ahead, like the woman on the towel, her eyes squinted because of the glare. Frozen on her full, red lips was a hesitant smile.

Once again Sakina Bano sought her son's figure among the throng near the water's edge. At first the brightness of the sun blinded her and she couldn't see where he was. She strained her eyes, shielding them from the sun with a hand on her forehead. And finally she spotted him. He and Jamil were talking to some people. A dark man and a dark girl. The son and daughter-in-law of the woman in the *sari*. Were they acquaintances then, perhaps friends? The four of them laughed like old friends, the girl standing so close to Raza he must surely be able to see her half-naked breasts. The poor boy!

They had begun to walk toward where she and Hameeda were seated. Raza was going to introduce his friends to his mother. How was she to conceal her discomfort at the woman's mode of dress?

"*Ama*, I want you to meet Ajit and Kamla. Ajit works at Ethan Allen with me. Kamla wants you to come to their house for dinner next Sunday."

Hameeda was also introduced. Kamla made a joke about "the shy new bride," Hameeda showed her pretty teeth in a smile, and then Kamla said, "You have to come, Auntie." Sakina Bano wondered why Raza appeared so comfortable in the presence of a woman who was nearly all naked. Even her loincloth was flimsy. Granted it wasn't as bad as some of the others she had been seeing around her, but it was flimsy nonetheless.

"Yes, it's very nice of you to invite us. It's up to Raza. He's usually so busy. But if he is free. . ."

"Of course I'm free next Sunday. We'd love to come, Kamla."

Kamla said, "Good! I'll introduce you and Auntie to my mother-in-law after a swim. Coming?" She laid a hand on Raza's arm and Sakina Bano glanced away, just in time to catch Hameeda's smile of surprise. Well one's son can become a stranger too, even a good son like Raza.

"Sure. *Yar*, Ajit, are you and Kamla planning to go to the late show?"

"Yes we are. You? Do you have tickets?" Ajit wasn't a bad looking boy. But he didn't measure up to Raza. No, Raza's nose was straight and to the point, his forehead wide and his eyes well-illuminated. But he had changed somehow; she felt she was distanced from him. A son is always a son, she thought and smiled and nodded again as Ajit and Kamla uttered their *Namaste's* and returned to the water with Raza and Jamil.

"*Khalaji*, why don't we wet our feet before we go? Hameeda suddenly asked her.

"Wet our feet?"

"Yes, *Khala*. Just dip our feet in sea water. Come on. You're not afraid of the water, are you?"

"No, child." She wasn't afraid. Her mind was playing tricks with her, filling her head with thoughts that had no place there. A change was welcome. "Yes, why not?" she said, as if speaking to herself. When she attempted to get up she found that her joints had stiffened painfully. "Here, girl, give me your hand." She extended an arm toward Hameeda. Why not, especially since they had come so far and she had suffered the heat for what had seemed like a very long time.

Hameeda had rolled up her *shalwar* almost to the level of her knees. How pretty her legs are, the skin hairless and shiny, like a baby's, and not skinny at all, Sakina Bano mused in surprise, and how quick she is to show them.

She must do the same, she realized. Otherwise Hameeda would think she was afraid. She pulled up one leg of her *shalwar* tentatively, tucked it at the waist with one swift movement of her right hand, then looked about her sheepishly. Hameeda was laughing.

"The other one too, *Khala!*"

Who would want to look at her aged and scrawny legs? And her husband was not around to glare at her in remonstration. Gingerly the other leg of the *shalwar* was also lifted and tucked in. How funny her legs looked, the hair on them all gray now and curly, the calves limp. Now both women giggled like schoolgirls. And Raza would be amused, he would think she was having a good time, Sakina Bano told herself.

Raza and Jamil burst into laughter when they saw the women approach. They waved. Sakina Bano waved back.

Holding the front folds of her *shalwar* protectively, Sakina Bano strode toward the water. As she went past the other woman in the *sari* she smiled at her. The woman gave her a startled look, and then, dropping the hand with which she had been shielding her eyes from the sun, she let her arm fall away from her knees, and following Sakina Bano with her gaze, she returned her smile.

"Wait for me," Sakina Bano called to Hameeda in a loud, happy voice, "wait, girl."

6

◆≪≫◆

Strategies for Growing Old: Basha Is a Survivor

*For Basha, the central figure in this selection, the struggle for survival in America
has not ended though she has lived in this country for more than half a century.
With the initial shock of immigration long past and the stressful years of childrearing finally at an end, many immigrant women face the economic and physical
problems of old age alone, their husbands and lifelong friends dead, their children
far away. Unlike the lands in which many immigrants were born, contemporary
America does not honor its elderly; there are few socially approved roles for an old
woman with a foreign accent. Yet women like Basha have successfully coped with
aging, developing strategies to maintain their dignity and self-respect. Anthropol-
ogist Barbara Myerhoff documents some of these strategies in* Number Our Days,
*the study from which this selection was taken. Myerhoff spent several years ob-
serving and participating in the life of a Jewish senior citizen center in southern
California. Here she describes how Basha, "the survivor," maintains her independence as long as she can, surrendering it only when she must and in her own
way—among her friends, with humor, and with a continuing commitment to life.*

> Every morning I wake up in pain. I wiggle my toes. Good. They
> still obey. I open my eyes. Good. I can see. Everything hurts but I
> get dressed. I walk down to the ocean. Good. It's still there. Now
> my day can start. About tomorrow I never know. After all, I'm
> eighty-nine. I can't live forever.

Death and the ocean are protagonists in Basha's life. They provide points
of orientation, comforting in their certitude. One visible, the other in-
visible, neither hostile nor friendly, they accompany her as she walks down
the boardwalk to the Aliyah Senior Citizen's Center.

Basha wants to remain independent above all. Her life at the beach de-
pends on her ability to perform a minimum number of basic tasks. She must
shop and cook, dress herself, care for her body and her one-room apartment,
walk, take the bus to the market and the doctor, be able to make a telephone
call in case of emergency. Her arthritic hands have a difficult time with the
buttons on her dress. Some days her fingers ache and swell so that she cannot

Source: From *Number Our Days* by Barbara Myerhoff. Copyright 1978 by Barbara
Myerhoff. Reprinted by permission of the publisher, E. P. Dutton.

fit them into the holes of the telephone dial. Her hands shake as she puts in her eyedrops for glaucoma. Fortunately, she no longer has to give herself injections for her diabetes. Now it is controlled by pills if she is careful about what she eats. In the neighborhood there are no large markets within walking distance. She must take the bus to shop. The bus steps are very high and sometimes the driver objects when she tries to bring her little wheeled cart aboard. A small boy whom she has befriended and occasionally pays often waits for her at the bus stop to help her up. When she cannot bring her cart onto the bus or isn't helped up the steps, she must walk to the market. Then shopping takes the better part of the day and exhausts her. Her feet, thank God, give her less trouble since she figured how to cut and sew a pair of cloth shoes so as to leave room for her callouses and bunions.

Basha's daughter calls her once a week and worries about her mother living alone and in a deteriorated neighborhood. "Don't worry about me, darling. This morning I put the garbage in the oven and the bagels [rolls] in the trash. But I'm feeling fine." Basha enjoys teasing her daughter whose distant concern she finds somewhat embarrassing. "She says to me, 'Mamaleh, you're sweet but you're *stupid*.' What else could a greenhorn mother expect from a daughter who is a lawyer?" The statement conveys Basha's simultaneous pride and grief in having produced an educated, successful child whose very accomplishments drastically separate her from her mother. The daughter has often invited Basha to come and live with her, but she refuses.

> What would I do with myself there in her big house, alone all day, when the children are at work? No one to talk to. No place to walk. Nobody talks Yiddish. My daughter's husband doesn't like my cooking, so I can't even help with meals. Who needs an old lady around, somebody else for my daughter to take care of? They don't keep the house warm like I like it. When I go to the bathroom at night, I'm afraid to flush. I shouldn't wake anybody up. Here I have lived for thirty-one years. I have my friends. I have the fresh air. Always there are people to talk to on the benches. I can go to the Center whenever I like and always there's something doing there. As long as I can manage for myself, I'll stay here.

Managing means three things: taking care of herself, stretching her monthly pension of three hundred and twenty dollars to cover expenses, and filling her time in ways that have meaning for her. The first two are increasingly hard and she knows that they are battles she will eventually lose. But her free time does not weigh on her. She is never bored and rarely depressed. In many ways, life is not different from before. She has never been well-off, and she never expected things to be easy. When asked if she is happy, she shrugs and laughs. "Happiness by me is a hot cup of tea on a cold day. When you don't get a broken leg, you could call yourself happy. . . ."

Basha dresses simply but with care. The purchase of each item of clothing is a major decision. It must last, should be modest and appropriate to her
age, but gay and up-to-date. And, of course, it can't be too costly. Basha is
not quite five feet tall. She is a sturdy boat of a woman—wide, strong of
frame, and heavily corseted. She navigates her great monobosom before her,
supported by broad hips and thin, severely bowed legs, their shape the heritage of her malnourished childhood. Like most of the people who belong to
the Aliyah Center, her early life in Eastern Europe was characterized by relentless poverty.

Basha dresses for the cold, even though she is now living in Southern
California, wearing a babushka under a red sunhat, a sweater under her
heavycoat. She moves down the boardwalk steadily, paying attention to the
placement of her feet. A fall is common and dangerous for the elderly. A frac-
tured hip can mean permanent disability, loss of autonomy, and removal
from the community to a convalescent or old age home. Basha seats herself
on a bench in front of the Center and waits for friends. Her feet are spread
apart, well-planted, as if growing up from the cement. Even sitting quite
still, thereisan air of determination about her. She will withstand attacks by
anti-Semites,Cossacks, Nazis, historical enemies whom she conquers by out-
living. She defies time and weather (though it is not cold here). So she might
have sata century ago, before a small pyramid of potatoes or herring in the-
marketplace of the Polish town where she was born. Patient, resolute, she is
a survivor. . . .

Basha had decided that she could no longer live on her own. A series of
blows had demoralized her: an obscene phone call, her purse had been
snatched, her new dentures could not be made to fit properly causing her
endless digestive problems, then she lost her Social Security check and took
this as a final sign that she was no longer able to take care of herself. If she
waited much longer, it might be too late—she might become really dependent
and she dreaded her friends' pity more than leaving them and the community.
Sonya scolded her. "Look here, Basha. I don't like this attitude of yours. I've
known you for thirty-eight years and you were always a brave woman. You're
giving up and there's no excuse for it." But Basha was resolute. She was going
to an old age home twenty miles away and would probably never see the Center again. From time to time a few friends would find ways to visit her there,
and phone or send notes, but she knew this was all she could hope for in sal-
vaging ties that had endured for three decades. She had had her hair washed
and set in a beauty parlor for the first time in her life just before she left.

A few days before her departure, Basha invited Olga, Sonya, Hannah,*
and me to her room for tea. She had packed nearly everything. The room was
oppressively clean. Basha was not ordinarily a neat housekeeper. Her room

---

*Friends from the Aliyah Center.

had been crammed with the material remains of her own and her parents' lives. Photographs of everyone but her father—who had been unwilling to "become an idol" by having his picture taken—hung on the walls, alongside a night school certificate, an award for completion of a course from the Singer Sewing Machine Company, and her Graduation-Siyum diploma.** Books, newspapers, greeting cards, buttons, and scraps of material had mingled unselfconsciously on every surface. . . .

Everyone made much over Basha's new hairdo. Pleased and proud, she refused our compliments. "A dressed-up potato is still a potato," she quoted in Yiddish. "You shouldn't be taken in by an old lady. . . ."

I sat in Basha's kitchen thinking about how ingenious and resourceful these old women were, and they thought so, too, it was clear. "Basha, darling," Olga said, "you will be all right wherever you are. Above all, when you get to the new home you should adapt yourself. The worse part will be having a roomate. If you're lucky you won't end up with someone who snores all night. Try to be cheerful. And you could do like I do in the Guest House. Whenever I want a snack, I go into the kitchen and make jokes with the girl there. If you get people to laugh, they help you and they won't pity you neither. Last week I went to the doctor. They put on me one of those foolish paper robes. I had everybody in stiches. I told them if they would give me a broom I would fly away to the Witches' Sabbath. If people see you're a person and not a ghost, they do nice little things for you."

"That's right. Adapt and have a sense of humor about you," said Hannah. "When I was to go to the hospital I spent two days cooking. My neighbor comes in and says, 'Hannah, what are you doing? Are you planning on having a party or going for an operation?' I'll tell you, dear, I says, 'I'm going to cook all this food and freeze it. If I come back, I'll have what to eat, nourishing food to recover on. If I don't, my friends should have all the best food to eat for my wake, just the way I would cook it myself.' She got a kick out of that."

The women were describing some of the strategies they had cultivated for coping with their circumstances—growing old, living alone and with little money. Each in a different way, with a different specialization had improvised techniques for growing old with originality and dedication. For these women, aging was a career, as it had been for Jacob, a serious commitment to surviving, complete with standards of excellence, clear, public, long-term goals whose attainment yielded community recognition and inner satisfaction. . . .

They had provided themselves with new possibilities to replace those that had been lost, regularly set new standards for themselves in terms of which to measure growth and achievement, sought and found meaning in their lives, in the short run and the long.

**From an adult education program given at the Aliyah Center.

The elders were not deluded and knew quite well the difference between careers in aging and those in the outside "real world of work." Thus, Sadie, whose career was composing and singing her songs, said, "Myself, when I sing I am in glory. My only regret is I never had the chance for a real career. I had talent but I had to sacrifice. I had to choose between myself and my children. But now when I sing I try to get better all the time, and then I really lose myself." There were many other careers: Basha's ceaseless efforts on behalf of Israeli causes; Gita's passion for dancing; the involvement of many of the women with the [Center's] philanthropic work; Hannah's devotion to the pigeons she fed every day, gathering huge bags of crumbs from neighbors, stores, and restaurants. Olga told and retold a cycle of highly polished, nearly invariant stories about herself that showed how she handled hostility and indifference with courage and dignity; these tales become her special lifework.

Sonya was just as proud of the neat, well-spelled minutes that she kept so faithfully for Center meetings. And she made truly elegant dresses out of scraps and castoffs that she bought in rummage sales, her self-satisfaction doubled because the money she laid out for materials went to Israel.

And for all of them, getting up each morning, being independent, living up to their goals, despite incredible odds, managing for themselves . . . demanding and getting satisfaction from a hardhearted or indifferent doctor or welfare official—these, too, should be counted as successful examples of the lifework of aging.

"Even though Sonya is mad at me for leaving, she should know that I wouldn't let myself sink into a vegetable," sighed Basha, pouring tea into our glasses, "I wouldn't pretend to you it's all easy. The home took all my savings. All right, what would I do with three thousand dollars? They charged my children five hundred dollars each, even my son-in-law who doesn't like me. They take my monthly check from now on. I wouldn't complain about it. My books I gave to the Center, there's no room for anything in that place. My clothes, I sent almost everything to Israel. A few little things I have saved. . . . It's time to begin now a different life. In this I'm prepared. But I'll tell you what worries me. It isn't going to be easy to make new friends. My hearing and eyes aren't so good anymore. If I don't go soon, I wouldn't recognize a new friend if I could find one. I'll tell you what is the worst that could happen. If no one speaks Yiddish, I don't know how I'll manage. Somehow, no matter how bad things are, when I hear Yiddish, something in me goes free, and everything changes around. Without this I would just dry up."

"Basha," Sonya said, "where do you think you could go and find not even one old Jew? We're the world's best wanderers. We turn up everywhere. Maybe you'll be lucky. Your roomate knows Yiddish, she doesn't snore, and she's not Litvak either." We all laughed and raised our tea glasses, making a toast to Basha and to life.

PART III

Work

"Must work—no work, no eat," explained a widow with two young children.[1] Not all immigrant women were this desperate, but for many survival was inescapably linked to work. Part III documents the work immigrant women did and the conditions under which they did it.

In 1930 the Women's Bureau published a study of 2,146 foreign-born working women in Philadelphia and the nearby Lehigh Valley. The study provides insight into the motives and problems of the many immigrant women throughout the nineteenth and twentieth centuries who added paid employment to the unpaid work of homemaking and childcare.[2] Not surprising, the study concluded that economic necessity was the main motivation. Single women who had to depend upon their own earnings usually started paid employment immediately after they arrived, often in jobs previously arranged for by friends and relatives already in the United States. Married women who entered the job market were likely to do so later.

Married women took jobs because their husbands were sick, injured, unemployed, or "no good . . . drinks and spends his own money."[3] More often, they did so because their husbands' earnings were inadequate. In 1925, 60 percent of all working men in Philadelphia earned less than $25 a week, while the cost of a "minimal standard of decency" for a family was from $30 to $35 a week. As one husband put it, "She works so we can live."[4]

When the immediate needs of survival were met, many women remained in the job market to earn a "cushion" against emergencies, or to provide a better standard of living for themselves or their children. Even young brides seemed preoccupied with saving for old age: "We don't want to be on the city. Plenty widows have no money. This in my mind, then, to work as long as I can."[5] Better housing and education for the children were common goals. "My boys must go to high school," explained one woman in the Woman's Bureau study. Another worked to help her daughter through business college. One widow worked a ten-hour day to keep a daughter in normal school. "I no care how long I work if she can teach."[6]

Some women worked because they were accustomed to sharing economic burdens with their husbands. Women from many different cultures had kept gardens and livestock, sold farm products, handicrafts, and other merchandise in village markets, or worked sporadically or regularly as servants or agricultural laborers to contribute to the family livelihood.[7] Some of these women continued their old roles in the new country because, as one put it, "Could I sit and watch my man do it all?" Husbands often expected no less: "If woman does not help, bad for man."[8]

Finally, a few women worked simply because they wanted to—and sometimes despite their husbands' objections. "Why sit around and not have any money?" asked the working wife of a bricklayer well able to support the family alone. "Nothing especially to keep me at home. No baby. I like to work," said another. "I'm happiest when working."[9]

Occupational Choices

From the mid-nineteenth century to the closing decade of the twentieth immigrant women have worked outside the home for the reasons cited by the Women's Bureau study—to survive, to provide security for themselves and their families, and, in some cases, because they wanted to. A recent study of Punjabi women in the canneries of California suggests two additional reasons: these women enjoyed the sociability of the assembly line and liked the enhanced power their earnings gave them in the family. "Now my husband, he listens to me when I say something; when I want to buy something, I do; when I want to go in the car, I go."[10]

Occupational choices were influenced by a woman's family status; the education, skills, and attitudes she had acquired in her homeland; the time and place of her immigration; and the opportunities extended or withheld by the American society. Typically, single women entered domestic service or factory work, while women with family responsibilities took in sewing or laundry, kept boarders, or operated small businesses from their homes. Finnish farm women used old world dairying skills in Minnesota, Bohemian women who had made cigars in Bohemia continued to do so in Philadelphia or Chicago, and Puerto Rican women skilled in needlework entered the garment industry of New York City. On the other hand, women who left rural homelands to settle in industrial cities found it necessary to learn new skills.

Women in cities dominated by "heavy" industry, such as Pittsburgh, had fewer opportunities for employment than women in cities with more diverse economies, like New York or Philadelphia. Sometimes ethnic cultural values restricted employment opportunities. Traditional southern Italian women, for instance, avoided occupations such as domestic service that removed them from the protection of fathers, husbands, or other male relatives. More often, occupational choices were limited by the prejudices of employers. Black women who immigrated from the Caribbean in the early twentieth century were barred on grounds of race from virtually every job except domestic work. Slavic women were hired for jobs in stockyards and foundries, often at great cost to their health, because of the stereotype that they were capable of work "physically too heavy" for others.[11] Race and sex discrimination confined most Asian-American and Mexican-American immigrants of recent decades to domestic work or low-paid, menial jobs in garment "sweatshops" and other factories, restaurants, and hotels. "If you're brown or a woman, you work for years and never get promoted," said a cannery worker.[12]

Immigrant women encountered discrimination based on appearance and age as well as sex and ethnicity. Desirable service jobs went to the young and the attractive. Factory foremen often refused to hire women older than thirty-five or forty, regardless of their skills and experience. An immigrant woman, unemployed after twenty-eight years of restaurant work, commented bitterly, "When we are young and strong, it is all right in America, but we wear out pretty soon, then what?"[13]

Rural Work

In the nineteenth century, when land was plentiful and relatively cheap, more than half of all immigrant women (particularly Scandinavians and Germans) settled in rural areas. Historian Theodore Blegen describes the life of a Norwegian farm woman on the Great Plains in the 1840s:

> The farmer worked hard, but his wife worked harder. She did the housework, cared for the children, prepared the meals, helped to care for the cattle, pigs, sheep, and chickens, milked the cows, churned the butter, made the soap, did the canning in summer and fall, prepared cheese, carded and spun the wool, wove cloth, dyed it with homemade dyes, knitted and sewed clothing, mended mittens and socks. On occasion she pitched in and helped to rake hay or load the grain. . . . She bore children year after year, and she cared for the sick when her home was struck by disease. She got little leisure or relaxation. . . . Mrs. Gro Swendson, who loved to read . . . was obliged to get in most of her reading during her confinements.[14]

Some rural families maintained gardens and livestock while moving in and out of the paid labor force in nearby industries or commercial farms. This was the situation of Katharina Heunsaker, a German immigrant in *The Joppa Door*, a novel by Hope Williams Sykes. Katharina, whose efforts to feed her six children during hard times are described in the first selection, drew upon skills learned in Germany, used her children as a labor force, and took pride in her success.

In the early twentieth century Japanese women grew fruit and vegetables on the west coast, while European women engaged in truck farming in the east. In the decades that followed, large numbers of Mexican women entered the country as migrant farm workers. Following the crops and living in barracks provided by their employers, often without running water, heat, or electricity, women grew from childhood to adulthood without adequate schooling or health care. As the nation became increasingly urban, the number of immigrant women in agriculture declined. By the last third of the century the majority of Mexican-American women, like their European and Asian counterparts, had moved to the city.

Professions

On the frontier and in urban ghettos, immigrant women commonly treated the physical and psychological illnesses of neighbors and friends who lacked access to or confidence in male physicians. Following traditions handed down through generations, folk healers like Mexican-born Teresa Urrea relied on their knowledge of herbs, hygiene, and human nature and on strong, cheer-giving personalities. A few acquired formal training in midwifery, nursing, or medicine before or after coming to the United States. One of the first formally trained "regular" physicians was Prussian immigrant Dr. Marie Zakrzewska. The second selection describes her life as director of a hospital and clinic for women in New York City in the 1850s.

In the early twentieth century journalist Hutchins Hapgood noted women physicians, dentists, and lawyers among the Jewish immigrant population of the lower east side of New York. Large numbers of physicians and nurses immigrated from Korea, the Philippines, India, and other Third World countries after the passage of the immigration law of 1965, which gave preference to professionals. Jewish immigration from the Soviet Union in the 1970s and 1980s included physicians, engineers, chemists, and other professional women. Although some foreign-trained professional women were able to find appropriate employment in the United States, language and certification problems led to years—sometimes a lifetime—of underemployment for many others.

Probably the single largest profession for foreign-born women has been teaching. Women who emigrated from English-speaking countries or who came young enough to speak unaccented English and who were able to stay in school long enough could become teachers in a public school system that was expanding during most of the nineteenth and twentieth centuries. Religious orders gave immigrant and second-generation women opportunities for education and professional employment in nursing, social work, and missionary work as well as teaching—opportunities not readily available elsewhere. In Detroit in 1907, teaching nuns accounted for two-thirds of all professionals, male or female, in the Polish community.[15]

Providing Services

Lacking the education necessary for professional careers, many women supported themselves by providing services. With their husbands or alone, they peddled food or dry goods or operated steamship ticket agencies, employment bureaus, delicatessens, laundries, restaurants, or beauty shops. Some cared for neighbors' children as well as their own. Many washed, cooked, and cleaned for boarders who shared their cramped living space and helped pay the rent. Finnish women who operated boarding houses helped Americanize their clients and, because of their influence and prestige, served as spokespersons for their communities.[16] West Indian domestics in New York City saved and sometimes pooled their money to become owners of "brownstone" apartment buildings. A second-generation Jewish writer remembers a great aunt who sold brandy in the basement of her brownstone during Prohibition.

The most common service provided by immigrant women was housework—without pay in their own homes or for wages in the homes of others. Unlike their native-born counterparts, immigrant "housewives" have usually had to learn new ways of doing familiar tasks. The third selection describes the problems faced by early twentieth-century women from rural Europe adjusting to housework and childcare in the tenements of urban, industrial America.

Housework was especially burdensome to women who held outside jobs as well. A few husbands helped. More often, women relied on young daughters or did everything themselves, working night shifts and caring for their households by day or working day shifts and doing housework at night. A textile worker in the Lehigh Valley described her routine: "Everything I do—wash, iron, cook, clean, sew. . . . Get up at 4:30, feed the chickens, make the breakfast, get ready the lunches, and it is time to start to work. Six o'clock come home, make eats for children, washing at nighttime, and make clothes for children."[17]

Housework for wages—domestic service—was the dominant occupation of Irish, German, Scandinavian, Bohemian, Mexican, and Slovak women in 1920 and an important occupation for Latina and West Indian women in recent decades. In the nineteenth and early twentieth centuries, women became live-in domestics because housework was the only work they knew; because it offered room, board, information about America, and a chance to save money; or because they had no other skills. In recent decades Latina and West Indian women became live-in domestics even when they had other saleable skills because it was the only way they could obtain the employer's sponsorship that would enable them to immigrate or, if they were already in the country illegally, to obtain legal permanent residency ("green card" status). The latter practice became more difficult after 1986, when a new immigration law made it illegal for employers to hire undocumented workers.

The Women's Bureau study of 1930 reveals that more women quit domestic work than any other job because of the long hours, heavy work, lack of freedom, and isolation. "So much to do—not go to church. . . . I so lonesome, I cried all the time," complained a Polish live-in domestic at the turn of the century.[18] The fourth selection shows that the problems of West Indian domestics half a century later were strikingly similar. Unlike most earlier domestics, however, who were usually young and single, West Indian domestics were often mature women with children.

Employment in Industry

As the United States became an industrial giant in the late nineteenth and early twentieth centuries, the percentage of foreign-born women employed in agriculture or domestic work decreased and the percentage employed in manufacturing grew. In 1900 half of all the nation's domestic workers were foreign-born, but three-quarters of female factory workers were immigrants or the daughters of immigrants.[19] While Irish, German, and Scandinavian women still clustered in domestic work, most French Canadians, Poles, Jews, and Italians worked in industry. Women wove textiles, made clothing, cut glass and metal, shaped bolts and screws, twisted electrical cable, rolled cigars, packed soap, canned vegetables, and, more recently, assembled electronic and computer parts in factories. They sewed, knitted, embroidered, packaged, and assembled "sundries" at home. The fifth selection describes the lives of "typical" European-born industrial workers in the early twentieth century.

Industrial employment at the turn of the century meant long hours, dangerous conditions, and low wages. Child labor was common, and piecework kept wages at the barest subsistence level. In 1905 laundry workers in Illinois were hospitalized from exhaustion after working sixteen to twenty hours a day in the heat and dampness of steam-filled plants.[20] Job-related illnesses and injuries were common. In 1911, 146 workers died in the Triangle Shirtwaist Fire; they were unable to escape the burning building because doors had been locked to keep workers in and union organizers out. In 1902 the highest-paid woman in the Pittsburgh canneries earned less than the lowest-paid man. The men hosed down their work area, but the women spent four hours on their hands and knees on Saturday afternoons scrubbing the tables and floors.[21]

By mid-century, factory legislation and the labor movement (in which immigrant women played an important role) had raised wages, shortened hours, and alleviated many of the horrors of earlier years. But immigrants continued to encounter abuses in the workplace. Forty of sixty-three Texas employers investigated by the Department of Labor in 1979 were paying alien workers less than federal minimum wages, failing to pay for overtime, or not paying fully for hours worked.[22] Child labor and sweatshop conditions were common in the garment industry on both coasts. Lacking English language skills and job alternatives and fearing deportation (even if they were legal), many Chinese, Mexican, Central American, and other foreign-born women remain vulnerable to exploitation by employers in their own community and in American society at large.

Arts and Letters

Despite many obstacles, immigrant women of exceptional talent have worked in music, literature, and the arts. A few have attained fame in the wider American community—sculptor Elisabet Ney, opera singer Adelina Patti, concert pianist Teresa Carreno, and film maker Maya Deren. Most have won acclaim within their own communities. Poets, novelists, and journalists published in their native languages for an ethnic public and, less frequently, in English for the wider American public. Russian-born poet Marya Zaturenska won a Pulitzer Prize in 1938. Ethnic theater, in immigrant languages and later in English, offered nineteenth- and early-twentieth-century women a livelihood, public recognition, and the opportunity to engage in a nontraditional life-style with relative impunity. Despite the competition of movies and television, women like Cuban-born playwright Dolores Frida, who tells her story in the final selection, continue to be "theater workers." Like Frida, artists, authors, and actors worked not only to support themselves, but also to express themselves.

Social Mobility

"When I left Vietnam, I didn't have anything. Now I can go to school, look for a job, save money. Here I can do everything," said a Vietnamese refugee, expressing the hope for a better life that has brought many women, past and present, to the United States.[23] Most women wage earners had to start at or near the bottom of the American socioeconomic ladder, and most remained there despite years of work, sacrifice, and saving. For a minority, however, there was social mobility. Industrial workers moved up to skilled or, more rarely, supervisory positions. Women who immigrated very young were sometimes able to leave manual labor for more prestigious (though not necessarily more lucrative) positions in offices, shops, or women's professions. Some women moved from labor to relative leisure through marriage to an upwardly mobile man.

Even when they remained in the same menial job year after year, most immigrant women took satisfaction in the results of their labor. They considered themselves fortunate if they could support their aging parents, educate their children, or contribute to the purchase of a home, perhaps the first the family had ever owned. For these women, as for their more "successful" counterparts, work was worthwhile and the American dream a reality.

Notes

1.   Caroline Manning, *The Immigrant Woman and Her Job*, United States Department of Labor Women's Bureau Bulletin no. 74 (Washington, D.C.; U.S. Government Printing Office, 1930), p. 57.

2.   Ibid.

3.   Ibid., p. 52.

4.   Ibid., pp. 49, 53.

5.   Ibid., p. 56.

6.   Ibid., p. 59.

7.   Emiliana P. Noether, "The Silent Half: Le Contadine Del Sud before the First World War," in *The Italian Immigrant Woman in North America*, ed. Betty Boyd Caroli, Robert F. Harney, and Lydio F. Tomasi (Toronto: Multicultural History Society of Ontario, 1978), pp. 3–12; Grace Abbott, *The Immigrant and the Community* (New York: Century, 1917), pp. 57, 61–62, 64; and Mark Zborowski and Elizabeth Herzog, *Life Is with People: The Culture of the Shtetl* (New York: Schocken, 1969), p. 131.

8.   Manning, *Immigrant Woman*, p. 53.

9.   Ibid., p. 57.

10.   Marcelle Williams, "Ladies on the Line: Punjabi Cannery Workers in Central California," in *Making Waves: An Anthology of Writings by and about Asian American Women*, Asian Women United of California (Boston: Beacon Press, 1989), p. 157.

11.   Abbott, *Immigrant and the Community*, p. 65.

12.   Williams, "Ladies on the Line," p. 156.

13.   Manning, *Immigrant Woman*, p. 111.

14.   Theodore C. Blegen, *Norwegian Migration to America: The American Transition* (Northfield, Minn.: Norwegian-American Historical Association, 1940), p. 48.

15.   Peter A. Ostafin, "The Polish Peasant in Transition: A Study of Group Integration as a Function of Symbioses and Common Definition" (Ph.D. diss., University of Michigan, 1948), p. 83, as cited in Thaddeus C. Radzialowski, "Reflections on the History of the Felicians in America," *Polish American Studies* 23, no. 1 (Spring 1975): 22, 27.

16.   Walter Mattila, *The Boarding House Finns* (Portland, Oreg.: Finnish American Historical Society of the West, 1972), p. 4.

17.   Manning, *Immigrant Woman*, p. 120.

18.   Ibid., p. 60.

19.   Carpenter, *Immigrants and Their Children*, p. 290.

20.   Florence Kelley, "Industrial Democracy," *Outlook*, December 15, 1906, p. 926, as cited in Barbara Wertheimer, *We Were There: The Story of Working Women in America* (New York: Pantheon, 1977), p. 215.

21.   Wertheimer, *We Were There*, p. 219.

22.   John M. Crewdson, "Inquiry in Texas Finds Employers Cheating Aliens," *New York Times*, October 28, 1979.

23.   *Newsweek*, September 10, 1979, p. 22.

1

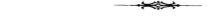

"Better We Glean Than Our Children Starve"

This selection, from Hope Williams Sykes' 1937 novel The Joppa Door, *describes work done by German-born Katharina Heunsaker, who immigrated to frontier Utah shortly after her Russian-born husband's conversion to the Mormon faith. Like many rural families, the Heunsakers depended upon cash earnings as well as upon their garden and livestock for survival. When hard times deprived the family of Herr Heunsaker's wages, Katharina used her skills and ingenuity and the meager resources available to her to provide food and even Christmas presents for her family. Accustomed to deferring to her husband, she defied him when she felt this was necessary to insure the welfare of her six young children.*

Hope Williams Sykes was a teacher who lived and worked among German-Russian immigrants in the sugar-beet-growing area of Colorado. The Joppa Door *was based upon a life story told to her by an elderly German-Russian immigrant woman, who read the finished manuscript and acknowledged its authenticity.*

A panic sits upon the land. Herr Heunsaker does not have the work at the foundry. Once again he goes to a farm, but he gets no money. Sure, I am glad this day that we have our home.

Herr Heunsaker comes home tired from his working. "Katharina, it is the end of the world. War is all they talk of, and panic is in the land. . . . Sure, it is the end." He puts his face in his hands.

"We have to feed our children," I say.

"Enough grain goes to waste in these American fields to feed a hundred starving people." Herr Heunsaker says. "Such a waste do these farmers make. Along the ditch banks and in the corners they never cut the grain."

"In Germany when I am a girl, we glean the fields. Each green weed and each head of grain we save." Long I stand and look out from my kitchen window.

"We do not glean fields here," Herr Heunsaker says jumping up from his chair. "We live like Americans."

Source: Hope Williams Sykes, *The Joppa Door* (New York: G. P. Putnam's Sons, 1937).

"Better we glean than our children starve," I say. "In the morning I see Brother Beekman. He has the large fields of wheat and of barley at the edge of town. I take the children with, and we gather the grain that is wasted."

"Katharina! You do not work like the ox of the field." Herr Heunsaker is so mad. "I do not have my woman—"

"In your pride you let your children starve?" Straight I look into Herr Heunsaker's deep brown eyes. I see the great hurt in them. It is a sad day when a man knows he cannot feed his little children.

This next morning I talk with Brother Beekman. With kindness he smiles upon me. "Welcome you are, Sister Heunsaker, to the gleanings from my field. For the poor and the stranger are the gleanings. After we have cut the grain, you may come into my fields."

"I thank you so much," I say, and I turn quick away for I do not want him to see my tears.

When the harvesters have left the fields, I hitch our horse to the buggy. With my six little children I go into the country. With our hand sickles we cut the grain and tie it in small bunches like in the Old Country. The sun shines bright and I think how such fresh air is good for my little ones. So happy are they. My baby, Lael, chases butterflies, and laughs with her hands stretched out far. Near two she is, and lovely like a flower. My Thyrza and Etta, and tiny Johanna work so busy. Much help they are. And my two boys. Ach, such men as they will make. My Gustave. My Philip.

"When I am a little girl, we go out into the fields. So many brothers and sisters I have. We laugh when we glean." I laugh softly and tell my little ones of Germany. I do not tell them I am bitter against the farm when I am young. I think how all youth is bitter against work and hard times, and doing without. Sure, it is right. The world goes on with the young people wanting better things.

Soon we have our buggy piled high with grain. Such a great load of barley. I think how I will roast the grains in the oven, and they will make the good barley coffee for our breakfast.

"Mamma! Mamma! Come, look what is here." Gustave stands far down the field. We all go to where he is, and, here in the great ditch which has gone dry, lies such a fish. Never before do I see such a great fish. . . .

"Lay it down, Gustave. It is spoiled. We cannot eat it."

"Such good it would be to eat." Gustave cries great tears. Sure, he is small, but he knows that food is precious in these hard times.

On the way home we have to go through the streets of the town. I look straight ahead. I do not let my little children notice how some people look on us with staring eyes. Sure, I know they think we are foreign people with the queer ways.

This night Herr Heunsaker comes home on a wagon. "A whole load of potatoes I get for pay, Katharina," he shouts.

"What we do with them?" I say.

"We eat them. What you think?" Herr Heunsaker laughs. But I do not laugh. Already we have some potatoes from our own garden, and we cannot eat a wagonload of potatoes, and we have no place to keep them. Our cellar and our sheds are filled with grain I have gleaned, and with carrots and with all vegetables which we pick on the shares from farmers.

I am turning in my bed, thinking of these potatoes, when all at once I think of my mother. I remember how times are hard in Germany and how once my mother is without starch and she grinds potatoes and pours cold water over and the starch comes out.

When I am putting the breakfast on the table, I tell Herr Heunsaker about my mother's starch. "We grind the potatoes. In the evenings when our work is done we can do it," I say.

I let the water stand on the potatoes which we grind fine in a grinder. When the starch is settled to the bottom of the tub, I pour the water off and let the starch dry hard. We break it into great chunks and put it away. I use it in my cooking, and in starching my children's clothes and my dresses. But I think always how Herr Heunsaker does things without thinking. Sure, he has the great mind, but not such good judgment to go with.

I do not like to keep my children out of school, but I think now we must have food to eat. Each day I take them all with me, and we gather apples on the shares, and then we peel them and dry them. We pick the corn when it is soft and dry it also. Ach, such a work we have putting fruit to dry and vegetables in the dugout for the winter, but soon winter will come and the children will be in school. Though panic is in the land, our cellars will be full. We will not starve.

In the evenings Herr Heunsaker sits long and studies. He buys such a book on how to raise chickens. He reads it aloud to me, and tells me how there is much money in chickens if a man follows the rules. Many nights he reads in this book and shows me the pictures of Buff Orpingtons, Rhode Island Reds, and Wyantdottes.

"We don't raise Leghorns. Too little and skinny, they are. They don't have the meat on their bones. We get the heavy chickens. Such money we make!" There is great excitement in Herr Heunsaker's voice. Soon he comes home with six fancy chickens. But he gets tired of them, and it is for me to look after the chickens.

The children bring home great wooden barrels from the stores in town, and we scrub them out good and stand them in the sun. Then the next day we scrub them again and stand them in the sun. Three, four times we do this, and when they are clean and sweet smelling, we slice the cabbage and fill the barrels. Such good sauerkraut it makes.

"I tell you, Katharina, in Russia we put the big green apples in with the sauerkraut. Sauerapples we call them. Ach, but they are good." Herr Heunsaker licks his lips, and his eyes look hungry. "I find some green apples and we put in the barrels."

"You do not put apples in my good sauerkraut," I tell him. I put the great stones on the tops of the boards in the barrels and he cannot put apples in. Such queer ways he brings from Russland, anyway. Not good German ways.

Near Christmas time I think how we have nothing. Never before do my children go without some little thing. I think—what can I do? My rags I look through and find some pieces of silk that a good neighbor gives to me. From these I make dolls for my Johanna and my Lael. For Etta and Thyrza I make some bright mittens from yarn Frau Cable gives me long ago. For the boys— what will I make? Sure there is nothing. Then I think of this black coat that Frau Cable gives to me to wear that first year I am in this country. Sure, I make my boys some caps. Good black caps they will be, with ear muffs to turn down so they keep their ears warm, and cardboard in the bills to make them stiff.

In the nighttime after the children are in bed, I make Christmas cookies, Sprengerle, and honey cakes. On the night before Christmas Day Herr Heunsaker helps me, and we put plates on the table, with bright red apples, the dolls, the mittens, and the caps on, also. In the center we pile the Christmas cookies. Sure, it is a good table for our little ones.

"It is a good country. Our America." Herr Heunsaker speaks with reverence. Then he bends his head in prayer and tells of his thankfulness. I bow my head with him.

In the cold days that follow, before the spring comes, we give of our abundance to others who do not know how to glean the fields, and to save, and to live with plenty when there is nothing.

2

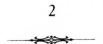

A Physician in the "First True 'Woman's Hospital' in the World"

Marie Zakrzewska, a Polish immigrant who came to the United States in 1853 to become a physician (see the third selection in Part 1), received her medical degree and practiced her profession when women physicians were a curiosity. Zakrzewska

Source: Marie Zakrzewska, *A Woman's Quest: The Life of Marie Zakrzewska, M.D.*, ed. Agnes C. Vietor (New York: D. Appleton, 1924), pp. 209–19, 228–32.

found gender to be a greater handicap in her professional life than foreign birth: landlords refused to rent office or living space to a "lady doctor." A feminist as well as a physician, she joined forces with two pioneer American-born physicians, Elizabeth and Emily Blackwell, to establish a woman's clinic, hospital, and training school for nurses in New York City in 1857. The following excerpt from Zakrzewska's autobiography describes her first year as director of "this primitive, first true 'Woman's Hospital' in the world, where her daily responsibilities included shopping, meal planning, and sewing, as well as the teaching and practice of medicine.

We at once entered into negotiation for the house we had in view and obtained the refusal of it for the 1st of March, 1857. We also ordered the twenty-four iron bedsteads needed, for the sum of one hundred dollars, and all the ladies went to work begging and preparing house linen, so that when the year closed we held a most joyful New Year's Day, and received so many congratulations that we actually thought ourselves in the command of thousands of dollars.

The house was an old-fashioned mansion of the Dutch style, at the corner of Bleecker and Crosby Streets, just at the outer end of what was called the "Five Points," fully respectable on the Bleecker Street side, and full of patients and misery on the other side and at the rear. And we spent the few weeks which elapsed before we could begin to arrange it in getting the good will of editors, ministers and business men, in order that we might procure the means for carrying on a charity for which we had nothing but an empty purse.

Dr. Blackwell's influence among the Quakers, many of them rich, and Miss Mary L. Booth's indefatigable notices in the newspapers, opened to us the ways of procuring the necessary materials for the dispensary, which occupied the lower front room. It contained a consulting desk, an examination table behind a large screen, shelves for medicines and a table for preparing the ingredients of prescriptions. . . .

The second floor was arranged for two wards, each containing six beds; while the third floor was made into a maternity department, the little hall room serving as a sitting room for the physicians. Open grate coal fires provided the only heat throughout the house.

The fourth, or attic floor contained four . . . sleeping rooms. . . .

Into this primitive, first true "Woman's Hospital" in the world, I moved in March, superintending all its arrangements, with the kind assistance of a few ladies appointed by the now organized board of directors. We ventured to hire one servant to clean, wash and do general work, as I was the only inmate until the house was regularly and formally opened on May 1, 1857. . . .

A sign on the front door told the purpose of the house, (and) . . . before a month had passed, we had our beds filled with patients and a daily attendance of thirty and more dispensary patients. Drs. Elizabeth and Emily Blackwell and myself each attended the dispensary two mornings in the week, from nine to twelve, while four students from the Philadelphia college came to live in the hospital in the capacity of interns, apothecaries and pupils of nursing. . . .

We also had two nurses, one for the general wards and one for the maternity department. They were both unskilled and considered the training as more than sufficient equivalent for their services, receiving simply an allowance of two dollars per week for their necessary clothing. Thus we kept true to our promise to begin at once a system for training nurses. . . .

As for myself, I occupied a peculiar position. I was resident physician, superintendent, housekeeper and instructor to the students of whom none was graduated, so that I had the full responsibility of all their activities, both inside and outside the little hospital. In order to give an idea of the situation, I want to relate from my notes the record of one day of my work.

At 5:30 A.M., I started in an omnibus for the wholesale market, purchasing provisions for a week, and at 8:00, I was back to breakfast. This consisted, for all inmates except patients, of tea, bread and butter, Indian meal mush and syrup, every morning except Sundays when coffee and breakfast bacon were added.

After breakfast, I made my visit to the patients in the house with two of the students, while the other two students attended upon Dr. Blackwell in the dispensary. Then a confinement case arrived and I attended to her, giving orders to students and nurses. After this, I descended into the kitchen department, as the provisions had arrived, and with the assistance of the cook I arranged all these so as to preserve the materials, and I settled the diet for all as far as possible.

I then took another omnibus ride to the wholesale druggist, begging and buying needed articles for the dispensary and the hospital, arriving home at 1:00 P.M. for dinner. This consisted every day of a good soup, the soup meat, potatoes, one kind of well-prepared vegetable, with fruit for dessert. . . .

After dinner, I usually went out to see my private patients, because receiving no compensation I depended upon my earnings for personal needs. On this day, however, I was detained by the confinement case mentioned and could not go out till 5:00 P.M., returning at 7:00 P.M. for tea. This always consisted of bread and butter, tea and sauce or cheese or fresh gingerbread. After again making the rounds of the patients in the house, it was 9:00 o'clock.

Then the students assembled with me in the little hall room, I cutting out towels or pillow cases or other needed articles for the house or the patients, while the students folded or even basted the articles for the sewing machine as they recited their various lessons for the day. After their recital, I gave them verbal instruction in midwifery. We finished the work of the day by 11:30, as I never allowed any one to be out of bed after midnight unless detained by a patient.

This day is a fair illustration of our life. If I had not food to provide, it was something else; if not drugs, it was drygoods; and if neither, I attended the dispensary at least two forenoons, and if either of the Drs. Blackwell was prevented by private business from attending her regular forenoon, I attended in her place.

The strain upon us all, added to the very meager diet, was immense, and it became a necessity to provide relaxations. So I arranged that during the summer, once a month, we all went on a picnic during an afternoon in the hills across the Hudson; and in the winter, once a month, we went to a good theater which was near by. . . .

From May 1, 1857, to May 1, 1858, . . . the average morning dispensary attendance was thirty; while the in-door patients were about one hundred during the year. But we had a very large out-door practice, one of the four students alone, Dr. Mary E. Breed, attending fourteen cases of childbed in one month; while I was often sent for in the night to assist them with advice when their knowledge was not sufficient.

The practical gain to these young women was so great that they were not only devoted, hardworking and conscientious in their professional duties, but they were more than willing to bear great physical discomfort, as well as the ridicule which they encountered when they attempted to demand the recognition and the respect due to their calling. Everywhere among the better situated people, they met with discouraging remarks and questions, giving evidence that the opinion was that the practice of medicine by women would, in the course of time, be impossible, even if the present few were received as exceptions, or as the novelties of a fad. And the greatest tact was called for in accommodating ourselves and our work to the need of even the poorest people. . . .

The need for the friendliness of the police towards us I can illustrate here also. A woman died in the hospital after childbirth. We had informed the many relations whom the poor and forsaken usually possess of the seriousness of the case. There was always one woman of the kinship at the bedside of the patient for about sixty hours before the death, which took place in the forenoon.

It was not an hour after this sad occurrence before all the cousins who had relieved each other at the bedside appeared, with their male cousins or husbands in working attire and with pickaxes and shovels, before our street door, demanding admission and shouting that the female physicians who resided within were killing women in childbirth with cold water.

Of course, an immense crowd collected, filling the block between us and Broadway, hooting and yelling and trying to push in the doors, both on the street and in the yard; so that we were beleaguered in such a way that no communication with the outside was possible. We could not call to the people who were looking out of the windows in the neighboring houses, our voices being drowned by the noise of the mob.

At this juncture the policeman who had charge of Bleecker Street and the one from Broadway came running up to the scene. On learning the complaint of the men, they commanded silence and ordered the crowd to disperse, telling them that they knew the doctors in that hospital treated the patients in the best possible way, and that no doctor could keep everybody from dying some time. . . .

Perhaps nobody, nowadays, can understand the willingness and devotion of the women who assisted me in carrying on this primitive little hospital: who were willing to work hard, in and out of hours; who fared extremely plainly and lodged almost to uncomfortableness; yet who felt that a good work was being accomplished for all womankind. And this was true of all—students, nurses and domestic help.

We had constant applications from students to share in the experience of practice which we offered, and who were willing to live outside in order to attend the dispensary; while the number of patients in daily attendance at this latter increased so rapidly that we had to establish the rule of locking the door against admission after a certain hour.

Among the applicants were all sorts of extremists—such as women in very short Bloomer costume, with hair cut also very short, to whom the patients objected most strenuously; others were training as practitioners in a water-cure establishment, and wished to avail themselves of our outdoor practice in order to introduce their theories and methods of healing. In fact, we were overrun with advisers and helpers whom we had to refuse. Popular prejudices could be overcome only in the most careful and conservative manner; and even our most ardent friends and supporters shared to a certain degree in the feeling of uncertainty as to the success of our experiment.

Personally, I received during this year great comfort in the acquaintances and lifelong friendships gained. And the recollection of these friends calls forth such a deep feeling of gratitude . . . that I consider it worth while to have lived if for no other reason than to realize through them the goodness of womankind.

So the year closed upon us as one which had brought great satisfaction in all we expected to gain, professionally and as bearers of a new idea. Youth was with us all, and our hopes of success knew no limit. . . .

Still, there was a dark side to my experience during that year. The sick headaches, to which I had been subject off and on since childhood, came upon me quite often and very unexpectedly, evidently due to the overstraining of all my forces, physical and mental, and I was quite often obliged to relinquish some very important duties.

Before leaving this year's record, I must add a few remarks concerning our work, that is, mine and that of the ten or twelve students who had been connected with the Infirmary now for twenty months.

The prejudice against women physicians was by no means confined to that stratum of society where education and wealth nurtured the young. We found it just as strong, through habit and custom, among the working people and among the very poorest of the poor. Their coming to our dispensary was not *a priori* appreciation of the woman physician, but was the result of faith in the *extraordinary*, just as now faith-curers with other claims are sought and consulted in illness.

Our work was that of real missionaries. Even among the well-to-do and intelligent, little or nothing was known of hygiene. If "a goneness in the stomach" was felt, whisky, brandy or a strong tonic was resorted to for relief. Diet, rest and the sensible use of water were never considered.

So among the poor we found everywhere bad air, filth and utter disregard of food. And sponges, as well as soap, were carried in the satchels of our young medical women along with the necessary implements of the physician. And the former were given to the patients' friends, after showing them the use of water and soap in fever cases as well as in ordinary illness. It was an innovation in the minds of the people, the teaching that sick people must be bathed and kept clean, and that fresh air was not killing.

The good results obtained by the addition of these sanitary auxiliaries whose use was permitted only through our persuasion, created almost a superstitious faith in us and resulted in sending to us patients from a distance of ten and twelve miles from Bleecker Street. This made increased demands on our physical and nervous powers, for we made it a point not to refuse any person if it were at all possible to see her.

Thus we placed foundation stones here and there all over Manhattan Island upon which to build our superstructure of medical practice by women.

3

"The Duties of the Housewife Remain Manifold and Various"

Immigrant women spent hours each day doing housework—cooking, shopping, washing, ironing, scrubbing. Little girls helped their mothers as soon as they were able and children as young as ten or twelve sometimes managed the entire house-

Source: Sophonisba P. Breckinridge, *New Homes for Old* (New York: Harper and Brothers, 1921), pp. 43–46, 54–66, 87–88, 117–23, 134–37.

hold for wage-earning mothers. *Adults worked in their own homes or the homes of others (or both), and even boarders were expected to help with the housework. Native-born Americans who complained about "dirty" or, more politely, "inefficient" immigrant homemakers or domestic servants usually knew little about immigrant women and their problems. In this passage from her 1921 book,* New Homes for Old, *sociologist Sophonisba Breckinridge describes the many difficulties, economic and cultural, encountered by the immigrant homemaker in the urban tenements of the early twentieth century.*

The grandmothers and maiden aunts, who were part of the group in the old country, and who shared with the mother all the work of the household, are not with them in this country. . . . It is perhaps the grandmother that is missed the more, because it was to her that the mother of a family was wont to turn for advice as well as assistance. . . .

This decrease in the number of people in the household is not compensated for by the diminution in the amount of work. . . .

The duties of the housewife may not be as many, but the work they involve may be more. This is true, for example, in the matter of feeding the family. In Lithuania soup was the fare three times daily, and there were only a few variations in kind. Here the family soon demands meat, coffee, and other things that are different from the food she has cooked in the old country. . . . Occasionally the situation is further complicated by the insistence of dietetic experts that the immigrant mother cannot feed her family intelligently unless she has some knowledge of food values. In other words, the work of the housewife was easy in the old country because it was well done— if it was done in the way her mother did it—and conformed to the standards that she knew. It could thus become a matter of routine that did not involve the expenditure of nervous energy. Here, on the other hand, she must conform to standards that are constantly changing, and must learn to do things in a way her mother never dreamed of doing them. . . .

In spite of all that has been taken out of the home the duties of the housewife remain manifold and various. She is responsible for the care of the house, for the selection and preparation of food, for spending the part of the income devoted to present needs, and for planning and sharing in the sacrifices thought necessary to provide against future needs. She must both bear and rear her children. The responsibilities and satisfactions of her relationship with her husband are too often last in the list of her daily preoccupations, but by no means least in importance. . . .

The Care of the House

The foreign-born housewife finds this work particularly difficult for many reasons. In the first place, housekeeping in the country from which she came was done under such different conditions that it here becomes almost a new problem in which her experience in the old country may prove of little use. . . .

Lithuanian women . . . have pointed out that at home most of the women worked in the fields, and that what housekeeping was done was of the simplest kind. The peasant house consisted of two rooms, one of which was used only on state occasions, a visit from the priest, a wedding, christening, or a funeral. In summer no one sleeps in the house, but all sleep out of doors in the hay; in winter, women with small children sleep inside, but the others sleep in the granary. Feather beds are, in these circumstances, a real necessity. Thus the bed that is found in this country is unknown in Lithuania, and the women naturally do not know how to care for one. They not only do not realize the need of airing it, turning the mattress, and changing the bedding, but do not even know how to make it up properly.

The Italian women, especially those from southern Italy and Sicily, have also spoken of their difficulties in housekeeping under new conditions. In Italy the houses even of the relatively well-to-do peasants, were two-room affairs with earthen floors and little furniture. The women had little time to give to the care of the house, and its comfort and order were not considered important. . . .

The experience in doing the family washing is said to typify the change. In Italy washing is done once a month, or at most, once a fortnight, in the poorer families. Clothes are placed in a great vat or tub of cold water, covered with a cloth on which is sprinkled wood ashes, and allowed to stand overnight. In the morning they are taken to a stream or fountain, and washed in running water. They are dried on trees and bushes in the bright, Italian sunlight. Such methods of laundry work do not teach the women anything about washing in this country, and they are said to make difficult work of it in many cases. They learn that clothes are boiled here, but they do not know which clothes to boil and which to wash without boiling; and as a result they often boil all sorts of clothing, colored and white, together. In Italy washing is a social function; here it is a task for each individual woman. . . .

Demands of American Cookery

Cooking in this country varies in difficulty in the different national groups. In the case of the Lithuanians and Poles, for example, the old-country cooking is simple and easily done. Among others it is a fine art, requiring much time and skill. The Italian cooking, of course, is well known, as is also the Hungarian. . . .

It is not always easy to transplant this art of cookery, even if the women had time to practice it here as they did at home. The materials can usually be obtained, although often at a considerable expense, but the equipment with which they cook and the stoves on which they cook are entirely different. The Italian women, for example, cannot bake their bread in the ovens of the stoves that they use here. Tomato paste, for example, is used in great quantities by Italian families, and is made at home by drying the tomatoes in the open air. When an attempt is made to do this in almost any large city the tomatoes get not only the sunshine, but the soot and dirt of the city. . . .

With this lack of experience in housekeeping under comparable conditions, the foreign-born housewife finds the transition to housekeeping in this country difficult at best. As a matter of fact, however, the circumstances under which she must make the change are often of the worst.

Even a skillful housewife finds housekeeping difficult in such houses as are usually occupied by recently arrived immigrants.

Water Supply Essential

In the first place, there is the question of water supply. Cleanliness of house, clothing, and even of person is extremely difficult in a modern industrial community, without an adequate supply of hot and cold water within the dwelling. We are, however, very far from realizing this condition. In some cities the law requires that there shall be a sink with running water in every dwelling, but in other cities even this minimum is not required. The United States Immigration Commission, for example, found that 1,413 households out of 8,651 foreign-born households studied in seven large cities, shared their water supply with other families. . . . It is a great handicap to efficient housekeeping if water has to be carried any distance. Further inconvenience results if running hot water is not available, which is too often the case in the homes of the foreign born.

Cleanliness is also dependent, in part, upon the facilities for the disposition of human waste, the convenient and accessible toilet connected with a sewer system. These facilities are lacking in many immigrant neighborhoods, as has been repeatedly shown in various housing investigations. For example, in a Slovak district in the Twentieth Ward, Chicago, 80 per cent of the families were using toilets located in the cellar, yard, or under the sidewalk, and in many cases sharing such toilets with other families.

There is also the question of heating and lighting the house. Whenever light is provided by the oil lamp, it must be filled and cleaned; and when heat is provided by the coal stove, it means that the housewife must keep the fires going and dispose of the inevitable dirt and ashes. . . .

Overcrowding Hampers the Housewife

The influence of overcrowding on the work of the housewife must also be considered in connection with housekeeping in immigrant households. That overcrowding exists has been pointed out again and again. Ordinances have been framed to try to prevent it, but it has persisted. In the studies of Chicago housing a large percentage of the bedrooms have always been found illegally occupied. The per cent of the rooms so occupied varied from 30 in one Italian district to 72 in the Slavic district around the steel mills. The United States Immigration Commission found, for example, that 5,305, or 35.1 per cent, of the families studied in industrial centers used all rooms but one for sleeping, and another 771 families used even the kitchen.

Crowding means denial of opportunity for skillful and artistic performance of tasks. "A place for everything and everything in its place," suggest appropriate assignment of articles of use to their proper niches, corners, and shelves. One room for everything except sleeping—cooking, washing, caring for children, catching a breath for the moment—means no repose, no calm, no opportunity for planning that order which is the law of the well-governed home. . . .

The housework for the foreign-born housewife is often complicated by other factors. One is the practice to which reference has been already made of taking lodgers. . . . Usually the boarder or lodger pays a fixed monthly sum—from $2 to $3.50, or, more rarely, $4 a month—for lodging, cleaning, washing, and cooking.

Women Work Outside the Home

Another factor that renders housekeeping difficult is the necessity of doing wage-paid work outside the home. . . .

Many women who worked outside the home did their housekeeping without assistance from other members of the family. This meant that they had to get up early in the morning and frequently work late at night at laundry or cleaning; 49 women, for example, washed in the evening; 25 washed either Saturday, Sunday, or evenings. . . . Now the foreign-born housewife, like other housewives, has certain resources of money and time and strength, and these she wishes to distribute wisely. But she labors under many disadvantages. . . .

Unfamiliarity with Money

In the first place, her income is in an unfamiliar form. There is first the fact that the money units are strange to her. . . .

In the second place, for many there is the difficulty growing out of the exclusive dependence upon money payments, when before there were both money and the products of the land.

It is then peculiarly difficult to value in terms of the new measure those articles with which one has been especially familiar under the old economy.

For example, when vegetables and fruits have been enjoyed without estimating their value, it is difficult to judge their value in money. While meat was before thought out of reach, it may be purchased at exorbitant rates under the new circumstances, because one has no idea of how much it should cost. Evidence as to this kind of difficulty is found among all groups. It takes the form, sometimes, of apparent parsimony, sometimes of reckless and wasteful buying.

The Neglected Art of Spending

Saving is the problem of *over there*, and of the future. Spending is the problem of *here* and *now*, and in the expenditure for present needs as well as in saving for future wants the foreign-born housewife meets with special difficulties. She is handicapped by the kinds of places at which she must buy, because of language, custom, and time limitations, as well as the grade of article available. . . . In shops kept by her co-nationals she will naturally have the utmost confidence. This puts the small neighborhood stores in a position of peculiar privilege, and makes it doubly easy for them to take subtle advantage of the unwary customer. . . .

There is also the question of the means with which to buy. An Italian mother says that she buys at the chain store when she has the cash, and at other times in the Italian stores where, although the prices are higher, she can run a charge account. The system of buying on credit at the local store is spoken of as practically universal in all the foreign-born groups.

Even the skilled housekeepers have little experience in buying. At home they were used to storing vegetables in quantities; potatoes in caves, beets and cabbage by a process of fermentation, other vegetables and fruits by drying. In the United States this sort of thing is not done. There is, in the first place, no place for storage, and the initial cost of vegetables is high and quality poor, and the women know nothing of modern processes of canning.

New Fashions and Old Clothes

Then there is the unsolved problem of clothing. As in the case of food, so with dress; the general effect of the organization of the department stores in the different neighborhoods can be only misleading and confusing. Many misleading devices that would no longer deceive the older residents are tried again on the newcomer. . . .

The foreign born are faced with a particularly difficult problem. They often come from places where dress served to show where one came from, and who one was. In the United States, dress serves to conceal one's origin and relationships, and there results an almost inexorable dilemma. Follow the Old-World practice, and show who you are and where you come from, and the result is that you remain alien and different and that your children will not stay with you "outside the gates." Or follow the fashion and be like others, and the meager income is dissipated before your eyes, with meager results. The Croatians have emphasized the waste of American dress and the immodest styles often worn, while the Italians have chiefly dwelt upon the friction between parents and children. . . .

Shoes are particularly a source of difficulty, both those for the younger children and those for the older boy or girl who goes to work. In some neighborhoods where the older women go barefooted and are thought to do so because they wish to cling to their Old-World customs, they are simply saving, so that the children may wear "American shoes. . . ."

The Care of the Children

The care of the children is the most important of the mother's duties. It cannot be thoroughly done under modern conditions unless the mother has leisure to inform herself about conditions surrounding her children at work and at play, and to keep in touch with their interests, especially as they grow older. It includes caring for their physical wants, bathing them and keeping them clean when they are little, feeding them, providing their clothing, taking care of them when they are sick; it also includes looking after their education and training, choosing the school, seeing that they get to school regularly and on time, following their work at school as it is reported on the monthly report cards, encouraging them to greater efforts when their work is unsatisfactory, praising them when they do well, and, above all, giving them the home training and discipline that they need.

Learning to Play

One of the needs of the growing child that is much emphasized in modern ideas of child culture is an opportunity for wholesome play. The foreign-born mother, from a rural district in Europe, where children were put to work helping the parents as soon as they could be in any way useful, frequently does not recognize this need, and hence does not even do those things within her power to secure it. From some opportunities which she and the children might enjoy together, she is cut off by lack of knowledge of English. A Bohemian woman, for example, said that she did not go with her husband and the children to the moving pictures, as she could not read the English explanations and often did not understand the pictures.

Even when the need is recognized it is still a very difficult problem. In the old country, when the child was too little to work, he could play in the fields quite safe, in sight of his mother at her work. In the city, however, especially in the congested districts, which are the only ones known to immigrants when they first come, the child cannot play [safely]. . . .

4

——◆——

"With Respect and Feelings": Voices of West Indian Child Care and Domestic Workers in New York City

From the Irish "girls" of the nineteenth century to the Latina and West Indian women of the late twentieth, many immigrant women have supported themselves through domestic work. The technology has changed, but the long hours, poor pay, and low status of this stereotypically women's work remain. This shortened version of a longer article is based on interviews with ten West Indian women, most of them mothers, who immigrated in the 1970s and 1980s to provide a better life for themselves and their families. The names of the women interviewed have been changed to protect their anonymity. They had held a variety of jobs before immigrating, including teaching, clerical work, factory work, and petty trading. They became household workers in the United States primarily because before the immigration law reform of 1986 this was a fairly simple path to obtaining a green card, that is, permanent legal residency in the United States. Women were allowed to enter the country to become live-in domestics, a category of workers in short supply, in return for the employer's sponsorship for a green card. Although the employers were supposed to follow government regulations concerning wages and hours, the sponsorship situation could and often did result in exploitation of the immigrant.

Here women describe their experiences as working mothers in a job "many times devalued as it passed from one woman to another along class, racial, ethnic, and migration lines." Jamaican-born Joyce Miller voices a theme common among all the women: "I'm not looking for them [American employers] to shower us down with money, with clothes, but with a little respect and feelings."

Learning to Be "Maidish"

This is not something I thought I would ever do for a living. If somebody had said to me "You're going to clean somebody else's house to make money," I'd say, "Come off it." I had an attitude about that but then after I really thought about it, I said if this is

Source: Abridged from Shellee Colen, " 'With Respect and Feelings' ": Voices of West Indian Child Care and Domestic Workers in New York City," in *All American Women: Lines That Divide and Ties That Bind*, ed. Johnnetta B. Cole (New York and London: Free Press, 1986), pp. 46–70. © Shellee Cohen 1985

what I have to do, I'm going to make the best until the situation changes . . . [Monica Cooper]

After three weeks on her first job here, Marguerite Andrews, a thirty-three-old former school teacher supporting four children, spoke of her adjustment. Although she had an "understanding," "good" employer, becoming a domestic worker and moving from the relative autonomy and high status of teacher to a subordinate, if not subservient, position was difficult.

> I'm not yet really adjusted to it. . . . She's not bossy or anything like that. But within myself I figure I should be more, I can't explain. . . . I don't like to use the word "maidish," but I should put myself all out to do everything. But you know this will have to take some time. . . .

Living In and the Sponsor Job

Everyone described sponsor jobs as the "worst," especially those which are live-in. Sponsored jobs on a live-in basis greatly exacerbate problems structural to domestic work. Although some employers seek to avoid exploitation and some are unaware of the impact of their behavior on the worker, many take advantage of the sponsorship situation, the workers' vulnerability, and their lack of experience with codes of behavior here. Exploitation may involve long hours, abysmal pay, a heavy work load, and particular attitudes and behaviors exhibited toward the worker.

Joyce Miller worked at her live-in sponsor job from 1977 to 1981. The couple for whom she worked, on the edges of suburban New Jersey, owned a chain of clothing stores. The wife worked part-time in the business and devoted the rest of her time to shopping for antiques, decorating, attending cooking classes, entertaining, traveling, and participating in her children's school. Joyce worked sixteen hours or more a day, was on call twenty-four hours a day, seven days a week, caring for the large house and three children for $90 a week ($110 at the time she quit). When she took a day off to see her lawyer, that day was deducted from her salary.

> The working situation there [was] a lot of work. No breaks. I work sometimes till 11 o'clock at night. . . . I get up early in the morning and I get up at night to tend the baby. I wash, I cook, I clean.

As Joyce began to get "enlightened" (her words) to her own exploitation, her employer became upset.

When Dawn Adams, who was at the time undocumented, quit a short-lived suburban job, her employers threatened to report her to the Immigration and Naturalization Service. Others told of similar intimidation that plays on undocumented West Indian women's sense of vulnerability. This itself is heightened by occurrences such as INS raids at the Port Authority bus terminal on Sunday nights and Monday mornings to "catch" undocumented domestic workers returning to suburban jobs from their day off. . . .

Isolation from kin, friends, and community is a painful consequence of many live-in jobs. Immersion into a foreign world aggravates the loneliness and demoralization of many new migrants. Janet Robinson said that her first employer was good, "But I was very homesick and lonely." Those in isolated suburban areas often fared the worst. Those in the city and especially those who got away on days off to their "own" community fared better. Marguerite Andrews squeezed just enough out of her paycheck to escape from her Park Avenue live-in job to a furnished room in Bedford-Stuyvesant every weekend. Joyce Miller found that the isolation of a black woman living in a white world had other consequences when people mistook her for a convict from the nearby prison when she did the shopping in town. When faced with a snowstorm on her day off, Monica Cooper paid several times her normal bus fare to "get out" of her suburban live-in job and come to New York. As she said, "There's no way on earth I'm going to have a day off and stay in there. . . ."

Respect, the Asymmetrical Relations of "Doing Domestic"

Class, sex, race, and migration have shaped the asymmetrical social relations for much domestic and child care work in the United States, from the first African house slaves to the Irish immigrant "servants" of one hundred years ago and to contemporary Salvadoran, West Indian, and other workers. The worker is thus categorized as "other" (as defined by the dominant white male society), increasing the separation between employer and employee as well as the potential for exploitation. Marguerite Andrews states that "The racial thing really gets me down. I'm treated this way because of race. The only difference between us [Marguerite and her employers] is race." While race may be a major difference, it does not exist apart from sex, class, and migration for West Indian women of color in creating "otherness" which reflects and reinforces the particular asymmetrical social relationships of the work. . . .

In discussing the asymmetrical relations, every woman spoke most about the lack of respect shown to her by employers. What the worker experiences as lack of respect often appears to be efforts to depersonalize the very personal relations involved in the work and to dehumanize the worker in a variety of ways.

The low esteem for housework and for those who perform it was noted by some women as the "worst part." As Beverly Powell said,

> When people look down on you for cleaning up their messes, then it starts hurting. The worst thing is when they look at you as stupid, maybe not stupid, but as a damn fool. You should treat people

> exactly as how you want to be treated. We can't all be doctors or
> lawyers, someone has to clean up the dirt. I am a hard worker. I
> want a little consideration. If I'm paid $1,000 for work but treated
> like dirt, it will pay the bills, but forget it.

Like other West Indian domestic workers, Monica Cooper took pride in
her housekeeping but resented her employers' distancing and denial of her
as a person.

> It was like because I am the employee, because of what I'm doing,
> somehow I was looked down on. I was a good housekeeper. Because
> that's how I am. Whatever it is I do, I love to do my best. And I did
> my best. . . . But . . . there is a blockage in between. It's like she
> and I are O.K., but if a friend comes by, you feel the difference:
> "Oh, now she's the housekeeper."

Whatever the relationship otherwise, it is depersonalized as it is presented
beyond the household.

Clothing is one of the clearest forms of depersonalization. While for
some women uniforms provide an inexpensive mode of dress that saved their
own clothes for "after work," most who were asked to wear uniforms resented it. Judith Thomas "hardly ever wore the uniform because it was
white" and therefore impractical for both child care and housework. . . .

In the context of racial segregation, uniforms function to unmistakably
identify people of color as service workers, the only roles which would justify
their presence in otherwise all white settings.

Food and eating are other arenas of dehumanization and depersonalization. Some employers left food for the worker to prepare for the children but
none for the worker herself, though she might work an eight- to twelve-hour
shift. One worker was accused of consuming "too much" of a particular
food, milk, which she never drank. When one woman on a live-in job ate
some pork chops which had been in the refrigerator for several days while
her wealthy corporate executive employers dined out, she was informed that
several pork chops were "missing" and that she should "find" them. With
her own money, the worker replaced what she ate and no comment was
made. . . .

Joyce Miller spoke of the classic situation in which, as a live-in worker
for a young, wealthy family, she ate separately from the other members of the
household.

> I couldn't eat with them at the table. . . . I have to eat after they
> finish eating. . . . And then I eat in the kitchen. There are a lot of
> people who do that because they want us to know that we are not
> equal. . . .

Judith Thomas spoke of the depersonalization, trivialization, and lack of
respect involved in being treated like a child on a live-in job.

It was another hard thing that as a woman, a mother, responsible for home, with a husband, and to come here to New York City and have to be living with people. . . . It was definitely hard for me. You know at times they would talk to you as though you were just some little piece of a girl. It was really humiliating at times. . . . Most of the time they wouldn't see me as that [fully adult] person. . . . A couple of times I really had to tell them that. I really had to say, "Well, I want to be treated as a full adult. . . ."

In contrast, women spoke of "good employers" who are "fair," who "understand," who "have genuine human affection" and who "treated me like a human being." Besides attempting to minimize the material exploitation and disrespect on the job, some employers helped out in medical and family crises and tried to assist in the worker's education or self-development. Dawn Adams' sponsor employers, a theatrical lighting designer and her photographer husband living in Greenwich Village, was "the best person to work for." She was "willing to help" Dawn attend college by offering to continue to pay her a full-time rate though Dawn would attend classes in the morning while the child, for whom Dawn was primarily responsible, attended nursery school. Another woman who worked for this employer concurred with Dawn. Janet Robinson spoke highly of several of her employers including her current ones, two lawyers. Beverly Powell likes her current employers, involved in theater, who pay her overtime and treat her well. Those whose employers are regularly absent from the home, especially for their own full-time employment, fare the best. However, rarely did anyone speak of any employer without ambivalence. Even when airing a complaint, many workers said something like "she has her good side. Regardless of everything else, I think she's O.K." The flip side is also true. As several women said, "Nobody's perfect." Joyce Miller was often "confused" by the very friendly relations with her sponsor employer who "told [her] everything," always included her in dining and most other activities, yet paid her poorly. The basic outlines of the job include the inherent contradictions of employer/employee relations, including lack of respect, in a personalized context.

"One of the Family": Manipulation, Trust, and Distrust

The highly personalized relations of domestic work, especially that which is live-in, produce such phrases as "like one of the family." Joyce Miller said,

Whenever they want you to give your all in their favor, or anyway to feel comfortable to do what they want you to do, they use the words "we are family." That's the one I hate. "You are one of the family." That's not true. That's a password as sorry . . . if you're one of the

family, don't let me eat after you. . . . They say it to make you feel
O.K., but at the same time, they're not doing the right thing.

The ideology of family is used to manipulate the worker. Often used to explain why members of the *same* family should sacrifice for one another, here
it is used to encourage people who are *not* family members to perform tasks
or to tolerate treatment that may be exploitive. The image of family is called
up to soften the edges of wage labor in personalized situations.

The image of family is most pervasive in child care. Most of the women
in this group were hired primarily to care for children, which they preferred
to their secondary housework responsibilities. Janet Robinson said "I love
the kids" and was echoed by many others who take pleasure in their relationships with the children.

Emotional vulnerability and exploitation are risks in child care situations, especially in conjunction with separation from one's own children.
Some children received no parental discipline when they teased, hit, spit at,
or were otherwise rude to the workers. When told that "Janet will clean it
up," children learned to expect others to clean up after them. Several women
mentioned that the parents were jealous of worker/child relationships. A jealous parent humiliated one worker by ordering her to her room when the employer's child sought comfort from the worker after being scolded by the
parent. Relationships with the children often lead women to stay longer on
jobs than they would otherwise; they sometimes return to visit children once
they have left. . . .

Monica Cooper spoke about a major element in child care employment,
trust. . . . Though entrusting her with the care of their children for four
years including while they were vacationing in the Caribbean, Monica's employers' trust vanished when she gave two-weeks notice.

> Everything was O.K. For four years I was with them and they
> trusted me and . . . all of a sudden . . . they couldn't find this and
> they couldn't find that. . . . Now that I'm leaving they're going to
> miss a [gold] chain [necklace] and they're going to miss a slip, and
> they're going to miss everything else.

While all wage-working mothers balance work and family responsibilities with some difficulty in contemporary capitalist society, child care and
household maintenance are stratified by class. The resources on which
women have to draw engender different ways of handling their work and family duties. While both employer and employee may work to support their
households, the wages, working conditions, and nature of kin and household
responsibilities of these West Indian women mean that they have to juggle a
different set of responsibilities in a different material and social context than
their employers. . . .

With their wages, women support at least two households, in full or in part: their own in New York, and one or more composed of kin (possibly including their children) in their home country. New York housing takes the biggest bite our of their wages. Lawyers' fees, for those who hire them for their own or their children's green cards, are another major expense. Every woman sends remittances regularly. Dawn Adams was not unusual in remitting at least half of her earnings every other week to support her mother and two daughters, before her daughters joined her. Like others, she sent both money, for living expenses and her daughters' school expenses, and barrels, packages filled with food, clothing, and household goods, basic nonluxury items either unavailable or exorbitantly priced in the home country. . . .

Many women spoke about the inconsiderateness of the unpredictably shifting schedules and the impact on their lives. Dawn Adams was regularly requested to remain late just as she prepared to leave, which often interfered with her "after work" plans. Several times her employers returned very late, which, for Dawn and other women, meant later and therefore longer and more dangerous subway rides home. As she said, "It seems as if it never bothered them [that] when they were in their house, I had to be on the streets." These schedule extensions left less time in which women could accomplish their own household and kin responsibilities, be with children, other kin, or friends, or just relax. As Beverly Powell said, "No matter how well paid I am, I want a little time to myself. . . . She doesn't even think of the child that I have. And then she talks about loyalty. . . ."

While child care arrangements across town were difficult, those across oceans were more so. These women with young children present paid a large part of their salaries to a local babysitter, often another West Indian, who took several children into her apartment. Many women reported a variety of problems that occur in this situation. Children left at home when a mother migrates are generally kept by kin, often a mother or sister, or friends. Although the mother provides as best she can, her children may feel emotionally or materially deprived, and the situation may be stressful for her, the children, and the caretakers.

This balancing is not without its emotional costs. The pain and loneliness of leaving children was central to these women's experiences. As Dawn Adams said, "What could be harder than me leaving my kids in St. Vincent and coming here to work, not seeing them. I don't see them for about two and a half years after that last night I slept in the house with them." When Beverly Powell described getting into bed at night and wondering if her daughter had been bathed and was asleep yet, she spoke for many women who reported crying themselves to sleep many nights, missing their children and wondering about their welfare. Joyce Miller was "so very, very lonely" for her son that she said, "I think I give them [her employer's children] more because I just think of them as my own. Just 'cause I was lonely, I gave them all I have. . . ."

[After they got green cards, most workers left live-in positions and either moved out of paid household work altogether or took live-out jobs in which their primary responsibility was child care. Some remained in these jobs indefinitely. Others planned to change to different kinds of work, usually in the predominantly female fields sometimes referred to as the pink-collar ghetto.]

Leaving domestic work for the pink-collar ghetto may not seem to offer much, but it holds promise for many domestic workers. When Dawn Adams' $25 raise was rescinded a few months after it was given, because her employer, though a "good person to work for," had difficulty paying it, she had had enough. She found a bank teller job with regular hours, wages, and raises, and began college study toward a business and management degree. Though she took an initial pay cut, the job provides medical and dental benefits for herself and her children, who arrived in New York five months later. Judith Thomas, who earned her certification as a nursing aide, began looking for a job with medical and dental benefits for herself and her daughters soon after their arrival. No longer "frustrated" doing housework "because of circumstance," Monica Cooper expresses the optimism of many as she prepares for a singing career and does temporary clerical work: "Now I'm doing what I want to do because that's what I choose to do. At this point in my life, I'm not settling and doing anything that I don't want to do." Few are able to avoid doing things they do not want to do, but many are pleased to leave the particular constraints and exploitation of domestic work. Their balancing act as wage-working mothers continues as they enter another world of women's work.

5

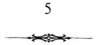

The Immigrant Woman and Her Job:
Agnes D., Mrs. E., Angelina, Minnie, Louise M., and Theresa M.

In the opening decades of the twentieth century, large numbers of foreign-born women entered industrial occupations. The following case histories are taken from the 1930 Women's Bureau study of immigrant women wage earners in Philadelphia and the Lehigh Valley. As the case histories suggest, immigrant industrial

Source: Caroline Manning, *The Immigrant Woman and Her Job*, United States Department of Labor Women's Bureau Bulletin no. 74 (Washington, D.C.: U.S. Government Printing Office, 1930), pp. 13–17

workers were a varied group, including single and married women, with children and without, young and old. For most of the women in this study, work was not a temporary expedient but a long-term commitment. Their attitude toward their work varied from resignation or resentment to pride in their skills. Immigrant women and their daughters were more likely to be in the industrial labor force than white mainstream American women, who dominated "white collar" clerical and sales occupations. The entry of foreign-born women into the labor force during the period of heavy immigration at the turn of the century accounted for much of the rise in women's employment that took place between 1890 and 1910.

Agnes D.

In 1905 Agnes D, aged 17, accompanied by a friend, left her farm home in Galicia bound for America, thinking she would make more money and have an easier time in the land of opportunity. Her sister, who had come to Philadelphia some time before, secured the first job for Agnes as a domestic worker at $4 a week, but she found it so hard that after two months she left it. Her sister then took Agnes to an agency and for a fee of $1 Agnes was placed as a kitchen maid in a restaurant. Here her working day was from 5 A.M. to 11 P.M. Much of the time her hands were in hot water and the continuous standing made her feet tired and sore, but she hesitated to give up the job, since her sister had paid a fee to secure it for her, and she kept hoping that she would mind it less if she gave it a good trial. In about a year, having secured another job through the help of a friend, she quit the restaurant and began work "painting leather" (seasoning) in a tannery, at $6 a week. She continued at this place for about eight years, until she married in 1914. Her husband proved to be no good and worked very irregularly, so in 1921, when the eldest boy was 7 years old and the children could shift for themselves, she returned to her old job in the tannery, where she is still employed. When she has a full week she can earn as much as $17, but lately business has been too bad and she has forgotten what a full pay envelope looks like. She takes pride in her work and regrets that she can never do "measuring," as she does not know her "numbers." Measuring is one of the most desirable jobs in a leather plant, as the skins are measured automatically by a machine, which records their surface in square inches. The operator merely feeds the hides into the machine and copies the measurement, but Agnes can neither read nor write the numbers, for she has never attended school.

For three years this worker has been the chief support of the family, although the husband helps intermittently. She is concentrating all her energy to make ends meet, working by day in the tannery and by night at home, where, in addition to the housework for her own family, she washes for a lodger.

Mrs. E.

Mrs. E. told a most unusual story of a long life spent as a cigar maker. She is still rolling cigars, with a background of about 40 years of cigar making in the United States and years of work in the same trade in Germany. Mrs. E.'s brother in this country kept writing to her, and "something did drive me like to come. I don't know if it was lucky or not, but anyway in 1885 had we come to America." Since her husband was a slow worker, it was necessary for Mrs. E. to go to work in the new country, and she has worked ever since except for interruptions due to slack times, strikes or occasional change of job when shop conditions did not suit her, always sharing the support of the family with her husband.

Widowed, and 81 years old, she still cares for her little home and works in the shop daily from 9 to 5—shorter hours than formerly. "If I can't make a living from 9 to 5, some one else can do it." She earns only $8 or $9 a week but feels quite independent though her children see to it that she does not need anything.

Angelina

Thirteen years ago Angelina, then a girl of only 16, anxious to see the world, came with some neighbors to her cousin's in New York. She thought she knew what life in America would be like and only in a vague sort of way did she expect to work, but she supposed her money would buy beautiful clothes and that her life would be like that of the women in restaurant scenes in the movies. When, the day after she arrived, her cousin spoke quite emphatically about her going to work, she was surprised, but it was an even greater surprise when she found that she could not get the kind of work she wanted. She had started to learn dressmaking in Italy, but her cousin told her it was altogether different here, where each person makes but one special part of the dress and work is so scarce one has to take whatever can be found. So her cousin took her that day—her second in the United States—to an underwear shop and she was given pressing of corset covers, at 3 cents a dozen. Her first pay was $3.15. Adjustment to her work and her new life was difficult and she did not always succeed in keeping back the tears. She, who had come to this country to make and wear pretty clothes, never had a shirt waist that cost over $1 in the five years before she was married. . . .

Then she had five happy years in her own home and forgot about work in the shop. But tragedy overtook the family and since 1922 her husband has been in a sanitarium and she is back again at her old job, the sole support of herself and two little children. There is no tone of complaint in her voice as she describes the routine of her day's work—preparing the breakfast, dressing the children and taking them to the neighbor's, and starting for the shop by 7 in the morning; then, after a long day at the machine, home again to prepare more food and care for the children.

Minnie

Another case of disillusionment was that of a young Jewish girl who had been induced to come to the United States by her sister. Unlike Angelina, who succeeded in taking care of herself and her children, Minnie has failed often to be even self-supporting. She arrived in August, 1921, and was immediately put to work in her brother-in-law's small store. She had had six years' experience in a store in Warsaw, but this was different. "I slaved here seven days a week. I was always in the store, early and late—sometimes more than 12 hours a day." For 10 months she endured it, grateful to her sister for work. Then the bottom dropped out and she became ill—first a patient in a hospital ward, then in a free convalescent home, and now in a boarding home for working girls. During much of the past two years she has been "on the city," as she expressed it, and she kept repeating "I must cover my expense." At the time of the interview she was making an effort in spite of homesickness and "many worriments" to be self-supporting by making lamp shades at $10 a week. Most of the girls in the shop were pieceworkers, but Minnie was not strong enough to hurry, so the boss gave her a "particular job" and paid her "straight," which she regards as a great advantage, as "piecework would kill me."

Once Minnie managed to go to night school for three weeks. She is sensitive about her lack of English: "Not very good language, so I can't hope for nice store job," although she feels she could do the work in a store better than anything else.

Louise M.

"Everybody else was going," so Louise M. a child of 14, left her poor home in Poland in 1905 to come with an uncle to the United States. For two years she tried her fortune in several housework jobs, but she was never satisfied, and as soon as she was 16 she went to a clothing factory and secured work as a sewing-machine operator. For six years she experienced the ups and downs in this industry—sometimes she waited in the shop for work and sometimes she waited at home; sometimes her pocketbook was empty, some weeks the pay envelope had $3, other weeks, $12. Probably her best job was pressing shirt waists, "folding and pinning them just as you buy them in the store," and for this she was paid at the rate of 15 cents a dozen. She was glad enough to give up this struggle for marriage and never expected to be a wage earner again.

But in the depression after the war the little fruit stand in which they had invested all their savings failed, and she returned to work—any kind of work, in a laundry on the mangle feed, in a restaurant kitchen, office cleaning. This last she particularly disliked. Her comments about it were: "Four car fares a day; that's too much. Marble floors. Just so much to scrub, and if you stopped five minutes you couldn't finish on time." She vowed she would not go back to that for $20 a week. At the time of the interview she was operating a drill press—a job that paid her $16 to $21 a week. She was delighted with the work and did not plan to give it up. "You feel different— you feel that you are just like everybody else. You ain't got to be ashamed. You feel like a different woman; you aren't near so tired." The joy in her job almost overshadowed the fact that this house was the first in which she had ever lived where there was no sink and no water, and she was happy that her earnings could provide the necessities. "You have to have plenty milk for the children. From week to week you just keep going."

Teresa M.

Although Teresa M. was only 12 years old when she came to America, she can not read English; however, she speaks it better than do most of her neighbors. In Hungary there were cigar factories near her home and she was glad to find them here and eager to get to work; so her father helped her to find a job as a roller in a cigar factory and there, except for the interruptions of childbearing, she has been during the last 20 years. Altogether, she estimates that she has lost about 4 years from work during her 14 years of married life. "My man made me stay home for babies," and there had been five, although only three are living.

In spite of the 20 years, most of which had been spent in only two shops, she still was keen about working and was contented with her job. "I can always have my place. If I do not feel so good and stay home a day, I phone the boss and he says, 'All right, I'll get another roller in your place to-day but be sure you come back.' If we work, then the boss he likes."

Her husband also is thrifty and has one of the few steady jobs in a wire mill. There is an air of prosperity about their home and garden. Her husband could support the family, Teresa says, but they couldn't have things "nice" unless she worked; and she took the visitor to see the cellar, that had been cemented recently and paid for with her earnings—$200. There is electricity in the house, a washing machine, and modern plumbing.

The fact that her husband helps her with the housework, with the washings, and "sometimes he cook" makes it possible for Teresa to do two jobs. She says she could not do it "without my man, in everything he help," nor could the husband have such an attractive home if Teresa had not helped as a wage earner also.

She intends to continue working, hoping to be ready to meet adversity when it comes, for "everybody sick or old some day." She also hopes some day "to sit and rock on the porch like other ladies. I'll be old lady then."

6

———⟨≈⟩———

"I Consider Myself a 'Theater Worker'. . ."

Despite parental objections and financial difficulties, exceptional immigrant wo-
men built satisfying careers in the arts. Some became actresses, playwrights, and im-
pressarios in the hundreds of ethnic theaters that sprang up across the nation from the
mid-nineteenth century to the present. Performing in native languages and later in
English, these popular, community-based theaters offered immigrant audiences en-
tertainment, education, and insight into their own lives. "I did not get into the the-
ater for the 'let's-put-on-a-show' fun of it," writes contemporary playwright Dolores
Frida, "but because I had something to say about immediate and relevant issues."

Although ethnic theater peaked in most European immigrant communities in
the opening decades of the century, it continues to grow in the expanding Asian and
Hispanic communities as the century nears its close. In this "testimonio," Cuban-
born Dolores Frida describes her work in the contemporary Hispanic theater and
her hope that the arts, especially the theater, can promote understanding between
minorities and mainstream America.

O ver ten years ago, when my first play was produced in New York City,
I dragged my whole family down to a dank basement in the Lower East
Side to see it. My mother, who never really understood what I did in the
theatre, said to me after the show was over: "Todo estuvo muy bonito, m'ija,
pero, en todo eso que yo vi, ¿qué fue exactamente lo que tú hiciste?" [That
was all very nice, dear, but what exactly did you do in what I just saw?]

I explained to her that I had written the play, that I was the *dramaturga*.
She just said, "ahhh," and shook her head.

I fantasized about her, next morning, telling her coworkers at that factory in Brooklyn where she used to sew sleeves onto raincoats all day long,
"¿Oye, Rosalía, tú sabes que mi hija, la mayor, es dramaturga?" And Rosalía
answering, "¿Dramaturga? ¡Ay pobrecita! Y eso, ¿tiene cura?"

["Hey Rosalia, did you know that my oldest daughter is a dramaturga?"
"Dramaturga! Poor thing! Can it be cured?"]

Source: Dolores Frida, "The Show Does Go On" (Testimonio), in *Breaking Bound-*
aries: Latina Writings and Critical Readings, ed. Asuncion Horno-Delgado, Eliana Or-
tega, Nina M. Scott, and Nancy Saporta Sternbach, eds. (Amherst: University of
Massachusetts Press, 1989) copyright (c) 1989 by the University of Massachusetts
Press pp. 181–86.

My mother passed away three years ago, and I regret I never took the time to explain to her what being a *dramaturga* meant to me, and why it can't be "cured," that once bitten by the love of the theatre, you are infected with it for the rest of your life.

Now it is too late to share with her why I put up with the long hours, the lack of money, the unheated basements: the thrill of opening night, the goose pimples when an audience laughs at the right lines, or when you can hear a pin drop at the right moment.

It is not too late to share some of it with you.

I didn't start off as a playwright. As a teenager, I wrote poems and short stories that nobody read. In fact, nobody knew I wrote them because I didn't tell anyone. Writing poetry wasn't the "in" thing among my peers. I am from a small town where there was one single bookstore and one single library, which was closed most of the time—I don't know why, maybe because it was right next door to the police station. . . .

One thing we didn't have in Caibarién, Cuba, was a theatre. I didn't get to see a live play until I came to New York. That was in 1961. It was a musical, and I became fascinated forever with the idea of people bursting into song and dance at the least provocation.

The first play I wrote—*Beautiful Señoritas*—was a play with music. And I wrote it in English.

In 1976, I went to Caracas, Venezuela, to cover an International Theatre Festival for *Visión*, the Latin American news magazine. It was my first festival and I enjoyed every minute of it. I saw plays from over thirty different countries, many in languages I did not understand. But one peculiar thing caught my attention: not one of those plays dealt with "the women's issue." At the time, I was quite involved in the women's movement in New York and knew that *la liberación femenina* was also being hotly debated in Latin America and Europe. Yet, the stages of an international theatre festival didn't reflect it. I decided, then and there, that when I got back to New York I would write a play about women. And I did.

Beautiful Señoritas was produced by DUO Theatre in 1977. It was a modest one-act musical play that poked fun at long-standing Latin women stereotypes—from Carmen Miranda to Cuchi Cuchi Charo to suffering, black-shrouded women crying and praying over the tortillas to modern-day young Latinas trying to re-define their images. The play was extremely well received—it went on to have many productions throughout the country, including a special performance at the National Organization for Women's national convention in San Antonio, Texas, in 1980.

From then on, most of my plays have been about the experience of being a Hispanic in the United States, about people trying to reconcile two cultures and two languages and two visions of the world into a particular whole: plays that aim to be a reflection of a particular time and space, of a here and now.

I consider myself a "theatre worker" rather than a "theatre literata." Theatre is not literature; theatre is to be "done," not read, seen, not imagined. Theatre is people. Theatre is team work. We need each other: playwright, director, designers, actors, choreographers, technicians, carpenters, composers, ticket takers, audience. We don't exist without each other. And I have tremendous respect and admiration for the skills and talent of everyone involved in bringing a production to the stage. I love actors. I adore choreographers. I am awed by composers and musicians. Directors? Putting your play in the hands of a good director who has vision and understands your work—well, that's icing on the cake. Good directors, however, are few and far between.

The first thing I did at Teatro the Orilla, a collective theatre group in New York's Lower East Side, was to sweep the floor and collect tickets at the door. Then I ran the sound equipment, made lights from empty tomato juice cans and supermarket light bulbs, went shopping for costumes and props, filled out endless forms for grant money, and then, only then, I began to think I could write a play that would appeal to that particular audience: people who had never been to a theatre before.

My theatre life came into being soon after various Hispanic theatre groups began to get established, thanks to newly available public funds in the late sixties and early seventies. It was all part of a process, a side effect of the ethnic and racial reaffirmation that followed the black civil rights movement, the women's liberation movement, the anti-war demonstrations.

I did not get into the theatre for the "let's-put-on-a-show" fun of it, but because I felt I had things to say about immediate and relevant issues and I wanted to say them with comedy, with music, with songs. Live.

Besides those already mentioned, I have also written about gentrification (*Savings*), about anti-poverty agencies (*The Beggars' Soap Opera*), about Hispanic theatre itself (*La Era Latina*), about Latin soap operas and nuclear war (*Pantallas*), about cultural assimilation (*Boltánica*). Waiting their turn are plays about AIDS (so many of my friends are gone) and teenage pregnancy (What happened to women's liberation? Have we failed the younger generation of women?). . . .

I define Hispanic American theatre, or literature, as that written by Hispanics living and working in the United States whose subject matter, whether written in Spanish or English or both, reflects their expressions in this country in the same manner that, before us, the Jews, the Irish, the Italians documented their experiences and their histories that came to be part of *the* history of this nation. . . .

Millions of Americans live next door to a Rodríguez or a Fernández. They go down to the corner bodega and buy Café Bustelo and Goya Beans.

They eat tacos and enchiladas (big and small) as if there were no tomorrow. They work shoulder to shoulder with millions of Hispanics at every level, every day.

However, in the schools, in the universities, these same Americans learn nothing about those strangers they ride the elevator with. They are not taught who they are, what they think, why they came here.

This is the place, and this is the time. And theatre, and painting, and dance, and poetry can help bridge that gap.

In the theatre, we have that saying—you know the one: "The show must go on. . . ." Soon Hispanics will be the largest ethnic minority in the U.S. Our presence here promises to be a long-running engagement—despite the bad reviews we get most of the time, despite the problems we may have with the lights, and the curtain and the costumes, and the enter and exit cues. Despite all that, this show will go on, and you might as well get your tickets now.

PART IV

Family

Once between us the Atlantic,
Yet I felt your hand in mine;
Now I feel your hand in mine,
Yet between us the Atlantic.[1]

As Israel Zangwill's poem suggests, immigration could have an enormous and sometimes devastating impact upon family life. Frequently, the move to a new country and a new culture altered the relationship between the immigrant woman and those closest to her: her parents, her husband, her children. Part 4 explores the many ways immigration affected women's experiences within the family.

The Single Woman

For young, unmarried women immigration meant, first and foremost, separation from parents. Often this separation was physical but not emotional; the women devoted themselves to the financial support of loved ones overseas and worked and waited for the time when they could bring their families to the United States. In the initial selection a nineteenth-century Irish priest described the sacrifices Irish immigrant women made to help their poverty-stricken families.

Contemporary social scientist Robert E. Kennedy suggests, however, that the Irish immigrant may have been ambivalent in her feelings about home and family. In nineteenth-century Ireland, women worked longer hours than men, and mothers doted upon their sons, not their daughters. Women were given less food than men, a situation reflected in their higher child mortality and shorter life expectancies: "Daughters would have been unaware of these indices, but they were not unaware of their low status vis-a-vis their brothers and of their future low status as wives. . . . The uncommonly high number of single women in the Irish immigration may be seen as an early Women's Liberation Movement."[2] By working in the United States to support their families back home, Irish and other immigrant women could fulfill the obligations of dutiful daughters while enjoying greater freedom and independence. When a woman brought her parents and siblings to the

United States, moreover, her roles as wage earner and "Americanized" sponsor and advisor of the newcomers gave her increased status within the family.

Some single immigrants lived the solitary, self-sacrificing lives described in the first selection, but most looked for fun, relaxation, and male companionship in America as they had in their homelands. Immigration complicated social life. In an old world village, a woman knew the local men well. Courtship took place at traditional times and places under the watchful eyes of family and community. In early twentieth-century America, however, very young and inexperienced women were left to manage their own social relationships with men met casually at work or in the local dancehalls. Poverty, loneliness, and a desire for American style romance combined, in many cases, with lack of information about their own bodies made these women vulnerable to sexual exploitation and to accidental pregnancy, as described in selection 2.

Ignorance caused unwanted pregnancies in the late as well as the early twentieth century. A 1990 survey of 374 immigrant Latinas found that over half had little knowledge about their reproductive systems; they "just didn't look down there."[3] In 1991 author Carla Trujillo noted that "good" Chicanas were expected to suppress all sexual feelings, or, better still, not have them: "This generates a cloud of secrecy around any sexual activity, and leads, I am convinced, to our extremely high teenage pregnancy rate, simply because our families refuse to acknowledge the possibility that young women may be sexually active before marriage."[4]

A special category of foreign-born women who "went wrong" were prostitutes. An investigation by the United States Immigration Commission in 1907 revealed that immigrant women were seduced, tricked, or forced into prostitution by organizations that preyed on their vulnerability. The commission blamed the traffic on "the keepers of houses, the pimps, and the procurers" rather than the women. However, they failed to acknowledge the role played by poverty and by the double standard, which convinced "fallen" women that they had no future among "respectable" people.

Most single immigrants, even those who "went wrong," were successful in beginning new lives in America. The vast majority eventually married, meeting their future mates at work, in the neighborhood, or through church or ethic institutions. Many were determined to choose their own husbands without the traditional parental guidance, to marry for love as they assumed "real" Americans did. In practice, however, friends, relatives, co-workers, professional matchmakers, and advertisements in the ethnic press helped women find husbands of the "appropriate" ethnicity, religion, region, and class—and continue to do so. In the 1980s two popular Indian newspapers, *India West* and *India Abroad*, carried several columns of marriage ads in every issue.[5]

The Married Woman

In the societies from which most pre-1965 (and some post-1965) immigrants came, marriage was a social and economic arrangement between the families of the bride and groom rather than a romantic union between two individuals. Sex roles and marital obligations varied with ethnic, religious, and class background, but they were usually clearly defined and enforced by relatives and the community. Immigration challenged the stability of this traditional arrangement, however, by removing the married couple from the supportive network of family and community, by making new demands upon them, and by suggesting the possibility of choice and change.

The long separations that sometimes accompanied immigration strained many marriages. Separated for months, even years, each spouse might worry that the other had found someone else. Some southern Italian men left their marriages unconsummated before immigration; if their wives were unfaithful, they would know about it!

Marriages that survived long separations sometimes fell apart when the family was reunited. A wife who had assumed control of the family during her husband's absence might not want to relinquish her new role. More often, problems reflected differences in the pace of Americanization. A newly arrived wife might find her husband so Americanized in appearance and behavior that she no longer felt comfortable with him. He might find her old-fashioned and drab. Sometimes it was the wife who, having learned American ways in domestic service, considered her husband old-fashioned and unappealing. Elderly Chinese men who took advantage of post-World War II immigration laws to marry young women from Hong Kong found their brides startlingly different from their idealized memories of Chinese women. A modern bride from Hong Kong shocked her elderly Chinatown husband with a most untraditional ultimatum: "Move out of this delapidated apartment by Tuesday, or I get a divorce."[6]

Poverty and crowded living conditions placed additional strain on marriages, as did the presence of boarders in the household. Unemployed husbands who might have been held to their responsibilities by social pressure in their homelands deserted their families in the United States. "I was left without a bit of bread for the children, with debts in the grocery store and the butchers, and last month's rent unpaid," a woman with three small children wrote bitterly to the Jewish *Forward* in 1910. She offered to sell her children, "not for money, but for bread, for a secure home where they will have enough food and warm clothing for the winter."

Women of all ethnic groups were left to fare for themselves due to desertion, divorce, and, more frequently, the death of the husband. Widowhood was common among nineteenth- and early- twentieth-century immigrants because of disease and industrial accidents and among recent refugees because of the violence they had fled. After the initial shock and disbelief, most frontier widows learned to cope on their own with crops, livestock, growing children—and loneliness. Over a century later, Cambodian refugee widows in the Bronx faced difficulties that were both similar and different.

> for these years I take welfare and food stamps and stay at home. My friends tell me that I am still pretty and I have sometimes boy-friends—although it is difficult to be a widow with no children be-cause married Cambodian women cannot control their husbands around widow ladies and they get very jealous. . . .
>
> Many widow women live together because the rent is high, and for protection.[7]

Immigration led to subtle changes in sex roles and in the distribution of power within a marriage. In many cases, the changes worked to the woman's advantage. In traditional well-to-do Chinese families, for example, the bride entered her husband's household virtually as a servant to his fam-ily. In the United States, the absence of the husband's extended family and, until the mid-twentieth century, the scarcity of women could raise the wife's status considerably. Immigration also improved the status of Syrian, Domin-ican, Cuban, and other women who, typically, had not been wage earners in the homeland but whose earnings in the United States were critical to the survival and social mobility of the family. Selection 3 shows how new eco-nomic (and other) roles increased Syrian women's influence and power within the family.

In some cases immigration worked to women's disadvantage. For exam-ple, the decision-making power eastern European Jewish women had exer-cised eroded as newly prosperous husbands pressed their wives to abandon their traditional, productive economic roles and adopt the ornamental and less powerful role of American "lady." Working-class Jewish women did not suffer a comparable loss, however, since their active contribution to the fam-ily livelihood continued.[8]

Women's economic contributions to the family were not the only deter-minant of their status, however. As the fourth selection about a traditional Japanese family in California shows, geographic, ideological, and personality factors could keep a wife subservient regardless of her contribution to the family livelihood. A study of clients at the Center for the Pacific Asian Fam-ily in Los Angeles between 1978 and 1985 showed that many Asian immi-grant husbands became physically abusive when their wives became wage earners. Feeling insecure and "out of control" in a new environment, the husbands were afraid that they would lose their "accustomed privileges and esteemed place" if their wives assumed greater independence.[9]

The records of domestic courts and charity workers, past and present, overemphasize family pathology and underemphasize the soundness of most marriages. If immigration could shatter a poor marriage, it could strengthen a good one. Away from the expectations and interference of parents and traditional communities, husbands and wives were free to appreciate one another as individuals and to develop a more personal relationship. Necessity sometimes loosened the rigidity of traditional sex roles. On the frontier husbands helped their wives in childbirth and nursed them in sickness. In the cities husbands and wives worked side by side in laundries, restaurants, and other small family businesses. Crises such as unemployment or the death of a child could drive couples apart, but they could also strengthen the ties between the couple who endured and survived them together. Undoubtedly many women shared the feelings of this East European Jewish woman about her marriage:

> I really can't express . . . what love is. . . . They say like Romeo and Juliet and Elizabeth Browning. I don't know. Whether you get used to a person, whether it's physically, I really don't know. . . . I know that I looked up to my husband. . . . He respected me and I respected him. I guess love comes, with caring and doing things for each other. . . . He had a hard life and I had a hard life. . . . We worked together and loved being together.[10]

And if the first marriage failed, many immigrant women, like their American-born counterparts, were prepared to try again. "I loved him and I thought to myself, 'I'll take a chance,' and I did. We're honeymooning for thirty-three years now."[11]

Motherhood in America

Immigration affected the relationships between mothers and children and raised questions about the desirability of motherhood itself. In the traditional, agricultural societies from which many immigrant women came, large families were considered a gift from God, a proof of the husband's virility, and an economic asset. Although the pressure of population on food supply challenged this view for many women even before immigration, the view persisted. It was reinforced for women who immigrated to the nineteenth-century American frontier, where children were a valuable addition to the family labor force.

Among women immigrating to urban, industrial America, however, pregnancy was sometimes greeted with ambivalence or dismay. Poverty, crowded tenements, the cost of feeding, clothing, and educating children in the city, and the difficulty of protecting and supervising them made large families undesirable. The hope for social mobility and a better life for the children already born, often the main reason for immigration, also militated against having many children.

While educated, middle-class women in the United States and other industrial countries in the early decades of the twentieth century had access to birth control, most immigrant women, like other poor women, knew of no way to avoid pregnancy except by avoiding sexual relations. In desperation, women resorted to makeshift and dangerous illegal abortions. A Jewish woman from eastern Europe described the experiences of her mother and aunt, experiences familiar to poor women of many backgrounds:

> In my family we were all brought up very modest, so we don't talk about it, but the big trouble was always sex. It's hard to imagine what those women went through. . . . I must have been about five years old. My sister [had] just died, a very slow death, we didn't have enough food for her. . . . My mother didn't want any more children. I heard a funny sound and crept out in the middle of the night. My mother was lifting up a heavy barrel full of pickles and dropping it again and again. Somehow I found out it was to get rid of her baby. . . . In those days they had abortions like I wouldn't describe them here. My mother's sister died of that, she had fourteen abortions and eight children at forty. They knew none of the children would have a chance in life if they kept on that way, so she wouldn't go to her husband anymore. . . . I heard her tell my mother that if she wasn't a Jew and it wasn't against the law, she would hang herself.[12]

Margaret Sanger's campaign to disseminate information on birth control was stimulated by the suffering she saw in the immigrant ghettos of the early twentieth century. Her first clinic was opened—and welcomed—in a heavily Italian and Jewish neighborhood in Brooklyn, New York.

United States Immigration Commission studies based on the census of 1900 show that immigrant women had more children than the native-born, bearing a child on the average of once every 3.2 years, as opposed to 5.3 years for the native-born white women of native parentage.[13] In 1910 Syrian and Lebanese families in Springfield, Massachusetts, had a mean of ten children.[14] Statistics such as these reflect not only the unavailability of birth control, but also early marriage, religious beliefs that condemned interference with "natural" marital sex, and cultural traditions that greatly valued motherhood. A study showing that Italian-born women had a higher birth rate in Chicago than in the homeland suggests still another reason for large families: optimism about the future in the new environment.[15]

Finally, many immigrant women had large families because they found children a source of great personal joy and satisfaction. Children provided love, warmth, and laughter. Their companionship helped to compensate for the loss of friends and relatives left behind in the homeland. Children's achievements, in fact, children's very existence, justified the daily hardships of immigrant life and offered hope for the future. Women like Katharina in selection 5 centered their lives around their children and sometimes were fortunate enough to see their own youthful ambitions fulfilled by their daughters and sons.

Whether immigration led to larger or smaller families, it undoubtedly complicated childrearing. In many cases the relatives who had shared in the care of small children in the homeland were no longer available, leaving the mother to handle this time-consuming responsibility alone. Most immigrant women were too poor to afford babysitters, and the women of some ethnic groups, such as the Chinese, rarely used sitters even if they could afford them. However great their love for their family, many women must have experienced feelings like those of this mid-twentieth-century Chinese immigrant mother of ten:

> I don't have many friends. . . . We talk about trivia. If you want me to talk about serious things, I don't know how. . . . The other women go to the movies or the Chinese Opera, but I stay home all day. I don't go to the movies or anywhere. Who would take care of the kids? I have to cook . . . wash the clothes, then the day is gone. . . . To tell the truth, the children are so small, it will be a long time before it's my turn to go out. When will it ever be my turn?[16]

Childcare was even more of a problem for women who worked outside the home. Although a few churches and settlement houses offered day care in the early twentieth century, most women had no access to such facilities. Desperate mothers locked young children in the apartment while they worked night shifts or left toddlers in the care of brothers and sisters who were not much older. Many post-1965 immigrants have tolerated oppressive conditions in ethnically owned workplaces because they were allowed to keep their children with them.

Many immigrant mothers brought from their homelands distinctive patterns of childrearing reflecting life-styles and values different from those of mainstream America. While Anglo-American families typically encouraged independence, Japanese mothers typically encouraged dependence, using the threat of banishment from the family circle to enforce good behavior.[17] While most Anglo-American families taught children to stand up, perhaps even to fight, for their rights, traditional Chinese mothers taught their children to suppress anger and aggression and to "give up pleasure or comfort in favor of someone else."[18]

The generation gap was exacerbated by cultural conflict. When the school, the media, or "all the other kids" encouraged children to rebel against ethnic customs and values, mothers felt that not only an argument, but an entire way of life was being lost. Mothers from Puerto Rico, where unmarried girls were carefully sheltered, were appalled by their daughters' demands to go out unchaperoned.[19] A Vietnamese refugee told an interviewer that her greatest cultural shock was hearing the young daughter of her sponsor shout back at her mother. "When I heard this I was in total disbelief. You see, obedience is taught to be a virtue in our culture. Well, I thought this was a terrible, horrible thing." As mothers became more accustomed to American life, conflicts with children became less intense. The Vietnamese women who was shocked by the behavior of her sponsor's daughter noted that when her own daughter shouted at her a few years later, she took it in stride. "I was prepared. I'd learned enough."[20]

In some cases, there was little or no conflict between the generations on important matters, especially if the children were foreign-born and had spent a significant part of their childhood in the homeland. When researcher Rita Simon studied mother-daughter pairs among recent Vietnamese and Soviet Jewish immigrants, she found the generations in agreement on virtually all educational and family goals.[21]

Alternative Life-Styles

Although most immigrant women lived in traditional nuclear families, a significant minority did not. Some remained single by choice, finding friendship, warmth, and emotional support from women, men, or both outside of marriage. For members of religious orders, the sisterhood served as a surrogate family. Many professional women and women who devoted themselves to causes such as socialism or trade unionism formed warm, supportive ties with colleagues who shared their commitments.

The gay rights movement and other social changes of the 1960s and 1970s encouraged lesbians, always present in the immigrant population, to become visible, vocal, and politically active. As Chilean-born author and lesbian mother Mariana Romo-Carmona suggests, visibility had costs:

> Today, while walking to work through a crowded Manhattan street, I opened a letter from my godmother. After almost twenty years, the strong affection I feel for *mi madrina* comes rushing back into my heart. In her letter she tells me about her daughters, their life in Santiago [Chile], and that she wants to know more about my life. . . . Folding the letter in my knapsack, I wonder how much longer I could feel loved by mi madrina if she know I was a lesbian—would I cease to exist for her?[22]

Immigrant lesbians, like their native-born counterparts, encounter ridicule, scorn, and sometimes violence from a homophobic American society.

They also face special problems as immigrants. In many Asian and Hispanic communities, homosexuality is either not recognized at all or is seen as the result of abandoning one's heritage. "Being gay is a white disease," said the shocked parents of a Korean lesbian. "We're Korean; Korean people aren't gay."[23] Because of the closeness of their families, Latina lesbians find it especially difficult to hide their sexual preference. If they come out, however, they risk the loss of ties that are central to their lives. They also forfeit all chance for leadership in their ethnic communities.[24] Triple outsiders by virtue of race, gender, and sexual preference, Asian and Latina lesbians have difficulty finding a community in which they are fully accepted. These and other issues are explored in the sixth selection.

Government Policy and Family Life

While many of the changes in the immigrant woman's family life were the result of acculturation, others were stimulated by government policy. Welfare payments, food stamps, and other financial benefits available to recent immigrant and refugee families have been very helpful, especially in the initial periods of resettlement. Some other policies have been misguided or even destructive. The federal policy of resettling refugees from Southeast Asia in small nuclear family groups has made it easier to recruit American sponsors. However, it ignores and thus helps undermine the importance of the large extended family in these cultures. Probably the most extensive—and destructive—government policy affecting immigrant families was the racist internment of Japanese-Americans during World War II. The final selection in Part 4 describes the disintegration of Japanese family life in these "relocation" camps.

Notes

1. Israel Zangwill, "Sundered," in *A Treasury of Jewish Poetry*, ed. Nathan and Maryann Ausubel (New York: Crown, 1957), p. 33.

2. Robert E. Kennedy, Jr., *The Irish: Emigration, Marriage, and Fertility* (Berkeley: University of California Press, 1973), pp. 52–60.

3. Lourdes Arguelles, "A Survey of Latina Immigrant Sexuality," paper presented at the National Association for Chicano Studies Conference, Albuquerque, New Mexico, March 29–April 1, 1991, as cited in Carla Trujillo, ed., *Chicana Lesbians: The Girls Our Mothers Warned Us About* (Berkeley: Third Woman Press, 1991), p. 186.

4. Trujillo, *Chicana Lesbians*, p. 192.

5. Rashmi Luthra, "Matchmaking in the Classifieds of the Immigrant Indian Press," in *Making Waves: An Anthology by and about Asian*

American Women, ed. Asian Women United of California, (Boston: Beacon Press, 1989), p. 338.

6. Betty Lee Sung, *Mountain of Gold: The Story of the Chinese in America* (New York: Macmillan, 1967).

7. John Tenhula, ed., *Voices from Southeast Asia: The Refugee Experience in the United States* (New York: Holmes and Meier, 1991), pp. 118–19.

8. Charlotte Baum, Paula Hyman, and Sonya Michel, *The Jewish Woman in America* (New York: Dial Press, 1976).

9. Nilda Rimonte, "Domestic Violence among Pacific Asians," in *Making Waves,* p. 329.

10. Sydelle Kramer and Jenny Masur, eds., *Jewish Grandmothers* (Boston: Beacon Press, 1976), p. 100.

11. Ibid., p. 71.

12. Barbara Myerhoff, *Number Our Days* (New York: E. P. Dutton, 1978), pp. 232–33.

13. *Reports of the Immigration Commission,* Vol. 2, Senate Document 747, 61st Congress, 3rd session (Washington, D.C.: U.S. Government Printing Office, 1911), pp. 499–501.

14. Naseer H. Aruri, "The Arab-American Community in Springfield, Massachusetts," in, *The Arab Americans: Studies in Assimilation,* ed. Elaine C. Hagopian and Ann Paden (Wilmette, Ill.: Medina University Press International, 1969), p. 59.

15. Arnold M. Rose, "Research Note on the Impact of Immigration on the Birth Rate," *American Journal of Sociology* 47 (1942): 614–21.

16. Victor G. and Brett de Barry Nee, *Longtime Californ': A Documentary Study of an American Chinatown* (Boston: Houghton Mifflin, 1972), p. 268.

17. Harry H. L. Kitano and Akemi Kikumura, "The Japanese American Family," in *Ethnic Families in America: Patterns and Variations,* ed. Charles H. Mindel and Robert W. Habenstein (New York: Elsevier, 1976), p. 52.

18. Lucy Jen Huang, "The Chinese American Family," in ibid., pp. 134–36.

19. Joseph R. Fitzpatrick, "The Puerto Rican Family," in ibid., pp. 211–12.

20. Tenhula, *Voices from Southeast Asia,* p. 26.

21. Rita J. Simon, "Refugee Families: Adjustment and Aspirations: A Comparison of Soviet Jews and Vietnamese Immigrants," *Ethnic and Racial Studies* 6 (October 1983): 492–503.

22. Juanita Ramos, comp. and ed., *Compañeras: Latina Lesbians (An Anthology)*, (New York: Latina Lesbian History Project, 1987), pp. xx.

23. Pamela H., "Asian American Lesbians: An Emerging Voice in the Asian American Community," in *Making Waves*, p. 284.

24. Oliva M. Espin, "Cultural and Historical Influences on Sexuality in Hispanic/Latin Women," in *All American Women: Lines That Divide, Ties That Bind*, ed., Johnnetta B. Cole (New York and London: Free Press, 1986), p. 281.

1

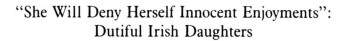

"She Will Deny Herself Innocent Enjoyments": Dutiful Irish Daughters

As the following reading illustrates, immigrant women, although separated by thousands of miles from their families, were often emotionally and psychologically very close to those families. Here the Reverend John Francis Maguire, an Irish Catholic clergyman who visited Irish communities in the United States in the mid-nineteenth century, describes, effusively but accurately, the devotion with which Irish women worked to support their parents and siblings in Ireland and the heroic (and often successful) efforts they made to reunite the family in America. For many Irish, Scandinavian, and German women in the nineteenth century and for their Slavic, Jewish, black and Latino counterparts in the twentieth, immigration to America was not an escape from the family but rather an act of loyalty to the family and a commitment to its future.

The great ambition of the Irish girl is to send 'something' to her people as soon as possible after she has landed in America; and in unnumerable instances the first tidings of her arrival in the New World are accompanied with a remittance, the fruits of her first earnings in her first place. Loving a bit of finery dearly, she will resolutely shut her eyes to the attractions of some enticing article of dress, to prove to the loved ones at home that she has not forgotten them; and she will risk the danger of insufficient clothing, or boots not proof against rain or snow, rather than diminish the amount of the little hoard to which she is weekly adding, and which she intends as a delightful surprise to parents who possibly did not altogether approve of her hazardous enterprise. To send money to her people, she will deny herself innocent enjoyments, womanly indulgences, and the gratifications of legitimate vanity; and such is the generous and affectionate nature of these young girls, that they regard the sacrifices they make as the most ordinary matter in the world, for which they merit neither praise nor approval. To assist their relatives, whether parents, or brothers

---

Source: Reverend John Francis Maguire, *The Irish in America* (1868; reprint, New York: Arno, 1969), pp. 315, 319–21.

and sisters, is with them a matter of imperative duty, which they do not and cannot think of disobeying, and which, on the contrary, they delight in performing. . . .

Resolving to do something to better the circumstances of her family, the young Irish girl leaves her home for America. There she goes into service, or engages in some kind of feminine employment. The object she has in view— the same for which she left her home and ventured to a strange country— protects her from all danger, especially to her character: that object, her dream by day and night, is the welfare of her family, whom she is determined, if possible, to again have with her as of old. To keep her place, or retain her employment, what will she not endure?—sneers at her nationality, mockery of her peculiarities, even ridicule of her faith, though the hot blood flushes her cheek with fierce indignation. At every hazard the place must be kept, the money earned, the deposit in the savings-bank increased; and though many a night is passed in tears and prayers, her face is calm, and her eye bright, and her voice cheerful. One by one, the brave girl brings the members of her family about her. But who can tell of her anguish if one of the dear ones goes wrong, or strays from the right path!—who could imagine her rapture as success crowns her efforts, and she is rewarded in the steadiness of the brother for whom she feared and hoped, or in the progress of the sister to whom she has been as a mother! . . .

Whether the money is given as the price of the passage out, or in the form of a ticket paid for in America, and thus forwarded to Ireland, or is sent as a means of supplying some want or relieving a pressing necessity, practically there is no more thought of it by the donors. It not unfrequently happens that tickets are returned to the donors, the persons to whom they were sent having changed their minds, being unwilling or afraid to leave the old country for a new home. But the money—recouped through a friendly agent—is almost invariably sent back, with a remark somewhat in this form: 'I intended it for you any way, either in ticket or in money; and if you won't take it in ticket, why you must in money. It is yours, anyhow, and no one else is to have it.'

As a rule, those who are newly come send more and make greater sacrifices to bring out their relatives, or to assist them at home, than those who have been longer in the country: the wants of the family in the old country are more vividly present to the mind of the recent emigrant, and perhaps the affections are warmer and stronger than in after years, when time and distance, and the cares or distractions of a new existence, have insensibly dulled the passionate longings of yore. But thousands—many, many thousands—of Irish girls have devoted, do devote, and will devote their lives, and sacrifice every woman's hope, to the holiest, because the most unselfish, of all affections—that of family and kindred. . . .

2

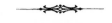

Unmarried Mothers

Not all young women who immigrated to the United States alone led the exemplary lives of the Irish girls described by Reverend Maguire in the preceding selection. The unmarried mother was a common "problem." In this 1921 publication, prominent social worker Grace Abbott, director of the Immigrant's Protective League of Chicago, describes environmental factors contributing to these pregnancies and makes a plea for their prevention by the improvement of this environment. Abbott's condemnation of the moral "double standard" and her advocacy of women holding positions of authority in the Immigration Service were views considered liberal by most of her early twentieth-century contemporaries. More radical observers, however, both in Abbott's day and more recently, would disagree with her idea that an unmarried mother was "disgraced and ruined." Despite social disapproval and economic hardship, many unwed mothers, like the Bohemian woman whose story Abbott tells, were successful in establishing stable one-parent (and sometimes eventually two-parent) families for the rearing of their children.

There are many explanations for the fact that the immigrant girls sometimes become unmarried mothers. The conditions under which most of these immigrant girls must live are far from satisfactory. While many of them come to relatives or friends who can give them the care and protection they need, many of them must live among strangers upon whom they have no claim. Because more men than women emigrate to this country, the families with whom they live usually have, in addition to the girl, three or four men lodgers. The Immigrants' Protective League has found in its visits to the newly arrived immigrant girls that about one half of the Polish, Lithuanian, Slovak, and Russian girls who come to live with relatives find themselves one more in a group of boarders. Sometimes all the other boarders are men; and the girl innocently does not see that because of the congestion and the consequent lack of privacy and the restraints which privacy exercises, she is quite unprotected against herself and the people with whom she lives.

There is the greater helplessness which is due to their ignorance of English; there is also the more dangerous environment in which they live, for it

Source: Grace Abbott, *The Immigrant and the Community* (New York: Century, 1921), pp. 69–80.

is near an immigrant or colored neighborhood that disreputable dance halls and hotels are usually tolerated. Moreover, their recreational needs are less understood than those of the native-born American, and the break with the old-world traditions has left them with fewer standards of discrimination.

At home, the girls have been accustomed to out-of-door dances and sports. In Chicago, when Saturday night comes, the demand for some sort of excitement after a hard and uneventful week, has become too strong to be ignored. But the danger is that because of her physical and nervous exhaustion and her demand for acute sense stimulation, the girl will become an easy victim for the unscrupulous. The neighboring saloon keeper, alert to the business side of her needs, is constantly seeking to attract her to the dance hall which he conducts in the rear of his saloon. At its best, such a dance adds to the nervous demoralization which began with the girl's overfatigue. At its worst, it leaves her disgraced and ruined. . . .

Sometimes the girl is not morally safe in her place of work. The Polish girls who work in restaurants seem to be in special danger. They usually resist at first, but often in the end find themselves unfortified against the combination of force and persuasion which is exerted sometimes against them by the restaurant keeper or a fellow employee. . . .

But it is not always a restaurant employee. American foremen in factories sometimes abuse a power which is more absolute than any man should have the right to exercise over others, and on threat of dismissal the girl submits to familiarities which if they do not ruin her cannot fail to break down her self-respect. One does not need to be told how serious the situations is when a young immigrant girl explains that she has learned how to "get on with the boss" and "take care of herself" at the same time.

Occasionally a girl who has preferred housework in the belief that it would give her a "good home" is ruined by some man in the family for whom she has worked. One young Bohemian girl comes to my mind in this connection. She had had a very hard life at home where a drunken and brutal father's control had been followed by that of a brother no more considerate. She came to America before she was twenty, expecting to earn enough to send for her mother so that the old woman might spend her last years free from the sort of abuse she suffered at home. The fulfillment of this dream was delayed by the great misfortune that came to the girl, although her dream did in fact eventually come true. With a courage that humbled those of us who listened, she explained that she must have a good job so that she could support her baby and bring her mother to America. During the years that we watched her in her successful struggle to accomplish this great task, we realized that although, as the girl mourns, the baby "hasn't got a name" it has at least a good mother.

Promise of marriage may, of course, be a factor in cases of the betrayal of American girls, and the foreign girl, whose village experience has not prepared her for the easy way in which men can disappear in the United States, is more easily victimized through her affections.

A study of the pathetic stories of the betrayal or the weakness of these girls makes it clear that the prevention of delinquency among immigrant girls presents no entirely new or indeed unusual problems. It is the same story of the desire for affection, together with loneliness, lack of knowledge of herself, and long hours of hard, montonous work. The difference between the temptations which meet the American country girl who comes to the city and those of the immigrant girl, is in the main, one of degree and not of kind. . . .

Much official attention has been given to the means of preventing immoral women and girls from coming into this country. Stirred by the stories that oriental women were being brought into the United States under contract for immoral purposes, Congress passed an Act in 1873 aimed especially at breaking up this "trade." The Immigration Law of 1903 excluded "prostitutes and persons who procure or attempt to bring in prostitutes or women for the purpose of prostitution." The language of the law was made more inclusive in 1907. Those entering in violation of this law were made deportable if their presence in the country was discovered within three years after their coming. In 1910, in accordance with the agreement reached at the Paris Conference on the suppression of the "White Slave Traffic" of 1904 and in part as a result of the investigation of the United States Immigration Commission, a further act was passed making it a felony "to persuade, induce, or coerce" any girl or woman to come to the United States for any immoral purpose. . . . The Immigration Law was also amended the same year so that any alien girl or woman who is an inmate of a house of prostitution or is employed in any place frequented by prostitutes, may be deported regardless of the length of time she had been in the United States [Act of March 26, 1910].

These laws applied the double standard of morality in the tests for exclusion and deportation. The man who profits by the social evil or who brings a girl into the country for immoral purposes is subject to punishment, but the man who is himself immoral is not regarded as an "undesirable" immigrant.

In so far as the Immigration Law breaks up the trade in women, in so far as it sends back home girls whose mothers and friends are in Europe and whose reformation, in consequence, will be more probable in Europe than in the United States, we can feel that the law is both useful and humane. But in its enforcement, it often means that we deny girls who have made some serious mistake at home the chance which they need to begin a new life here in the United States. For example, a few years ago, a young Austrian whose military service was uncompleted could not, therefore, marry the girl with whom he had lived and who was about to become a mother. They came to the United States that they might marry and their child be legitimate. The man was admitted but the girl was excluded. She was unmarried and her condition apparent, and as a matter of routine ruling she was denied admission. The young man had no relatives in this country. He was coming to Chicago because his one acquaintance in the United States lived in Chicago. He was overwhelmed by the excluding decision and told his story to the first sympathetic listener he met in Chicago. Special appeals from Chicago women resulted in reversing the decision. The woman was admitted and married on the day of her arrival in Chicago. And most people would probably agree that the moral level of the United States is not raised by the kind of harshness in judging others which an excluding decision such as this one showed.

Under this law, it is also possible to deport girls who are not citizens, although they have been in the United States since they were little children, whose ruin has been accomplished here, whose parents and all those who might help them back into an honest life are in the United States. Some Russian-Jewish girls, under exactly these circumstances, were recommended for deportation. Added to the family separation, these girls were ordered returned to a country in which religious prejudice made their outlook the more uncertain. In such cases, the United States was merely insuring that the girls would continue their immoral life by sending them away from any possible sources of help to live in what was to them, in spite of their citizenship, an alien country. And after these girls had been banished, could any one feel that the country was safer when the men and the conditions responsible for their ruin were left here in the United States—a menace to other girls, both immigrant and American?

There is no reason to feel that the moral health of the country will be promoted by special severity in dealing with the immigrant girl who has gone wrong. From the standpoint of the welfare of the community, attention could be much more profitably directed toward helping her to meet the difficulties she now encounters in the United States.

For this reason, it is to be regretted that the administration of the immigration law is so entirely in the hands of men. The women in the Immigration Service are "matrons"—the cross between a housekeeper and a chaperon who is rapidly disappearing in the best public and private institutions. Without the same pay as inspectors, these matrons are not expected to measure up with the men in intelligence and ability, although they often do. But they have, largely for these reasons, not been able to make much impression on the "Service" and have not secured the adoption of standards of comfort and consideration which trained women could institute in a place like Ellis Island, where so many thousands of women and children are detained each year. . . .

The same measures have not been taken by private as well as public agencies to safeguard the immigrant that have been taken to protect the American girl. Boarding clubs, which are among the first kindly expressions of interest in the American girl, have not, except in a very few instances, been provided for the immigrant. Agencies which are trying to help girls who have made some misstep have usually not felt it necessary to employ women able to speak the language of the immigrant or to understand her social traditions.

The immigrant girl has a long and hard road to travel. She suffers from the industrial and legal discriminations which are the common lot of working women. In addition, she much overcome the stupid race prejudice which leads many Americans to conclude that she suffers less from shame and humiliation than do other women and girls. Without trade training and with little education, as a rule, she begins at the bottom industrially, where, if the wages of the men are low, the wages of the girls are still lower.

And yet, in this struggle in which they are so handicapped, these girls are winning little by little—often at a terrible cost to their health and, in consequence, to the health of the children they will bear in the future. There are many who are moved only by this danger to the future generations. But for the girls of this generation, we should ask more leisure, better pay, better homes, and more sympathy before they are too old and broken to enjoy the fruits of their toil and of their eager sacrifices.

3

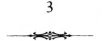

Syrian Women in Chicago: "New Responsibilities . . . New Skills"

In the empirical study from which this excerpt is taken, Safia F. Haddad questioned fifty immigrant and second-generation Syrian-American husbands and wives in Chicago about their respective roles in work, control of family finances, social life, community activities, and the rearing and disciplining of their children. She found that immigrant as well as second-generation wives were in the paid la-

In the traditional, rural society of the homeland, according to Haddad, husbands dominated work, family life, even the disciplining of the children, while wives, though respected as mothers, had little opportunity for independent activity.

Source: Safia F. Haddad, "The Woman's Role in Socialization of Syrian-Americans in Chicago," in *The Arab Americans: Studies in Assimilation,* ed. Elain C. Habopian and Add Paden (Wilmette, Ill.: Medina University Press International, 1969), pp. 84–101. Reprinted by permission.

Haddad attributes the improved status of wives to the new demands of the modern American industrial city, and to the Syrians' desire for social mobility. Lacking industrial skills, capital, and a knowledge of English, husbands commonly used peddling as an entry into the American economy; this occupation enabled their wives to become "junior partners" rather than subordinates in the family enterprise, and helped stimulate further changes.

The Woman in the Family

The Syrian immigrant [man] took easily to peddling. By the very nature of his trade and the small income he could draw from it, he gradually realized that he should have a partner. He naturally preferred a partner who could be subordinated to him and who would be unquestionably trustworthy. The nature of his trade also called for a partner who could have access to American homes. There was clearly one answer: his wife had to peddle also.

Once in this country, the Syrian woman used and adapted all the skills she had been taught in the rural society, plus a few more. She baked and sold Syrian bread to wealthy Syrian families, to other ethnic homes, and to some American homes. Sometimes she made aprons or other small items that she sold. If her husband could manage to handle a broader variety of merchandise, she helped with those too. Almost immediately her spatial world changed considerably. She went farther from home every day, and by virtue of her trade she learned to know her way around. Most important, she was learning English at the same time as, and as well as, her husband.

It was significant that 90 percent of the Syrian men in the foreign-born generation in Chicago reported that their wives had done, or were still doing, some work outside of home. . . .

The wife's work outside the home played an important part in breaking the patriarchal status of the man within the family. No longer the sole breadwinner, the husband could not remain the uncontested lawmaker and principal organizer of all household activities as in the homeland. . . .

At the beginning of a Syrian family's stay in Chicago, money, even in the case where the wife was working, was to a great extent controlled by the husband. But even the woman immigrant, especially if she was employed outside of home, gradually managed to break this control. When she brought cash home she expected to be consulted on most financial transactions dealing with the household. If she was working with her husband in his own business, chances were that she handled most, or at least part, of the accounts.

Moreover, within an intricate American economic and urban society the Syrian man had to be away from home the best part of the day. Thus he was compelled to rely on his wife as the family's purchasing agent. Although the "allowance" system still prevailed in some cases, especially among families in the foreign-born generation, at the time of this study it was usually extended to give the wife the prerogative of making all necessary purchases. This often included purchasing the children's and even the husband's clothes, a responsibility customarily reserved exclusively to men in the rural areas of the homeland. Syrian men with wives who worked at the time of this study explained that the husband remained the main, although not the sole, breadwinner for the family. However, the economic management of the household by the wife represented a great advance over the economic behavior of the Syrian woman in rural areas of the homeland. It also meant that the woman in assuming new responsibilities had acquired new skills necessary for cultural survival in an alien environment.

By the same token, responsibilities and individual freedom in economic matters had altered the position of women relative to their husbands. They were becoming at least the junior partners in the family units, and this, especially in the case of foreign-born women, had the effect of drawing them a little closer every day to American middle-class behavioral modes.

[Here the author describes the transition from traditional sex-segregated social activities, such as the all-male coffee houses, to American-style "couple" social activities. She also describes women's increased participation in community organizations. Both developments reflected the rising status of the immigrant woman.]

Parents and Children

The rural background of the families under consideration made the father the leading figure in the parent-child relationship. In the homeland the father had three major controls over his children—economic, educational, and recreational. By the time this study took place, however, the patriarchal aspect of the parent-child relationship within the Syrian family in Chicago was found to have undergone evident changes.

As a consequence of the family's inclusion in an American urban socioeconomic system, American-born Syrian children were no longer socialized primarily by a society of fathers. The father's traditional authority over the children and the household in general was shaken by factors beyond his control.

Caught in the gears of an urban civilization with all the characteristics of the highly diversified American culture, the Syrian father lost most of the means in his command to exert his authority over the children. He seemed to have lost ground to three main authorities, namely the mother, the American school, and the American society at large as represented by the child's peer group and social cliques. For the purpose of this study, only the mother's new role relative to the children will be discussed.

The child, of course, continued to remain dependent upon the livelihood provided by the father as the major breadwinner for the family, but immediate subordination of the child to the father in extensive areas of behavior no longer existed in the traditional, rural sense. Gradually some of the child's dependence on the father shifted to the mother. Even when the women were assuming only secondary controls over the children, in their everyday sustained expression these controls exceeded the father's final control. As in most American families, Syrian children in Chicago grew up mostly under the mother's supervision. As a general rule, the Syrian mother's relationship to the children gradually took on shades characterizing American ways of life.

This was exemplified in three major areas of the parent-child relationship, namely disciplining of the children, the sharing of activities with the children, and the school.

Disciplining the children was not only one of the most important duties of the father, but was also the symbol of his authority as head of the household and leader of an economic and social nucleus. The woman's role toward the husband and the children was traditionally considered a nutritive one, answering to the physical and emotional needs of the children. In the United States the woman's new or rather modified roles within the family have had a significant bearing on the mode of socialization of the children.

Faced with a complicated economic system where the responsibilities of earning a living are diversified and extensive, the father could not work in the proximity of his home, and could not be in any contact with his children for the best part of the day. Under such circumstances it was necessary that he relinquish to his wife some of his traditional responsibilities within the home. At first he made her only his representative while he was away. Gradually, however, the mother assumed more and more one of the father's prerogatives as disciplinarian. . . .

The sharing of activities with the children, particularly outside the home, is significant when one considers that, following the American middle-class behavior pattern, the mother's role here was predominant. Syrian fathers in Chicago were found to spend a good deal of time with their children, but in neither generation involved in this study did one find fathers alone sharing activities with their children outside of home, as was the father's prerogative in the homeland, especially where adolescent boys were concerned. Moreover, whenever possible mothers of Syrian families assumed the American way of life in assuming direction of most, if not all, of the children's activities. She became the more important figure in the child's social and recreational life by supervising his activities and by trying to a large extent to either select or screen his friends. . . .

Finally, the American school called upon the mother in matters regarding the children. Should any problem arise within the school, the principal's office, the nurse's office, or the guidance personnel would call for a conference with the mother. Whether she is being interviewed by the teacher, signing report cards, fulfilling her duties as a "room mother," or helping with the school's picnic, the Syrian woman is constantly told that the American environment is supporting her in the real governing of the children's lives.

4

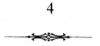

"Once You Marry Someone It Is Forever"

Immigration did not always raise the status of women in their families, even if they became wage earners. Michiko Tanaka, the central figure described here, immigrated to California in the 1920s and worked until a few years before her death in 1989. Though her many years of paid labor often saved her thirteen children from hunger, her harsh and domineering husband made all family decisions. Isolation from her parents, whose higher status might have protected her, contributed to this woman's apparent powerlessness, as did her acceptance of traditional Japanese ideology about women's roles.

The youngest daughter, Akemi Kikumura, published her mother's oral history, aptly titled Through Harsh Winters, *and, in the final chapter, reflected on that history. In the excerpt that follows, mother and daughter speak in turn. The excerpt suggests the strength of character that enabled this (and other) outwardly submissive woman to endure a life of hardship. It suggests, too, the power of the American environment on even the most conservative family. "Mama" was unable to transmit the traditional Japanese view of marriage to three of her American-born daughters, Yoko, Hana, and Keiko, all of whom divorced their husbands. Willingly or unwillingly, most immigrant women, like Michiko Tanaka, eventually made concessions to "changing times."*

A Mother Speaks

I was lonely [in California]—not a single relative. It might have been different had I been with someone I liked, but Papa never treated me gently. We never had conversation. We just worked and had babies.

Papa and I were not well suited for each other. He used to remind me that he wanted to marry his brother-in-law's daughter from a previous marriage. She was a rare beauty and a geisha, trained and quite accomplished in

Reprinted by permission of the publisher from *Through Harsh Winters: The Life of a Japanese Immigrant Woman,* by Akemi Kikumura. Copyright © 1981 by Chandler & Sharp Publishers, Inc. Pp. 40–41, 96–98, 101–4.

the arts. A person like that could have earned a living in America by teaching; Papa would have been well off. They would have been well suited to each other because Papa himself had an artist's spirit. He loved to entertain.

While in the company of others, Papa overflowed with laughter, but the minute he came home, he became *yakamashi* [stern, fault-finding]. At home he disciplined the children. He got angry if they used one word of English: "Use Japanese!" he admonished. "You go to school and learn English. A Japanese is no good unless he can speak Japanese." Even if I wanted to speak English, I couldn't. He wouldn't let me. "The children will naturally learn English," he said. Therefore at home they received discipline in Japanese: the language, social graces, practical wisdom.

He was severe. If I sat around not taking care of the household chores after coming home from work, he would say, "Don't go to work. After the household chores are taken care of, then go to work." He believed that a woman should never be idle for one minute. In the mornings, if I didn't come to the kitchen with my hair fixed neatly, he would get angry. Or if I came with slippers, he would say, "Go back into the bedroom and fix your hair and get dressed before you come out again." After marrying Papa, I have never risen after the sun was up. Even now, past four in the morning I can't stay in bed.

It has been that way between Papa and me ever since we got married. He never treated me well . . . birthdays . . . presents . . . clothes . . . who ever heard of such things? If I went into town, it was because my children were sick—not to have fun. But once I got married, I never entertained the thought of divorce. As long as he brought home enough to feed the children, I didn't care. Even if he was gone for a month, I didn't complain as long as my children could eat. . . .

The most important thing to remember for a woman is her role: to marry and raise children. To be happy is to have a good husband and fine children.

Between husband and wife it is not enough to have love . . . the meaning is deeper. That's why it is not good to get married young. Me, I married without thinking. I looked at marriage in a shallow light. I didn't like him much . . . I just wanted to come to America. I was too young, and when you are young, your thoughts are thin. But I never looked at another man while Papa was alive. Even after . . . and there were many who wanted to marry me. My daughters may be divorced but I continuously stayed married to Papa. I did what I had to, forgetting about myself and doing for my children.

Once you marry someone it is forever. You must think like that—that's how deep the meaning of marriage is. It is like religion: You promise *kamisama* (god) that you marry until death do you part. Promises are exchanged in front of *kamisama*, and if you divorce, you break that vow. That's the purpose of a marriage in a church.

I'm saying things from the Meiji Era [1868–1912]. Today people have different ideas. They do what makes them happy. . . .

I think that I am to blame that my daughters are divorced. If Papa were alive, nothing like this could have happened, but it is because of me and the changing times. . . .

A Daughter Reflects

In Japan, both ideal and law assigned women to a social position far inferior to that of the men: Men made the important decisions and women subordinated their wishes and needs to those of the household. But regardless of the society or time period, a strong-willed, wise, or beautiful women was not easy to dominate. In Mama's family, her mother made all the important decisions concerning the business. Her astute mind and business acumen was the bargaining power that she had with her husband. Mama recalled, "She could add up 20 items in her head without an abacus. Everything she touched turned to gold and everything Father meddled with became worthless." Other men recognized her capabilities and would come to consult with her about their investments.

But as for Mama, her bargaining position was minimal. She was totally subordinate in her relationship with Papa. If she had remained in Japan, her formal education and the family's social position could have been her bargaining tools. But being in a foreign country, far away from her family ties, confronted with strange ways and new situations, and unfamiliar with the English language, she became even more dependent on a strong-willed man who dominated practically every sphere of family life.

Mama and Papa fought incessantly. She would nag Papa about his gambling, making him even more furious and triggering off another round of arguments. After surviving a barrage of caustic abuse and ridicule, Mama would make excuses for his temper and even manage to laugh. This rankled her children: "How can you laugh! How could you humor Dad after he has treated you like that? How could you even touch him? We can support you. Why don't you leave him!"

Mama would quietly listen, then remark: "You children are young and impetuous. No matter if he drinks or gambles, he is still your father." For despite all the arguments, Mama did have a special love for him. When Papa wasn't gambling, he filled the house with laughter. He had a way of creating excitement and making the mundane seem extraordinary. He turned hard work into a game, everyday cooking into a festivity, rattlesnake meat, spoon turtle, and jackrabbit into delicacies. But that was only when he wasn't gambling. . . .

Concealing one's emotions was something that Mama and Papa both practiced and impressed upon their children. Yoko remarked, "If you are terribly upset and you just slapped several of your kids and were screaming at your wife, the minute somebody steps in the house, you turn on a smile . . . see?. . ."

Mama agreed that negative feelings must be concealed before others: "The worst thing to do is show an angry face. You must present a happy face. If something gets you angry to the stomach, or you are very depressed, you should at least recognize another's presence, otherwise you are discourteous. Our Papa said even if you fight to a point where you are both falling out the window, a woman must show a smiling face to other people." Concealing one's real emotional feelings was particularly useful while dealing with the white majority. To show a "good face" as a representative of the Japanese in general insured greater acceptance by the majority society.

Above all, a woman had to hold her man up high in public. Under the surface of Mama's outward submissiveness was a person whom Papa could always count on for inner strength and courage. When the money was all spent from gambling and no prospects of work lay ahead, she was the one that Papa sent out to borrow money. Papa would indulge in his gambling with the security of knowing that Mama would never desert the children and would somehow find a way to provide for them. . . .

Papa engaged Mama to do the distasteful or fearful things which he didn't want to face himself. [For example] when the family lived on the Kettleman Ranch, a fire enveloped the bath house at night and threatened to spread to the other buildings. The only source of water was a well, dug 15 feet deep and 30 feet in diameter. The motor to the pump rested at the bottom of the well. "Old woman," commanded Papa. "Go down and start the pump." Mama climbed down the dark pit. Somebody had to do it, but it wasn't going to be Papa.

Mama was also the person that Papa could turn to for emotional support. She appreciated his frustrations while dealing with the white society. "A man holds the biggest task of going out to face the world and bringing home the money," she would remark. She recognized his need to feel as though he had control over his environment. At home she would soothe his frustrations and uplift his ego through praise.

"My, you sure can talk," she encouraged when Papa came home from the market after negotiating his crops. "You are really a tough one . . . you really buffaloed them! Show me again how you did it." Papa would oblige without any further encouragement. Turning his back to her to fall into character, he then assumed his "Humphrey Bogart" stance, one of his favorite movie characters.

Mama was someone that Papa could always depend on. She was the one who provided the emotional security for the entire family. While Papa was volatile, unpredictable, and unyielding, Mama was patient, dependable, and forgiving. Just before his death, he would admit to her that "Without you, I could have never made it. . . ."

Papa was the one to be respected, feared, obeyed and pleased. Papa was the "superior" one—smarter, more glib, tall in stature, assertive, arrogant, proud, dominant—more American; Mama was the one to be pitied—weak, humble, self-effacing, nonassertive, submissive, agreeable, easy to please— more foreign. It took many years before her children could view her differently. After raising their own children, they saw that it took strength, not weakness, to persevere in her marriage and stand by Papa's side when all seemed hopeless, to subordinate her personal desires to those of her family. . . .

Yoko eventually married the man of whom the family disapproved. Even after the family moved to Los Angeles, her brother continued to forbid her to see them. Her marriage dissolved after 20 years: "He never forgot the bitter feelings aroused by the entire incident," she offered as an explanation for their divorce. The family suffered a great deal of sadness and guilt from the conflict and learned a costly lesson: Strict enforcement of the traditional rules will divide the family and threaten the stability of the household.

Years later, Mama expressed to Yoko the guilt that she continued to bear. She blamed herself for Yoko's divorce, for she believed that if she had been more understanding and supportive of her daughter's decision then the conflict which was to develop in their marriage could have been resolved.

But Mama's life up until the time of the incident with her daughter was dominated and determined by men. She chose the more familiar, traditional path—entrusting authority into the hands of her son—which had its rewards of social and economic security in old age. Her expected female behavior from childhood to adulthood had been conditioned on subservience to the male; the expectation that she would live with her son, who would take care of her in old age, influenced her decision to side with him in the conflict. To revise her behavior, assert her authority, and suddenly assume the role of decision-maker and enforcer within the family, could justify punishment in old age and jeopardize the security that she found in placing family decisions in the hands of the head of the house.

In a subsequent situation with her daughter Hana, Mama chose not to follow traditional role expectations in order to avoid the mistake she had made with Yoko. However, failure to do so was also a source of much internal conflict. Mama admitted that one of the things that she would like to do over again involved her action (or inaction) when her daughter Hana got a divorce. Mama wished that "I could have influenced her enough so that I could have said, 'No! You have to stay married.' and she would have listened." Instead, Mama did not intervene in her daughter's decision. Implicitly she knew that her daughter would follow through with the divorce despite her objections. If she had forcefully intervened, threatening her daughter with expulsion from the family, it could have meant an irreparable schism between mother and daughter.

Later, with Keiko's divorce, Mama found a way to fulfill both new and old role expectations. The following is an account told by Keiko just prior to her divorce:

> I got a call early in the morning from my mother-in-law telling me that Mom was there with Kenji's wife. I was surprised . . . didn't know how they even got there. It must have cost her over $20 in cab fare alone. Got to the house and the air was reeking with incense. As soon as I entered, Mom hit me and told me to quickly go and kneel at the *obutsudan* [Buddhist altar] and pray. I didn't get mad at her because I understood that this is how she had to act in front of my in-laws to save face. She felt so bad that her daughter was the cause and culprit of all this grief. By the time we returned to my house, Mom was talking sanely. She told me, "Keiko-chan, you know why I had to hit you in front of the in-laws." But she still couldn't understand, just as my in-laws, why I wanted a divorce. For the Issei, the only good reason for a divorce would be if the man was a drunk, a gambler, or if he fooled around with other women. Even then, a woman should go *gaman* [endure, tolerate] and sacrifice her own happiness for the sake of the children.

Mama managed to fulfill old role expectations and to save face by going through the formalities of trying to control her daughter's decision and by openly admonishing her for her "disgraceful" actions; she fulfilled new role expectations by supporting her daughter in her decision despite her own personal objections. Within the process, Mama did not change her values. She stood fast to her belief that a woman should endure regardless of her dissatisfactions and place family and children above all other considerations.

5

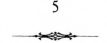

The Vine and the Fruit

As already noted, many immigrant women had large families, sometimes because they were ignorant of effective family planning methods, and sometimes because many children meant companionship, joy, and hope for the future. In the following

Source: Hope Williams Sykes, *The Joppa Door* (New York: G. P. Putnam's Sons, 1937), pp. 223–27, 243, 247–57.

two excerpts from The Joppa Door *(see Part 2), novelist Hope Williams Sykes captures the many dimensions of motherhood in her portrayal of a traditional family-centered German immigrant, Katharina, mother of nine. Sykes describes Katharina's problems—her fear that she will be left behind as her family becomes Americanized, her sadness when she realizes that there will be no more babies to care for, her loneliness as children leave home, her desolation at the death of a child (an event that was not uncommon in the nineteenth and early twentieth centuries). Sykes also captures the joy Katharina finds in the daily routines of family life—her pleasure in the companionship of her children, her satisfaction in doing things for them, and the intense pride she feels in their accomplishments.*

"My Familié *Is Growing Up"*

My *familié* is growing up, and, as I sit in my chair knitting, a desolate feeling is in my heart. Around the table they are gathered; their heads bend low over their books. Herr Heunsaker sits with them. They show him the things they read. He laughs. He argues. He is one of them. Sure, he is a smart man. He has the good mind. The children have the good heads. So much they all study. In the lamplight their faces are quiet with thoughts that I know not. Sure, I am on the outside, and I can do nothing about it.

I hold small Peter on my lap. He is my last baby. In my heart I know it. Nine children do I have. My William is six and goes this year to school with the others. Tight I hold Peter in my arms. Ach, he is the sweet-faced one. Only one year. I love him much. What I do when he gets big?

Thyrza sits at the sewing machine making herself such a dress of brown and white checks. My Thyrza is the smart one. Already she is through her high school and taking the cooking and sewing at the college. So fast her fingers go in and out with the needle. So quick her feet go on the pedal of the sewing machine.

Some neighbor children come into our kitchen. Two girls and three boys. The children have so many friends. Soon they are in the front room singing at the organ. Herr Heunsaker sings with them. I lay my Peter in his bed, and go sit in the front room with my knitting. So lovely are their voices all together. But I wait to listen for my Lael to sing. Such a voice I have never before heard. It has a sweetness not of this earth.

Sure, I must raise many vegetables this summer so I can sell much. Singing lessons my Lael must have. Such a voice must not be wasted. And my Johanna must go to high school.

My Gustave. Such a deep blue sweater I am knitting for him to wear to the school where he studies medicine. Strong hands. Strong doctor hands he has, and he has the good heart, the spirit of service, also. So many times I listen when he is talking with his father. Sure, I do not understand all the words, but I know what they speak about. Of healing and of service, and of high faith. . . .

"Mamma, come sing with us just this once," my Lael calls from the organ where Johanna is playing for her.

"Yes come on, Mrs. Heunsaker, I bet you have a good voice." A neighbor girl comes to me and tries to make me come to the organ.

"Ach, not. I cannot sing," I say.

"You used to sing to us in German when we were little," Etta says.

"I do not sing American good," I say.

"We'll sing it in German," Johanna begs.

"Not tonight," I say. I smile upon all of them. "Better I like to hear you sing." Sure, they must not know how much singing means to me. I cannot make myself sing. Better they think I am dumb than foolish. I can understand this English language, and I know many words in my mind, but I am afraid to speak. I am not sure when I speak them right. . . . I look on my hands. Short and wide they are and coarsened from much work. I cannot play the organ. I cannot sing, even. I do not know how to make leaves into tea. My hands do not have the healing in them like Herr Heunsaker's. Hard, they are with no softness. Sure, all my hands know is to glean in the field, to knit, to keep a house, and to cook for my husband and my children, and now my *familié* grow away from me. . . .

My Peter starts to school. I stand here in my front yard and watch him go. He is the last of my children, and now, I am alone. I go back into the house. So quiet it is. No one to talk to. No small boy asking for a piece of brown bread with butter and honey on. I walk through the house. I go upstairs and make their beds and stand long looking at them. Downstairs I go once again. Hard I scrub my kitchen floor. I make a soup for their dinner. Once again I find myself standing still in the middle of my kitchen with my hands doing nothing. Sure, I cannot do this. I go outside and sit on a box in the chicken yard and pound out seeds from great heads of sun roses. I talk to my red chickens but all the time it is as if I am listening for small Peter's voice talking also.

The morning is but half gone. I think—what will I do? Here I am not old. Many years I have yet to live, and I have nothing. There is nothing for me to do now when my *familié* is grown up. Always I work for them. Always I think on them.

I gather all the stockings that have holes in them. And here in the morning I sit and darn. Never before do I do this. How I stand all these days? Better I get some yarn and crochet my Thyrza a pocket book. She says just yesterday when she comes home for a visit she needs one for her new suit. I will get the yarn this afternoon.

At noon the children come home laughing. Ach, once again I am happy with them, but they eat so fast, and they are soon gone. I go to town in the afternoon and get the yarn for Thyrza's purse. I come home, and sit and crochet on it. But the stillness is so still; I cannot sit here. I go out in my garden and pick the vegetables so I cook them for our supper. I do not live until the children come running in from their school.

Peter shows me his book. "This is 'Cat,' mamma. See I know the words already." Peter laughs and shows me the pictures in his book.

"Cat," I say and laugh with him.

"You can learn it, too, mamma." Peter looks into my face with his blue eyes shining.

"Sure, I learn to read with you," I say.

"Why you need to learn English? You have your German Bible, and the German magazine that I order for you these many years," Herr Heunsaker speaks sharply.

"I learn with Peter," I say. I cannot tell him I have to learn English. Sure, I cannot stay outside my *familié*. Someway I have to stay with them.

The older children smile on me, and sometimes they laugh when I am learning the words with Peter. I make my face say nothing. Sometimes I smile back at them, and say, "I show you I am not so dumb."

With stubbornness I set my mind to this learning. I say the words slowly after Peter, and I look close on these letters. So fast as Peter I learn the reading.

The second winter he is in school, I am doing much better with my reading. When they are all gone to school, I look on the books that Herr Heunsaker reads, and on the books my children have learned from. . . . Such a happiness is in me when I find a word that I know. Soon I shall be reading these books that my husband and my children read.

The third year comes. My Peter and I are learning our lessons. Sure, I love him much. Never before do I have so much time to look after my little ones. My Peter is my baby. I talk much with him. The others talk things I do not understand, but my Peter and I understand each other.

Ice comes upon the ponds. The children go skating and small Peter begs for skates also. I do not like to see him go out in the cold, but he must grow into a man. Sure, he cannot always be hanging to his mother's apron strings.

The evening comes when small Peter comes home wet to his knees. "What you do, Peter? You fall in the water?" I take his clothes quick off of him. So cold is his small thin body. He is shaking and his lips are blue. . . .

Such a sickness my Peter has, and he does not get better. All winter he is thin, and his body aches. I have to keep him out of school. I read his little books to him at home. I play games with him. But he cannot run. His heart pounds so hard. His face is so white. Sure, my heart aches for him these days.

So anxious I am. I talk to the doctor, but he says words I do not know. "Rheumatic heart." I do not know what it is. I talk to my Gustave.

"Say it so I know it, Gustave."

"His heart is tired, mother. When he has the bad sickness his heart works too hard like you do when you work too hard in the garden, and it does not get rested."

"You think he does not get well, Gustave?" Sure, I look close into the face of this oldest doctor son of mine. Such a sadness in his eyes.

"He does not get well, mother." So quiet my Gustave speaks the words.

"I know it from the first, Gustave. I think I die when he dies. Sure, I do not want to live without him. I love him much." I turn and walk away and out into the yard. I cannot let my Gustave see my tears. I cannot go into the bedroom and let my small Peter see my tears. I must not make him afraid to die. I must not let him know how I shall miss him.

When my Gustave goes back to the city where he is studying to be a doctor, I go up to my Peter. I sit on the side of his bed. Quiet I hold his hand. So thin. So weak it is. So thin is his body. His poor little legs, they cannot run any more. Only his stomach is big and the rest of him does not grow.

I smile into his face. Quiet he smiles back at me. Sure, I love him much.

"You think I will walk again?" he says. Never before does he ask me. Sure, I cannot lie to him. Peter and I, always we understand each other.

"Feet hold us to the earth Peter. Heavy things they are. I think it be nicer to have wings. Such lovely wings. Like a bright angel. A bright angel. Think how lovely it will be, Peter, to be a bright angel."

Long he looks into my face, then he smiles. "A bright angel," he says, then he turns his face into the pillow.

I stand here beside his bed, and I can do nothing for him. But like my heart is breaking it is.

"A *bright angel.*"

My Peter is gone. I walk my house alone. I stand in the middle of my house. I look at my hands. Wide I spread my fingers. Like my two hands are my *familié*. So close they are to me. My nine children and my husband. And now my Peter is gone. It is like the littlest finger is gone from my hand. I work. I use my two hands, but always it is like one finger is gone. Never can it be the same again. A part of me is gone, when my small Peter goes from me.

I know only I must live so I see him again.

"Sure, It Is Good to Be Working for My Children Once Again"

We build a new house. Sure, I do not ever think I have a new house.

"What you think of this plan, Katharina?" Herr Heunsaker draws lines on a paper. "Here is a front room, and we make a fireplace in the side. Always I think how I will sit before a fire that burns open." So excited is Herr Heunsaker's voice. . . .

"We have to have plenty of bedrooms so the children have a place to come," I say.

"What we need with bedrooms? Thyrza is married. Etta is married. Johanna is married. Philip is married. Gustave is away in the city with his doctoring. Only Emil and William are home. Lael takes her singing in New York." Herr Heunsaker laughs at me. I sit with my crocheting in my hands.

Sure, he speaks the truth. My *familié* is grown up. I can only sit here and crochet a bedspread of fine thread for my Thyrza, who likes the fine things in her home.

"We put two bedrooms on the upstairs so if they come home, they have a place to sleep," Herr Heunsaker says.

"Better we make it three," I say. But all the time I am thinking how I do not need a fine house now. When my children are little and need the nice home, we do not have it. When they should have the rooms by themselves, they do not have them. Sure, life is queer. It gives us not the goods things when we can use them. . . .

It is Christmas and my children come home. My Lael comes, and my Gustave, and my Philip, and all the others.

In the evening we sit here around our fireplace for our house is done for two months now. Ach, so beautiful is my Lael.

"Mother, I remember how you used to raise vegetables and how we peddled them. And the money you spent on singing lessons for me." There are bright tears behind my Lael's dark eyes.

"Sure, I know it," I say and nod my head. With love I smile upon her.

"Tonight, I will sing for you. Johanna, you play for me. It will be like old times." My Lael stands up.

"I like better the organ than the piano," I say.

"I like the organ, too," my Lael says. Sure she is the great singer. In great churches of the East she sings. And in the opera, they say. But I know not of it.

This night I sit in my chair, and for once I do not make my hands do any work. I sit in silence to hear my girl sing, my Lael.

Near taking my heart out of me, she does. So sweet. So high, she sings, and she looks into my eyes as she sings. To me she sings. Ach, foolish that I am. I cry. I cannot keep the tears away.

That I should live to hear my girl sing. Like I could never sing, she sings. In her I live in song. Such music. It breaks the heart to hear it. Through my tears I smile upon her.

There is a silence when she stops her singing.

I sit here among my children. Sure, it is good to have them all around me again. And it is as if small Peter is here, also.

My Gustave turns from the window where he is standing. There are tears in his eyes. "It is good that one of us reaches the heights." He looks with love on his sister Lael. "We used to glean the fields all together."

"*Ja*," I say, "I remember the hard days, but I had you children around me. It was not so bad." I smile and get up from my chair.

"I remember how you do not like my barley coffee. Tonight I make you coffee from the store, but for your father I make the barley coffee." Sure, it is good to be working for my children once again.

6

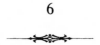

"We Want to Give a Complete Picture of Who We Are"

Not all immigrant women have lived in traditional families. The social changes of the 1960s and the gay rights movement enabled immigrant lesbians to speak and write about their lives. One result was the publication of several anthologies, including Compañeras, *an anthology by and about Latina lesbians, many of them political activists ("compañera, companion, friend, lover, comrade in struggle. . ."). These readings, both from* Compañeras, *provide different but complementary insights about women who love other women. The first, "Palm Sunday 1981," is a personal view, a poem about the bond between two women, the hostility they encounter, and their hopes for the future. "I am Mexican, born in El Paso, Texas and raised in Ciudad Juarez, Chihuahua until I was nine," writes the poet, "Lorenza," who came out as a lesbian at the age of twenty. The second, by Chilean-born author and lesbian mother Mariana Romo-Carmona, is the introduction to the anthology. It gives an overview of the experiences of Latina lesbians with their lovers, families, and communities. Romo-Carmona writes about the double marginality—by ethnicity and sexual preference—of Latina lesbians. She urges them to unite, as other groups have, to struggle for equality and to build a Latina lesbian community in the United States and Latin America.*

Source: "Introduction" was first published in *Compañeras: Latina Lesbians (An Anthology)* Juanita Ramos, ed. (New York: Latina Lesbian History Project, P.O. Box 627, New York, NY 10009, 1987), Library of Congress Catalog Card Number: 87-82402.

Palm Sunday 1981

2:00 A.M. N.Y.C. No. 6 IRT

Lorenza

Two women holding hands
in the New York City Subway System
is too powerful an act

Listen to the rumble of society
shaking at its base
to the screeching brakes
to stop the numbness
to open metal lids
only for a moment
to stare

Laughter in the subway system
carries the message of a dying world
yet wisdom—amidst morbid ridicule—prevails
"Those two women must be together, man.
Face it. This is reality.
This is reality"

A knowing smile between two women
two women who hold hands
each other's heartbeat
who share the loving bond
of an unbroken grip
who share the burning fire
of directed anger

A steady walk
a steady glance
into a nearing future
of holding on
of holding up
the rest of the world

Introduction to Compañeras

Compañeras . . . at home I read the stories again and again, feeling moved to
the depth of my soul by the same discovery each woman makes when she tells
her life story. It is difficult at first to express what it means for us to come
together, but it is there in the words of our sisters: we, as Latina lesbians

have recognized ourselves, have reached for each other, for the people of our lands, and now we seek to establish a community of Latina lesbians that extends from country to country. . . .

THE OTHER SIDE/DEL OTRO LADO

The women who speak in this book were either born in the United States of Latino or mixed parentage, migrated to the U.S. as young girls with their parents or as adults, or have spent some time connecting with other Latina lesbians before going back to Latin America. *Compañeras* speaks with the voices of Latina lesbians who are puertorriqueñas, chicanas, cubanas, chilenas, hondureñas, brasileñas, colombianas, argentinas, peruanas, and nicaragüenses; women who met to speak about what it implies to be both Latina and lesbian in our communities, whether we live in Latin America or the U.S.

Within this context we grapple with our identity, as lesbians who challenge the patriarchal expectations of white, North American society, and Latin American culture; and as Latinas who, by our very existence defy the widespread belief that the U.S. is a white world.

As Latina lesbians, sometimes we live in a suspended state, without a name, finding no reflection of ourselves. Other times, names have been given to us that distort who we are.

In white North American Society, our names are not pronounced, alway misspelled and chopped in half because they don't fit in any form created for anglo names. When we are *officially* recognized we are given a derivative name—Hispanic, a distillation which refers to the language most of us speak, a by-product of the country that colonized us before the U.S. did. This is a reflection of the subordinate political, cultural, racial and economic position Latinos in this country are forced to occupy. At the same time in our countries and communities of origin, many of us are seen as foreigners because we speak another language and have developed some different cultural ways.

As lesbians, we are also seen as foreigners. Our sexuality and lifestyle are regarded as abnormal, and most people would prefer that we did not exist [we] . . . speak of this rejection, the pain of being sent to mental institutions, of being forced to leave our countries, and for many the pain of self-destruction. As Chicana writer Gloria Evangelina Anzaldúa puts it, we are "always pushed to the other side . . . al otro lado."

For many of us the process of acquiring an identity as a lesbian is closely tied to coming to terms with our racial and cultural identity. The conflicts experienced on all these levels simultaneously, produces the feeling of being torn into different pieces. Julia Pérez, describing the conflicts around being Black and Puerto Rican, says, "Puerto Ricans would say to me, Tú eres negra" and Black North Americans would say to me, "You're Puerto Rican." Avotcja, reflecting on the way in which she and other contributors have come to reaffirm their identity in spite of pressures to deny different parts of themselves, states, "What they see is what they get!" "I'm not only a lesbian, but also a Rican who happens to be a Black woman."

COMING OUT/SALIENDO DEL CLOSET

The issue of being able to express the meaning of our lives is an important one for Latina lesbians, because as lesbians, we are seen mainly through our sexuality. With this view, we lose our perception of ourselves as women and as Third World/People of Color, as we are explained away as a phenomenon alien to our culture. When heterosexuals write or speak about us, no matter how sympathetic, they focus on what is exceptional about us *in spite* of our sexuality. We may be redeemed to human status *even though* we are lesbians. If the discussion is negative, the focus is on our failure to achieve acceptability *because* of our sexuality. In either case, we are an extreme, good or evil, never evaluated in terms of our net worth, our potential as human beings. By speaking about ourselves, we want to give a complete picture of who we are.

Coming out means that we stake our ground, and we claim that territory for ourselves both as Latinas and as lesbians, whole persons who live and work in the context of a community. But coming out is a process that involves a series of personal conflicts and choices. As Hilda Hidalgo states, it first involves recognizing that we are "different," "que sentimos atracción emocionaly físcia hacia personas de nuestro propio sexo."* . . . We speak about that process: painful, joyous, confusing, affirming.

The process of coming out is also one that does not end after a set period of time. The fear of telling the truth to a favorite Tía, or una mejor amiga, and being rejected, is repeated each time we are faced with the choice to speak or not. When we weigh the benefits of being silent and saving other people from the shock, or ourselves from the pain, we internalize the hatred against us. In essence, we begin to believe that our lives are less important, and we continue to hide a part of ourselves.

But the women we really are can only live if we break open the secret. How many daughters, mothers, sisters, godmothers and grandmothers, aunts, cousins and best friends have lived and died unknown? Each woman's forced silence was a denial of her existence, as if she never loved another woman, never rejoiced in their union, or cried for her, or waited for her to come home. Saliendo del closet is ultimately helping to create support for *all* that we are, to create a Latina lesbian community.

LOVERS AND FRIENDS/*AMANTES Y AMIGAS*

The first thing we know about each other is our love for women, and this is the knowledge that thrills us, makes us warm and open in each other's company, makes it easy to hold out our hands and embrace another Latina les-

---

*"that we feel emotional and physical attraction towards people of our own sex."

bian at first meeting. And yet, there is such fear that this tender trust be broken for it is not to everyone that we can speak freely about our lives. To be a lesbian means to be forever measuring the impact of our truth on other people. Being in love with women, a feeling that seems so natural to us, is not a feeling that is supported or celebrated. The birth of a new love, the anniversary of a love that endures, the conflicts of women that may grow together as lovers, or apart, the break-up of a friendship that held so much promise, all this happens almost entirely in silence.

The existence of a group of friends, of a community of women who share our perspective, is necessary for our development. In our discussions with each other, we've learned that living unrecognized and living in secret can make us feel like our relationships are not important, or not very real, and it becomes increasingly difficult to develop the lasting bonds that people need in their lives. Our lovers and our friends, *"las buenas amigas,"* as they are known to our family or significant straight people, are a central part of our lives, and yet must remain at the periphery of the daily choices we make, even in the way we prioritize our lives.

Although not all relationships between women develop amidst unsurmountable obstacles, the anonymity we may choose for protection can keep us unknown to one another. . . .

As our networks of support grow wider and stronger, we begin to question the negative images of lesbians we've internalized; to explore how to deal with violence, with jealousy and possessiveness, and with patterns of behavior that may be destructive.

Meanwhile, lesbians are subject to violence in every aspect of our lives—a woman can be queerbashed walking home from work, torn away from her lover by force, fired from her job, beaten by a jealous man, all for loving a woman. The pressure to be silent is still very strong, and often the consequences of loving are very painful. . . .

FAMILIES/*FAMILIAS*

For those of us who live in the U.S., our Latina identification is crucial. The pride in ourselves is what allows us to confront and survive the various forms of discrimination we face when dealing with the white North Americans who, by no means, see it to their advantage to regard us as equals in "their" society. However, when we turn to our families for support, we often find that we can only get it if we are willing to repress our lesbian selves.

For many of us, the introduction to a marginalized existence occurs in the family, as this is often the place where we first learn about violence and sexual abuse, as well as about home, love and security. It is also within our family where we first acquire a notion of sexual roles, and what is expected of us as women. As Latinas, we are supposed to grow up submissive, virtuous, respectful of elders and helpful to our mothers, long suffering, deferring to men, industrious and devoted. We also know that any deviation from these expectations constitutes an act of rebellion, and there is great pressure to conform. Independence is discouraged, and we learn early that women who think for themselves are branded *"putas"* or *"marimachas."*

Being a lesbian is by definition an act of treason against out cultural values. Though our culture may vary somewhat from country to country, on the whole, to be lesbians we have to leave the fold of our family, and seek support within the mainstream white lesbian community. In *Compañeras* we see that Latino families react in different ways to our lesbianism, from the very unusual support to the more common outright rejection. Our choice of lifestyle—to leave the family, to live with women or alone, is seen as adopting foreign ways, as being headstrong, too independent, and these qualities are associated with being "less feminine." But the fact is that the place where we have learned to be who we are is the family. Our role models have been the women in our family who have been passive and supportive, as well as strong and independent.

Odilia Mendez says it in this way, in her poem "Mother":

> I grow older and I'm not like the other girls.
> I'm a woman in your image and you've made me strong.
> You've taught me to fight my battles.
> You don't expect me to make tortillas
> but to think about who first made tortillas
> and what the future holds for the tortilla.
> And my relatives laugh at you for not preparing me
> to be a good wife.

The process of leaving home, whether symbolic or actual, is unsettling and difficult. After the initial relief we experience in being among lesbians, we find that within the white community there is no way to express our identity as Latinas. As we mature and come to find our own ways of defining a family, alone, with our children, with our friends, in non-monogamous relationships or with one lover, it remains difficult to find acceptance for the lifestyle we have chosen.

Those of us who are mothers, or may choose to have children in the future, appear as a contradiction in terms. To this day there is no support for lesbian motherhood, or motherhood without the presence of a man to legitimize the relationship. Women have historically lost their children to the male system, lesbians or not, because children are seen as the property of the father along with the woman who produced them.

Having a child taken away, or living in fear of losing her, tears away at a woman's spirit. When motherhood is called into question because we are lesbians, it is not because our ability as mothers is deficient, but because we have ceased to be useful as a breeder of children to a man. We constitute an unarguable threat to the status quo; and sometimes our own families act in collusion with the state to deprive us of the right to raise our own children.

Whether or not we come out to our families, we ultimately challenge every aspect of a woman's role, and have to face the consequences imposed on us. As a result, our experience with our families changes us. The compromises and struggles we wage here, perhaps for the remainder of our lives, prepare us for the next step.

THE STRUGGLE CONTINUES/LA LUCHA CONTINUA

The heritage of Latin America has been one of constant struggle, achieving liberation from Spain and Portugal only to become part of the warehouse that feeds the first world market. As Latina lesbians who live in the U.S., we form part of the so-called minority population composed of Blacks, Asians, Native Americans and Latinos who live in the "belly of the beast," and who strive each day for increased political and economic power.

Individually, we have formed part of groups that organize against U.S. intervention in Central and South America, we are civil rights workers and activists, and we have joined coalitions to defend human rights on an international level. As lesbians, however, we have just started to come together. Our energy is divided along many issues that demand that we repress part of our identity in order to be accepted. This is where the struggle really begins, and we need each other to withstand the pressure. . . .

Black, white, Asian and Native American women, lesbian and heterosexual, have formed groups and continue to gather together, encouraging other women to unite. We also need to communicate with each other to survive, learn how to create and maintain our unity in order to struggle for our rights, and those of our people, and eventually, for our development, more than just survival.

The need to unite with other Latina lesbians in order to create our own support networks, becomes imperative. . . . Each day that passes, we are getting closer to knowing each other, discovering our history in the legacy left to us by the lives of Latina lesbians who lived before us, reaching out to our compañeras all over the U.S. and Latin America, and recording our current history in books, artwork, slideshow documentaries, so that collectively we may never cease to exist again. . . .

We have a burdensome past to unlock, weighed down with traditional expectations. But we have a future as powerful as the impulse to know each other—¡p' afuera y p'alante, compañeras!

7

A Family Disrupted:
"*Shikata Ga Nai*—This Cannot Be Helped"

In 1942 a hundred thousand first- and second-generation Japanese-Americans were evacuated from their west coast homes, interned in "relocation centers" (race tracks, fair grounds, and stock exhibition halls), and then imprisoned in detention camps for the duration of World War II. In the following selection, a Japanese-American woman describes the impact of this experience on herself, her foreign-born mother, and her entire family.

Ordered by the American military, approved by President Franklin Roosevelt, and upheld by the Supreme Court, the evacuation was a response to wartime hysteria, unfounded fears of sabotage, and longstanding prejudice against Asian-Americans. The Federal Reserve Bank estimated the financial loss to the Japanese-American community at about $400 million. The emotional and psychological costs, of which one of the greatest was the destruction of traditional family life, are suggested in this selection.

The shacks were built of one thickness of pine planking covered with tar-paper. They sat on concrete footings, with about two feet of open space between the floorboards and the ground. Gaps showed between the planks, and as the weeks passed and the green wood dried out, the gaps widened. Knotholes gaped in the uncovered floor.

Each barracks was divided into six units, sixteen by twenty feet, about the size of a living room, with one bare bulb hanging from the ceiling and an oil stove for heat. We were assigned two of these for the twelve people in our family group; and our official family "number" was enlarged by three digits—16 plus the number of this barracks. We were issued steel army cots, two brown army blankets each, and some mattress covers, which my brothers stuffed with straw. . . .

The people who had it hardest during the first few months were young couples, . . . many of whom had married just before the evacuation began, in order not to be separated and sent to different camps. Our two rooms were

Source: From *Farewell to Manzanar* by Jeanne Wakatsuki Houston and James D. Houston, published by Houghton Mifflin Company. Copyright © 1973 by James D. Houston. Reprinted by permission.

crowded, but at least it was all in the family. My oldest sister and her husband were shoved into one of those sixteen-by-twenty-foot compartments with six people they had never seen before—two other couples, one recently married like themselves, the other with two teenage boys. Partitioning off a room like that wasn't easy. It was bitter cold when we arrived, and the wind did not abate. All they had to use for room dividers were those army blankets, two of which were barely enough to keep one person warm. They argued over whose blanket should be sacrificed and later argued about noise at night—the parents wanted their boys asleep by 9:00 P.M.—and they continued arguing over matters like that for six months, until my sister and her husband left to harvest sugar beets in Idaho. It was grueling work up there, and wages were pitiful, but when the call came through camp for workers to alleviate the wartime labor shortage, it sounded better than their life at Manzanar. They knew they'd have, if nothing else, a room, perhaps a cabin of their own. . . .

Months went by, in fact, before our "home" changed much at all from what it was the day we moved in—bare floors, blanket partitions, one bulb in each compartment dangling from a roof beam, and open ceilings overhead so that mischievous boys like Ray and Kiyo could climb up into the rafters and peek into anyone's life. . . .

I was sick continually, with stomach cramps and diarrhea. At first it was from the shots they gave us for typhoid, in very heavy doses and in assembly-line fashion: swab, jab, swab, *Move along now*, swab, jab, swab, *Keep it moving*. That knocked all of us younger kids down at once, with fevers and vomiting. Later, it was the food that made us sick, young and old alike. The kitchens were too small and badly ventilated. Food would spoil from being left out too long. That summer, when the heat got fierce, it would spoil faster. The refrigeration kept breaking down. The cooks, in many cases, had never cooked before. Each block had to provide its own volunteers. Some were lucky and had a professional or two in their midst. But the first chef in our block had been a gardener all his life and suddenly found himself preparing three meals a day for 250 people.

"The Manzanar runs" became a condition of life, and you only hoped that when you rushed to the latrine, one would be in working order.

That first morning, on our way to the chow line, Mama and I tried to use the women's latrine in our block. The smell of it spoiled what little appetite we had. Outside, men were working in an open trench, up to their knees in muck—a common sight in the months to come. Inside, the floor was covered with excrement, and all twelve bowls were erupting like a row of tiny volcanoes.

Mama stopped a kimono-wrapped woman stepping past us with her sleeve pushed up against her nose and asked, "What do you do?" "Try Block Twelve," the woman said, grimacing. "They have just finished repairing the pipes."

It was about two city blocks away. We followed her over there and found a line of women waiting in the wind outside the latrine. We had no choice but to join the line and wait with them. . . .

It was an open room, over a concrete slab. The sink was a long metal trough against one wall, with a row of spigots for hot and cold water. Down the center of the room twelve toilet bowls were arranged in six pairs, back to back, with no partitions. My mother was a very modest person, and this was going to be agony for her, sitting down in public, among strangers.

One old woman had already solved the problem for herself by dragging a large cardboard carton. She set it up around one of the bowls, like a three-sided screen. . . . Mama happened to be at the head of the line now. As she approached the vacant bowl, she and the old woman bowed to each other from the waist. Mama then moved to help her with the carton, and the old woman said very graciously, in Japanese, "Would you like to use it?"

Happily, gratefully, Mama bowed again and said, "*Arigato*" (Thank you). . . .

Those big cartons were a common sight in the spring of 1942. Eventually sturdier partitions appeared, one or two at a time. . . .

Like so many of the women there, Mama never did get used to the latrines. It was a humiliation she just learned to endure: *shikata ga nai*, this cannot be helped. She would quickly subordinate her own desires to those of the family or the community, because she knew cooperation was the only way to survive. At the same time she placed a high premium on personal privacy, respected it in others and insisted upon it for herself. Almost everyone at Manzanar had inherited this pair of traits from the generations before them who had learned to live in a small, crowded country like Japan. Because of the first they were able to take a desolate stretch of wasteland and gradually make it livable. But the entire situation there, especially in the beginning— the packed sleeping quarters, the communal mess halls, the open toilets—all this was an open insult to that other, private self, a slap in the face you were powerless to challenge.

At seven I was too young to be insulted. The camp worked on me in a much different way. I wasn't aware of this at the time, of course. No one was, except maybe Mama, and there was little she could have done to change what happened.

It began in the mess hall. Before Manzanar, mealtime had always been the center of our family scene. In camp, and afterward, I would often recall with deep yearning the old round wooden table in our dining room in Ocean Park, the biggest piece of furniture we owned, large enough to seat twelve or thirteen of us at once. A tall row of elegant, lathe-turned spindles separated this table from the kitchen, allowing talk to pass from one room to the other. Dinners were always noisy, and they were always abundant with great pots of boiled rice, platters of home-grown vegetables, fish Papa caught.

He would sit at the head of this table, with Mama next to him serving and the rest of us arranged around the edges according to age, down to where Kiyo and I sat, so far away from our parents, it seemed at the time, we had our own enclosed nook inside this world. The grownups would be talking down at their end, while we two played our secret games, making eyes at each other when Papa gave the order to begin to eat, racing with chopsticks to scrape the last grain from our rice bowls, eyeing Papa to see if he had noticed who won.

Now, in the mess halls, after a few weeks had passed, we stopped eating as a family. Mama tried to hold us together for a while, but it was hopeless. Granny was too feeble to walk across the block three times a day, especially during heavy weather, so May brought food to her in the barracks. My older brothers and sisters, meanwhile, began eating with their friends, or eating somewhere blocks away in the hope of finding better food. The word would get around that the cook over in Block 22, say, really knew his stuff, and they would eat a few meals over there, to test the rumor. Camp authorities frowned on mess hall hopping and tired to stop it, but the good cooks liked it. They liked to see long lines outside their kitchens and would work overtime to attract a crowd.

Younger boys, like Ray, would make a game of seeing how many mess halls they could hit in one meal period—be the first in line at Block 16, gobble down your food, run to 17 by the middle of the dinner hour, gulp another helping, and hurry to 18 to make the end of that chow line and stuff in the third meal of the evening. They didn't need to do that. No matter how bad the food might be, you could always eat till you were full.

Kiyo and I were too young to run around, but often we would eat in gangs with other kids, while the grownups sat at another table. I confess I enjoyed this part of it at the time. We all did. A couple of years after the camps opened, sociologists studying the life noticed what had happened to the families. They made some recommendations, and edicts went out that families *must* start eating together again. Most people resented this; they griped and grumbled. They were in the habit of eating with their friends. And until the mess hall system itself could be changed, not much could really be done. It was too late.

My own family, after three years of mess hall living, collapsed as an integrated unit. Whatever dignity or feeling of filial strength we may have known before December 1941 was lost, and we did not recover it until many years after the war, not until after Papa died and we began to come together, trying to fill the vacuum his passing left in all our lives.

The closing of the camps, in the fall of 1945, only aggravated what had begun inside. Papa had no money then and could not get work. Half of our family had already moved to the east coast, where jobs had opened up for them. The rest of us were relocated into a former defense workers' housing project in Long Beach. In that small apartment there never was enough room for all of us to sit down for a meal. We ate in shifts, and I yearned all the more for our huge round table in Ocean Park.

Soon after we were released I wrote a paper for a seventh-grade journalism class, describing how we used to hunt grunion before the war. The whole family would go down to Ocean Park Beach after dark, when the grunion were running, and build a big fire on the sand. I would watch Papa and my older brothers splash through the moonlit surf to scoop out the fish, then we'd rush back to the house where Mama would fry them up and set the sizzling pan on the table, with soy sauce and horseradish, for a midnight meal. I ended the paper with this sentence: "The reason I want to remember this is because I know we'll never be able to do it again."

PART V

Community Life

It is if I am alone and can never find comfort. I want to reach out my
hands. There is nothing to reach to. Nothing. Nothing. My heart is
as desolate as the mountain of Zion where only the foxes walk.[1]

Fortunately, most women did not have to face their problems alone. In
time of need they turned to others for food, clothing, shelter, comfort,
companionship, and moral support. Part 5 documents the kinds of aid
women received from friends, neighbors, ethic institutions, and the larger
American community.

The Community

Because separation of the sexes in work and recreation was often customary
in the homeland, many women found it natural to rely upon other women.
They turned first to mothers, godmothers, sisters, and aunts and, when relatives were not available, to neighbors who spoke their native language.
Common hardships created bonds between women who would have been
separated by class and life-style in the homeland, and the widely shared experiences of marriage and motherhood enabled many women to understand
and to help one another. For example, the first selection in this part describes
the emotional support as well as the medical care one woman offered another
who was going through childbirth on the Minnesota frontier. It also shows
that mutual need could foster an otherwise unlikely relationship between a
respectable housewife and a former prostitute.

Less dramatic but equally important was the everyday sharing of food,
household equipment, and information. Anzia Yezierska's short stories and
novels about Jewish immigrants at the turn of the century show women moving freely in and out of each other's kitchens and lives. The poor and the
desperate borrowed cooking pots and wash boilers and poured out their troubles while those less poor and desperate offered not only coffee and cake but
also understanding, encouragement, and sound advice. In the following passage from Yezierska's novel, *Bread Givers*, Sara Smolinsky tells how an experienced neighbor, Mahmenkah, helps her impoverished mother arrange a
room for boarders.

"You could charge your boarders twice as much for the sleeping if you give them a bed with springs,. . ." said Mahmenkah.
   "Don't I know. . . . But you have to have money for it."
   "I got an old spring in the basement. I'll give it to you."
   "But the spring needs a bed with feet."
   "Do as I done. Put the spring over four empty herring pails,
and you'll have a bed fit for the president. Now put a board over the
potato barrel, and a clean newspaper over that, and you'll have a
table. All you need yet is a soapbox for a chair, and you'll have a
furnished room complete."
   Even Mother forgot for a while her worries, so like a healing
medicine was Mahmenkah's sunshine.[2]

Women shared information about educational opportunities, jobs, and
the reliability of shopkeepers, social workers, teachers, and politicians as
well as about details of household management and childcare. Individually
or in groups, they were often able to recognize and help those in need of
food, medical care, or emotional support. Friendship groups ministered to
their own needs as well as to the needs of others. Author Paule Marshall describes one such group; in the 1930s her mother and other domestic workers
from Barbados gathered every day in her kitchen after "scrubbing floor" in
white women's kitchens to drink tea and talk.

They talked endlessly, passionately, poetically, and with impressive
range. No subject was beyond them. . . . the talk that filled the
kitchen those afternoons was highly functional. It served as therapy, the cheapest kind available to my mother and her friends. Not
only did it help them recover from the long wait [for prospective
employers] on the corner that morning and the bargaining over
their labor, it restored them to a sense of themselves and affirmed
their self-worth.[3]

Women's Organizations

Recognizing the inadequacy of spontaneous sharing, immigrant women institutionalized self-help by forming women's organizations on a local and, in
some cases, a national basis. An example of a local self-help institution was
the Finnish Woman's Cooperative Home, established in 1910 by Finnish
"live-in" domestics who pooled their money to rent an apartment for common use. By 1920 the home had four hundred shareholders, a four-story res-
idence accommodating more than forty women, and a building fund of a
thousand dollars:

Besides dormitory space and a few private rooms, it has a general living room, where the girls may receive men friends, and which contains a small library . . . there is a sewing club . . . for which music and lectures are provided . . . special parties are held. The dining room is open to the public as a restaurant. . . . There is an employment bureau, which is kept busy by housewives in search of domestic workers. Everything is done by these Finnish servant girls themselves.[4]

Some women's organizations, like the Finnish Cooperative Home, grew out of the self-help efforts of recent arrivals. Others were organized by well-established immigrants and second-generation women for the benefit of recent arrivals. The Polish Women's alliance, described in the second selection, was one of the largest, with strong ties to the international feminist movement of the early twentieth century as well as to Polish nationalism. The Slovenian Women's Union was less ideological. Organized in 1926, its purpose was "to unite the Slovenian women living in America, to assist in their social, moral, and intellectual education, to foster American and Slovenian ideals, to encourage participation in American civic affairs, to help members to become American citizens, and to arrange an adequate interment for its deceased members."[5]

As new groups entered the country, new organizations emerged. In the 1980s highly educated, often professional women from south Asia (mainly India) formed local women's organizations. While all of these organizations were concerned with the status of women, their priorities differed. Some worked with sister organizations overseas to promote women's rights in the homeland. Others, including a lesbian group, focused on establishing a visible ethnic or sexual preference group identity. Others addressed specific problems in their communities such as domestic violence and unequal economic opportunities, offering information, counseling and crisis intervention, and social services.

Women's organizations varied in structure and program according to the social class, ethnic background, interests, and needs of their members. For cultural and economic reasons, southern Italian, Greek, and Asian women were less likely to be involved in the early decades of the twentieth century than Polish, Finnish, Jewish, and Arabic women. The poorest and most recently arrived women of every group often lacked the time and energy to participate. Well-established professional women also had trouble participating because many were already juggling the demands of family and career. Another obstacle was male opposition. A founder of the Slovenian Women's Union noted that "men eyed it as an intrusion into their domain and as something totally unnecessary. . . . A woman's place was in the home, taking care of the husband, the children, and the boarders."[6] Half a century later, "lack of support from spouses" remained a problem for the Asian Indian Women's Network of Los Angeles.[7] Despite these problems and obstacles, membership was widespread. Women joined because the organizations offered them economic benefits (insurance plans and, often, scholarships for young people), cultural and educational activities, magazines or newsletters, the opportunity to meet new people and to socialize, and the opportunity to acquire administrative, financial, and political skills.

The Ethnic Community

Women were served by ethnic institutions other than women's organizations. The most important of these was probably the ethnic church. For some women, religious institutions were of minimal importance. Some Puerto Rican women, though nominally Catholic, ignored parish life; the religion of Orthodox Jewish women focused on home rather than synagogue observances; and radical women of diverse origins were often hostile to organized religion. Still, the ethnic church played a central role in the lives of millions, including women from China, Japan, the Scandinavian countries, Ireland, southern and eastern Europe, the Caribbean, and Mexico.

Religious services provided spiritual strength, solace, and a link to the homeland. "O, so we find ourselves again in a new, holy Germany," a nineteenth-century woman rejoiced, discovering that the hymns, devotions, even the statue of Mary in her New York parish had been imported from Germany.[8] Church activities also provided an important social outlet, in some communities one of the few available to "respectable" women. Parish charities distributed food, clothing, and fuel, and the larger denominations established hospitals, orphanages, schools, employment bureaus, and "shelters" to serve their various ethnic constituencies; clergy offered advice on personal problems. In the twentieth century, churches and synagogues sponsored the resettlement of refugees from Germany, Hungary, Russia, and Vietnam.

Women benefited from sickness and burial insurance and from the social and educational programs of lodges and mutual-benefit societies, often participating through their husbands' membership or through women's auxiliaries. In 1925 there were over thirty such societies among the relatively small West Indian community of New York City, while larger immigrant communities had dozens, even hundreds in a single city.[9] Other ethnic institutions that served women were newspapers (including some edited by women), which offered advice on homemaking, childcare, Americanization, and, in some cases, feminism; cultural and literary societies, which provided opportunities for self-expression; and theaters, which offered education, sociability, and escape from the problems of everyday life. Special agencies met special needs. In the early 1920s the Central Japanese Association met Japanese brides arriving in San Francisco when the grooms were sick or lived far away. A National Desertion Bureau helped Jewish women locate missing husbands.

Far from being passive beneficiaries, women helped to create and sustain the ethnic institutions that served them. The fund raising and other supportive activities of "ladies aids" and auxiliaries were vital to the survival of ethnic churches and lodges. Orphanages, hospitals, and other institutions that served immigrant women were often founded and administered by other immigrant women of the same ethnicity and religion, though usually not the same social class. Soon after their arrival in New York in 1846, the Irish Sisters of Mercy established a residential shelter for "poor women of good character," mostly Irish, teaching them household skills and placing over eight thousand in jobs in a five-year period.[10] Elizabeth Fedde, a member of a Lutheran religious sisterhood, organized a comprehensive charity system for Norwegian immigrants in New York in the late nineteenth century, including "outdoor" relief, hospital facilities, and an ambulance service.

Immigrant women were instrumental in founding and sustaining cultural as well as charitable institutions, institutions that served not only women but all members of the community. Feminist author and playwright Theofilia Samolinska was a founder of the Polish National Alliance, one of the largest ethnic organizations, as well as the Polish Women's Alliance. Among the many women leaders in ethnic theater were Antonietta Pisanelli Alessandro, founder of the Italian theater in San Francisco, and Miriam Colon, founder of the Puerto Rican Traveling Theatre of New York. Women of many ethnic communities established not only theaters but also clubs, choirs, choral groups, dance groups, and summer camps that provided recreation for people of all ages and helped to preserve cherished ethnic traditions.

The American Community

Because the resources of the ethnic community, like those of individuals, were inadequate, immigrant women turned to the larger American community. While illness, unemployment, or the injury or death of a husband could reduce any woman to destitution, those most likely to seek public assistance were the elderly, newcomers, and single mothers. Public and private charities have often been quicker to help women than men, believing women to be natural dependents and therefore innocent victims of lazy, intemperate, or vicious husbands or fathers. In the early twentieth century aid to immigrant women was seen as a means of preventing prostitution and as an investment in the mothers (or future mothers) of future American citizens.

The form American assistance took depended more upon mainstream ideology than upon the needs of immigrant women. In the nineteenth century poverty usually was blamed on bad habits and depraved character. Consequently, the poor were usually incarcerated in grim, vermin-infested poorhouses and subjected to a rigorous, regimented, and sex-segregated regime of work, prayer, and sermons. A commission that investigated poorhouses in New York State before the Civil War reported that "common domestic animals are usually more humanely provided for than the paupers."[11] Many women preferred prostitution or semistarvation to life in these institutions.

Outdoor relief as an alternative to the poorhouse grew almost accidentally from the evangelistic activities of home missionary societies before the Civil War. Shocked by the terrible living conditions of the immigrant and native-born poor, the New York City Mission Society, the New York Female Moral Reform Society, and similar organizations began to distribute food and clothing as well as religious tracts and to advocate better housing and sanitation as well as moral improvement. Believing that women were more easily converted than men, missionaries paid special attention to them, providing "outdoor" opportunities to learn skills and earn money in sponsored workshops and residential shelters.

While the idea that poverty was caused by viciousness or laziness was never totally abandoned, the twentieth century saw less emphasis upon religious conversion and more emphasis upon improvement of the environment. Influenced by the Social Gospel popular at the turn of the century, some of the larger urban churches opened nurseries, kindergartens, clinics, classes, and other services in immigrant neighborhoods as a demonstration of Christian concern. The Salvation Army, the YWCA, the Daughters of the American Revolution, and other mainstream organizations also turned their attention to the immigrant.

The most widely publicized helping agency at the turn of the century was the settlement house. Sponsored by churches, synagogues, universities, or secular philanthropies and staffed primarily by college-educated, native-born women, settlements worked to "uplift" the urban poor through Americanization. Working mainly with women and children, settlements provided food and fuel in emergencies, but their main focus was on services such as day nurseries, kindergartens, milk stations, penny banks, libraries, sports, vocational and English classes, and a variety of clubs. Hundreds of immigrant women and their daughters belonged to women's clubs sponsored by settlement houses. In addition to providing places for women to socialize, women's clubs sponsored by settlements provided women with information on health, child care, and civic issues and, in some cases, helped them participate in local political campaigns.

In the opening decades of the twentieth century, charity work became increasingly professionalized, and social welfare became a political issue. Armed with new "scientific" studies (often conducted at settlements), professional social workers joined religious leaders, women's clubs, and others to lobby successfully for widows' pensions and workmen's compensation programs. In the decades that followed, social security, Aid to Dependent Children, food stamps, Medicare, and Medicaid were added to the list of government programs potentially useful to immigrant women. Federal funds as well as voluntary agencies assisted refugees.

Receiving Help

Destitute women were often pathetically grateful for the food, fuel, or medical care provided by individuals and agencies. Sick and lonely newcomers appreciated sympathy from helpers who could speak their language. Elizabeth Fedde's diary describes the response to her visits in 1883 to Scandinavian women in a public charity hospital: "A sick woman said to me: 'How good God is to me! He hears my sighs in a strange land and sends one to whom I can talk,' and she burst into tears; I stayed a long time with her. Another said, 'Oh, how I have waited for you!' "[12] The third selection describes the many benefits an Italian immigrant received from a Chicago settlement house in the early twentieth century, as well as her devotion to that institution and its staff.

More often, however, religious, ethnic, class, and other differences created barriers between helping agencies and women in need. So many Protestant mission societies demanded church or Sunday school attendance as the price of assistance that many Catholic and Jewish immigrants avoided all church-related agencies, including the YWCA and the Salvation Army. The failure of social agencies to hire foreign-born case workers or interpreters destroyed their usefulness to women who spoke little or no English. In 1920 New York City had one Italian-speaking social worker to serve a thousand families; Philadelphia had one social worker who spoke Italian and a little Polish to serve 526 Italian, 229 Polish, 69 Russian, and 45 other Slavic families.[13]

Many women were alienated by lack of sensitivity to their cultural background. Institutions serving eastern European Jewish women sometimes failed to provide kosher food, an omission that made them unacceptable to a large proportion of their potential clientele. Women avoided helpers whose zeal for Americanization and "scientific" methods of homemaking and childcare made them disdainful of time-honored old world traditions. Enrico Sartorio, a Protestant clergyman in the early twentieth-century Italian community, describes the encounter of southern Italian women with such "helpers":

Social workers burst into their homes and upset the usual routine of their lives, opening windows, undressing children, giving orders not to eat this and that, not to wrap babies in swaddling clothes. . . . The mother of five or six children may, with some reason, be inclined to think that she knows a little more about how to bring up children than the young-looking damsel who insists upon trying to teach her how to do it.[14]

Help often came at the price of humiliation, as described in the fourth selection. Women whose circumstances made them temporarily unable to support themselves were often treated like irresponsible minors. Destitute women in an antebellum New York shelter were required to wear clothes "suitable to the custom of the house," to give up snuff, alcohol, nicknames, loud laughter, and "the telling of indelicate stories," and to keep their rooms always open for the matron's inspection.[15] Twentieth-century women on public assistance found their budgets, homes, and personal lives supervised and subject to inspection at any hour of the day or night. Often women were helped inadequately or not at all. Amateur charities overlooked many of the neediest, and the complexity of twentieth-century bureaucratic rules and regulations discouraged many legitimate applicants. Stipends were often slow in coming or so parsimonious that the women who depended upon them were consigned to the grimmest poverty.

Some women benefited from the American relief system by using it selectively; for example, teenagers in Buffalo at the turn of the century flocked to settlement programs in basketball and cooking, but refused to attend classes in housecleaning.[16] Others manipulated the system, sending their children to Protestant day nurseries without joining the sponsoring church, getting multiple Christmas baskets from competing agencies, or supplementing meager welfare allotments with unreported part-time work. A few turned to political action, including the welfare rights movement of the 1960s, hoping to make the relief system more just and more humane for all Americans.

Community Workers

Other women have concentrated on providing alternatives. Energetic, dedicated immigrants (and daughters of immigrants) worked, and continue to work, within their ethnic communities, to provide women with practical assistance that is culturally acceptable, respectful of their autonomy, and responsive to their needs. One such woman is Korean-born Grace Lyu-Volckhausen, whose background and activities in behalf of Korean immigrant women are described in the fifth selection. First- and second-generation "community workers" have also reached out to communities other than their own, helping not only women but people of both sexes and all ages. In the final selection Chicana artist Judy Baca tells how she used mural painting to create unity and combat hopelessness among young people first in her own Los Angeles neighborhood and then in other Latino, Asian, and African-American neighborhoods across the city.

Many community workers were sensitized to the needs of others by their own experiences as "outsiders" and were conscious of their position as role models. These feelings were expressed by "Maria," a Puerto Rican social worker in the 1980s. Maria counseled teenage runaways from a variety of ethnic backgrounds, including some who were gay, who had been sexually abused, or who were drug addicts.

> I think my experiences as a Puerto Rican and as a lesbian can show other people that if I'm "making it," despite other people's prejudices, they too can make it. . . . I grew up with the stereotype that because I'm Puerto Rican I'm not capable of doing anything but carrying knives. As a lesbian social worker I have to cope with society saying I'm a freak, and belong in an institution myself. Meanwhile, I'm able to deal with people whose lives are falling apart. I'm able to give them supportive services and follow through with them.[17]

Although community work could be very rewarding, it also presented many problems. Women who were highly visible in their communities were often criticized for assuming public roles, a prerogative usually reserved for men. There were other sources of tension. Lyu-Volckhausen, Baca, "Maria," and many other community workers had received part or all of their education in mainstream institutions, which set them apart from most of the people they served. Moreover, their work often required them to mediate between mainstream officials and ethnic constituencies. A not uncommon result was criticism from both sides. Mainstream officials saw them as ethnic radicals, and envious members of their own communities accused them of "forgetting where you came from." Yet without education and the ability to deal with mainstream authorities, they could not have accomplished what they did. As Maria put it,

> you almost need to become part of the system to be able to come back and work with your own people. I've done a lot of work through the system, and I will never forget where I come from. . . .
>
> We have to understand one another and see each other as individuals who are struggling to fulfill our dreams and ideals, as we help our community.[18]

Notes

1. Hope Williams Sykes, *The Joppa Door* (New York: G. P. Putnam's Sons, 1937), pp. 158–59.

2. Anzia Yezierska, *Bread Givers* (1925; reprint, New York: George Braziller, 1975), pp. 14–15.

3. Paule Marshall, "From the Poets in the Kitchen," in Paule Marshall, *Reena and Other Stories* (New York: Feminist Press, 1983), pp. 5–7.

4. John Daniels, *America via the Neighborhood* (New York: Harper and Brothers, 1920), pp. 78–81.

5. Marie Prisland, *From Slovenia to America: Recollections and Collections* (Chicago: Slovenia Women's Union of America, 1968), p. 78.

6. Ibid.

7. Jyotsna Vaid, "Seeking a Voice: South Asian Women's Groups in North America," in *Making Waves: An Anthology of Writings by and about Asian Women*, ed. Asian Women United of California (Boston: Beacon Press, 1989), pp. 402–3.

8. Jay P. Dolan, *The Immigrant Church: New York's Irish and German Catholics, 1815–1865* (Baltimore: John Hopkins University Press, 1975), p. 77.

9. Ira De A. Reid, *The Negro Immigrant: His Background, Characteristics, and Social Adjustment, 1899–1937* (New York: Columbia University Press, 1939), p. 156; and Alice G. Masaryk, "The Bohemians in Chicago," *Charities*, December 3, 1904, p. 208.

10. Dolan, *Immigrant Church*, p. 132.

11. David J. Rothman and Sheila M. Rothman, *On Their Own: The Poor in Modern America* (Reading, Mass.: Addison-Wesley, 1972), p. x.

12. "Elizabeth Fedde's Diary, 1883–88," trans. and ed. Beulah Folkedahl, *Norwegian American Studies* 20 (1945): 184.

13. Sophonisba Breckinridge, *New Homes for Old* (New York: Harper and Brothers, 1921), pp. 282–83.

14. Enrico Sartorio, *Social and Religious Life of Italians in America* (Boston: Christopher, 1918), p. 58.

15. Terry Coleman, *Going to America* (New York: Pantheon Books, 1972), pp. 160–61.

16. Mary E. Remington, *Annual Report of Welcome Hall, 1909–1910* (Buffalo, N.Y.: Mathew Northrop, 1910), p. 12.

17. "Maria," "I'm Climbing That Mountain!" (oral history) in *Compañeras: Latina Lesbians (An Anthology)*, ed. Juanita Ramos (New York: Latina Lesbian History Project, 1987), p. 243.

18. Ibid., p. 244.

1

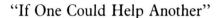

"If One Could Help Another"

Sharing the hardships and uncertainties of immigrations, women like Kristina and Ulrika in Vilhelm Moberg's novel, Unto a Good Land (the sequel to The Emigrants), reached out to one another. In the first excerpt the respectable wife Kristina recognizes the interdependence of all their traveling partners, including even the prostitute Ulrika, whom she had formerly scorned. Kristina helps Ulrika on the journey, and the two become friends. Several months later it is Ulrika's turn to help Kristina. In a passage describing a difficult childbirth in the isolation of the Minnesota frontier, Ulrika draws upon her own childbearing experiences to give Kristina medical care and emotional support that her husband cannot provide. The bond between Kristina and Ulrika, though fictional, is an example of the helping relationships that grew between many immigrant women, relationships that were sometimes institutionalized in women's clubs and charitable organizations.

"The Last Loaf"

The children whined for food, and for the third time since leaving Albany Kristina brought out the food basket. By now there was not much left of their provisions from Sweden—a couple of rye loaves, a dried sausage, the end of a cheese, and a piece of dried leg of lamb. But these were precious scraps and must be carefully rationed. They could buy no food in the railroad wagon; those without food baskets must starve.

From Karl Oskar's purchase in New York Kristina had saved two wheat rolls for the children, from one of the rye loaves she cut slices for her husband, brother-in-law, and herself, and among them she divided the sausage the best she could. The rye bread was dry and hard, and she had been unable to scrape away all the mildew. But they all ate as if partaking of fresh Christmas bread. . . .

Kristina's hand, still holding the bread knife, fell on her knee: there were two hungry people in her company who had nothing to eat, Ulrika of

---

Source: Vilhelm Moberg, *Unto a Good Land* (New York: Simon and Schuster, 1954), pp. 63–66, 212–23. Copyright © 1954 by, Vilhelm Moberg. Reprinted by permission of SIMON AND SCHUSTER, a division of Gulf and Western Corporation.

Västergöhl and her daughter Elin. They belonged to Danjel's household and she shared his food throughout the journey. But now their food basket was empty, now Ulrika and her daughter must sit and look on while others ate their meal.

Kristina could not help feeling sorry for her! as she now shared her food with all the others, could she pass by Ulrika and her brat? It said in the Bible to break one's bread with the hungry.

Kristina had only one bread loaf left, one single loaf. Must she cut this for the Glad One's sake? She had a hungry husband, brother-in-law with a heavy appetite, and three small children, lean and pale, who needed regular meals. She did not know when they might be able to buy more food. Could God mean that she ought to take the bread from her own poor children and give it to a person like Ulrika, a harlot, an evil creature? How she had insulted other women, this Ulrika of Västergöhl! How detested and looked down on she had been in the home parish! And how Kristina had suffered from being forced to travel in her company! If she now offered the infamous whore food from her own basket, then it would be as if she invited her as a guest to her own table. . . .

Kristina's heart beat faster, so greatly was she perturbed. Should she cut the last loaf—or should she save it? She had a vague feeling that what she did now would be of great importance to all of them. She had a foreboding that fundamental changes awaited them in this new land, everything seemed different from home, they were forced to act in new and unaccustomed ways. And as they now were driven through strange country, with everything around them foreign and unknown, they were more closely united—it seemed more and more as if they were one single family. . . .

Kristina's hand took a firmer hold of the knife handle—but this was the children's bread. They were weak and needed every bite. She thought, you cannot take it away from them! To cut that bread is like cutting your own flesh. The Glad One is big and strong, vulgar and forward, she will always manage, she'll never starve to death. It's different with your helpless little ones. If there were plenty of food, more than they needed, then . . . Now—never!

But it couldn't go on like this. They couldn't continue to hurt each other. They were all of them poor wretched creatures, lost in the New World; no one knew what awaited them in this new country, no one knew what they might have to suffer. One loaf would save no one's life in the long run. And if one could help another . . . Help thy neighbor. The Glad One too was her neighbor. . . .

She took out the last loaf, cut generous slices, and handed them to Ulrika of Västergöhl and her daughter: Wouldn't they please share her bread? It was old and dry, but she had scraped off the mildew as best she could. . . .

Kristina herself began to eat and she wondered: What would the people at home think of this? What would they say, if they could see her cut her last loaf from home in order to share with Ulrika of Västergöhl, the parish whore?

Childbed in the North American Forest

[Several months later . . .]

"It's my time, Karl Oskar."

"Do you think so?"

"Yes. It couldn't be anything else."

He looked at her in foolish surprise. "But—isn't it too soon?"

"Fourteen days too soon."

"Yes, that's what I thought. . . . Then we must get someone right away!"

He had just finished pulling off his boots, now he pulled them on again quickly. Where could he find a woman to help? Who out here could act as midwife? At home she had had both her mother and mother-in-law at her childbeds. But here—a married woman, a settler woman who spoke their language—there was hardly a one. . . .

"I had better get Swedish Anna. But it will take a few hours."

"You needn't go so far," Kristina said. "Get Ulrika."

"What? Ulrika of Västergöhl?

"Yes. I asked her at the housewarming."

"You want the Glad One to be with you?"

"She promised me."

Karl Oskar was stamping on his right boot, and he stopped, perplexed: The Glad One was considered as good as anyone here, no one spoke ill of her now. Both he and Kristina had made friends with her, had accepted her in their company. But he had not imagined that his wife would call for Ulrika of Västergöhl to be with her at childbed, he had not thought she would want her so close. Yet she had already bespoken her—the woman she had wanted to exclude as a companion on their journey. She would never have done this at home; there a decent wife would never have allowed the public whore to attend her at childbirth.

Kristina rose and began preparing the bed: "Don't you think Ulrika can manage?"

"Yes! Yes, of course! I only thought. . ." Perhaps it was as well, perhaps it was fortunate that she was within call when a midwife was needed. She should know the requirements at such a function, she had borne four children of her own, she should know what took place at childbirth. Ulrika had health and strength, she was cleanly. She would probably make a good midwife. She could help a wedded woman, even though all her own children had been born out of wedlock. What wouldn't do at home would have to do here; here each one did as best he could, and they must rely on someone capable, regardless of her previous life.

Karl Oskar now was surprised at himself for not having thought of Ulrika. "I shall fetch her as fast as I can run. . . ."

A hundred yards from the cabin they stopped short at the sound of a scream. Both listened intently; it wasn't a bird on the lake, it was a human voice, a voice Karl Oskar recognized: "It's Kristina!"

He ran ahead as fast as his legs could carry him. . . .

Kristina was lying on her side in the bed, her body twisting as she shrieked and moaned.

"Kristina! How is it?"

"It's bad. Where is Ulrika? I've been waiting so. . ."

"We hurried as much as we could." Karl Oskar took hold of his wife's hand: it was clammy with perspiration; her eyes were wide open, she turned them slowly to her husband: "Isn't Ulrika with you?"

Ulrika had thrown off her shawl and now stepped up to the bed, pushing Karl Oskar aside: "Here I am. Good evening, Kristina. Now we'll help each other."

"Ulrika! God bless you for coming."

"How far along are you? Any pushing pains yet?"

"Only the warning pains, I think. But—oh my dear, sweet Ulrika! Why did you take so long?. . ."

Ulrika pulled down the blanket and felt Kristina's body with her hands, lightly touching her lower abdomen; then she asked: Had the birthwater come, and how long between the last pains? While Karl Oskar undressed the children and tucked them in, and rekindled the fire, the two women spoke together: they understood each other with few words, they had gone through the same number of childbeds, four each; they were united and close through their like experience.

"It feels large," said Ulrika after the examination.

"I have thought—perhaps its twins."

"Haven't you had twins before?"

"Lill-Märta's twin brother was taken from us when he was fourteen days old."

"It runs in the family. Karl Oskar. Get me some light. Heat water over the fire. Be of some use!"

Ulrika assumed command in the cabin, and Karl Oskar speedily performed as he was told to do. It was not his custom to take orders, but tonight at his wife's childbed he was glad someone told him what to do.

From dry pine wood he made such a roaring fire that it lighted the bed where Kristina lay, comforted by her helping-woman in between the pains. . . .

Karl Oskar had never before been present at childbirth; at home the women had taken care of everything and never let him inside until all was over. He didn't feel too much for other people—sometimes his insensibility made him feel guilty—but his wife's cries of agony cut right through him, he could scarcely stand it.

"You look pale as a curd, Karl Oskar," said Ulrika. "Go outside for a while. You're of no use here. . . .

Karl Oskar Nilsson spent most of the night in the byre, lost and baffled, talking to his borrowed cow; he felt he had been sent to "stand in the corner," he didn't know what to do with himself. He had been told to go out— he was driven out of his own house and home. The Ljuder Parish whore was master in his house tonight.

After a few hours he went to inquire how the birth was progressing. Kristina lay silent, her eyes closed. Ulrika sat by the bed, she whispered to him: He must walk quietly, she had just gone through another killing pain. Things went slowly, the brat did not seem to move at all. The real birth-water hadn't come yet, and the pushing pains had not yet set in. This birth didn't go according to rule, not as it should; something was wrong. . . . But there was no use explaining to him; he wouldn't understand anyway.

"I wonder how long. . ."

No one could say how long it would take; maybe very long. . . .

Kristina had dozed off between the pains; she moaned at intervals: "Ulrika . . . Are you here?"

"Yes. I'm here. You want something to drink?"

Ulrika gave her a mug of warm milk into which she had mixed a spoonful of sugar.

Kristina dozed again when the pains abated. She had always had easy births—what she went through this night surpassed all the pain she had ever experienced in her young life. But she felt succor and comfort close by now: a little while ago she had been lying here alone in the dark, alone in the whole world, alone with her pains, no one to talk to—no one except her whimpering children. Now she had Ulrika, a compassionate women, a sister, a blessed helper.

There was so much she wanted to tell Ulrika, but she didn't have the strength now, not tonight. She had lived with Ulrika in bitter enmity—she remembered that time when Ulrika had called her a "proud piece." Ulrika had been right. She had been proud. Many times, at home, she'd met unmarried Ulrika of Västergöhl on the roads without greeting her. She was the younger of the two, she should have greeted her first with a curtsy. Instead she had stared straight ahead as if not seeing a soul. . . .

Yes, all this she must tell Ulrika—some other time—when she was able to, when this agony was over. Oh, why didn't it pass? Wouldn't she soon be

delivered? Wouldn't God spare her? It went on so long . . . so long. . . .
"Oh, help! Ulrika, help!"

The pains were upon her; she felt as if she were bursting into pieces,
splitting in halves lengthwise. A wild beast was tearing her with its claws,
tearing her insides, digging into her, digging and twisting. . . .

Ulrika was near, bending over her. The young wife threw herself
from side to side in the bed, her hands fumbling for holds. "Oh! Dear God!
Dear God!"

"The pushing pains are beginning," Ulrika said encouragingly. "Then
it'll soon be over."

"Dear sweet, hold me! Give me something to hold on to!"

Kristina let out piercing cries, without being aware of it. The billowing
pains rose within her—and would rise still higher, before they began to sub-
side. In immeasurable pain she grasped the older woman. She held Ulrika
around the waist with both arms and pressed her head into the full bosom.
And she was received with kind, gentle arms.

Kristina and Ulrika embraced like two devoted sisters. They were back
at humanity's beginning here tonight, at the childbed in the North American
forest. They were only two women, one to give life and one to help her; one
to suffer and one to comfort; one seeking help in her pain, one in compassion
sharing the pain. . . .

Ulrika was shaking Karl Oskar by the shoulder; he had dozed off
for a while. The night was far gone, daylight was creeping in through
the windows.

The midwife was calling the father—now she would see what use he
could make of his hands.

Kristina's body was now helping in the labor, Ulrika said. Her pushing
muscles were working, she was about to be delivered. But this last part was
no play-work for her; Karl Oskar might imagine how it would hurt her when
the child kicked itself out of her, tearing her flesh to pieces, breaking her in
two. While this took place it would lessen her struggle if she could hold on
to him, as she, Ulrika, had to receive the baby and couldn't very well be in
two places at the same time.

Karl Oskar went up to the head of the bed and took a firm hold around
his wife's shoulders . . .

"The head is coming! Hold her firmly. I'll take the brat." Ulrika's
hands were busy. "A great big devil! If it isn't two!"

Karl Oskar noticed something moving, something furry, with black,
shining, drenched hair. And he saw a streak of dark-red blood.

The birth-giving wife clung convulsively to her husband, seeking his
embrace in her deepest agony. Severe, slow tremblings shook her body, not
unlike those moments when her body was joined with his—and from moments of lust had grown moments of agony.

While the mates this time embraced, their child came into the world.

A hair-covered crown appeared, a brow, a nose, a chin—the face of a human being: Ulrika held in her hands a living, kicking, red-skinned little creature. . . .

"On the hearth! Hand me the wool shears, Karl Oskar!"

With the old, rusty wool shears Ulrika cut the blood-red cord which still united mother and child.

Then she made that most important inspection of the newborn: "He is shaped like his father. It's a boy! . . ."

She handed the child to the father; they had no steelyard here, but she guessed he weighed at least twelve pounds. Ulrika herself had borne one that weighed thirteen and a half. She knew; the poor woman who had to squeeze out such a lump did not have an easy time. Ulrika had prayed to God to save her—an unmarried woman—from bearing such big brats; the Lord ought to reserve that honor for married women, it was easier for them to increase mankind with sturdy plants. And the Lord had gracefully heard her prayer— He had taken the child to Him before he was three months old.

Thus for the first time Oskar had been present at childbed—at the birth of his third son—his fourth, counting the twin who had died. . . .

Ulrika warmed some bath water for the newborn, then she held him in the pot and splashed water over his body while he yelled. And her eyes took in the child with satisfaction all the while—she felt as if he had been her own handiwork.

She said: "The boy was made in Sweden, but we must pray God this will have no ill effect on him."

Kristina had lain quiet after her delivery. Now she asked Karl Oskar to put on the coffeepot.

She had put aside a few handfuls of coffee beans for her childbed; Ulrika had neither drunk nor eaten since her arrival last evening, they must now treat her to coffee.

"Haven't you got anything stronger, Karl Oskar?" Ulrika asked. "Kristina must have her delivery schnapps. She has earned it this evil night."

The delivery schnapps was part of the ritual, Karl Oskar remembered; he had given it to Kristina at her previous childbeds. And this time she needed it more than ever. There were a few swallows left in the keg of American brännvin Jonas Petter had brought to the house-warming.

"I think you could stand a drink yourself," Ulrika said to Karl Oskar.

She finished washing the baby and handed him to the impatient mother. Meanwhile Karl Oskar prepared the coffee and served it on top of an oak-stump chair at Kristina's bedside. He offered a mug to Ulrika, and the three of them enjoyed the warming drink. The whisky in the keg was also divided three ways—to the mother, the midwife, and the child's father. . . .

The child is handed to the mother—it had left her and it has come back.

All is over, all is quiet, all is well.

Kristina lies with her newborn son at her breast. She lies calm and silent, she is delivered, she has changed worlds, she is in the newly delivered woman's blissful world. It is the Glad One—the public whore of the home parish—her intimate friend, who has delivered her.

2

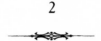

"Let Us Join Hands": The Polish Women's Alliance

There has been little research on immigrant women's organizations, though these organizations enrolled hundreds of thousands of women and played (and continue to play) important roles in the ethnic and American communities. Thaddeus C. Radzialowski's article on the largest Polish women's organization, excerpted below, is a welcome exception. Radzialowski describes the origins, activities, and ideas of the Polish Women's Alliance (ZPA), during the Progressive Era, the period of heaviest Polish immigration.

Radzialowski's article shows how immigrant women helped to educate and Americanize one another. His description of the ZPA's liberal political stance and its commitment to feminism is especially important because it destroys the stereotype of the European Catholic immigrant woman as unquestioningly subservient to the Church and impervious to the social causes that moved so many other American women during the Progressive Era. According to the ZPA journal, Glos Polek, the mere existence of the organization was a feminist statement: "Today's women who care about their independence understand that . . . only in a woman's organization will their ideas, their feelings and wills dominate." An understanding of the nationalist-progressive-feminist ideology of the ZPA at the turn of the century sheds light on the social and political commitments of contemporary Polish-American women like Barbara Mikulski of Baltimore, an activist in the Polish-American community, the Democratic party, and the women's movement. (See Part 8, selection 4.)

The Polish Women's Alliance was born at a meeting held in April, 1898, in the Chicago home of Stefania Chmielinska. This meeting was followed by a series of others in the spring and summer which culminated in the

Source: From *Review Journal of Philosophy and Social Science*, Volume 2, (Winter, 1977) No. 2, pp. 183–203. Reprinted by permission of author and publisher.

incorporation of a Polish Women Society with eleven charter members on August 5, 1898. . . . The organization grew to 21 groups in 1902 and 28 groups and 1400 members by June, 1903. It had acquired a charter and incorporated under the laws of the State of Illinois in 1902, and it had also established by that time a monthly newspaper *Glos Polek* (Voice of Polish Women) and a special Education Division *(Wydzial Oswiatowy)*. . . .

The women who founded and led the ZPA were initially drawn from the very small number of middle class women, many of whom had been educated in Europe, in the Polish immigrant community. . . .

The majority of the women who became members of the organization were, however, from the working class, although more than likely from the most literate and ambitious members of it. Many were doubtlessly attracted to the health and death insurance benefits available to members of the ZPA as well as the cultural activities of the organization. . . .

Stefania Laudyn, one of the most talented of *Glos Polek's* editors, clearly saw the organization as a unique fusion of women of the working class and the intelligentsia. In an editorial in *Glos Polek* she called for the solidarity of all Polish women:

> Let us join hands—women who do hard labor and women of words and thoughts—let us believe in each other, let us respect each other's work. . . . (Women of) all classes, ranks and conditions (forward) to the clearing of the road to enlightenment and the future! Let us not divide but unite; let us not destroy but shape and create what Polish women want and desire.

The single most important activity to which the Polish Women's Alliance devoted itself was the education of Polish women and children. This work was carried on in a variety of ways. The group established a reading room for women in Chicago which contained books, newspapers and journals, especially women's magazines from Europe and America. Staffed by volunteers the library was open two evenings a week for members. Through its Education Division, the Alliance conducted schools in Polish language, history, and culture and conducted summer camps for Polish immigrant children from the cities. Local branches of the Alliance and individual members who could afford it established schools in homes and meeting halls to teach girls and young women skills such as typing, sewing, and hat making so that they might enhance their chances of finding decent work. These informal schools also helped the young immigrant women to improve their literacy and to learn something about the national history and culture.

The ZPA's newspaper, *Glos Polek* (which reappeared as a weekly in 1910 after a seven years hiatus), was its most significant instrument of education and socialization of the immigrants. With a readership that far exceeded its membership (over 23,000 by 1917), the newspaper had an important impact on the women of the growing Polish American community. Its columns were given over to didactic articles on organizing and running a household, cook-ing, advice to consumers on a variety of matters, on health and how to main-tain it and on raising children. The newspaper also ran as part of its regular format features on the lives of famous women, especially Polish heroines and writers, signed articles on foreign and domestic affairs and poems, serialized novels and stories as well as a special children's "corner."

The history of women, their contemporary struggle for justice and rights in the western world and their problems in other parts of the world were central issues in the news columns, the signed articles and on the edi-torial pages of *Glos Polek*. The paper ran columns entitled "Women's Chron-icle" *(Kronika Kobieca)* dealing with the accomplishments of contemporary women from around the world and "From the Women's Movement" (Z. Ru-chu Kobiecego) which concentrated on news on the struggle for votes, ad-mission to universities, medical schools and law schools and other feminist issues of the day. Side by side with these regular features *Glos Polek* ran spe-cial stories on subjects such as the beginnings of a new role for women in Turkey, Persia, and China, on the history of women in medicine, especially on the work of Dr. Maria Zakrzewska, and on leaders of the battle for political rights such as the Pankhursts and Susan B. Anthony. On the edito-rial pages, the editors frequently commented on women's issues and the progress of feminist causes. The immigrant readers of the weekly edition of *Glos Polek* were probably as knowledgeable about the problems and activ-ities of contemporary women as any group of people in America. Further-more, they received the news in a context highly sympathetic to the political and social progress of women and in a newspaper controlled and run entirely by women.

In spite of the commitment to feminist causes and support for women's movements worldwide, the Polish Women's Alliance developed few contacts with feminist organizations and activists in the U.S. There appear to be sev-eral reasons for this failure to make common cause with their American sis-ters. First, they were separated from English speaking women by the barriers of language and culture. Second, the problems of the immigrant community were so massive and compelling that much of the energy of the Polish women had to be directed to their alleviation. Third, their feminism was inextrica-bly tied to a sense of Polish identity and nationalism. This gave their views an unusual perspective which their American sisters could not share nor per-haps even comprehend.

The leadership of the Polish Women's Alliance had a strong sense of themselves as members of both an oppressed sex and an oppressed people. The societies which repressed them as women also tried to crush them as Poles. They had a strong sense of special mission as a saving remnant to pre-serve a culture that was the object of systematic attempts at obliteration by Germans and Russians. We must "join together, organize" wrote the editor of *Glos Polek* in setting down the goals of the society in 1910, for "we believe profoundly and feel intensely in our Polish souls the command that the Polish woman must so protect the environment in which the souls of her loved ones develop" that they will "always remain faithful to fatherland and people."

The Polish Women's Alliance . . . developed a very ambiguous attitude toward the Catholic Church. On the one hand, the ZPA appeared to be favorably disposed to the Church. The ZPA publicly acknowledged the Church as the single most important agency in the Polish community and regarded it as crucial to preserving and propagating national identity and moral uplift among the immigrants.

However, the positivist tradition out of which the intellectual leaders came was strongly tinged by anti-clericalism . . . and the organization itself did not hold back from criticism or ridicule of the church hierarchy's position on women's issues. For example, in response to an editorial in the Dziennik Chicagoski, a newspaper edited by the Resurrectionist Fathers, which allowed that the "Church has nothing against and certainly does not condemn equal rights for women, except that it is necessary that women be mature enough for them," the editors of *Glos Polek* shot back defiantly:

> Ha . . . a people become ready for freedom when they get it, as the Negroes grew into it when they were emancipated, as the Chinese matured when they won freedom for themselves. In the area of rights everything must be taken and one must never wait to be given (them) for they will never be given. And so with Woman when she struggles for a right she must win it and take it.

The Polish Women's Alliance through its newspaper, its Education Division and its resolutions at national conventions took positions on a variety of public issues which clearly aligned it with the general currents of progressivism in the United States prior to World War I. In almost all areas the stands the Alliance took reflected its dual orientation. For example, the ZPA took strong and consistent stands against the liquor interests and urged sobriety on its readers and their families and prohibition on the society. On the one hand it opposed liquor because alcoholism among men led to abuse and neglect of women and children and, of course, this was a serious problem in the immigrant community. In addition, however, the Alliance also had a specifically nationalist response to the alcoholism problem. In an article entitled "Whiskey and We" (*Wodka i My*) *Glos Polek* saw the issue in terms of national survival. . . .

The Alliance newspaper followed the same pattern of double opinions in regard to its views of education. Strongly under the influence of Jean Jacques Rousseau, whom they quoted often, the editors of *Glos Polek* argued for summer camps in rural or wilderness areas as necessary for genuine education. Communing with nature, they felt, led to the development of the proper emotional and moral sentiments in the child. In the schools, *Glos Polek* favored a change from the harsh traditional regimen to a more humane system which treated each child as an individual and a thinking rational individual at that. The editors were totally opposed to physical punishment of the children in the schools and at home as well.

In regard to the education of women the Alliance took a strong feminist position. Women were to receive whatever education they wished and no educational institutions or courses of study should be closed to them. Women were urged especially to study science and mathematics even if they did not make careers in those areas for such knowledge was useful in modern life. . . .

In looking at education from the perspective of Polish immigrants, the women of the Alliance focused on its practical aspects. Poles should keep their children in school as long as possible for in the United States those people without education above the elementary level were doomed to spend their lives in manual labor. If the Poles were to succeed individually and collectively in America, they would have to take advantage of the educational opportunities the country offered. Keeping children in school had other benefits also. It kept them out of the hideous factories and sweatshops that exploited child labor and it provided the possibility of a future educated and professional class of American Poles who would enhance the good name of the group and who would preserve its culture and identity.

As Feminists, as representatives of an ethnic group whose members were largely laborers and as persons who believed in a progressive and humane society, the ZPA was often found championing the rights of workers, especially of women and children employed in the mines and mills. They reported many of the strikes of women workers and supported them enthusiastically. They deplored the "hunger and want" often facing strikers and condemned the "barbarous abuse" of women and children by the police during strikes. The condition of workers and the abuse and exploitation they suffered, especially Polish workers, led *Glos Polek* to a condemnation of the American industrial system and even of the country itself. After a disaster in the spring of 1911, in the Pennsylvania anthracite fields, the paper after denouncing the "indifference of the capitalists" asked rhetorically "How many of our brothers are lost in those gloomy pits, condemned to death by the frightful greed of the exploiters and the indifference of the government."

Earlier the same year *Glos Polek* in a tone of great bitterness noted that Poles brought to this country "their strength, health, youth," that "capital of our land" which "built the well-being and wealth of this nation." In return they received the lowest possible wages, discrimination, lack of rights and dangerous conditions which took their lives and crippled them. . . . In 1916, *Glos Polek* concluded sadly that "the lot of the workers is indeed heavy in the famous land of freedom. . . . The economy of this free country sacrifices a greater number of lives than the war in Europe."

The ZPA did not affiliate with any political party but it watched closely the positions taken by all the parties on women's issues. It probably agreed with the socialists more than with any other party and certainly had more faith in the sincerity of their belief in women's rights. . . .

The readers of *Glos Polek* were also treated periodically to an expose of the unfavourable stereotypes and the subtler forms of discrimination which resulted from the long subordination of women. It did not hesitate to attack the age old prejudices which men used to justify prostitution and refused to accept as valid images of women as temptresses who inspired lust and lured men to ruin. The terrible curse of venereal disease would only cease its ravages when men were willing to practice the same moral standards that they prescribed for women. This double standard which was symbolic and symptomatic of the social inferiority of women would only end when women assumed full equality. "The contemporary woman" wrote Dr. Budzinska-Terlecka in the pages of *Glos Polek*, "the liberated, awakened woman—a person in the full meaning of that word, does not recognize the double morality, which is lenient for men and absolutely rigorous for women. . . ."

In its first two decades of existence the Polish Women's Alliance grew from a handful of women to an organization of almost 24,000 women. As an insurance company run entirely by women it provided desperately needed health insurance to immigrant families and death benefits to husbands and orphaned children of its members. The grateful letters of bereaved husbands who received assistance and moral support from the women of the organization as well as an insurance settlement, testify to the effectiveness of the ZPA. As an ethnic organization it helped to socialize Polish immigrant women to the American city. It taught them new ways of cooking, cleaning, childcare, and explained health and hygiene to them. Through its newspaper and its local meetings it urged on its members the wisdom of saving for the future, avoiding needless spending, acquiring training and job skills, shunning gambling and excessive use of alcohol and other traits usually subsumed under the misnamed 'puritan ethic'. As a nationalist organization, it struggled to preserve national language and culture and teach them to immigrants who were denied the right to know them by foreign overlords. Finally, it sought to mobilize their energies to win back the homeland one day. As a Feminist organization, the ZPA educated its largely working class membership to the accomplishments of women in the past and present and to the potentialities of women in a future wherein 'the hitherto stunted soul of woman' was liberated and she took her place in human society as a full human being. Far more willing than their American counterparts to accept and even glory in women's 'traditional' roles as wives and mothers, the women of the Alliance nevertheless battled as fiercely for political rights and full educational and career opportunities for women. . . .

3

————◆◆◆————

Rosa and the Chicago Commons: "How Can I Not Love America?"

In recent years scholars have debated whether the middle-class Americans who worked in agencies that helped immigrants (and other minorities) were motivated by altruism or by a desire to satisfy their own egos and keep the poor "in their place." The next two selections provide contrasting views on the issue. Here Rosa, an Italian immigrant, describes her positive experiences at a Chicago settlement in the early twentieth century. Chicago Commons is Rosa's workplace, the center of her social life, the school in which she learns to speak English, and the caretaker of her family when she becomes ill.

That lady—she wore a nice red blouse—she got a little work for me in the new settlement house. I started to wash the clothes for the residents and cleaned around the building and helped the cook—anything they told me. But when I first started that job—scrubbing the floors in the Commons—I was still *so* afraid of the teachers. And one day, I didn't see it, but a hole in my apron caught hold of one of those iron curls on a big lamp that was standing on the floor and that lamp fell over. I heard the crash and I looked around and when I saw that beautiful pink glass lamp shade in a million pieces on the floor I fell over in a faint. I thought I would be put in jail! I thought I would be killed! Miss May and one other teacher, they came running to see what had happened. When they saw me there on the floor without my senses they woke me up and carried me into the kitchen and made me drink hot tea with sugar in it. "Rosa! Rosa!" they said. "Where are you hurt? Where did it hit you?" And when they learned that I had only fainted from scare because I had broken the pink glass lamp they started to laugh. "But Rosa," they said, "you did a good thing! That lamp was terrible! Somebody gave it

Source: ROSA: THE LIFE OF AN ITALIAN IMMIGRANT by Marie Hall Ets. Copyright © 1970 by the University of Minnesota. University of Minnesota Press, Minneapolis.

to us, so we had to keep it. But now it's gone and we won't ever have to see it again. You did good! We're glad it's broken!"

Think of those angel women! They didn't scold me or anything. They were giving me hot tea with sugar in it and patting my shoulder and telling me they were glad. How can I *not* love America! In the old country I would have been killed for breaking a lamp like that!

So after that time of the pink glass lamp I said to myself, "Oh, I hope I do my work good so I never have to leave this place! I'm never going to leave!" And I truly never did. Forty or fifty years I've been scrubbing the floors, cleaning the rooms, doing the cooking, and telling the stories in the Commons. I grew old with that building. I love it like another home. I know every board in the floors, and I think those little boards know me too. Now I am old, I only have the little job to do the cooking when the regular cook is off. But even if they didn't pay me I would not want to stop working in the Commons. Never! . . .

In that time us poor women, we didn't have any pleasures—no movies, no shows, no this, no that. . . .

Rushing-the-can like the men, that's all the pleasure the poor women had in that time. In the summer when it was so hot you couldn't stay in those buildings, the women and the boys and girls and babies were sitting down in the street and alley. All the women would bring down their chairs and sit on the sidewalk. Then somebody would say, "All the women put two cents and we'll get the beer." So everybody did and the children would run by the saloon and get the can of beer. . . . That's all the pleasure we had—the cool from the beer in summer. Even when we started the club in the settlement, the women in the alley were drinking beer.

After not long, one lady from the settlement house—she was American but she could talk German too—she asked me if I wanted to go round the neighborhood with her and ask all the women to come and start the woman's club. Those women didn't know what it was, but they wanted to come anyway. Oh, I remember there was one lady—everybody knew her—she was tall, tall, about six and a half feet, with red hair. She was really a lamp post on the street. That woman, for one dime she would choke the Devil, so stingy she was for the money. And bad! Everybody was scared of that lady. She had the saloon and she was getting drunk herself, and she was swearing terrible and chasing the children. She fought with everybody. Mis' Reuter, she said to me "We're going in the saloon and ask that lady."

"Sure not, Mis' Reuter!" I said. "If she comes in the club the other women won't—they'd be too scared."

But Mis' Reuter, I guess she went sometime when I didn't know it and asked that lady anyway, because one day here she was in the club. The other women were saying, "She's in our club? She's coming in our club? What are we going to do?"

That lady, in two or three weeks, she changed from a devil to a lamb—honest to goodness! She got good. When it was her turn she was the first one to go and wash the dishes and make the coffee. And she was talking nice to the women to make them laugh, so they would like her. She got to be the best one of all. And when she moved to California the woman's club were so sorry they gave her a big farewell party. . . .

In the first beginning we always came in the club and made two circles in the room. One circle was for those ladies who could talk English and the other circle was for the ladies who talked German. Mis' Reuter talked German to the German ladies, and Miss Gray talked English to the other ladies. But I guess they both did the same preaching. They used to tell us that it's not nice to drink the beer, and we must not let the baby do this, and this. Me, I was the only Italian woman—where were they going to put me? I couldn't talk German, so I went in the English Circle. So after we had about an hour, or an hour and a half of preaching, they would pull up the circle and we'd play the games together. All together we played the games—the Norwegian, the German, the English, and me. Then we'd have some cake and coffee and the goodnight song.

One nice lady, Miss Chase, she used to teach the girls and the women to sew. Some young girls were ready to get married and they had never held a needle before. And Miss Chase, she'd teach them to make their own wedding dress. She was teaching me to sew too. She was a wonderful lady, Miss Chase, but she died after one year. . . .

Pretty soon they started the classes to teach us poor people to talk and write in English. The talk of the people in the settlement house was different entirely than what I used to hear. I used to love those American people, and I was listening and listening how they talked. That's how I learned to talk such good English. Oh, I was glad when I learned enough English to go by the priest in the Irish church and confess myself and make the priest understand what was the sin! But I never learned to do the writing in English. I all the time used to come to that class so tired and so sleepy after scrubbing and washing the whole day—I went to sleep when they starting the writing. I couldn't learn it. They had the clubs for the children too; my little girls loved to go. And after a few years when they started the kindergarten, my Luie was one of the first children to go in. . . .

I have to tell about another good thing the settlement house did for me. That winter my [baby] Leo died we were still living in that little wooden house in the alley. All my walls were thick with frosting from the cold, and I got the bronchitis on the lungs, with blood coming up. So one of those good ladies from the Commons, she arranged and sent me to a kind of home in the country where people go to get well. They had the nice nurses in that place and they cured me up good. I had a good time there too—I was all the time telling stories to entertain the other sick ladies.

In those weeks I was gone, Chicago Commons helped my husband take care of the children, and my family moved into a good building. That building in front of where we were living had the empty rooms good and dry. But when my husband asked the manager, he said, "No, I don't let no Italians in!"

So Dr. Taylor, he went himself downtown, or someplace, and saw the owner to that building. The owner said yes, the manager has to let my husband in. The rent was no more, and there we were the only—or almost the only—Italian family in the neighborhood that time, and the Germans and Norwegians were afraid to let us come in their buildings. But Chicago Commons took care of us. . . .

4

"The Free Vacation House"

"The Free Vacation House," a short story by Anzia Yezierska, a Jewish immigrant, dates from the same period as the previous selection. But unlike Rosa, who expresses nothing but gratitude for the help provided by her neighborhood settlement house, Yezierska suggests that social workers were anything but helpful. These contrasting views of the interaction between immigrant women and American agencies are important because they were widely shared; many immigrants probably alternated between one view and the other. This selection, like the one before it, is important also because it provides insight into how it felt—and feels—to be helped.

How came it that I went to the free vacation house was like this:

One day the visiting teacher from the school comes to find out for why don't I get the children ready for school in time; for why are they so often late.

I let out on her my whole bitter heart. I told her my head was on wheels from worrying. When I get up in the morning, I don't know on what to turn first: should I nurse the baby, or make Sam's breakfast, or attend on the older children. I only got two hands.

"My dear woman," she says, "you are about to have a nervous breakdown. You need to get away to the country for a rest and vacation."

Source: Anzia Yezierska, "The Free Vacation House," in *Hungry Hearts* (Boston and New York: Houghton Mifflin, 1920), pp. 97–113.

"Gott im Himmel!" says I. "Don't I know I need a rest? But how? On what money can I go to the country?"

"I know of a nice country place for mothers and children that will not cost you anything. It is free."

"Free! I never heard from it."

"Some kind people have made arrangements so no one need pay," she explains.

Later, in a few days, I just finished up with Masha and Mendel and Frieda and Sonya to send them to school, and I was getting Aby ready for kindergarten, when I hear a knock on the door, and a lady comes in. She had a white starched dress like a nurse and carried a black satchel in her hand.

"I am from the Social Betterment Society," she tells me. "You want to go to the country?"

Before I could say something, she goes over to the baby and pulls out the rubber nipple from her mouth, and to me, she says, "You must not get the child used to sucking this; it is very unsanitary."

"Gott im Himmel!" I beg the lady. "Please don't begin with that child, or she'll holler my head off. She must have the nipple. I'm too nervous to hear her scream like that."

When I put the nipple back again in the baby's mouth, the lady takes herself a seat, and then takes out a big black book from her satchel. Then she begins to question me. What is my first name? How old I am? From where come I? How long I'm already in this country? Do I keep any boarders? What is my husband's first name? How old is he? How long he is in this country? By what trade he works? How much wages he gets for a week? How much money do I spend out for rent? How old are the children, and everything about them.

"My goodness!" I cry out. "For why is it necessary all this to know? For why must I tell you all my business? What difference does it make already if I keep boarders, or I don't keep boarders? If Masha had the whooping-cough or Sonya had the measles? Or whether I spend out for my rent ten dollars or twenty? Or whether I come from Schnipishock or Kovner Gubernie?"

"We must make a record of all the applicants, and investigate each case," she tells me. "There are so many who apply to the charities, we can help only those who are most worthy."

"Charities!" I scream out. "Ain't the charities those who help the beggars out? I ain't no beggar. I'm not asking for no charity. My husband, he works."

"Miss Holcomb, the visiting teacher, said that you wanted to go to the country, and I had to make out this report before investigating your case."

"Oh! Oh!" I choke and bit my lips. "Is the free country from which Miss Holcomb told me, it is from the charities? She was telling me some kind people made arrangements for any mother what needs to go there."

"If your application is approved, you will be notified," she says to me, and out she goes.

When she is gone I think to myself, I'd better knock out from my head this idea about the country. For so long I lived, I didn't know nothing about the charities. For why should I come down among the beggars now?

Then I looked around me in the kitchen. On one side was the big wash-tub with clothes, waiting for me to wash. On the table was a pile of breakfast dishes yet. In the sink was the potatoes, waiting to be peeled. The baby was beginning to cry for the bottle. Aby was hollering and pulling me to take him to kindergarten. I felt if I didn't get away from here for a little while, I would land in a crazy house, or from the window jump down. Which was worser, to land in a crazy house, jump from the window down, or go to the country from the charities?

In about two weeks later around comes the same lady with the satchel again in my house.

"You can go to the country to-morrow," she tells me. "And you must come to the charity building to-morrow at nine o'clock sharp. Here is a card with the address. Don't lose it, because you must hand it to the lady in the office."

I look on the card, and there I see my name wrote; and by it, in big printed letters, that word "CHARITY."

"Must I go to the charity office?" I ask, feeling my heart to sink, "For why must I come there?"

"It is the rule that everybody comes to the office first, and from there they are taken to the country."

I shivered to think how I would feel, suppose somebody from my friends should see me walking into the charity office with my children. They wouldn't know that it is only for the country I go there. They might think I go to beg. Have I come down so low as to be seen by the charities? But what's the use? Should I knock my head on the walls? I had to go.

When I come to the office, I already found a crowd of women and children sitting on long benches waiting. I took myself a seat with them, and we were sitting and sitting and looking on one another, sideways and crosswise, and with lowered eyes, like guilty criminals. Each one felt like hiding herself from all the rest. Each one felt black with shame in the face.

We may have been sitting and waiting for an hour or more. But every second was seeming years to me. The children began to get restless. Mendel wanted water. The baby on my arms was falling asleep. Aby was crying for something to eat.

"For why are we sittin' here like fat cats?" says the woman next to me. "Ain't we going to the country to-day yet?"

At last a lady comes to the desk and begins calling us our names, one by one. I nearly dropped to the floor when over she begins to ask: Do you keep boarders? How much do you spend out for rent? How much wages does your man get for a week?

Didn't the nurse tell them all about us already? It was bitter enough to have to tell the nurse everything, but in my own house nobody was hearing my troubles, only the nurse. But in the office there was so many strangers all around me. For why should everybody have to know my business? At every question I wanted to holler out: "Stop! Stop! I don't want no vacations! I'll better run home with my children." At every question I felt like she was stabbing a knife into my heart. And she kept on stabbing me more and more, but I could not help it, and they were all looking at me. I couldn't move from her. I had to answer everything.

When she got through with me, my face was red like fire. I was burning with hurts and wounds. I felt like everything was bleeding in me.

When all the names was already called, a man doctor with a nurse comes in, and tells us to form a line, to be examined. I wish I could ease out my heart a little, and tell in words how that doctor looked on us, just because we were poor and had no money to pay. He only used the ends from his fingertips to examine us with. From the way he was afraid to touch us or come near us, he made us feel like we had some catching sickness that he was trying not to get on him.

The doctor got finished with us in about five minutes, so quick he worked. Then we was told to walk after the nurse, who was leading the way for us through the street to the car. Everybody what passed us in the street turned around to look on us. I kept down my eyes and held down my head and I felt like sinking into the sidewalk. All the time I was trembling for fear somebody what knows me might yet pass and see me. For why did they make us walk through the street, after the nurse, like stupid cows? Weren't all of us smart enough to find our way without the nurse? Why should the whole world have to see that we are from the charities?

When we got into the train, I opened my eyes, and lifted up my head, and straightened out my chest, and again began to breathe. It was a beautiful, sunshiny day. I knocked open the window from the train, and the fresh-smelling country air rushed upon my face and made me feel so fine! I looked out from the window and instead of seeing the iron fire-escapes with garbage-cans and bedclothes, that I always seen when from my flat I looked—instead of seeing only walls and washlines between walls, I saw the blue sky, and green grass and trees and flowers.

Ah, how grand I felt, just on the sky to look! Ah, how grand I felt just to see the green grass—and the free space—and no houses!

"Get away from me, my troubles!" I said. "Leave me rest a minute. Leave me breathe and straighten out my bones. Forget the unpaid butcher's bill. Forget the rent. Forget the wash-tub and the cook-stove and the pots and pans. Forget the charities!"

"Tickets, please," calls the train conductor.

I felt knocked out from heaven all at once. I had to point to the nurse what held our tickets, and I was feeling the conductor looking on me as if to say, "Oh, you are only from the charities."

By the time we came to the vacation house I already forgot all about my knock-down. I was again filled with the beauty of the country. I never in all my life yet seen such a swell house like that vacation house. Like the grandest palace it looked. All round the front, flowers from all colors was smelling out the sweetest perfume. Here and there was shady trees with comfortable chairs under them to sit down on.

When I only came inside, my mouth opened wide and my breathing stopped still from wonder. I never yet seen such an order and such a cleanliness. From all the corners from the room, the cleanliness was shining like a looking-glass. The floor was so white scrubbed you could eat on it. You couldn't find a speck of dust on nothing, if you was looking for it with eye-glasses on.

I was beginning to feel happy and glad that I come, when, Gott im Himmel! again a lady begins to ask us out the same questions what the nurse already asked me in my home and what was asked over again in the charity office. How much wages my husband makes out for a week? How much money I spend out for rent? Do I keep boarders?

We were hungry enough to faint. So worn out was I from excitement, and from the long ride, that my knees were bending under me ready to break from tiredness. The children were pulling me to pieces, nagging me for a drink, for something to eat and such like. But still we had to stand out the whole list of questionings. When she already got through asking us out everything, she gave to each of us a tag with our name written on it. She told us to tie the tag on our hand. Then like tagged horses at a horse sale in the street, they marched us into the dining-room.

There was rows of long tables, covered with pure-white oil-cloth. A vase with bought flowers was standing on the middle from each table. Each person got a clean napkin for himself. Laid out by the side from each person's plate was a silver knife and fork and spoon and teaspoon. When we only sat ourselves down, girls with white starched aprons was passing around the eatings.

I soon forgot again all my troubles. For the first time in ten years I sat down to a meal what I did not have to cook or worry about. For the first time in ten years I sat down to the table like a somebody. Ah, how grand it feels, to have handed you over the eatings and everything you need. Just as I was beginning to like it and let myself feel good, in comes a fat lady all in white, with a teacher's look on her face. I could tell already, right away by the way she looked on us, that she was the boss from this place.

"I want to read you the rules from this house, before you leave this room," says she to us.

Then she began like this: We dassen't stand on the front grass where the flowers are. We dassen't stay on the front porch. We dassen't sit on the chairs under the shady trees. We must stay always in the back and sit onthose long wooden benches there. We dassen't come in the front sitting-room or walk on the front steps what have carpet on it—we must walk on the back iron steps. Everything on the front from the house must be kept perfect for the show for visitors. We dassen't lay down on the beds in the daytime, the beds must always be made up perfect for the show for visitors.

"Got im Himmel!" thinks I to myself; "ain't there going to be no end to the things we dassen't do in this place?"

But still she went on. The children over two years dassen't stay around by the mothers. They must stay by the nurse in the play-room. By the meal-times, they can see their mothers. The children dassen't run around the house or tear up flowers or do anything. They dassen't holler or play rough in the play-room. They must always behave and obey the nurse.

We must always listen to the bells. Bell one was for getting up. Bell two, for getting babies' bottles. Bell three, for coming to breakfast. Bell four, for bathing the babies. If we come later, after the ring from the bell, then we'll not get what we need. If the bottle bell rings and we don't come right away for the bottle, then the baby don't get no bottle. If the breakfast bell rings, and we don't come right away down to the breakfast, then there won't be no breakfast for us.

When she got through with reading the rules, I was wondering which side of the house I was to walk on. At every step was some rule what said don't move here, and don't go there, don't stand there, and don't sit there. If I tried to remember the endless rules, it would only make me dizzy in the head. I was thinking for why, with so many rules, didn't they also have already another rule, about how much air in our lungs to breathe.

On every few days there came to the house swell ladies in automobiles. It was for them that the front from the house had to be always perfect. For them was all the beautiful smelling flowers. For them the front porch, the front sitting-room, and the easy stairs with the carpet on it.

Always when the rich ladies came the fat lady, what was the boss from the vacation house, showed off to them the front. Then she took them over to the back to look on us, where we was sitting together, on long wooden benches, like prisoners. I was always feeling cheap like dirt, and mad that I had to be there, when they smiled down on us.

"How nice for these poor creatures to have a restful place like this," I heard one lady say.

The next day I already felt like going back. The children what had to stay by the nurse in the play-room didn't like it neither.

"Mamma," says Mendel to me, "I wisht I was home and out in the street. They don't let us do nothing here. It's worser than school."

"Ain't it a play-room?" asks I. "Don't they let you play?"

"Gee wiss! play-room, they call it! The nurse hollers on us all the time. She don't let us do nothing."

The reason why I stayed out the whole two weeks is this: I think to myself, so much shame in the face I suffered to come here, let me at least make the best from it already. Let me at least save up for two weeks what I got to spend out for grocery and butcher for my back bills to pay out. And then also think I to myself, if I go back on Monday, I got to do the big washing; on Tuesday waits for me the ironing; on Wednesday, the scrubbing and cleaning, and so goes it on. How bad it is already in this place, it's a change from the very same sameness of what I'm having day in and day out at home. And so I stayed out this vacation to the bitter end.

But at last the day for going out from this prison came. On the way riding back, I kept thinking to myself: "This is such a beautiful vacation house. For why do they make it so hard for us? When a mother needs a vacation, why must they tear the insides out from her first, by making her come down to the charity office? Why drag us from the charity office through the streets? And when we live through the shame of the charities and when we come already to the vacation house, for why do they boss the life out of us with so many rules and bells? For why don't they let us lay down our heads on the bed when we are tired? For why must we always stick in the back, like dogs what have got to be chained in one spot? If they would let us walk around free, would we bite off something from the front part of the house?

"If the best part of the house what is comfortable is made up for a show for visitors, why ain't they keeping the whole business for a show for visitors? For why do they have to fool in worn-out mothers, to make them think they'll give them a rest? Do they need the worn-out mothers as part of the show? I guess that is it, already."

When I got back in my home, so happy and thankful I was I could cry from thankfulness. How good it was feeling for me to be able to move around my own house, like I pleased. I was always kicking that my rooms was small and narrow, but now my small rooms seemed to grow so big like the park. I looked out from my window on the fire-escapes, full with bedding and garbage-cans, and on the wash-lines full with the clothes. All these ugly things was grand in my eyes. Even the high brick walls all around made me feel like a bird what just jumped out from a cage. And I cried out, "Gott sei dank! Gott sei dank!"

5

---◆◇◆---

"I Bridge a Gap Between Two Cultures":
Lyu-Volckhausen, Advocate for the Korean Community

Women who had experienced the "culture shock" of immigration themselves were often more sensitive and more effective than native-born Americans in helping newcomers adjust to the United States. Familiar with the native language and culture, and free of ethnic (though not necessarily class) prejudice, immigrant women were more likely than others to offer practical, culturally acceptable assistance. A few were trained social workers. More were relatives or volunteers for women's organizations. Some, like Grace Lyu-Volckhausen, were simply dedicated individuals with empathy, ideas, and the ability to make things happen.

Like many (but not all) community leaders, Lyu-Volckhausen had advantages—parents who set an example of public service, an excellent education (partly in the United States), and a financially and emotionally supportive husband. She developed her first project with friends around the kitchen table and maintained this down-to-earth approach, whether the issue was wages, wife abuse, or day care. She also maintained a scrupulous respect for the dignity and autonomy of the women she served.

A semicircle of 30 neatly dressed Korean women sit in the simple meeting room, heads bowed in prayer. On the wall in front of them is a faded picture of Jesus, to one side an old upright piano. Each woman's eyes are closed and on each lap is a hymnbook. But, standing to the other side, there is one highly incongruous participant: small, broad-faced, arms crossed stubbornly, eyes wide open and missing nothing, she waits slightly impatiently for the prayers to end and the meeting she had organized to begin. When it does, she steps forward, passes around a pile of Xeroxed sheets of paper and, in a voice as purposeful as a general, begins her talk.

This is Grace Lyu-Volckhausen, and she's at it again. The meeting she has called together this time is at the local Young Women's Christian Association in Flushing, Queens, a section of New York with a lot of Korean immigrants. It's a meeting for the board of directors of a 1,000-member YWCA program that Grace and three others organized from scratch five years earlier.

Source: Anne Field, "Organizer: From Sweatshop to Diplomatic Corps," *MS. Magazine,* November 1985, pp. 59–62. Anne Field is a New York-based writer and editor specializing in workplace and business issues.

But, before she has the women split up into small groups to encourage more discussion, she is giving a quick lecture on leadership and decision-making. It's something about which Grace knows a lot.

Indeed, since her days as a student activist in Korea in the late 1950s, Grace has spearheaded and arranged a dizzying array of services and programs that might have exhausted a less energetic woman years ago. At 47, Grace has not made any headlines, but her fierce commitment has touched the lives of countless immigrant women. Her special talent: translating a strange foreign culture into terms that the newly arrived can understand. "She does great things daily," says Edgar Romney, manager/secretary of the International Ladies' Garmet Workers' Local 23–25, who has worked closely with her.

Central headquarters is a cozy brownstone in an Italian section of Brooklyn that she shares with her husband of 17 years, William Volckhausen, her two teenage children, and her mother. From there, she has organized educational workshops, counseling centers, recreational facilities, day-care centers, union meetings. The common thread, she explains: "I bridge a gap between cultures. But I don't tell these women what to do. It's not fair to do that. It's a matter of giving them endless information."

That's why, for example, she translated a battered woman's handbook several years ago and ran it in one of New York's six Korean newspapers. The two-column piece featured household hints in one, and the translation in another. "Otherwise, the woman readers wouldn't have paid any attention," she explains. An updated translation is now on its way.

Throughout her career, Grace has been lucky to be married to a man who has fully supported her activities: William Volckhausen, the general counsel of the Dime Savings Bank of New York City, has provided for most of the family's finances. The bank itself has also provided supporting services, including use of its boardroom, for Grace's work. "I'm a firm believer in finding the right partner for your cause," she says. But Grace's role in the family may change as she assumes a new government position, working with the New York City Human Resources Administration as a liaison with community groups. She'll not only be contributing more financially, but she'll also have to juggle more apples at the same time.

In a culture in which women are taught subservence at an early age, Grace may seem an anomaly. Actually, she is the logical outcome of a highly unusual family. "For me, this isn't something new. It's something in the family," she says. Her maternal grandmother started a job-training program for peasant girls in the 1920s. Her mother was a founder of Korean women's groups and, at age 73, is still active in this country. Her father was a liberal member of the Korean government.

It's no surprise, then, that even as a college freshman at Seoul's Yonsei University, Grace caused a furor that her classmates will never forget. En-

raged that the school's bylaws wouldn't allow women to hold student government positions higher than vice president, she set out to overhaul the
rules. "All hell broke loose," she remembers. But after a year of constant
meetings, fights, discussions and deliberations with intransigent and often
flabbergasted male students, the laws were rewritten.

After graduation, she moved to New York to study international and human relations at New York University. A year later, in 1961, after the Chung
Hee Park military coup, Grace's father, a Park opponent, was caught up in
the political crisis. That was probably the turning point in her life. She
learned about it one morning through a story in the New York *Times*. "Suddenly, all my money was cut off. My telephone was tapped. I couldn't talk to
my family at all," she recalls. "You really grow up when you're thrown into
something like that." Fifteen years later, her father died.

Grace might have felt more stranded, but her unusually fluent command of the English language helped her through. Not that she didn't experience a healthy dose of culture shock. The first time she saw a couple
kissing in public, for example, Grace ran to her adviser in a tizzy. "I was so
embarrassed," she says. "But it put my adviser in stitches." She won a series
of scholarships and then took several college teaching jobs. It was through
one of them that she met her husband, a lawyer who is also an expert in Asian
affairs. "I had no intention of getting married at first," she confides, laughing. "I was too busy."

Over the next 10 years, she had two children and got involved in local
community activities. Then, two events occurred. Her doctoral thesis dealt
with women and cultural change. Through that work, she started her first
experiment in translating foreign cultures for recent arrivals. She started
teaching classes for the wives of diplomats stationed in this country to help
them handle the problems of cultural transition.

Then one day, Grace and three Korean friends came up with an idea
while sitting around the wooden table in her cluttered, comfortable kitchen.
In the 1960s, the American government had liberalized the quotas reg-
ulating the number of Asians allowed into the country. As a result, a flood of
Koreans had immigrated. Grace and her friends decided to organize an immigrant outreach center. They had all been active in the YWCA in Korea,
so the best place seemed to be the Y in Queens, an area jampacked with Korean residents.

Now, the organization offers a six-day-a-week program with Saturday
morning sewing classes for grandmothers, after-school recreation, a children's chorus, counseling for battered wives, and monthly discussion groups
on differences between women in American and Korean cultures. The facilities are simple—several rooms packed with tables, chairs, books, sewing
equipment, toys—and a special office for senior citizen activities. During a
recent tour, Grace showed a visitor one wall lined with photographs of a vegetable garden plot in Queens cultivated by elderly members.

Soon after starting the program, Grace was enlisted by the ILGWU to help unionize Koreans working for local contractors. Textile manufacturers hire these contractors to produce individual garments. Many are Koreans, and they hire mostly immigrant women to work for them. It's a group of women Grace had been concerned about for a long time. "If you go into some of these garment factories, you find that these are not uneducated farm women. Many of them are college graduates," she explains. "There are women doctors who have to work behind a sewing machine because they cannot speak the language." Grace's mission: to persuade contractors to trust the union and sign up with organized manufacturers, and to explain to women workers the benefits of unionization. Now, she holds nightime meetings for members every few months to answer questions and discuss health insurance benefits, schools, how to get medical checkups.

A tightly knit community with a deep distrust of unions, however, Koreans are a difficult bunch to convert. Grace arranges for union leaders to meet Korean contractors, many of whom suspect that all American labor unions are Communist fronts. Such meetings can be delicate arts of diplomacy, often discreetly taking place in the back of quiet restaurants. But Grace offers an irresistible commodity: access to information about industry trends and economics that the men, who are new to the country themselves, could never find out on their own. "For these men, I am a necessary evil," she says.

Grace's greatest challenge, though, is conveying an array of complicated information to the Korean women with whom she works. Through informal chats and formal meetings, she tries to make sense of the new culture for which most are totally unprepared. Although perhaps 80 percent of Korean immigrant women work in this country, for example, few ever held a job in the old country. The problems, she finds, are immense. Questions range from how to buy soap at a supermarket to how to cook a traditional three-course Korean breakfast and still have time to get to work. "The immigrant woman, on top of a new job, has to deal with her husband's pressures, her children's pressures, plus endless housework," says Grace. "It is so time-consuming to cook Korean food but that's what their husbands want." Even the simplest things can be unnerving. Grace recalls the woman who was rattled at the sight of fashionable women with chopsticks in their hair. "How would you feel if you saw people walking around with knives and forks on their heads?" she says.

At times, Grace receives emergency calls at home. Once, for example, a YWCA member telephoned with traumatic news. Her teenage daughter had come home with a boy to work on a science project and her mother had chased him away with a broom. Explains Grace, "It's a perfectly understandable event for a seventy-year-old Korean grandmother who sees a fifteen-year-old grandaughter with a fifteen-year-old boy in the same room. Confucius said that a woman and a man should not be in the same room after the age of seven.

"After I got the call from the mother, crying hysterically, I got a call from the daughter, crying hysterically. I told the girl, 'You and your grandmother are both absolutely right. But how would you feel if you had just moved to, say, Timbuktu at the age of seventy?' "

Part of Grace's time is taken up representing her community on the New York City Commission on the Status of Women and on the Mayor's Ethnic Council. But it's a special day-care proposal that, of all her achievements, Grace is the proudest. She developed it through Governor Mario Cuomo's Garment Advisory Council, a state governmental body that she was appointed to sit on. The group includes union, consumer, and industry representatives, some of whom were not enthusiastic about day care. Through two years of concerted cajoling and politicking, Grace persuaded the group to adopt a comprehensive service. But its implementation will require continued attention.

"They all said, we don't want to worry about babies. But I convinced them that mothers would be more productive if they knew their children were okay," she explains. Colleagues tell it another way. Says Betty Kaye Taylor, deputy commissioner of New York's labor department, "Grace did it by the sheer force of her personality. You simply have to yield to her indefatigable energy and determination to see things through."

That iron stubbornness will undoubtedly see Grace through her next project: writing a guide for recent Korean immigrants to be printed in installments in Korean newspapers over a six-month period and then compiled into a book. Says Grace, with typical determination, "The work I do comes from the heart. . . ."

6

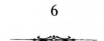

"People Who Do This Kind of Work
Are in Such Danger of Burnout":
Judy Baca, "Urban Artist"

Born in Los Angeles of "immigrant people," Chicana muralist Judy Baca used art to improve the environment and the lives of young people first in her own commu-

Source: Diane Neumaier, "Our People Are the Eternal Exiles." Interview with Judy Baca in *Cultures in Contention*, ed. Douglas Kahn and Diane Neumaier, © 1985 Real Comet Press, Seattle, WA. Interview © 1985 Diane Neumaier.

nity and then in minority communities all over Los Angeles. Baca's parents were afraid she could not earn a living as an artist, so she studied education and history as well as art. An "urban artist," she wanted her work to be accessible and useful to the public, including people like her Spanish-speaking grandmother, rather than locked away in galleries or private collections.

The passage that follows is from an interview originally published in 1985. Baca describes the urban conflict, decay, and political neglect that motivated her mural projects, and the satisfaction she got from those projects. She also describes her problems working with city bureaucrats and neighborhood people and directing other artists. Baca struggled to develop a leadership style that would be both democratic and effective. She also struggled with the sex role contradictions a Latina—or, indeed, any woman—faces in exercising authority.

I went to school in the sixties at the state university in Northridge, California, in the part of the San Fernando Valley which was all white. . . .

The moment I left my community to go to college, I was isolated from my own people because not that many of them went to college, and I was isolated from any sense of my own culture in the university system. . . .

When I got out of college I started teaching at a Catholic high school— in fact, the same school I went to—in a program called Allied Arts, an innovative teaching program which I designed to celebrate the different senses. The kids wrote music, learned basic drama, wrote poetry. We interrelated all the arts. It was a fabulous course for me to teach, because it pulled a lot of things together and helped me understand how to use different techniques to get a desired product. People made presentations using three art forms to express one idea. It took over the whole school and became an incredible event. . . .

I did my first mural there. I was trying to get team cooperation because there was a problem of division among kids coming from different neighborhoods. So I asked them to draw something together. We took a human figure, divided it up into parts, blew it up ten times its size, reconnected the parts, then dropped it out of a second-story window. Here was a sixty-foot person. It caused an amazing uproar. I saw that you could do an incredible amount of teaching with scale transformation. Changing scale in that way makes people perceive things differently.

Then I got hired in a program for the city with twenty artists. We were supposed to teach at parks all over the city. They looked at us and sent the black people to Watts and the Mexican people to East Los Angeles. So I ended up in East L.A.

I was given two classes, one at ten in the morning and another one at three in the afternoon. It was twenty-six miles from my home, so I would do my morning class and then hang out in the parks. I began to really watch street life. I saw young people, teenagers, adolescents, the throw-away people. Nobody wanted them in the parks; the Recreation and Parks Department had no programs planned for them because they were vandals, because they were involved in gang warfare. So they would play dominoes, drink wine, smoke dope, hang out in various corners. There was always this constant battle. The police would be called to get rid of them, and the kids would come back, like a flock of pigeons that fly up and land again. So I made friends with a lot of them. I met some kids who were involved in tattoo work. Of course, they were also writing all over the walls.

Visual symbols, calligraphy basically, were a focal point in their life on the street. You could read a wall and learn everything you needed to know about that community, about the guys or girls who hung out in the street—who they were, who they hung out with, what generation they were, how many of them had the same nickname—all in what they call *placayasos*.

I became something of an expert reader of street writing. I knew who was who in four or five different neighborhoods because I taught at different places. I realized *I* was moving from one part to the next, but they couldn't. They could not go five blocks without being in danger from other gangs. Some of the feuds were fifty or sixty years old.

That was my constituency. It's certainly not the whole of the Chicano community—I have to say that I get very perturbed when people perceive the Chicano community as being people who write all over the walls—but this is a street phenomenon that has been on the increase. In the sixties, it was more political slogans: now, it's about territory. It has to do with people saying, "Listen, I own nothing here. So I own your wall. Here's who I am." The tattoos are a whole thing, too. Kids with tattooed tears on their cheeks! What does that say about how the kids feel about themselves? What's going on for them is pretty rough, and its reflected in the highest dropout rate in the entire nation.

I said I wanted to form a mural team. Pretty soon I had a number of people who began to hang with me, who trusted me and would do something I asked them to do. At that point nobody knew what a mural was; it wasn't the phenomenon it is now. I had to explain that we were going to do a big picture on the wall. But I had to figure out how to get the wall back. It was marked. Who do I have to talk to to get permission to use this wall? So I said to the kids, "Listen, I'm going to take off your *placayasos*. Here's what we're going to do. Do you want to work with us?" It was like negotiating treaties.

The most important skill that I've had to develop in this work is to be able to deal with people in City Hall, then jump in my car, drive ten miles to the East Side, change into boots and jeans, and go sit on the curb with the kids. There are people who are bridge people, and my ability to move between those great extremes has made it possible for me to do what I do. Possibly, because I had a university education, because I became Anglicized to a certain degree, I was able to come back to my own community with more information and make things happen.

I formed my first mural team of twenty kids from four different neighborhoods. It was the first time in recent history that they had been able to put aside their differences and work together. That was in 1970. We did three pieces that summer, including *Mi Abuelita*, a giant three-sided bandshell with a grandmother image in it—my grandmother, actually. I had to do it on a volunteer basis, but I got the kids paid. . . .

People were amazed at our work. The *Los Angeles Times* ran sensational articles like "Teenage Youth Gangs Put Down Knives for Brushes." Terrible. The head of Rec and Parks came down to the site—the kids thought he was a narc, and he's lucky he got in and out of there—and said to me, simply, "How can we bottle and package what you do?" I began to understand that I was becoming to the City of Los Angeles a wonderful instrument of graffiti abatement. But I was accomplishing my goals at the same time by doing my own work in the street—which for me was clearly *not* graffiti abatement.

The group of people I was working with was very connected to and influenced by visual symbols—in tattoos, in the kind of writing that went on in the street—but there was no visible reflection of themselves in the larger community. Nothing of the architecture or visual symbols reflected the presence of the people—other than the graffiti. First it was a Jewish community, then Mexican people moved in. What I could see was that any population could move through the place without being reflected in it.

Symbols already had significance in this community, and it made sense to create another set of symbols acknowledging the people's commonality, the fact that they came from the same place and had a common culture. It seemed to me this could break down the divisions among these people, give them information, and change their environment. The murals have been clear forms of expression, reflecting the issues and needs as they see them.

In the first years of this work people came by and brought us food and beer, anything we needed. They would volunteer to help us. It was interesting, because there was a real division between the young people from the street and their families; their parents hated them for not being good Mexican kids and thought they had gotten completely out of control. It's that old country-new country stuff. . . .

But when the parents saw their kids doing something positive, connections among the family members began to develop again.

Few girls participated during that time. It was much easier organizing among the young men because girls were not allowed the same mobility. It has been a long process drawing the young girls in, but it's equal. It's taken this many years for that to happen. You see, Latin women are not supposed to be doing things like climbing on scaffolding, being in the public eye. . . .

I wrote a proposal, a very grandiose idea for a citywide mural program. It would incorporate forty murals a year covering a radius of over a hundred miles in every ethnic community of the city. And would cost in the area of $150,000 a year. They gave it to me.

It was a struggle for about six months. I had to appear in front of all types of committees. I would give my spiels over and over again about what it would do for senior citizens, children, professional artists, the black community, the Chicano community, the Asian community, the Korean community, the Thai community, the Chinese community. Then I spent the next three years of my life doing it—a real ordeal. They might give you the money, but they're not going to help you. In fact, they're going to get in your way at every turn. For example, suddenly they would say, "All people hired from now on must have tuberculosis tests." Try getting a thousand people tuberculosis tests who don't have transportation. Or, "All payments will take four to six weeks." The mural would be done in three or four weeks, then you'd get whole gangs of kids coming after you because you haven't paid them. Crazy stuff. That's when I learned administrative skills.

I also learned how to work in a multi-ethnic situation. I no longer was working solely in the Chicano community. I learned that organizing in the Chinese community is *radically* different than organizing in the Chicano community or in the black community. I realized that the Chicano staff was absolutely racist against blacks and saw how the black style of coming in and being able to articulate what's in their mural just turned off my staff, who wanted to veto every black mural that came through.

A lot of the murals done in that program were cultural kinds of pieces; even the tame ones were, in fact, important statements to announce—for example, the presence of Filipinos in a community where no one would acknowledge them. There was a piece on the landing of Filipinos in the Philippine islands, which was very similar to the Mexican legend of the Aztecs arriving in Tenochitilan. This is what gave me the idea about overlapping legends. I thought that was a wonderful thing; people could see how they all connected in some ways.

Some of the pieces were about police brutality and the open warfare that goes on between the police and the people in the communities. Some were about immigration, what the immigration authorities were doing, and the exploitation of illegal workers. Others were about drug abuse, including the government-supported influx of drugs into the communities and the *Las Tres* issue in Los Angeles, where three people were imprisoned for shooting a narcotics agent who was bringing narcotics into the community.

A lot of pieces were on gentrification and urban renewal, on how the developers' interests are taking people's homes away from them. . . .

It was truly an *amazing* experience. We were dealing with problems that are manifested in the whole society, going out into these communities and seeing how artists are treated. We did 250 murals (I probably directed around 150) and hired over 1,000 people. It wore me out—to death.

We were putting these pieces up all over the city, which was all fine and good. But at some point, because of the sun and the pollution, and because the murals were in poor communities that were subject to redevelopment, the murals would be torn down. Then the people would get up in arms. For example, somebody would start to paint out a mural when a building owner had changed, and fifty people would be out there with sticks wanting to beat up the guy. We had organized well in the communities, so they protected their murals. But we couldn't get money for maintenance, and it was very difficult to make building owners keep the pieces up.

I also saw artists do just *awful* things in the communities, like coming into an ethnically mixed community and, because the artist was Chicano, painting a Chicano piece with only Chicano kids. Sometimes they would incite people to attack a police officer; everybody would be beaten up and taken to jail—except the artist. Terrible things!

I couldn't handle it anymore. I couldn't control the quality of the pieces. I was tired of supporting other people, breaking my ass and killing myself, and being in this no-man's land position between the community and the city. The community perceived me as being part of the city bureaucracy, while the officials perceived me as being a flaming radical from the community!

I think I originally had the idea that leadership meant for me to be the person who created an environment in which other people could be creative. Now I acknowledge the fact that I usually have more experience than anyone else in my group, more mural experience. I've done a tremendous amount of work at this point. I've also watched a whole lot of other people do a tremendous amount of work. And I've made a lot of mistakes. Now, leadership means trusting my intuition, which I think is fairly highly developed, about how to deal with people.

I didn't like any hierarchy. I just thought that we should all be equal. But for now, I really can't say that's possible. I think if I worked in a situation where everybody raised the money, everybody had responsibility, and everybody had the same level of experience, it would be fine. But even then, the world outside would not relate to a collective answering a question. There's got to be one person who ultimately takes it on the chin. Maybe I'm getting tired, but I no longer want to take it for anybody else's mistakes besides my own. Also, when I don't listen to what I think, I screw up.

Of course, if a woman takes this on she's a bitch, a dyke, a macha, a demanding, difficult-to-work-with person—all those kinds of things. Those are stereotypes about what a woman is if she's a leader. I'm conscious all the time of my own body, of what it says to people when I'm talking to them, of the way that I use my words to communicate. I try to use all those parts and pull them together in a way that communicates from a soft place in myself—not the defense/fear place—what I think and what I care about, what I want other people to do and think and care about. They may not care, but at least I'm communicating my attitudes to them. That's how I feel I'm a leader. A lot of times I can plug into the psychology of a group, the overriding feeling, what they're creating for themselves—and pull it out and say, "Let's define it. What is it?" That's part of my role as a leader. So much of it is really being a good teacher. So much of it is drama, being some kind of theater person. But the other part of it is that although I take the consequences for the decisions, I often don't make a decision totally by myself. A lot of times I really am a catalyst, a facilitator. But the other part of it is, I often have to take the responsibility for making decisions myself.

The whole business of learning to be responsible is hard. I have gotten myself in a position a number of times where I've made myself sick. I had acute acrylic poisoning two years ago from mural paint. I was in intensive care with cardiac arrhythmia. I couldn't breath. . . . I've got to take care of myself. I'm working at it, but I find myself not doing it a lot of the time. It frightens me. That's part of being willful, pushing yourself when your body is telling you something else. We are not taught to be nurturing of ourselves. We're taught to sacrifice, particularly in my culture. The women put on the black mantilla, and they are the mourners and the producers and the nurturers. They make them and they bury them.

People who do this kind of work are in such danger of burnout, or absolutely destroying themselves. We have all those people who have wonderful capabilities out there, people who've been real instrumental in making things happen, and they all get beat up, literally beat up! There's something wrong with how we are perceiving ourselves. That's critical information.

PART VI

Education

All immigrant women suffered a double educational handicap—they were foreign-born and female. Some were also members of racial minorities. Part 6 explores the educational opportunities offered to immigrant women in the United States and women's responses to these opportunities.

The Nineteenth Century

In the predominantly rural America of the nineteenth century, schooling was not a requirement for economic survival. Nor was it seen as the critical factor in the Americanization of immigrants. Native-born Americans looked to time, America's "free institutions," and the frontier—or to immigration restriction—as much as to the schools to solve the "immigrant problem."

Night school or other Americanization programs for adults were virtually nonexistent until late in the century. Educational opportunities were not abundant for immigrant children either. Few immigrant girls could afford the private academies and convent schools that educated middle-class, native-born girls, even if they had been welcome. Some attended charity schools. Some attended Irish, German, Polish, or other ethnic or parochial schools, where the traditional religion, language, and culture were taught. (More girls than boys attended Catholic schools because some women's religious orders would not teach boys.) However, after mid-century, most immigrant girls, like most native-born girls, attended the new public schools.

Whether immigrant girls went to public, private, or parochial schools, their formal education was usually limited. Many teachers were poorly educated, and classes of fifty or sixty were not uncommon. Through most of the century the school term lasted only a few months, and children did well to attend three or four terms. Many did not attend at all. Their education came from their parents and from everyday life on the farm or on the city streets.

"Progressive" Education

Parents and communities were important educators in the twentieth century, too, as the first selection shows. They provided information, shaped atti-

217

tudes, and imparted values. In the twentieth century, however, a more complex urban society and a growing emphasis on credentials and expertise made formal schooling increasingly important. Moreover, in the twentieth century public schooling was viewed as the best means of Americanizing immigrant children and, through them, immigrant parents as well.

The arrival of the southern and eastern European immigrants at the turn of the century coincided with an enormous expansion of public and parochial schooling. Education became compulsory to age fourteen in most states, and the school year was lengthened. "Progressive" innovations such as kindergartens, vacation schools, extracurricular activities, and vocational education and counseling further extended the influence of public schools over children's lives.

Educational reformers of the early twentieth century introduced a variety of academic, commercial, and industrial curricula into the public schools to prepare children for their appropriate places in the new industrial economy. The place educators considered appropriate for immigrant women (indeed, all women) was the home. As one educator put it: "The daughters of Russian and Italian immigrants do not look upon teaching, bookkeeping, stenography, or shoptending as aims in life. They simply and openly desire a sound mind in a sound body, that they may make good wives and present their husbands with healthy sons."[1]

Given this widely shared view of immigrant girls' limited aspirations, public schools, settlement houses, and other agencies of Americanization provided programs emphasizing "domestic arts." Girls living in dark, crowded tenements without running water were taught to cook, clean, shop, sew, and care for children in the middle-class Anglo-American style. They were expected to use this knowledge to Americanize their homes, thus combatting the dirt, disease, crime, decline in family life, and other real and imagined urban ills attributed to immigrants. If necessary, they could also use this knowledge to earn a living in the few jobs seen as appropriate to their class and gender: garment manufacturing or domestic service. A 1929 teacher's manual suggested another use. Girls were to be taught careful budgeting, "how to plan in prosperity for the day of no income and adversity," so that families would not become public charges and hungry husbands would not turn to radical politics or lives of crime.[2]

The School Girl

The most immediate problem facing many immigrant school girls was language. Most schools offered no special help. New immigrants of all ages were usually placed in kindergarten or first grade—which many "overage" girls found humiliating—and promoted as they learned English.

"Occasionally, newly arrived immigrant children are put in classes organized for backward or subnormal children . . . and grave injustice is thus
done to both groups,"[3] wrote Grace Abbott in 1917, describing an abuse still
affecting African American and native American as well as immigrant children. A second abuse described by Abbott has also been widespread and
long-lived. "In our zeal to teach patriotism, we are often teaching disrespect
for the history and the traditions that the ancestors of the immigrant parent
had their part in making."[4] Children were routinely punished for speaking
their native language. Chinese children were routinely segregated.

School could be painful for the culturally different child. "I was often
ridiculed for the clothes I wore until I began to believe myself that the
dresses of other girls in school were by all means more proper than mine,"
wrote an Italian immigrant who went to school in the 1920s.[5] Four decades
later a Puerto Rican school girl hurried home each day to avoid having her
mother come after her. Unlike the other children's dignified, grey haired,
portly mothers, her mother was an "an exotic young beauty, [with] black hair
down to her waist and a propensity for wearing bright colors and spike
heels. . . . I was embarrassed to be seen with her."[6]

Discrimination in the classroom was common, especially in the case of
racial minorities, and could be devastating to children's self-image and academic achievement. Mexican-born Elizabeth Loza Newby described the
treatment she and other Mexican-American children encountered:

> Many of the teachers I had would make the Mexican students sit in
> the back of the room. And, since they could not understand what
> was being taught, they were allowed to draw or play games while
> the teacher concentrated on the other pupils. Such segregation in
> the classroom was very embarrassing and contributed greatly to the
> feeling of inferiority that was already so much a part of our lives.
> The back of the room became the place where the dummies sat.[7]

Some girls were "dummies" because hours of farm work, piece work, or
housework left them too tired to learn. Some fell behind because they missed
school frequently to care for younger children or to help their mother during
sickness or childbirth, responsibilities boys were not expected to shoulder.
Many cities that had special programs for truant boys had none for truant
girls.

Despite these and other problems, immigrant girls in the opening decades of the century usually adjusted to school more positively than their
brothers. Many loved school and cried when they had to leave, sometimes
before the legal age, to go to work. To girls from Poland, Sicily, or Greece,
the teacher was the model American "lady" (even though she was often Irish)
and teaching a favorite childhood ambition. Even the domestic science programs, despised by some, were welcomed by others. They were a relief from

unintelligible, uninspiring academic classes, and food and clothing made at school could be used at home.

Mary Antin (a Jewish immigrant who entered school at the age of twelve and later became a writer) remembered a favorite teacher who "aided us so skillfully and earnestly in our endeavors to 'see-a-cat' and 'hear-a-dog-bark' and 'look-at-the-hen' that we turned over page after page . . . eager to find out how the world looked, smelled, and tasted in the strange speech." Promoted to a higher grade, Antin carried all her books home each day, "not because I should need them, but because I loved to hold them. I loved to be carrying books. It was a badge of scholarship and I was proud of it."[8]

The Struggle for Higher Education

Girls who immigrated in the early twentieth century rarely went to college; most did not finish high school. Immigrant families with few resources preferred to invest in extra years of schooling for their sons rather than for their daughters. Between elementary school and marriage most young women entered the labor market, helping to support the family and sometimes subsidizing the education of their brothers.

Some parents discouraged higher education because they felt it would be wasted when their daughters married, or because it did not necessarily result in greater earning power. Teaching, the most popular career choice, was usually closed to girls with a foreign accent. "My daughter wanted to be a teacher. . . . I sacrificed everything to send her to high school and college. . . . And now after all the worries and sacrifices, she can't get a job in any school. Well, we . . . followed the American way . . . and what does it amount to?" said a disillusioned Italian immigrant mother.[9]

Some parents were afraid that the free co-educational atmosphere of the American educational institutions would endanger their daughter's reputation, jeopardizing her chances for a good marriage and damaging the honor of the family. These fears were especially common among traditional southern Italian families in the early twentieth century and, more recently, among Mexican, Puerto Rican, and other Hispanic families. They are reflected in the second selection.

Education of the Adult

Fears of immigrant disloyalty or radicalism during World War I and the postwar "red scare" fueled a campaign to Americanize adults as well as children. Public schools, corporations, churches, YMCAs and YWCAs, settlement houses, and other agencies sponsored educational programs for this purpose. Most of these programs were directed at men, whose potential for benefiting or harming the nation was considered greater. Women were included mainly to prevent their holding back the Americanization of the rest of the family.

At a time when women's roles were broadening, Americanization classes for adults reflected and reinforced gender stereotypes. Men's programs included classes in various trades, citizenship, and English, and a wide range of clubs, debating societies, and athletics. Women's programs concentrated on cooking and sewing, with the occasional addition of singing, dramatics, and typewriting.

A typical manual for night school English teachers suggested the following exercises for men:

> I wash my hands. I sharpen my pencil. I read a book. I come into the room. I go out of the room.

The parallel exercise for the women's classes was:

> I wash my hands. I wash the dishes. I set the table. I sweep the floor. I dust the furniture.[10]

Curriculum for women was often simple as well as narrowly domestic, reflecting educators' view that "the wives of the new immigration are far more backward than the men."[11]

Despite the stereotypes, some women had positive experiences with night classes in the public schools.

> We came to class a little shyly, but eagerly, and studied enthusiastically. . . . In addition to reading and writing we had spelling and pronunciation. . . . We also learned American songs which we sang at the top of our voices.
>
> With pleasure we expressed our appreciation to the patient and capable instructors with gifts of potica and lerofi [traditional foods] at Christmas as well as on their birthdays. . . .
>
> After attending evening school for three years, we received our "diplomas" with great pride and satisfaction.[12]

More often experiences were negative.

> When I went to work, I was determined to continue my studies at night school. . . . But I found that it was not the same as day school. The instructor seemed more interested in getting one-hundred percent attendance than in giving one-hundred-percent instruction. He would joke and tell silly stories. . . . I soon realized I was wasting my time, and so my attempt to continue my formal education came to an abrupt end.[13]

Consistently low registrations and high drop-out rates in these programs indicate that most women reacted negatively. Attendance was low, not because women were "backward," but because they were too busy or too tired, or because their husbands objected. Many found the programs condescending or irrelevant to their interests, which included far more than housekeeping—the arts, politics, social issues, the homeland, and the United States.

Formal schooling was important mainly for young, single, working women. Most women moved toward education and Americanization in other ways—through church activities, ethnic newspapers and theaters, and public libraries. Many attended classes, lectures, and cultural events (often in the native language) sponsored by nationalist societies, ethnic women's clubs, and labor unions. The International Ladies Garment Workers Union offered its members, mostly Jewish and Italian working women, classes in English and labor history, movies, tours of museums, theater performances (the opera *Aida* drew an audience of twenty thousand), reading rooms, and libraries.[14]

Immigrant memoirs and fiction show how desperately many women wanted to broaden their mental horizons. Some made their school aged children serve as tutors. Others taught themselves. In a short story by Polish-American author Monica Krawcyk, a Polish immigrant takes on extra domestic work to buy an encyclopedia for her husband and children:

> each morning after the family left, Antosia was down on her knees in the front room, looking over the books, studying the pictures, giving sound to the words. Sometimes she stayed with them so long that the bread dough was running out of the pan, or her lunch was late, or beds had gone unmade. . . . she could never get enough of them.[15]

Ethnic Schools

Many first- and second-generation immigrant girls who attended public schools also attended afternoon or weekend schools in their ethnic communities. Some of these supplementary schools were sponsored by churches or synagogues. Others, like the Japanese school described in selection 3, were secular. A few, like the Free Thought and socialist Sunday schools, were militantly atheistic. New schools opened as new groups arrived. According to sociologist Joshua Fishman, the number of ethnic schools tripled between 1960 and 1980, reaching a total of at least six thousand nationwide.[16]

Ethnic schools fostered community cohesion and helped children born in America or brought here at an early age to understand the language and customs of their parents. As the experience of Japanese-American Monica Sone in selection 3 suggests, however, most of these schools failed to fulfill the anti-assimilationist hopes of their founders; the attraction of mainstream American culture was too strong.

Continuity and Change

As a new wave of immigration, mostly Latina and Asian, arrived in the 1970s and 1980s, public schools, churches, and private and governmental agencies once again developed educational programs for immigrant women. As Gail Kelly's article on Vietnamese women refugees (selection 4) illustrates, these programs continued many of the undesirable features of their predecessors. Some neglected women. Those addressed to women often repeated the mistakes of their predecessors by incorporating stereotypical and inaccurate ideas about the needs of their clients. Heavily subscribed language and job training programs often gave preference to men, assuming, incorrectly, that ethnic traditions would keep women out of the work force. Job training for women focused on low-paid "pink collar" occupations.

In the post-1965 period, as at the turn of the century, many women did not participate in these programs, although more probably wanted to. Problems with transportation and childcare were common. "If only someone would help me babysit! . . . I would study all day long," said a Hmong woman in Fresno, California.[17] Some women were afraid to attend night classes. "Three times I tried ESL (English as a Second Language). No good. Many bad things happened to me here in America. . . . It is very dangerous at night," said a young Cambodian widow.[18] "It is not possible for me to learn good English and at the same time get a job," said another, noting that all her neighbors spoke Spanish. "Maybe I should learn Spanish."[19]

A major difference from previous periods was the presence in the late twentieth century of a much larger number of well-educated, professional women. These women spent years learning English (if they did not know it before), taking "refresher" courses, and studying for licensing examinations. Their lives illustrate the close connection between education and social mobility. "Magda," who immigrated from Argentina in 1988 at the age of forty-four, was a clinical psychologist with a doctorate and extensive teaching and research experience. In Miami she worked in a clothing store, carrying heavy boxes of jeans and then in a day care center until she learned enough English to get a job in a geriatric unit and enroll at the university. "I remember leaving at the end of the first day of classes with tears of joy in my eyes," she told an interviewer. "I still have a long way to go, but I am confident I will get there."[20]

The Latina and Asian girls who entered the public schools in the 1970s and 1980s had advantages not available to school girls in the past. They were placed with others their age rather than in first grade. Bilingual/bicultural education and other programs had been created to ease their language transition. Title IX, the result of the new wave of feminism, guaranteed them access to educational programs formerly reserved for boys.

However, problems remained. Teenaged refugees whose education had been disrupted for years found it difficult to do high school work and learn English at the same time. Shortages of funds and qualified teachers deprived many students of access to language programs, and many programs stopped short of providing the English fluency needed for higher education. Long and frequent trips to the homeland by Latina or Caribbean families could disrupt classwork. Racial incidents in the schools were not uncommon.[21]

As in the past, cultural conflicts interfered with education. Many Asian and Latina girls found that the individualism espoused in American schools conflicted with the great emphasis upon family cohesion in their cultures. Chinese and other girls from more authoritarian school systems were confused by the teachers' demands that they express their feelings and interests: "too much freedom is no freedom at all. We are constantly asked to make decision. . . . What do you want to do? Which one do you want? . . . It is so hard to make decisions. . . . I'm not used to it. . . . I even find it painful, so I wind up doing nothing."[22] Girls from societies that were reticient about sex could be uncomfortable with the outspokenness of their American classmates. Girls from hostile political cultures had to adjust to a country they had been taught to distrust. "I cried a lot at first and said, 'Why did they [parents] bring me here?' " admitted Aurora Campos, who arrived from Communist Cuba at the age of fourteen. It took her two years to conclude, "because it's better."[23]

Many Asian and Hispanic girls struggled in school and left (or dropped out) with poor language skills and poor prospects for the future. Others did well in subjects like mathematics, where knowledge from the homeland could be used and English was less important, but poorly in social studies, literature, and American history. A conspicuous minority, especially those who came from urban areas and whose parents were well educated, made astonishing progress, winning academic awards in high school and acceptance at prestigious colleges and universities. These students were motivated not only by personal ambition but also by a desire to fulfill their parents' hopes and dreams.

The strength of traditional sex roles for women in some immigrant societies caused conflicts for foreign-born girls who became acculturated to the more flexible sex roles offered by American society and the American school. Canthou Sam, a popular and successful Cambodian high school student who wanted to be an accountant, experienced this conflict. "A Cambodian woman is supposed to sit at home, cook, and clean house," she acknowledged. "[But] I want my own job, house, and car before I marry. I want to be independent. . . . It is very hard to be caught in the clash of cultures."[24]

For other girls, there was little or no conflict. A 1987 study by James R. Campbell found that traditional (in other respects) Chinese families in New York City encouraged their daughters as well as their sons to go to college and did not object to daughters choosing nontraditional (for women) fields. The study attributed this to the families' desire first for economic security and then for social mobility in the new country. Campbell's study also attributed it to the fact that most immigrant families were too poor and too busy to maintain the traditional separate female culture for their daughters. First- and second-generation Chinese girls in New York City chose mathematical and scientific fields as often as their brothers, and more often than mainstream American girls.[25]

Dreams and Realities

Many women whose formal education had been cut short by economic or family responsibilities had no desire to continue it later. For others, however, the desire for further schooling was a lifelong aspiration. Most early twentieth-century immigrants, like the Japanese poet whose work appears in the final selection, never had the time or the money to realize their educational aspirations. They saw their dreams fulfilled if at all, in the lives of their children and grandchildren.

A fortunate few, however, did achieve their goal. As older students began to appear on American campuses in the decades after World War II, these elderly foreign-born women returned to the classroom.

> I remember when I was a teenager, even younger, I said to my father, "I don't want any dresses, no clothes, nothing. Just send me to high school. They called it *gymnasiia* in Kiev. . . .
>
> I was after music. From my childhood I loved that. But of course the Revolution, interruptions . . . marriage . . . children. . . . But you know what? After my children grew up, I went to Chicago Musical College four or five years. I was the oldest student I think. I was a grandma already.[26]

Notes

1. Robert A. Woods, *Americans in Progress: A Settlement Study of Residents and Associations of the South End House* (New York: Riverside Press, 1903), pp. 303–4.

2. Pearl Idelia Ellis, *Americanization Through Homemaking* (Los Angeles: Wetzel, 1929), pp. 30–31.

3. Grace Abbott, *The Immigrant and the Community* (New York: Century, 1917), p. 224.

4. Ibid., pp. 226–27.

5. Leonard Covello, *The Social Background of the Italo-American School Child: A Study of the South Italian Family Mores and Their Effect on the School Situation in Italy and America* (Leiden: E. J. Brill, 1967), p. 338.

6.   Judith Ortiz Cofer, *Silent Dancing: A Partial Remembrance of a Puerto Rican Childhood* (Houston: Arte Publico Press, 1990), p. 126.

7.   Elizabeth Loza Newby, *A Migrant with Hope* (Nashville: Broadman Press, 1977), pp. 36–37.

8.   Mary Antin, *The Promised Land* (Boston: Houghton Mifflin, 1912), p. 215.

9.   Covello, *Social Background*, p. 317.

10.   Frederick Houghton, *Immigrant Education: A Handbook Prepared for the Board of Education* (New York, 1927), pp. 7–9.

11.   Peter Roberts, *The New Immigration: A Study of the Industrial and Social Life of Southern and Eastern Europeans in America* (New York: Macmillan, 1912), p. 286.

12.   Marie Prisland, *From Slovenia to America: Recollections and Collections* (Chicago: Slovenian Women's Union of America, 1968), pp. 56–58.

13.   Rose Schneiderman and Lucy Goldthwaite, *All for One* (New York: Paul S. Eriksson, 1967), p. 39.

14.   Fania Cohen, "Educational and Social Activities of the International Ladies Garment Workers Union," *American Federationist* 36 (1929): 1446–52; and "Twelve Years of Educational Activities of the International Ladies Garment Workers Union," *American Federationist* 36 (1929): 105–11.

15.   Monica Krawczyk, "For Nickels and Dimes," in *If the Branch Blossoms and Other Stories* (Minneapolis: Polanie, 1950), p. 94.

16.   Joshua A. Fishman, "The Americanness of the Ethnic School," in *Minnesota's Ethnic Language Schools: Potential for the 80s*, ed. Betty Ann Burch (St. Paul: Immigration History Research Center, University of Minnesota, 1983), p. 7.

17.   *Hmong Resettlement Study Site Report: Fresno, California* (Washington, D.C.: Office of Refugee Resettlement, 1984), p. 51.

18.   John Tenhula, *Voices from Southeast Asia: The Refugee Experience in the United States* (New York: Holmes and Meier, 1991), p. 117.

19.   Ibid., pp. 117–18.

20.   Zita Zanotti Cazzaniga, "Immigrant Women Interview Project," unpublished student interview, April 1992.

21.   Joan McCarty and John Willshire Carrera, *New Voices: Immigrant Students in the U.S. Public Schools* (Boston: National Coalition of Advocates for Students, 1988). See also Maxine Schwartz Seller, "Immigrants in the Schools—Again: Historical and Contemporary Perspectives on the Education of Post-1965 Immigrants in the United States," *Educational Foundations* (Spring 1989): 53–75.

22. Betty Lee Sung, *Transplanted Chinese Children*, report to the Administration for Children, Youth, and the Family, Department of Health, Education, and Welfare, City College of New York, 1979, p. 67.

23. Helga Silva, *Children of Mariel: From Shock to Integration: Cuban Refugee Children in South Florida Schools* (Washington, D.C.: Department of Education and Cuban-American National Foundation, 1985), p. 17.

24. Tricia Knoll, *Becoming American: Asian Sojourners, Immigrants, and Refugees in the Western United States* (Portland, Oreg.: Coast to Coast Books, 1982), p. 165.

25. James R. Campbell, Rosalind Wu, Jeanne Pizzo, and Francine Mandel, "Parental Adaptation," paper presented at American Educational Research Association annual meeting, April 10–14, 1987, Washington, D.C.

26. Sydelle Kramer and Jenny Masur, eds., *Jewish Grandmothers* (Boston: Beacon Press, 1976), p. 86.

1

———◆◇◆———

"The Lessons Which Most Influenced My Life . . .
Came from My Parents"

Polish-born Harriet Pawlowska attended public schools in Cleveland and Detroit, where she remembers receiving an excellent academic education. She also remembers the pain she felt when textbooks ignored or distorted Polish history and when teachers mangled the pronunciation of her name. These and other negative lessons about being Polish-American would recur throughout her adult life. Pawlowska learned respect for herself and pride in her Polish heritage, however, through a different set of lessons, a positive curriculum taught in the home rather than the school. Her family, particularly her father, introduced her to American life, to Polish history and culture, and to the ideals and values that shaped her life. As Pawlowska's memoir demonstrates, family, home, and neighborhood were important educational influences in the lives of many young immigrant women.

I cannot think of growing up in America without feeling the weight of my Polish heritage. Sometimes this weight has been a burden like a cross which I accepted as part of my birthright. Most of the time, however, it was as natural a part of my life as the sun which gave me warmth or the wind that blew my hair into my eyes as I ran across the schoolyard in a game of hide-and-seek.

Although I had excellent teachers from the first (my parents never gave any of us a chance to think otherwise), the lessons which most influenced my life and that of my sister and brother came from my parents. It is from them we learned who we were as Polish immigrants, what we stood for, and the need for beauty, integrity and joy.

Joy I associate with my mother. Each spring as the sun pours forth on Palm Sunday, Easter and Pentecost, I am filled with a happiness which can be traced like a delicate cord to my childhood when my mother set the scene for a joyful resurrection after a long and lean Lenten season. The house sparkled, the air was filled with the aroma of vanilla, raisins and eggs beaten into

Source: Harriet Pawlowska, "The Education of Harriet Pawlowska," in *Growing Up Slavic,* ed. Michael Novak (Washington, D.C.: EMPAC, 1976), pp. 21–27. Reprinted by permission.

prize babas (pastries), and we children were dressed in the best buttons and bows which her inventive mind and limited purse could afford. There must have been cloudy and cold spring days when the immigrants celebrated the coming of Christ's passion, but I don't remember them. Only recently on a beautiful day I remarked to a friend, "This Palm Sunday reminds me of my childhood, the sun, the joy of it, when my mother. . ."

Three years after we came to this country, my father bought a house on the outskirts of Detroit in a rapidly changing neighborhood. Yes, they moved out in those days too. The house was fifty dollars down, which he borrowed from a friend, and twelve dollars a month on a $1500 land contract. When I stood on the front porch I could look down a long row of porches exactly like ours. As a child, I was fascinated by this narrow canyon down which I could peer and watch people who were near yet separated from me by lines and spaces. Modern artists like to play with that idea. Picasso gave us illusions on this theme, but I had the real thing before me, immigrants like myself, but emigrated from Galicia, the slice that Maria Therese cut for herself. Our neighbors were small in stature, with music in their voices, a sing-song kind of melody when they spoke from these porches or over fences after church on sunny Sunday mornings. Evenings one could hear a fiddler, sitting on the porch steps, gently scraping his fiddle and coaxing a melancholy tune into the darkness. "He's lonesome for the old country," I thought. Years later when I was collecting folksongs, I came across one of those plaintive melodies. It was a love song.

Inside, the dining room table was the setting for my father's classroom, for he was a born teacher and raconteur, setting the mood for learning, giving his children what Detroit schools could not. When we were little children, he regaled our mother and us with tales of his experiences, taught us folksongs, played games of wit with us, teasing us with sleight of hand or a play upon words. As we grew older, there came a steady stream of Polish history, feats of honor, days of glory.

I remember when I was studying American history in the eighth grade, I came home with proud tales from America's past. Instead of listening to what *I* was "teaching" *him*, he matched each incident with one from Poland's past. The Polish constitution of May 3rd, he said, was as great if not greater, and he enumerated act and article which humanized the Polish land. I was angry with him in those days of my youth for his stubborn Polishness. Wasn't he an American now? Shouldn't he listen to my tales of America as I had to his about Poland? But I got over my youthful impatience and continued to drink in his lessons until that fateful day in high school when I purchased my first history book.

I didn't have time to look into it until after I had boarded the street car for home. I remember the excitement with which I opened the book to the index and ran my finger down the P's until I came to *Poland*. There was a foreboding of ill when I noticed only one page listed, but somewhere in my heart was a certainty, a fiery hope that many pages of Polish history followed that one page listed. I found the page. I can still see it, even though this happened long ago. One third of the page down there was a short paragraph dealing with the "sad" fate of a nation which because of misrule was partitioned by Russia, Germany and Austria. The rest of the page dealt with something else.

For a long time I couldn't bear to listen to anything my father had to say. I never told him what had happened . . . ever . . . even after I had recognized the treachery that writers of history can deal out. Nor have I been able to discuss Polish history with Americans, any phase of it, unless they are informed, and few are. I must say, however, that some modern historians take time to know the land and its people before they write. Several years ago when I began a study of modern Poland between the two World Wars as historians see her, I found some who wrote about Poland honestly and objectively, nor did they dismiss the subject in one short paragraph.

The tragedy of this experience had far-reaching effects upon me. Even today, I find myself snarling at friends who expect American acculturation to wipe out every vestige of Polish culture within me.

Not all lessons which my father taught had such tragic endings. There were those which dealt with personal integrity, which had life-long effect upon me. It was our custom to gather at the round dinner table not only to eat the simple food my mother prepared, but to exchange our day's experiences.

It was at mealtime that we learned of my father's joys and tribulations in the world of bricklaying: when the job would be a long one (O good!); when it was about to end and the search for a new one had to begin (O God, I can't look at my mother's face!); when rain or deep frost put a halt to work and pay (for years I couldn't face a rainy day without the blues); about the tools he used (how often I have felt that I could do a better job of whatever I was doing if only I had a level, a T-square or a *hebel*, a word that sounds more like home to me than plane); about masonry as an art (which I notice even in today's buildings); or the fun of everyday happenings with fellow bricklayers. We children had our turn too. We bragged a little, but on the whole our parents got a good picture of what was going on in our lives outside of home.

One day while I was walking home from school with my friend, Esther Richards, she confided that she planned to be a teacher when she grew up. "I'd like to be," I said, "but I can't." "Why not?" she asked. "Because I have a funny name," I replied.

Somehow Pawlowska seemed completely out of line with Cottrell, Cozy, Birkamp, Christman, Van Dyke, Reekie, McGreevey. At age ten, that was an impossible hurdle to leap, especially when Esther said, "You're right." We were both very sad.

I wore my martyr's mantle to the dinner table that evening. Waiting for the appropriate moment, I repeated my sad story to my parents, fully expecting everyone to break into tears, even my little brother who at six could demonstrate sympathy with eyes always filled with wonder.

My father's hazel eyes turned into cold steel. He stopped eating, his knife and fork poised against the edge of the table. "Don't ever let me hear *you*, or any of you" (he looked at each of us sternly), "say that again. If you don't become a teacher, it won't be because of your name. It'll be because there is something lacking here!" and he pointed to his chest.

A couple of years later, I brought a tale of personal triumph to the dinner table. I had asked Miss Clawson to change my mark in history from 2 to 1. In those days 1's were like today's A's. "You gave Pauline 1 and I think my work is as good as hers," I argued.

Well, that didn't impress my father. "If you thought you deserved the top grade, you should have proved the merit of your work. Never try to reach the heights by climbing on another's back. Pauline had nothing to do with it!"

Thus it was, step by step, he taught the parental curriculum assigned to him by natural responsibility. It had nothing to do with our being foreigners, but he wanted to help with the problems we had to face in life.

On Sundays we took street cars to Belle Isle bridge, then walked the wooden structure of that day to the band shell where we listened to an hour of lively music. When we told him of a students' art exhibit at Cass Technical High, he said, "Let's go." Somewhere in his shift from job to job, he came across the log cabin at Palmer Park and took us there for some early American history. The launching of a ship into the Detroit River at Ecorse was marked for a Sunday trip for the family. It mattered little that he was "Hey you! Cholly!" to most Americans. He was making this land his land and preparing his children for smooth assimilation. Life was a history book to be lived fully. Anything else was a dullard's way out. And if his way seems severe today, let me assure you that we never felt unloved or unappreciated.

I was fortunate in the schools I attended and the teachers who taught me. Only one showed rank prejudice, but that is an excellent average when one considers the years of schooling from first grade through graduate school at Wayne University. . . .

There must have been evidence of an insidious prejudice in Detroit of which I was not aware, however. One educator, Charles M. Novak, convinced the Detroit Board that if he were to take over the administration of the newly built school on Detroit's east side, he wanted a free hand to prove that the children of Detroit's east side foreign born were as responsive to higher educational standards as those in well-heeled, long time American neighborhoods. He asked for a free hand in selecting his staff. He sought out teachers with Polish backgrounds, and Polish was to be an elective in the language department. That is how I got to Northeastern High as you probably have guessed. My father read about the Polish language course, and off I went, changing street cars downtown for an hour's ride each way in my junior and senior years.

The experience was not to be forgotten. The teachers were enthusiastic. The students were alive *and* Polish, so many of them. There was a Polish librarian and a teacher of Polish. We were coming into our own, back there during World War I, I thought then. Like so many of the feminine surnames, mine was changed to an *ska* ending also, at the suggestion of my counsellor. Although students were called by their first names, surnames were not mangled, nor did teachers stumble over the class rolls at the beginning of the semester as they did over mine at Western High where I was the only Pole in the school. I always dreaded that hesitation over my name and then the inevitable "It looks like Pavlova but it isn't." It was at Northeastern that I was introduced to my first symphony. Little need be said about the leap from the fiddle and accordian of Home Street to Beethoven's Third in Northeastern's auditorium by the Detroit Symphony that day. It happened so easily, the liquid rhythm, the melodic flow taking me with it, and above all the harmony of many sounds blending, moving and blending—an unforgettable experience for a fifteen-year-old.

In evaluating my father's contribution to our bridging the gap between the two cultures, and his teaching of values against which we could measure our steps through life, I have often wished he had taught us to be aggressive. Much of what had slipped through our fingers was the result of frontal attacks or benign neglect which left us unprepared with defenses because we had been taught that worthy efforts would be met with rewards, and our personal integrity would bring honor to home, country and cultural roots. It hasn't been so. Sometimes the rewards came with strings attached which I could not accept. At other times, I took matters into my own hands, swallowed my pride and said in effect, "Look! This is my academic background . . . ," presenting an impressive list of accomplishments. The answer was an astonished "Why didn't you let me know before?" When I asked, "But don't you have my record?" the individual muttered something and set the wheels in motion.

Later when I was teaching in the high school where a large percentage of the student body was of Polish descent, I considered myself a natural candidate for promotion to counsellorship. It was this principal who was able to make snide remarks about the Polish community in my hearing and who threw the promotion application at me from across his broad desk with the remark, "It's not what you know; it's who you know that counts!" All this left me with the feeling that I was a 20th century freak unfamiliar with the rules of the game and that somewhere I had missed an important ingredient for success in the modern world. . . .

Although I no longer consider my name to be a funny one, I am constantly meeting people who do. The worst example occurred several years ago when a member of my church came to my door on a Sunday afternoon to pick up a donation which I had neglected to send in. This was one of the occasions when I was alert and met him head on. When I answered the doorbell, he politely bade me good afternoon and then uttered a garbled something which was supposed to be my name. I just shook my head no. He looked at his pad and tried again, coming out with something really ludicrous. "There is nobody by that name here," I said quietly. This time he glanced at our house number, then at his pad, then took a good look at the name. "I beg your pardon," he said, "Miss Pawlowska?" I ushered him in. Nothing was said about the little drama at the door. I gave him the check and we parted friends.

Like the Polish joke, garbling of Polish names and the remarks which often accompany introduction such as "I can't think of your name; it's so hard" (which mine isn't), or "I don't remember her name. It's kind of funny and hard to pronounce" have no place in the United States where Polish names have been part of American culture since Captain John Smith's time (although the glass blowers' names are recorded in Latin). As in the case of the gentleman cited above, it is almost always a matter of not looking carefully at the name of dismissing it immediately upon hearing its Polish sound as too unimportant to be concerned with.

The problems of acculturation have not lessened the quality of life in the United States, only outlined more sharply the roles assigned to us. As I look back, I see a rich variety in a kaleidoscope of scenes which comprise the early part of my life, from the leisurely walks in the parks of Cleveland where we spent the first three years in America and where my mother tried to continue what she had known in Warsaw; to the hurdy-gurdy life in Delray with its folk weddings and folksongs, its organ grinders and gypsies, the peddlers who carried packs filled with pins and needles, cologne and laces, and the peddlers in horse-drawn carts who called off their pungent vegetables and fragrant fruits in sing-song melodies. It was an all-Polish community where one could be baptized, fed, clothed, married and buried in the Polish language. We spent ten years there and I am grateful for the experience.

I am proud that Warsaw is my birthplace. I feel strongly the kinship to a valiant people. I am aware of the indestructibility of their nature and the creative force that gives their lives meaning. I love them deeply.

I am proud to be an American. I salute the great men and women of the past whose wisdom and moral courage laid the foundation for this great nation.

2

"An Impossible Dream":
The Struggle for Higher Education

*Sometimes the "hidden curriculum" of the ethnic family thwarted rather than en-
couraged the educational aspirations of immigrant women, as illustrated in this
chapter from the autobiography of the Mexican-born daughter of a migrant farm
worker family. Young Elizabeth Loza Newby describes the anguish she felt in
1966 when her "old country" father forced her to choose between the protection and
companionship of her family and the opportunity to acquire higher education. Such
a choice was especially painful for her because of the great importance placed upon
family ties in traditional Mexican culture.*

*Newby's father feared that college would corrupt his daughter's morals and,
more justifiably, that it would change her life-style and diminish his authority over
her. Though the chapter focuses on the daughter's dilemma, the dilemma of her
mother is equally poignant. At the risk of not seeing her daughter again, Newby's
mother encouraged her aspirations for a different and better life.*

As I grew up in both the American and Mexican cultures, I was able to
pick up the English language easily. Though Spanish was spoken at
home and I was comfortable using Spanish with my family and friends, I
knew that if I were to escape from the migrant life, I was going to have to
master English. Since I viewed education as the most important thing in my
life, I knew that I had to be able to speak and comprehend the language that
was used at school. With the help of some very special teachers and an understanding mother, I was able to break the cycle that has imprisoned so
many of my people.

At the end of my sophomore year in high school my father decided that
my education should be terminated. He thought that school filled me with
too many foolish ideas, such as going to college; and besides, school was too
worldly. My mother, on the other hand, always encouraged me to continue
my education and was happy that I stayed, but she hardly ever opposed
Dad's wishes. He was the ruler of the home, and he made sure that we knew
that. He did not see the need for me to continue my education: He had arranged a marriage for me when I was a child, and schooling was not neces-

---

sary for me to be a wife and mother. I had known of this arrangement for a long time, for my parents had talked of it incessantly after my fifteenth birthday. Of course, this marriage arrangement custom was and is very old and is hardly ever practiced anymore. But since my father was very "old country," he saw nothing wrong with this ancient custom.

The young man whose wife I was supposed to become was about twenty-eight years old. He came from a very old French and Spanish family of our native home in Mexico. The first time I saw him was on a rainy spring afternoon when I arrived home from school. As I opened the door to our home, I was greeted by five smiling brown faces. . . . The five people in the room were my mother and father, Pablo Rodriguez (the man I was to marry), and his mother and father. The Rodriguezes had traveled all the way from Mexico City to meet me and to take me back with them so that I could marry Pablo.

I was almost sixteen years old. I had had enough education and had developed enough determination to oppose my parents' wishes. . . . I immediately let my negative feelings concerning this arranged marriage be known to all in the room. . . . I was determined not to be forced into a marriage I did not desire just for the sake of tradition. Consequently, I objected and refused to marry the chosen young man.

This action brought shame and disgrace to my father and it was not to be forgotten. . . .

It is easy to see how difficult it was for me to get my father's permission to continue my education after what had occurred. Once again, I called on one of my teachers for counsel regarding my educational dilemma. Mrs. Gilmore, the teacher to whom I presented my problem, had been very good to me throughout my freshman and sophomore years in high school. I could always count on her for guidance, since she was understanding of my Mexican migrant background and knew about my father's "old country" ways. . . . Following a time of searching and consolation, she advised me to go to Mr. Mullen, the school counselor. . . .

When I arrived at the counselor's office, Mr. Mullen had my file on his desk and was going over my grades. He asked me to be seated. Following a few moments of silence as he studied my file, he leaned back in his chair and said, "Elizabeth, I believe it is possible for you to graduate next year if you can obtain your father's consent to continue in school. This offer is dependent upon two considerations: First of all, you must maintain an average of C or better; and secondly, you must have a better attendance record."

The first stipulation didn't bother me, but I worried about attendance. My parents had always kept me home from school whenever they needed me for babysitting, housework, or work in the fields. I knew that even if I did get permission to continue in school, regular attendance was going to be very difficult. I thanked Mr. Mullen for his help and left for home in a perplexed mood. I was happy about the possibility of graduating the next year, but I worried about obtaining my father's permission.

I told my mother the good news, and she was very pleased. She said she would try to help me convince Dad to let me finish school. Time was of the essence; if I were allowed to finish high school, I would have to work and earn some money for clothes and other school expenses. I had decided to ask Dad the big question that evening, and until he arrived home from work I stayed in my room and practiced on how I might approach him.

Finally, after supper, I decided to ask him my pressing question. My whole body was shaking and my voice quivered as I explained to him the possibility of my graduating from high school the next year, if only he would allow me to go. Afterward there was a long silence. My father then said, "You do have your nerve! After all the shame you have put me through these past few months, do you believe that you can still do whatever you want?" Mom and I sat in silence, afraid to respond.

I then decided that I had nothing to lose by my insistence; so I started to tell him of the magnificent opportunity I was being offered, which did not occur often enough for our people. . . . Talking back to one's father in our culture was just not done, and by so doing I was risking severe punishment. My father became very angry, stood up from the dinner table, smashed his half-smoked cigar in his plate, and slapped me across the face. He sent me to my room crying.

My dear mother settled him down, and the next day she assured me that I would be allowed to finish school. She said that my father had been reluctant to give his permission; but late that evening, following a convincing argument by my mother he had consented. She also said that she was counting on me not to disappoint her. I hugged her and told her not to worry. We then began to make plans for the completion of my last year in high school, sharing a mood of great happiness.

The last year of high school went by quickly. The work load was tremendous; the pressures were great; and my work at home was heavy. Often I stayed up late studying and got up early to do my chores before I left for school. Such was my routine, day in and day out. Mother did all she could to lighten my load, but I knew she couldn't do more. Besides, I did not want her to overwork. . . .

I took one day at a time; and finally, at the end of the year, I received my high school diploma. Tears were flowing from my eyes as I walked down the center aisle in the school gymnasium and proudly accepted my diploma from the school principal. It was a joyous occasion, and I can still remember the proud expression on my mother's face as she snapped one picture after another with a camera she had borrowed from a neighbor. . . .

It was a grand day of celebration; but even though it was a day to remember and the most exciting event that had ever happened to me up to that
time, a more profound life-changing event was about to occur.

Late one afternoon, within a week following my graduation from high
school, Mother greeted me at the door . . . holding a letter that was addressed to me from the school principal. She anxiously handed me the letter
and asked me to open it immediately. I was nervous and scared as I ripped
open the envelope, expecting to read the crushing news that there had been
a mixup in their records and that, for some reason, they were rescinding
my diploma. As I read the letter I discovered that I could not have been further from the truth. The note said that I was the recipient of a one-thousand-
dollar scholarship for college.

The feeling that I experienced at that moment is indescribable. This was
an impossible dream come true—an answer to prayer. At last I was being
given the opportunity to escape from my dreary migrant existence.

While most of my classmates were destined to go to institutions of
higher learning, I considered myself fortunate just to complete high school.
My sense of accomplishment, which my mother shared, is beyond expression
in words. For Mother it was a wonderful experience to see one of her children graduate from high school, let alone have an opportunity to continue
study in college. We were both ecstatic! . . .

Mom and I decided to select an institution near relatives, where I could
get help in obtaining employment or perhaps even stay with them while in
college. After much consideration we decided on a college in southern Texas,
where we had many relatives. We sent for an application and entrance papers
and made all the arrangements.

We knew it was going to be difficult to tell Dad; but at this point I felt
that I was in so much trouble with Dad from our previous problems that one
more defiant act on my part would not make me any less endearing. . . .

He was furious! He was, in fact, so upset that he could hardly speak.
The first thing he said was: "I knew I should never have let you go to school
this last year. I have been too free with you, and all I have received in return
is disgrace!" All this was beyond me, for I failed to see how going to college
could be rebellious or disgraceful; and I pointed this out to him. Nevertheless, he continued his tirade and gave me the longest lecture I had ever heard
on the evils of college and the terrible nature of career women. It seemed as
though he would never finish. Mom and I sat in grave silence until his tirade
ended. At this point we tried to tell him about the advantages of higher education and how I would be under the careful eye of relatives while I was in
college. This argument did not help, and he stormed out the door while we
stood there helpless. . . . He could not understand why I could not accept
the traditional life-style of the typical Mexican migrant girl. I know that he
loved me, but he just could not understand the changing times and felt

threatened by higher education. . . . Dad did not speak to me for the rest of the week. The following Sunday, the day before I was supposed to leave, he finally approached me. . . . He said, "I have given this matter much thought, and I have only one thing to say; so listen carefully for you will have to live with the decision you make. Once we terminate this conversation we shall never speak of it again." By this time my stomach was in knots, and I knew somehow this decision was going to hurt. Then, in the very brief statement he made next, my world came crashing down all around me, leaving me drained and speechless. He continued: "I have decided that you can give up all these foolish ideas about college and have the love and protection of your family, or you can go ahead with your foolish plans to enter college. But the minute you walk out our door, consider it closed to you forever."

I was numb. I couldn't believe what I was hearing. . . .

After Dad had left, Mom came in to comfort me. She placed her hands on my shoulders and said, "Elizabeth I know this is a difficult decision you have to make, but I want you to think about this: Don't let emotion and 'old country' traditions hinder your future. You *are* and *always will be* my daughter. Your father can never take that away from me. I want you to go and take advantage of this wonderful opportunity. Make us all proud. Your father is slow to change, but give him time and pray for him. Please go with my blessing."

With great reluctance I left home that last Monday of August 1966. It was the most difficult decision I had ever had to make, for I knew full well the consequences of being disowned. That day was a turning point in my life in that my family ties and relationships could never be the same again—I had lost my father forever. I was frightened and lonely as I boarded the bus for college, and my heart was heavy for Mom and the family. I knew that life would never be as it had so long been. Mine was a tearful and sad departure. I cried most of the way to Texas, thinking about the family which I had lost. . . .

When I arrived in Texas and no one was there to meet me at the station, I knew that one of my fears was already becoming a reality. I decided to call my aunt just in case she had not been sure of my arrival time. During our phone conversation, my aunt informed me that all of my relatives knew that I had been disowned by my family and consequently felt obligated to abide by my father's wishes. This meant, of course, that they would be unable to help me. While she felt sorry for me, she thought it best not to get involved with my family problem. She ended the conversation by wishing me the best. Under the circumstances, I was glad to have ended the conversation on this positive note. Feeling completely alone and lost, I hung up the phone.

Never in my life had I been so completely alone. In the cold and lonely atmosphere of the bus station, I tried to decide what to do next. The more I sat there, the more tempted I was to get on the next bus home and beg my father's forgiveness; but my pride would not let me do it. I reckoned with myself that I was going to have to make it alone, now or never. . . .

I walked toward the largest building on campus, hoping that I could find help from someone inside. As I entered the front door, I felt the cool blast of air conditioning on my tired, hot body. The trip down to Texas had been long and tiring, and the weather was hot and humid. These conditions, combined with lack of rest, caused me to feel somewhat faint.

I inquired at the reception desk, asking where I might find someone to whom I could talk concerning personal problems. . . . Following a brief wait, I was ushered in to see the dean. . . .

He looked as if he had been through a long, hard day, and I felt slightly guilty about burdening this man with some more problems. I found him to be very warm and understanding. The expression on his face as I told him my story showed a loving concern that I had witnessed many times before in past relationships with teachers.

He arranged for me to stay in the dormitory and to work for my room and board, finding me a job in the language department for $1.25 an hour. It wasn't much, but it was a beginning. . . .

My two college years were a learning as well as a frustrating experience. I was a country bumpkin, without even much farm experience, and my naïveté was obvious. In the beginning I was depressed and extremely homesick, and the drab gray color of my dormitory room did not help my spirits. The room looked bare and lifeless with the lone bed, desk, and lamp, but I could not get in the mood to fix it up and make it more lively. Mr room in fact reflected my personality during my college years in Texas. Most of my depression had stemmed from the crisis which I had experienced at home. I wrote to Mother frequently, but never once received an answer. Later I learned that my father had forbidden her to write me, under the threat of physical abuse. If I had known the circumstances, I would not have put Mother through such a strain.

Most of my time in school was spent in one of four places: the library, where I studied; the language department, where I worked; the cafeteria, where I ate; and my dormitory room, where I slept. This was my world, and the occasions when I ventured out of this self-imposed restrictive environment were rare.

The frustrations of wanting to learn and be a good student, but of feeling burdened by the conditions I left at home, caused me to contemplate suicide. Alone in my room at night, I envisioned different ways to take my own life, thinking that if I did kill myself I could get even with my father. . . .

I was finding the pressures of the outside world greater than I had expected them to be. I had left home after the start of the Vietnam War; and campus unrest, drugs, and hippie communes were all a part of my college experience. Confusion, along with unfamiliarity with campus life, was my constant companion. I was approached by all kinds of campus organizations, but I refused membership in them out of fear of being unacceptable to my peers. I kept pretty much to myself, as I had done in high school, and had only limited friendships. . . .

On the lighter side of my college life, in 1967 I ate my first hamburgers and french fries. This experience occurred when I was invited to dinner by a fellow student—my first date! I had a difficult time trying to decide whether to go on this first date; and Thomas, the young man who asked me out, seemed surprised at my innocence. . . .

After dinner, Thomas walked with me back to the dormitory, where we said goodnight. In a quick move that took me by surprise, he leaned down and gently kissed me on the cheek. I was stunned for a moment, but soon regained my composure and thanked him for the nice evening by shaking his hand. . . .

During my college years in Texas, I was also faced with the temptation to use drugs. . . . The temptation to join the crowd and take something to erase my problems, if even for a short while, was great; but I knew that once the power of the drug wore off, the problems would still be there. Though I was vulnerable, I was not weak enough to deny my responsibility and take the easy way out. There were numerous times when I was so low that nothing in life seemed to matter. Only with God's help was I able to survive those times of temptation and to reject the lower paths I could have followed.

Finally, after two years of agony and unhappiness, Dr. Cooper, one of my professors, called me into his office. . . .

He began our conversation with small talk about the weather and played with the items atop his desk in a fidgety manner. After about ten minutes he said abruptly, "Let's talk about your life, beginning with your life as a migrant, and your relationship to your family." We discussed my life from its start to the present for some two hours, then finally came to my future. My future was something I hadn't thought about since I had arrived on campus. Somehow my future had lost its importance during those two years. I really had no one with whom to share my dreams; beside, by that time, I wasn't dreaming much anyway.

Dr. Cooper informed me that I had no future unless I really wanted to have it. He said those magic words, "It's time for you to go home and make everything right with yourself and your family." I wanted desperately to go home, but I told him that I had been disowned and that this meant I was forbidden ever to go home again. He said, "This is 1968! No one gets disowned anymore. . . . Swallow your pride and be realistic. You are not functioning as a human. You are walking around like a zombie. Your mind is at home. Go home! This is the only way you are going to find peace of mind, and perhaps your future will be saved."

By the next day I was packed and ready to go. Dr. Cooper bought me a bus ticket home and drove me to the bus station. I am forever in debt to him for encouraging me to make the decision to return home. Finally, I was really on my way home! Just the thought was sweet and made me peaceful. I knew that I would not be well received by my father and brothers, but I was more than willing to face the consequences just to know and see for myself that those whom I loved were all right. The thought of going home was so wonderful that nothing could mar my joy and great expectation.

I had written to my mother earlier, informing her of my decision to come home. . . .

As the bus entered my hometown, many pleasant and not-so-pleasant memories entered my mind. Though I was beginning to feel like the prodigal returning home, somehow I could not feel guilty over what I had done. Those two years in Texas, however miserable they may have been, were growing years; and I knew that I would never again be able to live with my family.

As we neared the bus station, my heart was beating frantically as my eyes scanned the crowd of people in the depot. I was desperate as the bus came to a halt; there was still no sign of my mother. I disembarked and slowly made my way over to where the luggage was being unloaded. As I waited for the familiar sight of my worn, brown suitcase, I felt a hand upon my shoulder. I quickly spun around and was greeted with the warm loving smile and bright black eyes of my mother. It was the best therapy for my heart and soul just to see her and to hold her close. Following an exchange of hugs we began the short walk from the bus depot to our home.

When we arrived, my father would have nothing to do with me. He made it clear that I could stay only until I could find another place to live. I was prepared for this reaction and realized that my visit at home would be brief. After staying for two months and satisfying my mind on the condition of my parents and brothers, seeing for myself that all was as well as could be expected, I was ready to move on and to try to salvage my future. This time I knew that I could make it because I could be keeping close contact with Mother. Never again would I be alone.

3

The Stubborn Twig:
"My Double Dose of Schooling"

This passage from Monica Sone's memoir Nisei Daughter *describes the author's first encounter with an afternoon Japanese school, Nihon Gakko. A child in the years immediately preceding World War II, Sone lived in a hotel kept by her Japanese-born parents at the edge of a Skid Row neighborhood in Seattle. Considering herself a "Yankee," she was dismayed by her parents' insistence that she and her brother attend Japanese school.*

Like Monica Sone, thousands of foreign-born women, their daughters, and their granddaughters have attended afternoon, evening, or weekend schools sponsored by churches or organizations in the Japanese, Chinese, Korean, Scandinavian, Jewish, Greek, Czech, Ukrainian, and other ethnic communities. These schools offered a curriculum of ethnic language, history, and (usually but not always) religion, supplemented in recent years by "extracurricular" offerings such as art, music, dance, crafts, drama, cooking, summer camping, socials, trips to other nearby communities, even tours to the ethnic homeland. Ethnic schools were handicapped by lack of time, money, equipment, and qualified teachers, and children often resented the infringement upon their "free" time. Many, like Monica Sone, found the curriculum irrelevant to life in an America that does not encourage bilingualism or biculturalism. Some academic learning took place, especially among children whose parents used and valued ethnic language and culture. For most students, however, the greatest impact of the school lay in its reinforcement of ethnic identity and of social cohesion within the ethnic community.

The inevitable, dreaded first day at Nihon Gakko [Japanese school] arrived. Henry and I were dumped into a taxicab, screaming and kicking against the injustice of it all. When the cab stopped in front of a large, square gray-frame building, Mother pried us loose, though we clung to the cab door like barnacles. She half carried us up the hill. We kept up our horrendous shrieking and wailing, right to the school entrance. Then a man burst out of the door. His face seemed to have been carved out of granite and with turned-down mouth and nostrils flaring with disapproval, his black marble eyes

Source: From *Nisei Daughter* by Monica Sone. Copyright 1953 by Monica Sone. By permission of Little, Brown and Company in association with the Atlantic Monthly Press.

crushed us into a quivering silence. This was Mr. Ohashi, the school principal, who had come out to investigate the abominable, un-Japanesey noise on the school premises.

Mother bowed deeply and murmured, "I place them in your hands."

He bowed stiffly to Mother, then fastened his eyes on Henry and me and again bowed slowly and deliberately. In our haste to return the bow, we nodded our heads. With icy disdain, he snapped, "That is not an *ojigi*," He bent forward with well-oiled precision. "Bow from the waist, like this."

I wondered, if Mr. Ohashi had the nerve to criticize us in front of Mother, what more he would do in her absence.

School was already in session and the hallway was empty and cold. Mr. Ohashi walked briskly ahead, opened a door, and Henry was whisked inside with Mother. I caught a glimpse of little boys and girls sitting erect, their books held upright on the desks.

As I waited alone out in the hall, I felt a tingling sensation. This was the moment for escape. I would run and run and run. I would be lost for days so that when Father and Mother finally found me, they would be too happy ever to force me back to Nihon Gakko. But Mr. Ohashi was too cunning for me. He must have read my thoughts, for the door suddenly opened, and he and Mother came out. He bowed formally again, "*Sah,* this way," and stalked off.

My will completely dissolved, I followed as in a terrible nightmare. Mother took my hand and smiled warmly, "Don't look so sad, Ka-chan. You'll find it a lot of fun when you get used to it."

I was ushered into a brightly lighted room which seemed ten times as brilliant with the dazzling battery of shining black eyes turned in my direction. I was introduced to Yasuda-sensei, a full-faced women with a large, ballooning figure. She wore a long, shapeless cotton print smock with streaks of chalk powder down the front. She spoke kindly to me, but with a kindness that one usually reserves for a dull-witted child. She enunciated slowly and loudly, "What is your name?"

I whispered, "Kazuko," hoping she would lower her voice. I felt that our conversation should not be carried on in such a blatant manner.

"*Kazuko-san desuka?*" she repeated loudly. "You may sit over there." She pointed to an empty seat in the rear and I walked down an endless aisle between rows of piercing black eyes.

"Kazuko-san, why don't you remove your hat and coat and hang them up behind you?"

A wave of tittering broke out. With burning face, I rose from my seat and struggled out of my coat.

When Mother followed Mr. Ohashi out of the room, my throat began to tighten and tears flooded up again. I did not notice that Yasuda-sensei was standing beside me. Ignoring my snuffing, she handed me a book, opened to the first page. I saw a blurred drawing of one huge, staring eye. Right above it was a black squiggly mark, resembling the arabic figure one with a bar across the middle. Yasuda-sensei was up in front again, reading aloud, *"Meh!"* That was "eye." As we turned the pages, there were pictures of a long, austere nose, its print reading *"hana,"* an ear was called *"mi-mi,"* and a wide anemic-looking mouth, *"ku-chi."* Soon I was chanting at the top of my voice with the rest of the class, *Meh! Hana! Mi-mi! Ku-chi!"*

Gradually I yielded to my double dose of schooling. Nihon Gakko was so different from grammar school I found myself switching my personality back and forth daily like a chameleon. At Bailey Gatzert School I was a jumping, screaming, roustabout Yankee, but at the stroke of three when the school bell rang and doors burst open everywhere, spewing out pupils like jelly beans from a broken bag, I suddenly became a modest, faltering, earnest little Japanese girl with a small, timid voice. I trudged down a steep hill and climbed up another steep hill to Nihon Gakko with other black-haired boys and girls. On the playground, we behaved cautiously. Whenever we spied a teacher within bowing distance, we hissed at each other to stop the game, put our feet neatly together, slid our hands down to our knees and bowed slowly and sanctimoniously. In just the proper, moderate tone, putting in every ounce of respect, we chanted, *"Konichi-wa, sensei. Good day."*

For an hour and half each day, we were put through our paces. At the beginning of each class hour, Yasuda-sensei punched a little bell on her desk. We stood up by our seats, at strict attention. Another "ping!" We all bowed to her in unison while she returned the bow solemnly. With the third "ping!" we sat down together.

There was *yomi-kata* time when individual students were called upon to read the day's lesson, clear and loud. The first time I recited I stood and read with swelling pride the lesson which I had prepared the night before. I mouthed each word carefully and paused for the proper length of time at the end of each sentence. Suddenly Yasuda-sensei stopped me.

"Kazuko-san!"

I looked up at her confused, wondering what mistakes I had made.

"You are holding your book in one hand," she accused me. Indeed, I was. I did not see the need to using two hands to support a thin book which I could balance with two fingers.

"Use both hands!" she commanded me.

Then she peered at me. "And are you leaning against your desk?" Yes, I was slightly. "Stand up straight!"

"Hai! Yes, ma'am!"

I learned that I could stumble all around in my lessons without ruffling sensei's nerves, but it was a personal insult to her if I displayed sloppy posture. I must stand up like a soldier, hold the book high in the air with both hands, and keep my feet still.

We recited the Japanese alphabet aloud, fifty-one letters, over and over again. "Ah, ee, oo, eh, *OH!* Kah, kee, koo, key, *KOH!* Sah, shi, soo, seh, *SOH!*" We developed a catchy little rhythm, coming down hard on the last syllable of each line. We wound up the drill with an ear-shattering, triumphant, "Lah, lee, loo, leh, *Loh!* WAH, EE, OO, EH, OH! UN!"

Yasuda-sensei would look suspiciously at us. Out recital sounded a shade too hearty, a shade rhythmic. It lacked something . . . possibly restraint and respect.

During *kaki-kata* hour, I doubled up over my desk and painfully drew out the *kata-kanas*, simplified Japanese ideographs, similar to English block printing. With clenched teeth and perspiring hands, I accentuated and emphasized, delicately nuanced and tapered off lines and curves.

At five-thirty, Yasuda-sensei rang the bell on her desk again. "Ping!" We stood up. "Ping!" We bowed. "Ping!" We vanished from the room like magic, except for one row of students whose turn it was to do *otohban*, washing blackboards, sweeping the floor, and dusting the desks. Under sensei's vigilant eyes, the chore felt like a convict's hard labor.

As time went on, I began to suspect that there was much more to Nihon Gakko than learning the Japanese language. There was a driving spirit of strict discipline behind it all which reached out and weighed heavily upon each pupil's consciousness. That force emanated from the principal's office.

Before Mr. Ohashi came to America, he had been a zealous student of the Ogasawara Shiko Saho, a form of social conduct dreamed up by a Mr. Ogasawara. Mr. Ohashi himself had written a book on etiquette in Japan. He was the Oriental male counterpart of Emily Post. Thus Mr. Ohashi arrived in America with the perfect bow tucked under his waist and a facial expression cemented into perfect samurai control. He came with a smoldering ambition to pass on this knowledge to the tender Japanese saplings born on foreign soil. The school-teachers caught fire, too, and dedicated themselves to us with a vengeance. It was not enough to learn the language. We must talk and walk and sit and bow in the best Japanese tradition.

As far as I was concerned, Mr. Ohashi's superior standard boiled down to one thing. The model child is one with deep *rigor mortis* . . . no noise, no trouble, no back talk.

We understood too well what Mr. Ohashi wanted of us. He yearned and wished more than anything else that somehow he could mold all of us into Genji Yamadas. Genji was a classmate whom we detested thoroughly. He was born in Seattle, but his parents had sent him to Japan at an early age for a period of good, old-fashioned education. He returned home a stranger among us with stiff mannerisms and an arrogant attitude. Genji boasted that he could lick anyone, one husky fellow or ten little ones, and he did, time and time again. He was an expert at judo.

Genji was a handsome boy with huge, lustrous dark eyes, a noble patrician nose, jet crew-cut setting off a flawless, fair complexion, looking every bit the son of a samurai. He sat aloof at his desk and paid strict attention to sensei. He was the top student scholastically. He read fluently and perfectly. His handwriting was a beautiful picture of bold, masculine strokes and curves. What gnawed at us more than anything else was that he stood up as straight as a bamboo tree and never lost rigid control of his arms or legs. His bow was snappy and brisk and he always answered *"Hai!"* to everything that sensei said to him, ringing crisp and clear with respect. Every time Mr. Ohashi came into our room for a surprise visit to see if we were under control, he would stop at Genji's desk for a brief chat. Mr. Ohashi's eyes betrayed a glow of pride as he spoke to Genji, who sat up erect, eyes staring respectfully ahead. All we could make out of the conversation was Genji's sharp staccato barks, *"Hai! . . . Hai! . . . Hai!"*

This was the response sublime to Mr. Ohashi. It was real man to man talk. Whenever Mr. Ohashi approached us, we froze in our seats. Instead of snapping into attention like Genji, we wilted and sagged. Mr. Ohashi said we were more like *"konyaku,"* a colorless, gelatinous Japanese food. If a boy fidgeted too nervously under Mr. Ohashi's stare, a vivid red stain rose from the back of Mr. Ohashi's neck until it reached his temple and then there was a sharp explosion like the crack of a whip. *"Keo-tsuke!* Attention!" It made us all leap in our seats, each one of us feeling terribly guilty for being such an inadequate Japanese.

I asked Mother, "Why is Mr. Ohashi so angry all the time? He always looks as if he had just bitten into a green persimmon. I've never seen him smile."

Mother said, "I guess Mr. Ohashi is the old-fashioned schoolmaster. I know he's strict, but he means well. Your father and I received harsher discipline than that in Japan . . . not only from schoolteachers, but from our own parents."

"Yes, I know, Mama." I leaned against her knees as she sat on the old leather davenport, mending our clothes. I thought Father and Mother were still wonderful, even if they had packed me off to Nihon Gakko. "Mrs. Matsui is so strict with her children, too. She thinks you spoil us." I giggled, and reassured her quickly, "But I don't think you spoil us at all."

Mrs. Matsui was ten years older than Mother, and had known Mother's father in Japan. Therefore she felt it was her duty to look after Mother's progress in this foreign country. Like a sharp-eyed hawk, she picked out Mother's weaknesses. . . . It was impossible for us to remember the endless little things we must not do in front of Mrs. Matsui. We must not laugh out loud and show out teeth, or chatter in front of guests, or interrupt adult conversation, or cross our knees while seated, or ask for a piece of candy, or squirm in our seats. . . .

Mr. Ohashi and Mrs. Matsui thought they could work on me and grad-ually mold me into an ideal Japanese *ojoh-san*, a refined young maiden who is quiet, pure in thought, polite, serene, and self-controlled. They made little headway, for I was too much the child of Skidrow. As far as I was concerned, Nihon Gakko was a total loss. I could not use my Japanese on the people at the hotel. Bowing was practical only at Nihon Gakko. If I were to bow to the hotel patrons, they would have laughed in my face. Therefore promptly at five-thirty every day, I shed Nihon Gakko and returned with relief to an environment which was the only real one to me. Life was too urgent, too exciting, too colorful for me to be sitting quietly in the parlor and contem-plating a spray of chrysanthemums in a bowl as a cousin of mine might be doing in Osaka.

4

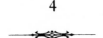

"I Am a Housewife":
English Lessons for Vietnamese Women

Now as in the past, most immigrant women remain untouched by official education and Americanization programs. During the mid-1970s, however, large number of Vietnamese women did encounter these programs in refugee camps while awaiting resettlement in the United States. Using oral histories and direct observation as well as camp newspapers, textbooks, official records, and other documents, com-parative education specialist Gail Kelly studied the programs provided for Viet-namese women in the large refugee camp at Indian Gap, Pennsylvania.

Kelly's finding, excerpted in the following selection, suggest unfortunate similarities between contemporary programs and those of the past. The experience of the Vietnamese indicates that official policy still considered the education of immigrant women less important than that of men. Moreover, the programs were still based on preconceived (and often inaccurate) ideas about ethnic culture and appropriate sex roles rather than on the real needs and interests of immigrant women.

_____
Source: Gail Kelly, "Americanization and Socialization of Vietnamese Immigrant Women," mimeographed, 1979. For expansion of this material, see Gail Kelly, *From Vietnam to America: The Chronicle of the Vietnamese Immigration to the United States* (Boulder, Colo.: Westview Press, 1977).

For centuries Vietnamese peasant women worked the land and engaged in petty trade, but constant war during the 1960's stimulated a vast migration to the cities. To sustain themselves and their families many of these peasant women entered the urban economy as petty traders, bar girls, laundresses, maids, and prostitutes. Middle-class women also came into the job market; their husbands' salaries were no longer sufficient to sustain the life styles to which they had become accustomed. Wives of prominent civil servants, university professors, and high-ranking military officers (groups well represented among the immigrants) opened knitting factories, worked as teletype operators, and the like. In many cases they provided the main income, since the men had either been killed or disabled in the war. Over twenty-one percent of all Vietnamese households that immigrated to the United States were headed by women who claimed to be the sole breadwinner of that household. Vietnamese female immigrants therefore had few expectations or experiences of life in which women were confined to narrow roles of housewife and mother. Only fourteen percent of Vietnamese immigrant women, in fact, reported their occupation as "housewife." As one middle-aged wife and mother of six expressed it, "I was a dog butcher in Vietnam; can I be a butcher here?"

There is no question that Vietnamese women in the camps wanted to learn what life in the United States would entail. They eagerly attended, or attempted to attend, cultural orientation lectures, English language classes, and whatever vocational training programs were open to them. They avidly read the bilingual daily *Dat Lanh (New Land)* which was full of advice on "how to live" in America.

The camp's programs could have served them better. All sources of information on new roles in the United States were mediated by Americans, and had been developed without any Vietnamese input. Moreover, all promoted a division of labor between the sexes foreign to most Vietnamese and more rigid than one would find among most American families. A survey of the English language classes reveals the program's overall inadequacies.

English Language Instruction and Women's Roles

English language instruction was the single largest educational program for Vietnamese in refugee camps. Initially, English classes were available only to men. Worried about overcrowding, American authorities deliberately barred women, arguing that since only the men would work in America (which they believed was consonant with Vietnamese culture), men should have first priority in obtaining quality instruction in relatively small classes. The Americans continued to discourage female attendance even after the camps began to empty. Camp officials and educators alike expressed the fear that male students might lose authority within their own families should they fail to acquire facility in English as rapidly as women. Despite such discouragement, Vietnamese women entered the classroom when authorities permitted.

The content of English language instruction reflected the concern of American immigration authorities and school personnel that male authority within the family be retained. Instructional materials used in class were of two kinds: an HEW-developed Survival English program and, used as a supplement, the Macmillan English language 900 Series. The Survival English course, taught at three levels, had sixteen lessons that covered topics such as Meeting Strangers, Finding a Place to Live, Occupations, Renting Apartments, Shopping, John's Interest, and Applying for Jobs. In all but two of the sixteen lessons conversations took place between a mythical "Mr. Brown" and "Mr. Jones," with "Mr. Jones" apparently playing the role of a Vietnamese refugee. In the lesson on occupations, for instance, Mr. Jones asks what kind of job he might find to support his wife and two children. Mr. Brown replies that he could work as a room clerk, salesman, cashier, laborer, plumber, bricklayer, cook, cleaning person, secretary, typist, seamstress, nurses' aide.

Women were present in the sixteen units of Survival English only in two instances: in a lesson on budgeting and shopping and in a lesson called "conversation." One lesson contained two lines about a Miss Jones. These lines were: "Miss Jones missed the bus to the Miss Universe competition," and "She is an attractive girl." The only other references to women in the entire curriculum occur in a set of drills on shopping. In the introductory classes a Mrs. Brown shops for dresses, shoes, food, aspirins, baby needs, and cosmetics while Mr. Brown shops for shirts, houses, cars, and furniture. The advanced classes elaborate on the divisions of labor between the sexes. A woman named Marie compares prices of food and other commodities, thereby saving her husband *his* hard-earned money. Moreover, Marie buys nothing but food without consulting her husband, Tim. Although she finds the best bargain in town on a sofa and sewing machine, she takes Tim to the store before making a purchase: The final decision is his.

The Macmillan English Language 900 Series, used as a supplement to the Survival English course, is designed for non-English speakers in general. These texts, interestingly enough, are quite different from the materials devised specifically for the Vietnamese. Women are more present in the texts, and more active. They travel, work, go to the doctor, shop, ask questions. Even so, women's roles are limited to those of wife and mother. In Unit 1 of Book Three (an intermediate-level text), for example, Judy talks with John about buying a new sofa. In Unite 2, Barbara and Ella talk about baking a cake for Harry, while Frank and Tom discuss hammers and nails; Unit 4, includes a discussion of marriage and bridal dresses, in Unit 5, Mr. James buys a house and Mabel has coffee klatches with her new neighbors; in Unit 8, on health and sickness, Dr. Smith and his female nurse give Mrs. Adams advice on her children's health and Mr. Lewis advice on his own health; in Unit 9, mother puts the children to bed and wakes them up while father goes off to work.

The curriculum materials used in teaching Vietnamese the English language, in sum, emphasize a strict division of labor between the sexes, preparing Vietnamese women not for the work place but for narrow social roles. In many course materials, women simply do not exist. When they enter the texts, they do so only as wife, mother, and shopper. It is of particular interest that the Survival English course, designed specifically for refugees, suggests occupations for Vietnamese men that traditionally have been reserved for American women. These include typist, seamstress, and nurses' aide, jobs at the very lowest ends of the American occupational and salary scales. In addition, it is Mr. Jones who finds out where stores are, gets a doctor, selects a church, locates the children's school, etc. In the Survival English materials, men take over not only traditionally female occupations, but virtually all other life functions as well.

Teacher-student interaction in class reflected the ideological bent of the texts. An incident in an English class designed for illiterates illustrates this best. This class had more women than any other I observed at Fort Indian Town Gap. (All other classes appeared to be predominantly male; advanced English classes included almost no women.) Because the students were illiterate, the instructor used no written materials. He introduced vocabulary by pointing to an object or a picture and teaching the English name for it. When pictures of objects were not available, he used charade. In one lesson, designed to help the Vietnamese describe their work skills to prospective employers, the teacher began with the phrase, "What kind of work do you do?" He then drew stick figures showing different kinds of work—ditch digging, selling, etc.—and named them all. After introducing phrases like "I am a ditch digger," "I am a mechanic," he asked each of his thirty or more students, "What kind of work do you do?" The first student to respond was a young man, obviously a former soldier. He responded by imitating a gun with his fingers and replied. "I rat-a-tat-tat." The teacher corrected him with, "I work with my hands." A middle-aged woman with lacquered teeth (indicating she came from a rural lower-class family) made a motion that looked like casting nets; she came from coastal Vung-Tau and had fished for a living. The teacher retorted with, "I am a housewife." The woman looked puzzled. The teacher then drew a stick figure on the blackboard representing a woman with a broom in her hand inside of a house. He repeated, "I am a housewife," pointing to the woman. The women in the class began a lively discussion in Vietnamese and started laughing. The teacher then drilled all the women with the phrase "I am a housewife."

America, it has often been claimed, is a plural society with little consensus on roles, values, and behavior. Not all programs Americans developed for Vietnamese attempted to deny women roles in the economy as well as in the household or prepare the Vietnamese elite for lower-class status. Programs that offered alternatives, however, were not compulsory as was English language instruction. Moreover, skill in English is crucial for entry into American society.

The Impact of Education

English language classes prepared Vietnamese women of all social classes to be wives and mothers of working-class men; that is, to be housewives rather than participants in the labor force, as most had been in Vietnam. Yet one year after the camps were closed, over 45 percent of Vietnamese female immigrants were employed in the American labor force, primarily in service occupations requiring a minimum of English language proficiency and work skills. This figure is comparable to the percent of American women in the work force. At the same time, however, Vietnamese male immigrants suffer from an unemployment rate that runs close to 40 percent.

These fragmentary data indicate that Vietnamese women did not blindly accept what the educational programs preached. Many did not become housewives, perhaps through economic necessity or the persistence of their own cultural norms. And, perhaps, because the refugee camps led them to expect less from American life than did their husbands and sons, they were happy to accept any job or role in American society.

5

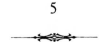

"Glad That I Am the Future"

In the poem that follows, a fifteen-year-old Cambodian refugee describes her feelings about high school in the United States. Like many recent immigrant students from Southeast Asia, she likes science better social studies. Her explanation for her preference is not the usual one that science (and math) requires less English fluency and offers better job opportunities. Her distrust of social studies is rooted in her family's refugee experience.

Source: From *Voices from Southeast Asia: The Refugee Experience in the United States,* by John Tenhula (New York: Holmes & Meier Publishers, Inc., 1991). Copyright © 1991 by Holmes & Meier Publishers, Inc. Reprinted by permission of the publisher.

Some immigrant parents have put great pressure on their children to achieve academically, to justify the suffering of immigration, to help the family succeed in a new land, and to reflect well on the ethnic community. In the post-1965 period this has been especially true among Asian immigrants. Some children have been uncomfortable with this pressure; a few have even committed suicide. However, the anonymous school girl who wrote this poem appears to have shouldered the burden willingly, glad to be the bearer of her family's hopes.

> Biology and math make me feel good.
> I hold them close like I would my mother
> when I was a young girl.
>
> Too much disaster is found in current events,
> I keep a distance—like the black plague is
> near or an ugly boy
> I am sad to hear of the journey to America,
> but glad that I am the future.

6

Unfulfilled Aspirations: "Never Used the Brush and Ink"

Some women were too busy or too isolated (or both) to pursue formal education, despite their strong desire to do so. Teiko Tomita was such a woman. Born in Japan in 1896, she was graduated from a girls' high school and earned an elementary school teaching certificate. She hoped to continue her studies. However, in 1921 she and her husband immigrated to the United States to farm on the remote Yakima Indian Reservation in the state of Washington. In the decades that followed she kept house in a primitive cabin, reared four children, worked the land, and, after internment during World War II, became a garment worker.

Tomita kept a record of her life by writing tanka, a traditional Japanese poem that concentrated complex subjects into thirty-one syllables arranged in five lines. This reading, from an article by Gail Nomura, includes three tanka that express Tomita's sadness at not having continued her education.

Source: Gail M. Nomura, "*Tsugiki*, A Grafting: A History of a Japanese Pioneer Woman in Washington State," in *Women in Northwest History*, ed. Karen J. Blair (Seattle: University of Washington Press, 1988), pp. 221–22.

Thoughts rise of the unfulfilled aspirations of youth. For Tomita those memories are of dashed hopes of continuing her studies. In a series of poems she recalls these hopes of scholarship, symbolized in a treasured box given to her as a graduation prize:

> As a lifetime memory
> Placed in a suitcase with love and care
> For thirty years
> A lacquer calligraphy box

She remembers the words that accompanied the prize—words admonishing her to continue to train her mind and soul. But since coming to America:

> Too busy were
> Thirty years of life
> In a foreign country
> Never used the brush and ink

There had never been time for her formal studies. She had written her tanka in isolation in the fields of Yakima. Even after moving to the Seattle area, though she had been able to join a tanka club, she had not been able to attend the monthly meetings. . . .

Her life, she said in an interview, could be summed up in one word, *isogashii*—busy, a life filled always with things she had to do. As for thoughts of the luxury of studies:

> Never to return are the days
> When I put my heart and soul
> In my studies only
> I grow old in a foreign country

PART VII

——◆——

Social and Political Activists

" "The foreign-born woman plays directly in American politics a part somewhat, but not much, more important than that played by snakes in the zoology of Ireland," stated a 1920 Carnegie Corporation report, reflecting the widespread view that the immigrant woman's world was limited to the kitchen, the nursery, and the church.[1] Poverty, lack of education, and the multiple burdens of housework, childcare, and paid employment deprived many immigrant women of the time, energy, and resources they would have needed for political activity. Moreover, most came from traditions that defined politics as a male sphere, a definition reinforced by American society and not yet abandoned. Nevertheless, some immigrant women have acted as agents of social and political change. Part 7 will explore their roles in the public arena of nineteenth- and twentieth-century America.

In some cases women had become politically active before leaving the homeland. The German revolution of 1848, Mexican revolutionary struggles of the early twentieth century, and battles for the independence of Ireland, Poland, and other suppressed nationalities influenced women before they came to the United States, as did the international feminist, socialist, anarchist, syndicalist, and trade union movements. Eastern European Jews were politicized by the struggle against the czar and by the rise of socialism, Zionism, and trade unionism. Finnish women were politicized by the struggle for a democratic constitution, including women's suffrage, in 1906 and by the Finnish civil war between Reds and Whites that followed the Russian Revolution.

Contact with American reform movements or their own experiences with the deficiencies of American life drew other women into the public arena for the first time. When Mary Harris Jones, Irish-born labor organizer, was working as a seamstress in Chicago in 1870, she was appalled by the contrast between "the poor shivering wretches, jobless and hungry, walking along the frozen lakefront" and the wealthy people whose luxurious clothes she sewed.[2] Jewish and Italian garment workers in New York were radicalized by the death of 146 co-workers in the Triangle Shirtwaist Fire of 1911.

Personal experiences activated more recent immigrants as well. Julia Tang, who was elected president of the San Francisco Community College

Board in the 1980s, was politicized when she faced discrimination for the first time as an eighteen-year-old immigrant. "I never faced degradation or racism in Hong Kong, where I was born and raised," she explained. "I became very angry. I thought, 'why should I be treated differently?' "[3] Immigrant lesbians asked the same question in a different context, and by the early 1990s were a visible presence in gay and lesbian rights movements. Identifying with the victims of the first atomic bombs, some Japanese and other Asian-Americans became antinuclear and peace activists.

Women were often moved to political action by concern for their children. A Finnish women's paper sponsored by the Industrial Workers of the World addressed this concern: "We think of our children's fate. . . . Capitalism crushes even young workers' lives and uses the best youths of the land like cattle in their bloody sports."[4] Sometimes the motivation was more personal. After her son was killed by a drunk driver, Irish-born Matilda Bradley Carse devoted herself to the temperance movement, serving for many years as president of the Chicago Central Women's Christian Temperance Union. Jessie Lopez de la Cruz, daughter of Mexican immigrants, describes the personal tragedies that led Mexican-American migrant farm women into the labor movement:

> I had a little girl who died in '43. . . . She was so tiny, only five months old. The cause was the way we were living . . . thousands of flies . . . no place to refrigerate the milk. . . .
>
> It was like that for all of us. I would see babies who died. It was claimed if you lifted a young baby up fast, the soft spot on its head would cave in and it would get diarrhea and dehydrate and die. . . . I know it wasn't that that killed them, it was hunger, malnutrition, no money to pay the doctors. When the union came, this was one of the things we fought against.[5]

Sometimes women made full-time careers of social and political activism. More often, they made brief forays into the public arena, becoming active when male leadership was lacking or when an issue affected their jobs or their domestic responsibilities. When a crowd failed to reach the proper pitch of enthusiasm at a Chicago rally for the release of Sacco and Vanzetti, an Italian woman, Aurora D'Angelo, about whom nothing else is known, called for action and led the demonstrators out of the hall.[6] Orthodox Jewish housewives in New York in 1902 organized a successful city-wide boycott to bring down the price of kosher meat because "Our husbands work hard. . . . They try their best to bring a few cents into the house. We must manage, spend as little as possible. We will not give away our last few cents to the butcher and let our children go barefoot."[7]

The Nineteenth Century

Immigrants were among the many women who helped shape ordered society out of the chaos of nineteenth-century frontier life. The first selection describes the activities of the resourceful Italian-born Sister Blandina Segale. Sister Blandina founded schools and hospitals to serve native Americans, Mexican-Americans, and mainstream Anglo-Americans in Colorado and New Mexico, and risked her life negotiating with outlaws to substitute the law courts for the lynch mob. Her activities were exceptional, but many foreign-born women worked with their American counterparts in less spectacular ways to create the public institutions that served nineteenth-century America on the urban as well as rural frontiers.

Immigrant women participated in the great reform movements—temperance, abolitionism, feminism, communitarianism—which swept across the United States in the decades preceding the Civil War. The energy for these movements came from two main sources: religious evangelism and secular, democratic humanitarianism. American-born reformers usually entered the public arena through church-affiliated temperance and other moral reform societies, as did some Irish and Scandinavian immigrants. The most prominent foreign-born reformers, however—Ernestine Rose, Marie Zakrzewska, and Mathilde Giesler-Anneke—came from a secular, even antireligious tradition. Rebels from girlhood against the religious and social restraints of Metternich's Europe, these women had education, self-confidence, personal autonomy, and, in the case of Rose and Giesler-Anneke, husbands supportive of their activities.[8] In antebellum America travel was dangerous as well as uncomfortable, and it was shocking for women to speak in public on any topic. Yet these women traveled all over the United States and gave public speeches challenging the rationality and justice of the most basic American institutions.

"I was a rebel at the age of five," said Ernestine Rose, daughter of a Polish rabbi. She rejected an arranged marriage, sued her father in the Polish courts for control of her inheritance, and left home forever at the age of sixteen. After several years in Germany and England, she came to the United States in 1836. Here she became an abolitionist, an advocate of Free Thought, and a colleague of Elizabeth Stanton and Susan B. Anthony in the women's movement, and led the campaign that gave married women in New York control over their own property. Rose was an accomplished speaker despite her foreign accent. The second selection is an excerpt from one of the many addresses on the rights of women that won her renown as the "queen of the platform."

Marie Zakrzewska's tireless activities to improve medical care for women and to open up professional opportunities for women physicians and nurses were supplemented by an active interest in women's suffrage and abolitionism. The latter led to friendships with American reformers Theodore Parker, Wendell Phillips, and William Lloyd Garrison. Far more radical was Mathilde Giesler-Anneke, a political refugee from the German revolution of 1848. She played a leadership role in the American women's movement, edited a German language feminist newspaper, and established an ungraded liberal arts school for girls in Milwaukee based upon the progressive principles of the German educational reformer, Friedrich Froebel. Giesler-Anneke believed that "the regeneration and emancipation of all people, regardless of race or sex, depended upon the replacement of capitalism by communism."[9]

Twentieth-Century Reformers

The passion for reform that energized so many Americans before the Civil War subsided in the decades that followed, only to revive again at the turn of the century in what historians have termed "The Progressive Era." By 1900 the United States had become the world's most productive industrial power, and its growing cities reflected the new extremes of wealth and poverty. America's coming of age as an urban, industrial nation and a world power inspired a variety of political and social reforms. Some of these reforms— Prohibition, restriction of immigration, and the destruction of the power of ward politicians (many of them representing ethnic communities)—had little appeal for immigrant women. Campaigns for better health care, housing, and working conditions, on the other hand, attracted their support, even their leadership.

In the Progressive Era as in the mid-nineteenth century, some immigrant women were conspicuous in movements for radical change. "Red" Finnish women in Minnesota attended IWW and Communist party meetings, participated in radical drama at labor halls, and trained radical youth. At least one Finnish woman ran for office on the Communist ticket.[10] German, Scandinavian, and Jewish immigrants including Theresa Malkiel, Meta Stern Lilienthal, Rose Pastor Stokes, Annette Konikow, and Meta Berger served on the Women's National Committee of the Socialist party, one-fourth of which was foreign-born.

The most famous—or notorious—of the radicals was the Russian Jewish anarchist Emma Goldman. Goldman advocated the replacement of all traditional political institutions, whether based on majority rule or military coercion, with voluntary, free associations. A proponent of "the propaganda of the deed" in her early years, Goldman was blamed for inspiring the assassination of President McKinley in 1900, a terrorist act with which she actually had no connection. In public lectures, leaflets, and a journal, *Mother Earth*, Goldman defended the civil rights of minorities, including homosexuals, espoused free love, disseminated birth control information (which resulted in a jail term), and organized resistance to the draft during World War I (see selection 3). Her antiwar activities led to her imprisonment in 1917 and deportation two years later.

Most immigrant women who were active during the Progressive Era were involved in mainstream rather than radical movements. Traditional responsibilities for home and children led many into neighborhood improvement, education, and child welfare. Women worked through settlement houses, consumer groups, and other organizations for improved city services and more healthful living conditions. Although most professional settlement workers were mainstream Americans, a few were immigrants. Bohemian-born Josephine Humpel Zeman, for example, was a staff member of Jane Addams' famous Hull House in Chicago, where she wrote articles for *Commons* and for the United States Industrial Commission on Immigration and Education on the working conditions of immigrant women in Chicago. Immigrant women were also prominent in tenant and consumer associations. As early as 1904 Jewish women were taking their landlords to court for housing abuses in New York City, and by the 1920s a city-wide tenant movement included Jewish, Irish, Italian, West Indian, and native-born women.

"Progressive" educational innovations in the public schools were carefully monitored by the education-minded Jewish women of New York City. Thousands rioted in 1906, stoning schools and smashing windows and doors because they thought the vaccinations performed by the new public health physicians threatened their children's lives.[11] A few years later, Jewish women joined in demonstrations that helped block the adoption of the innovative Gary plan, which they feared, with some justice, would dilute the academic content of their children's education.[12]

Although poverty forced many immigrant families to send underaged children into the factories, immigrant women were among the advocates of laws against child labor. In 1903 Irish-born Mary Harris Jones ("Mother Jones") led a protest march of child workers from Pennsylvania to President Roosevelt's summer home in New York (see selection 4). Remembering a childhood in which her widowed mother was barely able to keep the family together, Russian-born Sophie Irene Loeb Simon helped create New York City's Child Welfare Board and pioneered outdoor relief as an alternative to the institutionalization of children.

Radical women such as Emma Goldman and Mother Jones argued that basic economic change, not suffrage, was needed to improve the position of women in the United States. Other women, especially those active in trade unionism, supported the battle for the vote. Parades, petitions, demonstrations, and other political activities among immigrant Jewish women in New York City were critical in winning the city, and with it the state, for suffrage in 1917. Two immigrants, Russian-born Nina Samarodin and Polish-born Rose Winslow, were imprisoned because of national prosuffrage activism.

Winslow's account of her experience in prison with American-born radical suffragist Alice Paul is recorded in the fifth selection.

"Mainstream" Politics

In the nineteenth and early twentieth centuries few immigrant women had the time, money, and education—or the desire—to compete for elected "mainstream" office. In the mid- and late twentieth century, however, this began to change. In 1968 West Indian Shirley Chisholm became the first African-American woman to be elected to Congress. Although born in the United States, she had spent most of her childhood in Barbados, returning to New York City at the age of twelve. The fact that she was an "outsider" by race, ethnicity, and gender contributed to her willingness to "break the rules." Chisholm spoke out for abortion rights and against the Vietnam war before most other political leaders were willing to take these controversial positions. She was also a feminist. "Women are a majority of the population, but they are treated like a minority group," she wrote. "Of my two 'handicaps,' being female put more obstacles in my path than being black."[13]

Unlike Chisholm, most of the small number of immigrant women who held office did so on the local level. In Hawaii and on the west coast in the 1970s and 1980s a sprinkling of Asian women served on school boards and city councils. Taiwan-born Lily Chen of Monterey Park became the nation's first Chinese-American woman mayor, and Hong Kong-born Mae Yih served in the Oregon state senate. Most of these women entered politics hesitantly, to solve a particular problem rather than to build a career. Most drew strength from their families and from having overcome the difficulties of immigrant childhoods. Like other women in public life, they faced the problem of finding enough time for their families. As immigrants, they had to overcome ethnic stereotypes, including the belief that Asian women were passive and not suited for leadership. Many also had to overcome an upbringing that discouraged self-assertion. "At first you don't want to fight. You think, 'We are more dignified than that. Don't be rude, don't be so obtrusive,' " said Thelma Bucholdt, Filipino state legislator from an overwhelmingly Caucasian district in Alaska.[14]

Nationalist Activity

Political activism in the interests of the homeland has been widespread, cutting across ethnic groups and historical periods. As individuals and as members of organizations, immigrant women have raised money, distributed information, petitioned, marched, and lobbied for the independence of Ireland, Poland, Yugoslavia, the Ukraine, Korea, and other suppressed nationalities. Jewish women joined organizations such as Haddassah and Pioneer

Women to work for the rebuilding of a Jewish state in the Middle East and then to support the new nation of Israel. Even before the United States acquired Puerto Rico in 1898, Puerto Rican women on the mainland participated in movements to change the status of the island. They continued to do so through the twentieth century, some favoring statehood, others independence.

In the opening decades of the century women from the Caribbean joined societies "to promote the civic, political, economic, and social welfare of the Virgin Islands and their people whether at home or abroad."[15] West Indian immigrants also joined native-born black women to participate in the first mass movement for black nationalism and black pride, the Universal Negro Improvement Association founded by Jamaican immigrant Marcus Garvey in 1914. In selection 6, Amy Jacques Garvey, second wife of Marcus Garvey and a black nationalist leader in her own right, urges more women to assume leadership in the black nationalist cause. In the 1980s and 1990s Haitian women in New York and Florida demonstrated and campaigned on behalf of their homeland and other Haitians who were being refused admission to the United States.

The Labor Movement

Participation in the labor movement also cut across ethnic groups and historical periods. Everyone who participated in the early labor movement faced violent opposition from employers, police, and portions of the public, but women encountered additional difficulties. Women were more likely to be employed in unskilled, isolated, or temporary jobs unconducive to unionization. Hoping to leave work for marriage, many saw little reason to jeopardize present earnings for dubious future benefits by joining a union or striking. Moreover, with salaries 40 percent to 50 percent lower than those of their male counterparts, women found it difficult to pay union dues and to support themselves and their dependents during strikes. Finally, some husbands discouraged their wives' activism as inappropriate female behavior and as a disruption of family life.

The unions themselves were often inhospitable, if not hostile, to women. Many unions ignored or actively discouraged women's participation in the workplace because of traditional views on women's "place" and because of job competition. Male union officials sometimes favored protective legislation for women workers less as a means of benefiting women than as a means of discouraging their employment. A male culture predominated within the unions. Meetings were usually held at night in saloons or other places where many women felt uncomfortable. Women rarely became officers, even in unions such as the International Ladies Garment Workers Union, in which they constituted the great majority of the membership.

Women activists who married union officials were expected to give up their own positions in deference to their husbands, and usually did. Third World women workers had additional problems, as "white" union officials, male or female, often treated them with little respect.

Despite these obstacles, tens of thousands of immigrant women entered the public arena to fight for better wages and working conditions for their husbands and for themselves. The most colorful, effective, and beloved early labor organizer was Mary Harris Jones ("Mother Jones"), who unionized miners in Pennsylvania and West Virginia, and led their wives against police, scabs, and company officials with mops, brooms, pots, and crying babies as weapons. "With one speech she often threw a whole community on strike," wrote labor leader Tom Tippett, "and she could keep the strikers loyal month after month on empty stomachs and behind prison bars."[16] Similarly, "Big Mary" Septak rallied Hungarian, Polish, and Italian women armed with rolling pins and pokers in support of their striking husbands, brothers, and sons in the Pennsylvania coal mines in 1897. The authorities were bewildered by the "ill advised and unwomanly demonstrations" of Septak's "Amazons."[17]

Working women organized in behalf of their own jobs as well as those of their men. Irish and French Canadian women participated in strikes in New England mills in the decades following the Civil War. Bohemian women struck in New York in the 1880s against the oppressive tenement system in cigar making, an industry in which they were especially prominent. Irish-born Leonora Kearney Barry, a hosiery worker from Amsterdam, New York, became a full-time organizer and business agent for the Knights of Labor, America's first large-scale industrial labor union, in the 1880s. Barry helped organize skilled and unskilled women, conducted boycotts of nonunion goods, and established two cooperative shirt factories in accordance with the Knights' policy of seeking alternatives to the wage system. Attacked by a group of Catholic priests, she defended her right to labor activism "as an Irish woman, a Catholic, and an honest woman."[18]

Jewish women played a leading role in the struggle for unionization and better working conditions in the garment industries of early twentieth-century urban centers. They were joined by Italian and Irish women, by Mexican-American women, and in later years by West Indians and Puerto Ricans. In 1909 a Jewish teenager, Clara Lemlich, introduced the resolution for "the rising of the 20,000," an unprecedented general strike among the shirtwaist makers of New York. Polish women were the first to stop the looms and walk out of the factories in the famous textile mill strike in Lawrence, Massachusetts, in 1912. In 1982 Chinese garment workers in San Francisco organized a march and one-day strike, winning union contracts that helped thousands of women workers.

Organized by activists like Luisa Morenos, Emma Tenayucas, and Manuela Sagers, women from Mexico played an important role in the pecan shellers' strike in San Antonio in 1938 and other struggles for better working conditions. They continue to do so. The final selection documents the activities of Chicanas during a strike at the Farah garment factories in Texas. The Chicana strikers did more than change their working conditions. They also changed their feelings about themselves and those closest to them. Indeed, immigrant women of many ethnic groups have noted that activism widened their circle of friends, raised their self-esteem, and improved their status in the family and the community.

The labor movement illustrates the interrelation among activist causes. Some early twentieth-century trade unionists moved into the Socialist party or the Industrial Workers of the World. Others, like Rose Schneiderman, joined the Woman's Trade Union League, an organization founded by socially prominent mainstream women to provide education, strike funds, and moral and political support for women workers. Union women also moved into the suffrage movement and into national politics: Mary Anderson became head of the Department of Labor Women's Bureau in the 1920s and Rose Schneiderman became an advisor to President Franklin Roosevelt's New Deal.

The labor movement also illustrates the price women paid for their social and political commitments. Most full-time activists, women like Pauline Newman, Rose Schneiderman, and Mary Anderson, found that their careers precluded marriage and motherhood. Satisfaction in their work was accompanied by loneliness. "I have so many plans to carry out, so much work to do—work that shall live after I am gone" wrote Pauline Newman, "yet no one to help me, no one to advise me. Always alone. It is dreadful."[19] For Mexican-American labor leaders the price could be even higher. Luisa Moreno was deported in 1953, after twenty years of work for the development of her community.

The rank and file in labor and other movements also paid a price. During a strike or an organizing campaign, working women as well as leaders were insulted, beaten, or jailed. A pregnant Italian woman picketed during the Lawrence strike because "soldier and policeman no beat women. I got big belly"; she was beaten so severely that she lost the baby and almost died.[20] Women who cared for hungry children at home while encouraging their husbands to remain on the picket line week after week should also be considered activists. These women, too, paid a high price for their commitments. An organizer for the Women's Trade Union League asked the sick wife of a striker how she could bear the hardships of her children. The woman replied, "We do not live only on bread. If I cannot give my children bread, I can give them liberty."[21]

Progress was made in many of the causes for which immigrant women gave so much; yet too often victory remained elusive. The woman's suffrage amendment was ratified, but, as Emma Goldman had anticipated, discrimination against women continued. Child labor laws were enacted, wages rose, and working conditions in most industries improved; but in 1990 women, especially foreign-born and Third World women, still clustered in low-paying, nonunion jobs, earning 30 to 40 percent less than men. In 1958 an unsafe seventy-five-year-old textile finishing factory in New York City caught fire. The sprinkler system did not work and the fire escapes were inadequate. Twenty-four women workers burned to death. Ironically, a survivor of the Triangle Shirtwaist Factory fire that killed 146 women in 1911 found herself once against watching women's bodies being lowered to the streets. "What good have been all the years?" she demanded in anger and despair. "The fire still burns."[22]

Notes

1. John Pakner Cavit, *Americans by Choice* (New York: Harper and Brothers, 1922), p. 296.

2. Cecyle S. Neidle, *America's Immigrant Women* (New York: Hippocrene Books, 1975), pp. 118–19.

3. Judy Chu, "Asian Pacific American Women in Mainstream Politics," in *Making Waves: An Anthology of Writings by and about Asian Immigrant Women,* ed. Asian Women United of California (Boston: Beacon Press, 1989), p. 415.

4. Patricia A. Book, "Red and White: Sex Roles and Politics in a North American Finnish Community," paper presented at the Seventy-third Annual Meeting of the American Anthropological Association, November 20–25, 1974, p. 12. Book cites Robert E. Park, *The Immigrant Press and Its Control* (New York: Harper and Brothers, 1922), pp. 244–45.

5. Ellen Cantarow with Susan Gushee O'Malley and Sharon Hartman Strom, *Moving the Mountain: Women Working for Social Change* (Old Westbury, N.Y.: Feminist Press and McGraw-Hill, 1980), p. 118.

6. Jean Scarpaci, "La Contadina, The Plaything of the Middle Class Woman Historian," *Occasional Papers on Ethnic and Immigration Studies* (Toronto: Multicultural History Society of Ontario, 1978), p. 34.

7. Paula Hyman, "Immigrant Women and Consumer Protest: The New York City Kosher Meat Boycott of 1902," *American Jewish History* 70 (1980): 91–105. Hyman cites *Yiddishes Tagblatt,* May 15, 1902.

8. Sally Miller, *The Radical Immigrant* (New York: Twayne, 1974), p. 61.

9. Book, "Red and White."

10. Book, "Red and White," pp. 13–14.

11. *New York Tribune,* June 28, 1906.

12. Diane Ravitch, *The Great School Wars, New York City, 1805–1973: A History of the Public Schools as Battlefield of Social Change* (New York: Basic Books, 1974), pp. 224–25.

13. Shirley Chisholm, *Unbought and Unbossed* (Boston: Houghton Mifflin, 1970), p. 12.

14. Chu, "Asian Pacific American Women in Mainstream Politics," p. 413.

15. Ira De A. Reid, *The Negro Immigrant: His Background, Characteristics, and Social Adjustment, 1899–1937* (New York: Columbia University Press, 1939), p. 156.

16. Barbara Mayer Wertheimer, *We Were There: The Story of Working Women in America* (New York: Pantheon, 1977), p. 350.

17. Victor Greene, *The Slavic Community on Strike: Immigrant Labor in Pennsylvania Anthracite* (Notre Dame: University of Notre Dame Press, 1968), p. 143. Greene cites the *Wilkesbarre Record*, September 22, 1897, p. 1.

18. Wertheimer, *We Were There*, p. 189.

19. Ibid., p. 289. Wertheimer cites a letter from Pauline Newman to Rose Schneiderman.

20. Ibid., pp. 363–64.

21. Mary Anderson, *Woman at Work* (Minneapolis: University of Minnesota Press, 1951), p. 41.

22. Wertheimer, *We Were There*, p. 315. Wertheimer cites Leon Stein, *The Triangle Fire* (Philadelphia: J. B. Lippincott, 1962), p. 214.

1

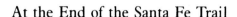

At the End of the Santa Fe Trail

Born in Cicagno, Italy, in 1850, Sister Blandina Segale immigrated to Cincinnati as a child and entered the Sisters of Charity mother house there at the age of sixteen. In 1872 the order sent her to the frontier mining town of Trinidad, Colorado. The following passage from her diary, At the End of the Santa Fe Trail, *demonstrates the resourcefulness and courage that made her an effective agent of change in a lawless frontier environment.*

Sister Blandina was later transferred from Trinidad to Santa Fe, where she built a trade school for Indian girls and a hospital for railroad workers. Her reputation for fairness among all elements of the population enabled her to negotiate peace treaties with outlaw bands and with Apache Indians. In 1894 she returned to Cincinnati, where she remained until her death in 1941. There she devoted herself to religious and educational work among recent immigrants, establishing three schools and four settlement houses to serve Italian and other populations. Widely respected for her activities in behalf of women and the young, she initiated successful court action against "white slavery" (prostitution) and served as a probation officer for the Cincinnati Juvenile Court.

One of my oldest pupils came to ask to have his sister excused from school. He looked so deathly pale that I inquired, "What has happened?" He answered, "Haven't you heard?"

"Nothing that should make you look as you do."

"Sister, dad shot a man! He's in jail. A mob has gathered and placed men about forty feet apart from the jail to Mr. McCaferty's room. The instant he breathes his last, the signal of his death will be given, and the mob will go to the jail and drag dad out and hang him."

"Have you thought of anything that might save him?" I asked.

"Nothing, Sister; nothing can be done."

"Is there no hope that the wounded man may recover?"

"No hope whatever; the gun was loaded with tin shot."

Source: Sister Blandina Segale, *At the End of the Santa Fe Trail* (Milwaukee: Bruce, 1948), pp. 59–63, 66. Reprinted by permission.

"John, go to the jail and ask your father if he will take a chance at not being hanged by a mob."

"What do you propose doing, Sister?"

"First to visit the wounded man and ask if he will receive your father and forgive him, with the understanding that the full force of the law be carried out."

"Sister, the mob would tear him to pieces before he was ten feet from the jail."

"I believe he will not be touched if I accompany him," I said.

"I'm afraid he will not have the courage to do as you propose."

"That is the only thing I can see that will save him from the mob law. Ask your father to decide. This is Friday. I'll visit the sick man after school this afternoon. Let me know if he will consent to go with me to the sick man's room."

Immediately after school, with a companion, I went to see the wounded man. Sister Fidelis had preceded me. She was writing a letter to his mother bidding her good-bye until they would meet where the Judge was just, and their tears would be dried forever.

I looked at the young man, a fine specimen of honesty and manliness. My heart ached for the mother who expected frequent word from her son, then to receive such news! To be shot unjustly, to die in a strange land, among strangers, so young!

As soon as Sister Fidelis and companion took leave of the sick man, the subject of the present visit was broached. The young man was consistent. He said, "I forgive him, as I hope to be forgiven, but I want the law to take its course."

Fully agreeing with him, he was asked: "Will you tell Mr. _____ this if he comes to beg your pardon?"

"Yes, Sister," he answered.

Friday evening the prisoner's son came to say his father was very much afraid to attempt to walk to Mr. McCaferty's room, but if Sister would walk with him, he would take the chance of having the court pronounce sentence on him.

Early Saturday morning we presented ourselves to the Sheriff in his office.

"Good morning, Sister!" was the Sheriff's pleasant greeting.

"Good morning, Mr. Sheriff. Needless to ask if you know what is taking place on our two principal streets."

"You mean the men ready to lynch the prisoner who so unjustly shot the young Irishman?"

"Yes. What are you going to do to prevent the lynching?"

"Do! What has any sheriff here ever been able to do to prevent a mob from carrying out its intent?"

"Be the first sheriff to make the attempt!"

"How, Sister?" Standing to his full height—he must be six feet four— he reminded me of a person with plenty of reserve strength, and on the *qui vive* to use a portion of it.

"The prisoner was asked if he would be willing to walk between the sheriff and Sister to the victim's sick bed and ask his pardon." The sheriff interrupted: "Sister, have you ever seen the working of a mob?"

"A few, Mr. Sheriff."

"And would you take the chance of having the prisoner snatched from between us and hanged to the nearest cottonwood?"

"In my opinion, there is nothing to fear." He straightened himself and looked at me, shrugged his shoulders and said, "If you are not afraid, neither am I."

We—the sheriff, my companion and myself—started to walk to the jail. All along the main street and leading to the jail were men at about a distance of a rod apart. These were the men who were to signal Mr. McCaferty's death by three taps of our school bell, in order that the mob might proceed to the jail, take the prisoner and hang him. Our group arrived at the jail, where we encountered the greatest discouragement. The prisoner saw us coming. When we got near enough to speak to him, he was trembling like an aspen. We saw his courage had failed him. We paused while we assured him he was safe in going with us.

He hesitated, then said: "I'll go with you." All along the road we kept silence, and no one spoke to us. When we got within a block of the sick man's room, we saw a crowd of men outside his door. It was at this juncture that my fears for the prisoner began. Intent upon saving our protégé from mob law, we hastened to the sick man's door. The crowd made way. Intense fear took possession of me. "Will the prisoner be jerked away when he attempts to enter his victim's room?"

The Sheriff and I remained at the foot of the few steps which led into the room. Meanwhile, I quietly said to the prisoner: "Go in," which he did, myself and companion following. The sheriff remained outside. The door was left wide open that those standing outside might hear the conversation taking place within.

The culprit stood before his victim with bowed head. Fearing a prolonged silence, I addressed the prisoner: "Have you nothing to say?"

He looked at the man in bed and said: "My boy, I did not know what I was doing. Forgive me."

The sick man removed the blanket which covered his tin-shot leg, revealing a sight to unnerve the stoutest heart. The whole leg was mortified and swollen out of proportion, showing where the poisonous tin had lodged and the mortification creeping toward the heart.

"See what you have done!" said the wounded man.

"I'm sorry, my boy, forgive me."

"I forgive you, as I hope to be forgiven, but the law must take its course."

I added, "Yes, the law must take its course—not mob law." Those outside the door with craned necks distinctly heard the conversation.

We returned to the jail where the prisoner was to remain until the Circuit Court convened. . . .

The Circuit Court came to Trinidad. At its sitting it sentenced the prisoner to ten years in the penitentiary. Mr. McCaferty had lived three days after being shot, hence the deed is called manslaughter, minimum, one year, maximum, ten years.

Shall I prophesy? The prisoner will be at large in less than two years. Yet this small unmapped town is making strides in the right direction.

2

"This Is Law, But Where Is the Justice of It"

Ernestine Potowski Rose (1810–1892) was born in Russian-controlled Poland. She was the only child of a rabbi who taught her the Torah and Talmud (Jewish religious law), an education usually reserved for boys. A rebel against the religious and secular world of her childhood, she rejected an arranged marriage and left home at sixteen, supporting herself in her travels through Europe on the proceeds of an air freshener she invented. In England she met Robert Owens, whose radical social philosophy influenced her own. She married an Englishman, William Rose, a talented silversmith and jeweler who supported her political activities and financed her lecture tours throughout her life.

Arriving in the United States in 1836, she focused her political activities on racial and sexual equity. A fearless abolitionist, she spoke out against slavery even in the South. She campaigned for property rights for women, women's suffrage, and easier divorce laws. Unlike most middle-class native-born feminists, she also favored a general reconstruction of American society. The following passage, from a speech at a women's rights meeting in 1852, illustrates the style and logic that made her successful with many audiences.

Source: History of Woman Suffrage, vol. 1, ed. Elizabeth Cady Stanton, Susan B. Anthony, and Matilda Joslyn Gage (New York: Fowler and Wells, 1981), pp. 237–341.

Here, in this far-famed land of freedom, under a Republic that has inscribed on its banner the great truth that "all men are created free and equal, and endowed with inalienable rights to life, liberty, and the pursuit of happiness" . . . even here, in the very face of this eternal truth, woman, the mockingly so-called "better half" of man, has yet to plead for her rights, nay, for her life. For what is life without liberty, and what is liberty without equality of rights? And so for the pursuit of happiness, she is not allowed to choose any line of action that might promote it; she has only thankfully to accept what man in his magnanimity decides is best for her to do, and this is what he does not choose to do himself.

Is she then not included in that declaration? Answer, ye wise men of the nation, and answer truly; add not hypocrisy to oppression! Say that she is not created free and equal, and therefore (for the sequence follows on the premise) that she is not entitled to life, liberty, and the pursuit of happiness. But with all the audacity arising from an assumed superiority, you dare not so libel and insult humanity as to say, that she is not included in that declaration; and if she is, then what right has man, except that of might, to deprive woman of the rights and privileges he claims for himself? And why, in the name of reason and justice, why should she not have the same rights? Because she is woman? Humanity recognizes no sex; virtue recognizes no sex; mind recognizes no sex; life and death, pleasure and pain, happiness and misery, recognize no sex. . . . Like him she enjoys or suffers with her country. Yet she is not recognized as his equal!

In the laws of the land she has no rights; in government she has no voice. And in spite of another principle, recognized in this Republic, namely, that "taxation without representation is tyranny," she is taxed to defray the expenses of that unholy, unrighteous custom called war, yet she has no power to give her vote against it. From the cradle to the grave she is subject to the power and control of man. Father, guardian, or husband, one conveys her like some piece of merchandise over to the other.

At marriage she loses her entire identity, and her being is said to have become merged in her husband. Has nature thus merged it? Has she ceased to exist and feel pleasure and pain? . . . And when at his nightly orgies, in the grog-shop and the oyster-cellar, or at the gaming-table, he squanders the means she helped, by her co-operation and economy, to accumulate, and she awakens to penury and destitution, will it supply the wants of her children to tell them that, owing to the superiority of man she had no redress by law, and that as her being was merged in his, so also ought theirs to be? What an inconsistency, that from the moment she enters that compact, in which she assumes the high responsibility of wife and mother, she ceases legally to exist, and become a purely submissive being. Blind submission in woman is considered a virtue, while submission to wrong is itself wrong, and resistance to wrong is virtue, alike in woman as in man.

But it will be said that the husband provides for the wife, or in other words, he feeds, clothes, and shelters her! I wish I had the power to make every one before me fully realize the degradation contained in that idea. Yes! He *keeps* her, and so he does a favorite horse: by law they are both considered his property. Both may, when the cruelty of the owner compels them to run away, be brought back by the strong arm of the law. . . .

Again, I shall be told that the law presumes the husband to be kind, affectionate, and ready to provide for and protect his wife. But what right, I ask, has the law to presume at all on the subject? What right has the law to intrust the interest and happiness of one being into the hands of another? . . . We have nothing to do with individual man, be he good or bad, but with the laws that oppress woman. We know that bad and unjust laws must in the nature of things make man so too. . . .

As long as woman shall be oppressed by unequal laws, so long will she be degraded by man.

We have hardly an adequate idea how all-powerful law is in forming public opinion, in giving tone and character to the mass of society.

Hence also the reason why we call on the nation to remove the legal shackles from woman, . . . it will have a beneficial effect on that still greater tyrant she has to contend with, Public Opinion.

Carry out the republican principle of universal suffrage, or strike it from your banners and substitute "Freedom and Power to one half of society, and Submission and Slavery to the other." Give woman the elective franchise. Let married women have the same right to property that their husbands have; for whatever the difference in their respective occupations, the duties of the wife are as indispensable and far more arduous than the husband's. Why then should the wife, at the death of her husband, not be his heir to the same extent that he is heir to her? In this inequality there is involved another wrong. When the wife dies, the husband is left in the undisturbed possession of all there is, and children are left with him; no change is made, no stranger intrudes on his home and his affliction. But when the husband dies, the widow, at best receives but a mere pittance, while strangers assume authority denied to the wife. The sanctuary of affliction must be desecrated by executors; everything must be ransacked and assessed, lest she should steal something out of her own house; and to cap the climax, the children must be placed under guardians. When the husband dies poor, to be sure, no guardian is required, and the children are left for the mother to care and toil for, as best she may. But when anything is left for their maintenance, then it must be placed in the hands of strangers for safekeeping!

According to a late act, the wife has a right to the property she brings at marriage, or receives in any way after marriage. Here is some provision for the favored few; but for the laboring many, there is none. The mass of the people commence life with no other capital than the union of heads, hearts, and hands. To the benefit of this best of capital, the wife has no right. If they are unsuccessful in married life, who suffers more the bitter consequences of poverty than the wife? But if successful, she can not call a dollar her own. The husband may will away every dollar of the personal property, and leave her destitute and penniless, and she has no redress. . . . This is law, but where is the justice of it?

3

---❖---

"In Memoriam—American Democracy"

B orn to a Russian-Jewish family in Latvia in 1869, Emma Goldman attended school in Königsberg, Germany, and completed her education in St. Petersberg by reading Russian radical authors such as Tchernyshevski, Turgenev, and the anarchist Peter Kropotkin. At sixteen she immigrated with an older sister to Rochester, where she sewed buttons on men's coats for $2.50 a week. At twenty she moved to New York to become a colleague of anarchists Johann Most and Alexander Berkman. Berkman became her lover as well as her political mentor.

A humanitarian and a critic of industrial society, Goldman believed that freedom and justice for the individual could be achieved only by the overthrow of all existing political and economic systems. She worked not only for anarchism, but also for civil liberties and women's rights, as illustrated in the following passage from her autobiography, Living My Life. Villified for her belief in free love as much as for her politics, she was arrested repeatedly and served three prison terms before being deported in 1919. Disillusioned with Bolshevik Russia, Goldman spent her last decades in western Europe. She died in 1940 in Canada while on a tour to raise money for the antifascist cause of the Spanish Loyalists.

M y lectures in New York that winter included the subject of birth-control. I had definitely decided some time previously to make public the knowledge of contraceptives, particularly at my Yiddish meetings, because the women on the East Side need that information most. . . .

My lectures and attempts at lecturing on birth-control finally resulted in my arrest, whereupon a public protest was arranged in Carnegie Hall. . . .

My trial, after several preliminary hearings, was set for April 20. On the eve of that day a banquet took place at the Brevoort Hotel, arranged by Anna

---

Source: Emma Goldman, Living My Life (1931; reprint New York: Dover, 1970), vol. 2, pp. 569–72, 597–603. Reprinted by permission.

Sloan and other friends. Members of the professions and of various social tendencies were present. Our good old comrade H. M. Kelly spoke for anarchism, Rose Pastor Stokes for socialism, and Whidden Graham for the single-taxers. The world of art was represented by Robert Henri, George Bellows, Robert Minor, John Sloan, Randall Davey, and Boardman Robinson. Dr. Goldwater and other physicians participated. . . .

Rose Pastor Stokes demonstrated direct action at the banquet. She announced that she had with her typewritten sheets containing information on contraceptives and that she was ready to hand them out to anyone who wanted them. The majority did.

In court the next day, April 20, I pleaded my own case. The District Attorney interrupted me continually by taking exceptions, in which he was sustained by two of my three judges. Presiding Judge O'Keefe proved to be unexpectedly fair. After some tilts with the young prosecutor I took the stand in my own behalf. It gave me the opportunity to expose the ignorance of the detectives who testified against me and to deliver in open court a defense of birth-control.

I spoke for an hour, closing with the declaration that if it was a crime to work for healthy motherhood and happy child-life, I was proud to be considered a criminal. Judge O'Keefe, reluctantly I thought, pronounced me guilty and sentenced me to pay a fine of one hundred dollars or serve fifteen days in the workhouse. On principle I refused to pay the fine, stating that I preferred to go to jail. It called forth an approving demonstration, and the court attendants cleared the room. I was hurried off to the Tombs, whence I was taken to the Queens County Jail.

Our following Sunday meeting, which I could not attend since my forum was now a cell, was turned into a protest against my conviction. Among the speakers was Ben [Reitman], who announced that pamphlets containing information about contraceptives were on the literature table and could be taken free of charge. Before he had got off the platform, the last of the pamphlets had been snatched up. Ben was arrested on the spot and held for trial.

In Queens County Jail, as on Blackwell's Island years previously, I saw it demonstrated that the average social offender is made, not born. One must have the consolation of an ideal to survive the forces designed to crush the prisoner. Having such an ideal, the fifteen days were a lark to me. I read more than I had for months outside, prepared material for six lectures on American literature, and still had time for my fellow prisoners.

Little did the New York authorities foresee the results of the arrests of Ben and me. The Carnegie Hall meeting had awakened interest throughout the country in the idea of birth-control. Protests and public demands for the right to contraceptive information were reported from numerous cities. In San Francisco forty leading women signed a declaration to the effect that they would get out pamphlets and be ready to go to prison. Some proceeded to carry out the plan and they were arrested, but their cases were discharged by the judge, who stated that there was no ordinance in the city to prohibit the propagation of birth-control information. . . .

In the excitement of the birth-control campaign I did not forget other important issues. The European slaughter was continuing, and the American militarists were growing bloodthirsty at the smell of the red stream. Our numbers were few, our means limited, but we concentrated our best energies to stem the tide of war. . . .

In the spirit of her military preparations America was rivalling the most despotic countries of the Old World. Conscription, resorted to by Great Britain only after eighteen months of war, was decided upon by Wilson within one month after the United States had decided to enter the European conflict. Washington was not so squeamish about the rights of its citizens as the British Parliament had been. The academic author of *The New Freedom* did not hesitate to destroy every democratic principle at one blow. He had assured the world that America was moved by the highest humanitarian motives, her aim being to democratize Germany. What if he had to Prussianize the United States in order to achieve it? Free-born Americans had to be forcibly pressed into the military mould, herded like cattle, and shipped across the waters to fertilize the fields of France. Their sacrifice would earn them the glory of having demonstrated the superiority of *My Country, 'Tis of Thee* over *Die Wacht am Rhein*. No American president had ever before succeeded in so humbugging the people as Woodrow Wilson, who wrote and talked democracy, acted despotically, privately and officially, and yet managed to keep up the myth that he was championing humanity and freedom.

We had no illusions about the outcome of the conscription bill pending before Congress. We regarded the measure as a complete denial of every human right, the death-knell to liberty of conscience, and we determined to fight it unconditionally. We did not expect to be able to stem the tidal wave of hatred and violence which compulsory service was bound to bring, but we felt that we had at least to make known at large that there were some in the United States who owned their souls and who meant to preserve their integrity, no matter what the cost.

We decided to call a conference in the *Mother Earth* office to broach the organization of No-Conscription League and draw up a manifesto to clarify to the people of America the menace of conscription. We also planned a large mass meeting as a protest against compelling American men to sign their own death-warrants in the form of forced military registration. . . .

I took the position that, as a woman and therefore myself not subject to military service, I could not advise people on the matter. Whether or not one is to lend oneself as a tool for the business of killing should properly be left to the individual conscience. As an anarchist I could not presume to decide the fate of others, I wrote. But I could say to those who refused to be coerced into military service that I would plead their cause and stand by their act against all odds.

A mass meeting was held. Almost ten thousand people filled the place, among them many newly rigged-out soldiers and their woman friends, a very boisterous lot indeed. Several hundred policemen and detectives were scattered through the hall. When the session opened, a few young "patriots" tried to rush the stage entrance. Their attempt was foiled, because we had prepared for such a contingency. . . .

The future heroes were noisy all through the speeches, but when I stepped on the platform, pandemonium broke loose. They jeered and hooted, intoned *The Star-Spangled Banner*, and frantically waved small American flags. Above the din the voice of a recruit shouted: "I want the floor!" The patience of the audience had been sorely tried all evening by the interrupters. Now men rose from every part of the house and called to the disturber to shut up or be kicked out. I knew what such a thing would lead to, with the police waiting for a chance to aid the patriotic ruffians. Moreover, I did not want to deny free speech even to the soldier. Raising my voice, I appealed to the assembly to permit the man to speak. "We who have come here to protest against coercion and to demand the right to think and act in accordance with our consciences," I urged, "should recognize the right of an opponent to speak and we should listen quietly and grant him the respect we demanded for ourselves. The young man no doubt believes in the justice of his cause as we do in ours, and he has pledged his life for it. I suggest therefore that we all rise in appreciation of his evident sincerity and that we hear him out in silence." The audience rose to a man.

The soldier had probably never before faced such a large assembly. He looked frightened and he began in a quavering voice that barely carried to the platform, although he was sitting near it. He stammered something about "German money" and "traitors," got confused, and came to a sudden stop. Then, turning to his comrades, he cried: "Oh, hell! Let's get out of here!" Out the whole gang slunk, waving their little flags and followed by laughter and applause.

Returning from the meeting home we heard newsboys shouting extra night editions—the conscription bill had become a law! Registration day was set for June 4. The thought struck me that on that day American democracy would be carried to its grave. . . .

Streams of callers besieged our office from morning till late at night; young men, mostly, seeking advice on whether they should register. We knew, of course, that among them were also decoys sent to trick us into saying that they should not. The majority, however, were frightened youths, fearfully wrought up and at sea as to what to do. They were helpless creatures about to be sacrificed to Moloch. Our sympathies were with them, but we felt that we had no right to decide the vital issue for them. There were also distracted mothers, imploring us to save their boys. By the hundreds they came, wrote, or telephoned. All day long our telephone rang; our offices were filled with people, and stacks of mail arrived from every part of the country asking for information about the No-Conscription League, pledging support and urging us to go on with the work. In this bedlam we had to prepare copy for the current issues of *Mother Earth* and the *Blast*, write our manifesto, and send our circulars announcing our forthcoming meeting. At night, when trying to get some sleep, we would be rung out of bed by reporters wanting to know our next step.

Anti-conscription meetings were also taking place outside of New York and I was busy organizing branches of the No-Conscription League. At such a gathering in Philadelphia the police came down with drawn clubs and threatened to beat up the audience if I dared mention conscription. I proceeded to talk about the freedom the masses in Russia had gained. At the close of the meeting fifty persons retired to a private place, where we organized a No-Conscription League. Similar experiences were repeated in many cities. . . .

The June issue of *Mother Earth* appeared draped in black, its cover representing a tomb bearing the inscription: "IN MEMORIAM—AMERICAN DEMOCRACY." The sombre attire of the magazine was striking and effective. No words could express more eloquently the tragedy that turned America, the erstwhile torch-bearer of freedom, into a grave-digger of her former ideals.

We strained our capital to the last penny to issue an extra large edition. We wanted to mail copies to every Federal officer, to every editor in the country and to distribute the magazine among young workers and college students. Our twenty thousand copies barely sufficed to supply our own needs. It made us feel our poverty more than ever before. Fortunately an unexpected ally came to our assistance: the New York newspapers! They had reprinted whole passages from our anti-conscription manifesto, some even reproducing the entire text and thus bringing it to the attention of millions of readers. Now they copiously quoted from our June issue and editorially commented at length on its contents.

The press throughout the country raved at our defiance of law and presidential orders. We duly appreciated their help in making our voices resound through the land, our voices that but yesterday had called in vain.

4

———◆———

The March of the Mill Children

"Whatever your fight, don't be ladylike," advised Mother Jones. Born in County Cork, Ireland, in 1830, Mary Harris Jones immigrated with her family at the age of seven. After a series of tragedies—her husband and four children died in a yellow fever epidemic in 1867 and her home and dressmaking business were destroyed by fire in 1871—she became an organizer for the Knights of Labor. Active into her nineties, she probably traveled farther and participated in more strikes than any other labor leader in the United States. Her exploits were legendary, the poor welcomed her into their homes, and trains carried her without charge from one strike headquarters to another. She lived more than one hundred years and died, appropriately, in the home of a miner in 1930.

Mother Jones was an ardent foe of child labor, which she had first observed in the mills of the South. Supporting a textile mill strike in Kensington, Pennsylvania, in 1903, she was appalled to find that 10,000 of the 75,000 mill workers were children, many of them maimed by machinery. She publicized their plight by marching them from Philadelphia to Oyster Bay, Long Island, President Theodore Roosevelt's summer home. In the following passage from her autobiography, she describes this march, which resulted in a new law against child labor in Pennsylvania.

In the spring of 1903 I went to Kensington, Pennsylvania, where seventy-five thousand textile workers were on strike. Of this number at least ten thousand were little children. The workers were striking for more pay and shorter hours. Every day little children came into Union Headquarters, some with their hands off, some with the thumb missing, some with their fingers off at the knuckle. They were stooped little things, round shouldered and skinny. Many of them were not over ten years of age, although the state law prohibited their working before they were twelve years of age.

The law was poorly enforced and the mothers of these children often swore falsely as to their children's age. In a single block in Kensington, fourteen women, mothers of twenty-two children all under twelve, explained it was a question of starvation or perjury. That the fathers had been killed or maimed at the mines.

Source: THE AUTOBIOGRAPHY OF MOTHER JONES, Third Edition, Revised, 1977. Published by Charles H. Kerr Publishing Company, Chicago.

I asked the newspaper men why they didn't publish the facts about child labor in Pennsylvania. They said they couldn't because the mill owners had stock in the papers.

"Well, I've got stock in these little children," said I, "and I'll arrange a little publicity."

We assembled a number of boys and girls one morning in Independence Park and from there we arranged to parade with banners to the court house where we would hold a meeting.

A great crowd gathered in the public square in front of the city hall. I put the little boys with their fingers off and hands crushed and maimed on a platform. I held up their mutilated hands and showed them to the crowd and made the statement that Philadelphia's mansions were built on the broken bones, the quivering hearts and drooping heads of these children. That their little lives went out to make wealth for others. That neither state or city officials paid any attention to these wrongs. That they did not care that these children were to be the future citizens of the nation. . . .

I called upon the millionaire manufacturers to cease their moral murders, and I cried to the officials in the open windows opposite, "Some day the workers will take possession of your city hall, and when we do, no child will be sacrificed on the altar of profit."

The reporters quoted my statement that Philadelphia mansions were built on the broken bones and quivering hearts of children. The Philadelphia papers and the New York papers got into a squabble with each other over the question. The universities discussed it. Preachers began talking. That was what I wanted. Public attention on the subject of child labor.

The matter quieted down for a while and I concluded the people needed stirring up again. . . . I asked some of the parents if they would let me have their little boys and girls for a week or ten days, promising to bring them back safe and sound. They consented. A man named Sweeny was marshall for our "army." A few men and women went with me to help with the children. They were on strike and I thought they might as well have a little recreation.

The children carried knapsacks on their backs in which was a knife and fork, a tin cup and plate. We took along a wash boiler in which to cook the food on the road. One little fellow had a drum and another had a fife. That was our band. We carried banners that said, "We want more schools and less hospitals." "We want time to play." "Prosperity is here. Where is ours!"

We started from Philadelphia where we held a great mass meeting. I decided to go with the children to see President Roosevelt to ask him to have Congress pass a law prohibiting the exploitation of childhood. I thought that President Roosevelt might see these mill children and compare them with his own little ones who were spending the summer on the seashore at Oyster Bay. . . .

The children were very happy, having plenty to eat, taking baths in the brooks and rivers every day. I thought when the strike is over and they go back to the mills, they will never have another holiday like this. All along the line of march the farmers drove out to meet us with wagon loads of fruit and vegetables. Their wives brought the children clothes and money. The inter-urban trainmen would stop their trains and give us free rides.

We were on the outskirts of New Trenton, New Jersey, cooking our lunch in the wash boiler, when the conductor on the interurban car stopped and told us the police were coming down to notify us that we could not enter the town. There were mills in the town and the mill owners didn't like our coming.

I said, "All right, the police will be just in time for lunch."

Sure enough, the police came and we invited them to dine with us. They looked at the little gathering of children with their tin plates and cups around the wash boiler. They just smiled and spoke kindly to the children, and said nothing at all about not going into the city.

We went in, held our meeting, and it was the wives of the police who took the little children and cared for them that night, sending them back in the morning with a nice lunch rolled up in paper napkins.

Everywhere we had meetings, showing up with living children, the horrors of child labor. . . .

I called on the mayor of Princeton and asked for permission to speak opposite the campus of the University. I said I wanted to speak on higher education. The mayor gave me permission. A great crowd gathered, professors and students and the people; and I told them that the rich robbed these little children of any education of the lowest order that they might send their sons and daughters to places of higher education. . . . And I showed those professors children in our army who could scarcely read or write because they were working ten hours a day in the silk mills of Pennsylvania.

"Here's a text book on economics," I said, pointing to a little chap, James Ashworth, who was ten years old and who was stooped over like an old man from carrying bundles of yarn that weighed seventy-five pounds. "He gets three dollars a week. . . ."

I sent a committee over to the New York Chief of Police, Ebstein, asking for permission to march up Fourth Avenue to Madison Square where I wanted to hold a meeting. The chief refused and forbade our entrance to the city.

I went over myself to New York and saw Mayor Seth Low. The mayor was most courteous but he said he would have to support the police commissioner. I asked him what the reason was for refusing us entrance to the city and he said that we were not citizens of New York.

"Oh, I think we will clear that up, Mr. Mayor," I said. "Permit me to call your attention to an incident which took place in this nation just a year ago. A piece of rotten royalty came over here from Germany, called Prince

Henry. The Congress of the United States voted $45,000 to fill that fellow's stomach for three weeks and to entertain him. His brother was getting $4,000,000 dividends out of the blood of the workers in this country. Was he a citizen of this land?"

"And it was reported, Mr. Mayor, that you and all the officials of New York and the University Club entertained that chap." And I repeated, "Was he a citizen of New York?"

"No, Mother," said the mayor, "he was not. . . ."

"Well, Mr. Mayor, these are the little citizens of the nation and they also produce its wealth. Aren't we entitled to enter your city?" [They were allowed to enter.] . . .

We marched to Twentieth Street. I told an immense crowd of the horrors of child labor in the mills around the anthracite region and I showed them some of the children. I showed them Eddie Dunphy, a little fellow of twelve, whose job it was to sit all day on a high stool, handing in the right thread to another worker. Eleven hours a day he sat on the high stool with dangerous machinery all about him. All day long, winter and summer, spring and fall, for three dollars a week.

And then I showed them Gussie Rangnew, a little girl from whom all the childhood had gone. Her face was like an old woman's. Gussie packed stockings in a factory, eleven hours a day for a few cents a day.

We raised a lot of money for the strikers and hundreds of friends offered their homes to the little ones while we were in the city.

The next day we went to Coney Island at the invitation of Mr. Bostick who owned the wild animal show. The children had a wonderful day such as they never had in all their lives. After the exhibition of the trained animals, Mr. Bostick let me speak to the audience. . . . Right in front were the empty iron cages of the animals. I put my little children in the cages and they clung to the iron bars while I talked. . . .

"Fifty years ago there was a cry against slavery and men gave up their lives to stop the selling of black children on the block. Today the white child is sold for two dollars a week to the manufacturers. Fifty years ago the black babies were sold C.O.D. Today the white baby is sold on the installment plan. . . .

"The trouble is that no one in Washington cares. I saw our legislators in one hour pass three bills for the relief of the railways but when labor cries for aid for the children they will not listen.

"I asked a man in prison once how he happened to be there and he said he had stolen a pair of shoes. I told him if he had stolen a railroad he would be a United States Senator.

"We are told that every American boy has the chance of being president. I tell you that these little boys in the iron cages will sell their chance any day for good square meals and a chance to play. . . ."

The next day we left Coney Island for Manhattan Beach to visit Senator Platt, who had made an appointment to see me at nine o'clock in the morning. The children got stuck in the sand banks and I had a time cleaning the sand off the littlest ones. So we started to walk on the railroad track. I was told it was private property and we had to get off. Finally a saloon keeper showed us a short cut into the sacred grounds of the hotel and suddenly the army appeared in the lobby. The little fellows played "Hail, hail, the gang's all here" on their fifes and drums, and Senator Platt when he saw the little army ran away through the back door to New York.

I asked the manager if he would give the children breakfast and charge it up to the Senator as we had an invitation to breakfast that morning with him. He gave us a private room and he gave those children such a breakfast as they had never had in all their lives. I had breakfast too, and a reporter from one of the Hearst papers and I charged it all up to Senator Platt.

We marched down to Oyster Bay but the president refused to see us and he would not answer my letters. But our march had done its work. We had drawn the attention of the nation to the crime of child labor. And while the strike of the textile workers in Kensington was lost and the children driven back to work, not long afterward the Pennsylvania legislature passed a child labor law that sent thousands of children home from the mills, and kept thousands of others from entering the factory until they were fourteen years of age.

5

Fasting for Suffrage: "We Don't Want Other Women Ever to Have to Do This Over Again"

Although Emma Goldman and Mother Jones viewed women's suffrage as irrelevant to basic social change, a mere plaything for the middle-class, privileged woman, other immigrant women activists did not agree. Among them was Polish-born Rose Winslow (Ruza Wenclawska). At the age of eleven Winslow was working fourteen hours a day in a hosiery mill in Pennsylvania. After tuberculosis forced her to leave the mill at nineteen, she became an organizer for the Consumers' League and a powerful force in the suffrage movement.

Source: Doris Stevens, *Jailed for Freedom* (New York: Boni and Liveright, 1920), pp. 187–91.

Suffragists increased their pressure on President Wilson during World War I on the grounds that they were denied at home the democracy America was supposedly fighting for abroad. Winslow was among the militant suffrage leaders—including Alice Paul, founder of the Woman's Party—arrested in 1917 and sentenced to seven months' imprisonment on the flimsy charge of obstructing traffic in front of the White House. The imprisoned women went on a hunger strike, and the authorities responded with brutality and force-feeding. Winslow's account of her confinement in the prison hospital, presented here, was smuggled to other suffragists and to her husband on tiny scraps of paper. On May 20, 1919, Congress finally passed the Woman's Suffrage Amendment, which was ratified by the last of the necessary thirty-six states on August 26, 1920.

"If this thing is necessary we will naturally go through with it. Force is so stupid a weapon. I feel so happy doing my bit for decency—for *our* war, which is after all, real and fundamental."

"The women are all so magnificent, so beautiful. Alice Paul is as thin as ever, pale and large-eyed. We have been in solitary for five weeks. There is nothing to tell but that the days go by somehow. I have felt quite feeble the last few days—faint, so that I could hardly get my hair brushed, my arms ached so. But to-day I am well again. Alice Paul and I talk back and forth though we are at opposite ends of the building and a hall door also shuts us apart. But occasionally—thrills—we escape from behind our iron-barred doors and visit. Great laughter and rejoicing!"

To her husband:—

"My fainting probably means nothing except that I am not strong after these weeks. I know you won't be alarmed.

"I told about a syphilitic colored woman with one leg. The other one was cut off, having rotted so that it was alive with maggots when she came in. The remaining one is now getting as bad. They are so short of nurses that a little colored girl of twelve, who is here waiting to have her tonsils removed, waits on her. This child and two others share a ward with a syphilitic child of three or four years, whose mother refused to have it at home. It makes you absolutely ill to see it. . . .

Alice Paul and I found we had been taking baths in one of the tubs here, in which this syphilitic child, an incurable, who has his eyes bandaged all the time, is also bathed. He was been here a year. Into the room where he lives came yesterday two children to be operated on for tonsillitis. They also bathed in the same tub. . . . Cheerful mixing, isn't it? The place is alive with roaches, crawling all over the walls, everywhere. I found one in my bed the other day. . . ."

"Alice Paul is in the psychopathic ward. She dreaded forcible feeding frightfully, and I hate to think how she must be feeling. I had a nervous time of it, gasping a long time afterward, and my stomach rejecting during the process. I spent a bad, restless night, but otherwise I am all right. The poor soul who fed me got liberally besprinkled during the process. I heard myself making the most hideous sounds. . . . One feels so forsaken when one lies prone and people shove a pipe down one's stomach."

"This morning but for an astounding tiredness, I am all right. I am waiting to see what happens when the President realizes that brutal bullying isn't quite a statesmanlike method for settling a demand for justice at home. At least, if men are supine enough to endure, women—to their eternal glory—are not."

"Yesterday was a bad day for me in feeding. I was vomiting continually during the process. The tube has developed an irritation somewhere that is painful.

"Never was there a sentence like ours for such an offense as ours, even in England. No woman ever got it over there even for tearing down buildings. And during all that agitation *we* were busy saying that never would such things happen in the United States. . . ."

"Mary Beard and Helen Todd were allowed to stay only a minute, and I cried like a fool. I am getting over that habit, I think.

"I fainted again last night. . . ."

"Don't let them tell you we take this well. Miss Paul vomits much. I do, too, except when I'm not nervous, as I have been every time against my will. I try to be less feeble-minded. It's the nervous reaction, and I can't control it much. I don't imagine bathing one's food in tears very good for one.

"We think of the coming feeding all day. It is horrible. The doctor thinks I take it well. I hate the thought of Alice Paul and the others if I take it well."

"We still get no mail; we are 'insubordinate.' It's strange, isn't it; if you ask for food fit to eat, as we did, you are 'insubordinate'; and if you refuse food you are 'insubordinate.' Amusing. I am really all right. If this continues very long I perhaps won't be. I am interested to see how long our so-called 'splendid American men' will stand for this form of discipline.

"All news cheers one marvelously because it is hard to feel anything but a bit desolate and forgotten here in this place.

"All the officers here know we are making this hunger strike that women fighting for liberty may be considered political prisoners; we have told them. God knows we don't want other women ever to have to do this over again."

6

---❧---

"Black Women of the World . . . Push Forward"

After the Woman's Suffrage Amendment, interest in public roles for women in the United States declined. However, Jamaican-born Amy Jacques Garvey continued to urge black women to assume leadership in public life, specifically in the black nationalist movement. Her views are expressed in the following 1925 editorial from Negro World, *the official newspaper of the Universal Negro Improvement Association.*

Amy Jacques Garvey was the second wife of Marcus Garvey, founder of the Universal Negro Improvement Association, a short-lived but influential movement that reached its peak in the early 1920s. The association attracted millions of followers, mainly urban, working-class blacks, by its platform of racial separatism, black pride, and political liberation of blacks in the United States, Africa, and throughout the world. Amy Jacques Garvey played an active role in the association as her husband's secretary and colleague, as editor and publisher of his ideas, as editor of the women's page of Negro World *for four years, and as a leader in her own right. In 1927 Marcus Garvey was deported after being convicted on a dubious charge of mail fraud. He died in London in 1940. Amy Jacques Garvey continued to write and work for black liberation in the United States, London, and Jamaica.*

The exigencies of this present age require that women take their places beside their men. White women are rallying all their forces and uniting regardless of national boundaries to save their race from destruction, and preserve its ideals for posterity. . . . White men have begun to realize that as women are the backbone of the home, so can they, by their economic experience and their aptitude for details participate effectively in guiding the destiny of nation and race.

No line of endeavor remains closed for long to the modern woman. She agitates for equal opportunities and gets them; she makes good on the job and gains the respect of men who heretofore opposed her. She prefers to be a bread-winner than a half-starved wife at home. She is not afraid of hard work, and by being independent she gets more out of the present-day husband than her grandmother did in the good old days.

Source: Amy Jacques Garvey, "Women as Leaders," editorial, *Negro World,* October 24, 1925.

The women of the East, both yellow and black, are slowly, but surely imitating the women of the Western world, and as the white women are bolstering up a decaying white civilization, even so women of the darker races are sallying forth to help their men establish a civilization according to their own standards, and to strive for world leadership.

Women of all climes and races have as great a part to play in the development of their particular group as the men. Some readers may not agree with us on this issue, but do they not mould the minds of their children the future men and women? . . . Many a man has risen from the depths of poverty and obscurity and made his mark in life because of the advices and councils of a good mother whose influence guided his footsteps throughout his life.

Women therefore are extending this holy influence outside the realms of the home, softening the ills of the world by their gracious and kindly contact.

Some men may argue that the home will be broken up and women will become coarse and lose their gentle appeal. We do not think so, because everything can be done with moderation. . . . The doll baby type of woman is a thing of the past, and the wide-awake woman is forging ahead prepared for all emergencies, and ready to answer any call, even if it be to face the cannons on the battlefield.

New York has a woman Secretary of State. Two States have women Governors, and we would not be surprised if within the next ten years a woman graces the White House in Washington, D.C. Women are also filling diplomatic positions, and from time immemorial women have been used as spies to get information for their country.

White women have greater opportunities to display their ability because of the standing of both races, and due to the fact that black men are less appreciative of their women than white men. The former will more readily sing the praises of white women than their own; yet who is more deserving of admiration than the black woman, she who has borne the rigors of slavery, the deprivations consequent on a pauperized race, and the indignities heaped upon a weak and defenseless people? Yet she has suffered all with fortitude, and stands ever ready to help in the onward march to freedom and power.

Be not discouraged black women of the world, but push forward, regardless of the lack of appreciation shown you. A race must be saved, a country must be redeemed, and unless you strengthen the leadership of vacillating Negro men, we will remain marking time until the Yellow race gains leadership of the world, and we be forced to subserviency under them, or extermination.

We are tired of hearing Negro men say, "There is a better day coming," while they do nothing to usher in the day. We are becoming so impatient that we are getting in the front ranks, and serve notice on the world that we will brush aside the halting, cowardly Negro men, and with prayer on our lips and arms prepared for any fray, we will press on and on until victory is ours. Africa must be for Africans, and Negroes everywhere must be independent, God being our guide. Mr. Black man, watch your step! Ethiopia's queens will reign again, and her Amazons protect her shores and people. Strengthen your shaking knees, and move forward, or we will displace you and lead on to victory and to glory.

7

"Why Did I Put Up With It All These Years?": The Farah Strike

As this reading will demonstrate, activism often changed the activists as much as the conditions they protested. In May 1972 four thousand garment workers struck against the Farah manufacturing plants in El Paso, Texas. Eighty-five percent of the strikers were Chicanas. Some were born in Mexico and some in Texas, but all were angry at the "racism, deprivation, and systematic oppression" they experienced in El Paso. The unionization drive and strike enabled them, usually for the first time, to give organized expression to their anger.

In 1977 Laurie Coyle, Gail Hershatter, and Emily Honig interviewed many of the strikers and wrote the longer article from which this reading is excerpted. The longer article describes the strikers' backgrounds. Some had seen their parents participate in bloody strikes in the mines of northern Mexico or had relatives in unionized plants in El Paso, but most knew little or nothing about labor history or union activities when the strike began. The article describes the conditions that caused the strike—low wages, deceptive "benefit" plans, unsafe working conditions, incompetent care from company medical personnel, and pressure and harassment from Anglo male supervisors. It also discusses the sometimes troubled relations between the strikers and the Amalgamated Clothing Workers of America.

This excerpt does not deal with these subjects. It focuses instead on the experiences of the women during the strike, and on how the strike changed the way they looked at themselves as Chicanas, as wives, as mothers, and as workers. The

Source: Laurie Coyle, Gail Hershatter, and Emily Honig, "Women at Farah: An Unfinished Story," in *Mexican Women in the United States: Struggles Past and Present,* ed. Magdalena Mora and Adelaid R. Castillo, Occasional Paper no. 2 (Chicano Studies Research Center Publications, University of California–Los Angeles, 1980).

reading begins several months before the strike, when a small group of elite male workers, the "cutters," launched a drive to organize the Farah plants.

Reactions to the organizing drive varied. Most women had little idea of what the activists hoped to gain from union recognition. Others were fearful—with good cause—of supervisors' retaliation. Furthermore, many workers believed what Willie Farah said about labor unions taking their money and benefits.

Even so, some women were moved by their fellow workers' persistence in the face of personal harassment and threats to their jobs. Several workers signed cards and began to talk to their coworkers about the new organizing drive. Efforts to sign up workers took place clandestinely because of the virulence of management tactics against the organizers. Women hid union cards in their purses, met hurriedly in the bathrooms and whispered in the halls to persuade the indifferent. The cafeteria was the heart of the organizing efforts. During lunch time, workers circulated among the tables to sound out each other's sentiments about the union. The first union meetings in people's homes were a completely new experience. "Oh, I did like them," a striker reminisced. "There was a lot of—you know, talking about new things, about the union. And especially, I felt that somebody was talking for us."

Management responded to organizing activities with a series of repressive measures . . . a striker recalled.

> They'd say, "Don't believe about the union, the union's a bunch of bullshit. They only want to take your money away." That's what they'd say. And I just heard them, and I didn't say anything. . . . But once they knew you were involved with the union, they'd start pressuring you. . . . Some of us just quit, some were fired. . . .

The activists who were fired went down to the union office and vowed to continue the struggle. One woman organized a group of students from a nearby high school to distribute leaflets in front of the Gateway, Paisano, and Third Street plants. They were insulted, their leaflets were torn up and thrown in their faces, and some of them were assaulted. But the woman came every day at 6:00 A.M. and stood her ground until the day of the walkout.

The Walkout

[A walkout in a Farah plant in San Antonio provided the spark that ignited the strike in El Paso]

When El Paso Farah workers learned of the San Antonio strike, their frustration with working conditions and with Farah's continued suppression of union activity exploded into a spontaneous strike. On May 9, the machinists, shippers, cutters, and some of the seamstresses walked out. The walk-out, which continued for almost a month, initially took the company by surprise. Women who had worked docilely at their machines for years, women who had been reduced to tears by a supervisor's reprimand, women who had never openly spoken a word in favor of the union, suddenly began to speak up.

> That day that we walked out, the supervisor saw that I had a little flag on. He went over and he looked at me, sort of startled, and he said, "You?" And I said, "Yes!" And he said, "What have we done to you?" I said, "Oh, I wouldn't know where to begin." He said, "We haven't done anything to you." I said, "But you have done a lot to all of the people around me. I've seen it going on. . . ."

For many women, the decision was a difficult one which took several days to make, while the management did its best to frighten or cajole the women who were still undecided. For all of the strikers, the day on which they decided to walk out remains a vivid and memorable one.

> I remember the first time of the walkout we were all in break, eat-ing, having some coffee. And then suddenly there was a whole bunch in the cutting room—the girls and everything. They went over to my table and said, "Alma, you've got to come out with us!" And I just looked at them. I was so scared I didn't even know what to do. What if I go and lose my thirteen years? So long, having se-niority and everything. I just looked at them and said, "Yeah, yeah, I'll go. I'll go." That's all I said. And I had a whole bunch of people sitting there with me and I said, "Let's go!" And one of them said, "Well, if you go, we'll go."
>
> So the next day I went and put pants on. I always wear dresses. I used to love to wear dresses. So I put some pants on and said, "I don't know what's going to happen. Maybe there's going to be fighting or something." You know, we were scared. . . . We were scared maybe they would beat us and everything. . . .
>
> So around nine o'clock I started gathering everybody. "We're going out! Right now! When you see me get off my machine." So you should have seen all those supervisors around me. . . . They said, "Alma, you're a good worker. We'll pay you what you want. Alma, the way you sew, the way you work, the way you help us." And I would just say, "Yeah, I know. I know." They thought I was going to stay there.
>
> At nine o'clock I got off [the machine]. I went to the restroom and I started telling everybody, "Let's go! . . ."
>
> Then I started walking through the middle of the—where all the people were working—they thought I was very happy [with

work at Farah]. And they started, "Alma! Alma!" And everybody started getting off the machines. I couldn't believe it. It was something so beautiful. So exciting. . . .

When I started walking outside, all the strikers that were out there, yelling, they saw me, and golly, I felt so proud, 'cause they all went and hugged me. And they said, "We never thought you were one of us" And I said, "What do you think? Just because I'm a quiet person?"

But it was beautiful! I really knew we were going to do something. That we were really going to fight for our rights.

As the walkout continued and spread beyond the shipping and cutting rooms, it began to include a wide variety of women. Some came from families with histories of union involvement, while others had no previous contact or experience with unions. Some who walked out had taken an active role in the union organizing campaign leading up to the strike, while others had never even signed a union card. For all of them, however, the act of walking out began a process of change in the way they looked at themselves and their work. . . .

The Strike

The strikers began to picket the Farah plants and local stores which carried Farah products. But in a town where many regarded Willie Farah as a folk hero, the strikers found that public reaction to the walkout was often hostile. One woman remembers that:

People were just very cruel. Everybody thought that Farah was a god or something. . . . I swear, they'd even turn around and spit on you if they could. There was one lady, I was handing out some papers downtown . . . and she got her purse and started striking me. . . . When she started hitting me, she said, "Ah, you people, a bunch of dumb this and that! Farah's a great man! . . ."

There was also considerable racism in the antiunion sentiment. Some members of the Anglo community felt that Mexican Americans were "aliens" and that Mexican American strikers were ungrateful troublemakers who should be dealt with severely. . . .

However, opinions about the strike did not simply divide along racial or ethnic lines. The strike split the Chicano community. Many workers at Farah crossed picket lines and continued to keep the plant operating. They were known as the "happies" because they wore buttons which featured a smiling face and the slogan, "I'm happy at Farah. . . ."

The strike divided families. Several women told of walking out while their sisters remained inside the plant. . . .

People on the picket lines faced continuing harassment from company personnel. Farah hired guards to patrol the picket line with unmuzzled police dogs. Several strikers were hit by Farah trucks, and one woman was struck by a car driven by Willie Farah's mother. Farah obtained an injunction limiting pickets to one every fifty feet; 1,008 workers were cited for violations, and many were ordered to report to the police station in the middle of the night and required to post four hundred dollars bond. One woman was jailed six times. (The Texas law which permitted such injunctions was later declared unconstitutional, and all charges were dropped.)

Support

Although the strikers suffered physical and psychological harassment from opponents of the strike, they also discovered new sources of support. The Amalgamated Clothing Workers of America sent organizers to El Paso, gave weekly payments of thirty dollars to each striker, administered a Farah Relief Fund, and sponsored classes for the strikers on labor history and union procedures. For many workers, the films shown by the union were their first exposure to the history of labor struggles in the United States. One woman was deeply moved by a film about a strike in Chicago; another striker especially liked the movie "Salt of the Earth," because it showed the role of Chicanas in a strike in New Mexico.

Immediately after the strike began, the union organized a national boycott of Farah pants which became a crucial factor in the success of the strike. . . .

[Support also came from the Catholic Church, local unions, and neighborhood merchants, who gave the strikers badly needed food.]

New Responsibilities

But the most profound changes among the Farah strikers began when they took on new responsibilities for organizing strike activities. Some women went to work for the union on a volunteer basis, writing strike relief checks, keeping records, and distributing the goods that arrived from outside El Paso. Almost immediately they began to realize that their capabilities were not as limited as they had been taught to believe. One striker asserted, "If I had not walked out, I would not have been able to realize all those things about myself."

You know, when we used to register the people from the strike, would you believe that we organized all those cards, all those people

on strike? And you know, not realizing, here you can do this anywhere! You can go to any office and sit down and work! You know,
you think to yourself, "How in the world did I ever think I couldn't
do anything?" This is one of the things that's held us back. We
didn't think we could do it. . . . Until you actually get there and sit
down and do it, and you find out, "I'm not so dumb after all!"

Other strikers went on speaking tours organized by the union or by
strike support groups to publicize the boycott and raise funds.

I had never travelled as much as I did when I was on strike. The
only place I had gone was to L.A., one time, but that was about all.
But I never thought that I could go to New York, or Seattle, or all
these places. To me it was just like a dream, something that was just
happening and I was going through, but I couldn't stop to think
about it. I just had to go and talk to those people about the
strike. . . .

One woman observed that antiunion harassment took similar forms all
over the country; when she stopped to talk to workers at a nonunion plant,
a supervisor appeared and shooed the workers back inside. When she spoke
on the East Coast she noticed that racial and ethnic differences often kept
workers isolated from one another. She returned to El Paso with a heightened
perception of the difficulties involved in building a strong union.

Financial Troubles

As the months wore on, strikers faced increasing financial hardship. The
union strike relief payments of thirty dollars a week were inadequate for
many families. In one household both husband and wife were on strike, and
there were eight children to feed and clothe. Unable to handle their house
payments, the family moved in with the husband's mother. The uncertainties
of the strike, the financial troubles, and the change in living arrangements
were a strain on the marriage. . . .

For single women workers living with their parents, the situation was
somewhat easier. Their parents supported them, and working brothers and
sisters often helped with car payments and other bills. But many single
women were themselves working to support widowed parents and younger
siblings. For them the strike meant financial desperation. . . .

[Although some strikers received food stamps, none were eligible for unemployment benefits.]

Because of these problems, it was imperative that strikers obtain contributions and money from other unions across the country. They staffed an
emergency committee which dispensed funds to strikers who could not meet

medical and other payments. They formed a Farah Distress Fund to supplement the fund-raising efforts of the union-sponsored Farah Relief Fund. They helped to arrange their own speaking tours in addition to speaking on the union tours. Strikers who did not need the groceries distributed by the union passed then on to those who did. But in spite of all these measures, their financial situation continued to decline. One ex-striker comments tersely, "A lot of people lost their homes, cars—you name it, they lost it."

Social Relations

If the strike created new pressures and anxieties, it also cemented new relationships. "The good thing about the strike," recalls one woman, "is that we started knowing a lot of people—what they felt, who they were, what their problems were." Women who had been too busy or too shy even to speak to their fellow workers found themselves involved in discussions and arguments. . . . Picket duty and strike support activists brought new groups of people together. . . .

The difficulties of being a striker in an antiunion town also inspired camaraderie. When groups of women were arrested for mass picketing and ordered to report to the police station, they took advantage of the inexperience of the police in dealing with female detainees, and created havoc.

> We got on the scale and they weighed us, and then they got our fingerprints, and they asked us how old we were, and then we used to say, "You really want to know?" And then they said, "What's your phone number?" "Ai, you *really* want to know!" We were just playing around. The jailman was going all kinds of colors, because he was an old man.

In working-class areas, particularly in the sprawling eastern end of town, many workers felt a sense of solidarity with their neighbors.

> Here the whole neighborhood, you know, the majority of us were on strike! . . . The guy on the corner was on strike, the girl across the street, . . . my neighbors in front—her father's always been fighting for unions. A lot of these things, I think, kind of made you feel good.

The Home

As women became more and more involved in running strike support activists, and as they developed new friendships among the strikers, they began to spend more time outside the home. This was a source of tension in many households. . . .

In some cases, differences of opinion about the merits of the walkout were fueled by financial insecurity. In other homes the husbands did not think that attending public meetings was an appropriate way for their wives to spend their time. . . .

But the women felt strongly enough about their involvement in the strike to put up a spirited defense of their activities.

> My ex-husband told me, "You're not gonna make it, and I'm not gonna help you!" And I said, "If God made it, and his followers made it, like Peter, he left his boat behind, his wife . . . everything, he left everything behind, all his belongings to follow God, yet he didn't die! Right now he's in better shape than we are. He's in heaven, holding that door—isn't that true!"

For many women the changes in their marriages were more profound than a few disagreements over meetings or money. The strike made them more confident of their ability to make decisions, and they began to question their own attitudes toward their husbands:

> Maybe it's just that the Mexican woman has been brought up always to do what somebody tells you, you know, your father, your mother. And as you grow up, you're used to always being told what to do. . . .
>
> For years I wouldn't do anything without asking my husband's permission. . . . I've been married nineteen years, and I was always, "Hey, can I" or "Should I . . ." I see myself now and I think, good grief, having to ask to buy a pair of underwear! Of course, I don't do this anymore. . . . [The time of the strike was] when it started changing. All of it. I was able to begin to stand up for myself, and I began to feel that I should be accepted for the person that I am. . . .

Women also consciously reevaluated their ideas about child-rearing and their hopes for their children. . . .

> My ideas are a whole lot different than they used to be. I want my kids to be free. I never want them to feel oppressed. I want them to treat everybody as an equal. . . . I don't think they should slight someone because he's black or he's any different than they are. . . .
>
> I want my daughter to be able to do what she's gotta do. . . . and not always comply to whatever her boyfriend or her husband [wants] . . . ; that she should be the person that she is. And I want my boys to be the person that they are. . . .
>
> You know, I think it [the strike] has made my kids more outspoken. . . . Maybe some people would call it disrespect. I don't.

Politicization of Women

The strike made women more conscious of political and social movements which they had regarded as "outside" and irrelevant to their own lives. These ranged from the support of local union struggles to the struggles of the UFW and Texas Farmworkers to the women's movement.

Recently, ex-strikers have also been involved in other unionizing drives. One woman who now works in a hospital is contemplating an organizing campaign among health care workers. Another has helped her father and uncles to begin signing up people at a bread factory. Several other women have joined a Texas Farmworkers support committee, which publicizes the working conditions of the farm workers and tries to raise funds for their unionizing campaigns.

People have also begun to discuss the women's movement in their homes. Although it is still perceived as a movement that is taking place somewhere outside of El Paso, it evokes both sympathy and support.

> Well, all of us women, we like it. And we sure would like to join them. Some of the husbands they don't like it at all. They're not happy about it. . . . [My husband] doesn't like it. . . . Sometimes [we argue] and my daughters help me, my daughters back me up. [My sons] like it too.

For all of the women, the strike made them more conscious of themselves as working people with interests distinct from other classes. One woman began to argue with her dentist, who complained to her that her strike was causing him to lose money he had invested in Farah Manufacturing Company. She commented that he could afford to lose money, and added,

> I happen to be of the working class, and I happen to be one of the minority (i.e., Chicana), that I feel work at the lowest type of job there is, and I feel that we have a right to fight.

For others the strike altered the way they looked at their jobs, and for the first time made them feel that their workplace was the site of an important struggle.

> I like being there. I like the challenge. You don't know what the next day's going to bring you. You might get fired! . . . I don't think I could see myself sitting there in back of a desk, answering phones. When you could be fighting somewhere else, in a grievance, fighting with your supervisors, giving them hell. . . .
> [Before the strike] it was just a job to go to.
> [In 1974 the strike was settled and a union contract negotiated].

After the Strike

In spite of their misgivings about the contract, and a pervasive feeling that the situation was no longer under their control, most strikers concluded that the contract was "all right for a first try," and that it was "a beginning." They realized that their fight for better working conditions was by no means over, but at least they now had the protection of a union and a grievance procedure. They were determined that they would no longer be intimidated by supervisors; if they were mistreated they were going to climb off their machines and protest. "I'm going to say something if I have to say it," one striker insisted. "And I'll be nice if they're nice. If they're not very nice I can also be very unnice. . . ."

While the Farah strike did not produce a strong, mature rank-and-file movement, it did help to create the conditions in which one can develop. The workers who made the strike were irreversibly changed by it. All of them say that they would organize and strike again. . . .

In the words of one striker:

I believe in fighting for our rights, and for women's rights. . . . When I walked out of that company way back then, it was like I had taken a weight off my back. And I began to realize, "Why did I put up with it all these years? Why didn't I try for something else?" Now I want to stay here and help people to help themselves.

The Chicanas who comprise the majority of strikers learned that they could speak and act on their own behalf as women and workers, lessons they will not forget.

PART VIII

Daughters and Granddaughters

Historian Marcus Lee Hanson suggests that the children of immigrants want to forget their heritage while the grandchildren want to remember it. Hanson's "law" is insightful, but it oversimplifies. Both the daughters and the granddaughters of immigrant women had mixed feelings about their heritage. Part 8 explores their struggle to come to terms with the past while meeting the demands of the rapidly changing present.

Growing Up: The Pain

"Stop calling me Chinese. . . . I'm American. My father happened to be born in China, but . . . I have no interest in China," insisted a Chinese-American woman, reflecting the widespread desire of immigrants' children to become as "American" as possible.[1] Taking on the ethnic and class prejudices of mainstream America, many American-born daughters were embarrassed by the foreign birth and working-class status of their parents:

> The language of my birth, Slovenian, did not pass my lips as I grew into womanhood. If someone did speak to me in that language, I might respond. More often I would not. . . .
>
> I became ashamed that my parents spoke "funny"; that we laughed too loud; that we drank homemade wine; that our walls were wallpapered in flower patterns; that we grew our own vegetables; that my father raised chickens in our garage; . . . that my mother never sat down to eat dinner with us (she cooked, served, ate when everyone was finished); that our clothes and our curtains and towels were homemade, some of them out of feed bags; . . . that we had linoleum floors.[2]

The American-born daughter's rejection of her ethnic background was encouraged, if not demanded, by the public schools and, indeed, by the entire society. In some cases it was also encouraged by immigrant parents, who purposely refrained from transmitting their "foreign" heritage to their children or who were unable to do so. Cut off from the culture of her parents but not integrated into mainstream Anglo-American culture, the daughter of immigrants was often ill at ease in both worlds. Selection 1, from Maxine Hong Kingston's autobiography *The Woman Warrior*, describes the pain of such a childhood of marginality.

Children of mixed marriages experienced additional dimensions of marginality. Pat Lichty-Uribe, the child of a Mexican mother and a Pennsylvania Dutch father, had the appearance and language to blend comfortably into Anglo-American society. She refused to do so, however, because "they would say racist things and look at me, expecting me to agree with them because they thought I was Anglo. My reaction was, 'Don't make assumptions about me because I look white.' Don't give me privilege on the basis of that.' If they were going to be racist, I did not want to pass."[3]

Poverty and disrupted family life as well as marginality were common sources of pain for daughters in immigrant families. A 1968 study estimated that 35 percent of the Puerto Rican population of New York City were receiving welfare under the Aid to Families with Dependent Children program.[4] A 1976 study of white working-class couples in San Francisco (mostly second-generation European Americans) revealed that 40 percent had at least one alcoholic parent and that almost as many were themselves children of divorce or desertion. Ten percent of the men and women had spent part of their childhood in institutions or foster homes because their parents were unable, unwilling, or judged unfit to care for them. Ten percent of the women had juvenile arrest records.[5] Many ethnic families who were approaching financial security in the 1920s were forced back into poverty by the Great Depression of the 1930s, or by inflation, recession, and "de-industrialization" in the 1970s and 1980s.

Nor was life necessarily easy in families working their way out of poverty. The second selection describes the tensions in an upwardly mobile Irish-American family in which a young daughter feels torn between her easy-going, earthy "shanty Irish" mother, who accepts her as she is, and rigid, social-climbing, "lace curtain" relatives who try to shape her in their image.

Moving "out" could be as painful as moving "up." Venturing out of their ethnic families and communities, American-born daughters faced ethnic and religious prejudice from other minority groups and from mainstream America. In selection 3 Selina, whose parents moved to New York City from Barbados, has an unexpected and shattering encounter with racism. Chicana poet Gloria Anzaldua, who had excelled in "the Gringo's tongue" at a "North American university," was ridiculed and told to "go back where you came from"—although her family had lived in southern Texas for six generations.[6]

Autobiographies and novels about ethnic life are filled with accounts of conflicts between foreign-born parents and American-born daughters who refuse to accept "old world" definitions of their roles and duties. Daughters fight for the right to go on American-style dates, to control their own wages, to choose their own friends, husbands, and life-styles. Unmarried daughters shock their parents by leaving home to establish independent lives. A Puerto Rican girl remembers her relationship with her mother with bitterness: "Contrary to popular belief, the Spanish Inquisition commenced the first time a Puerto Rican girl came home five minutes late. It was torture first, questioning later. . . . "I'm your mother!'—smack! 'Don't you forget that.' Did I really have to be reminded?"[7] What seemed oppressive behavior to a daughter was often a mother's attempt to protect her from the very real dangers of the streets. It could also be the mother's attempt to protect her from disappointment: "She taught me at an early age the rules of behavior I would have to follow if I wanted to survive in the real world. Rule Number One: Don't expect too much. 'Too much' meant what you wanted."[8]

Children of Jewish parents who survived the Nazi Holocaust and emigrated to America had a particularly difficult time. A psychiatrist who studied these children found that "the love and ambitions of whole families were resurrected in memory and imposed" on the child, who was treated "not as an individual but as a heavily invested symbol of the New World."[9] One young woman thwarted her parents' hopes by failing all of her college courses—except German. While the problems of the children of Holocaust survivors are unique, daughters in many immigrant families felt the pressure of parental expectations. The third selection describes a confrontation between a West Indian mother, who has sacrificed to give her daughter the opportunity for professional education, and the daughter, who wants to become "her own woman."

Growing Up: The Pleasures

Growing up in an immigrant family brought pleasure as well as pain. Autobiographies and fiction by second-generation women describe the warmth and security of close-knit families and neighborhoods with love and nostalgia. The sight, smell, and flavor of ethnic foods usually stand out in vivid detail: "the Christmas food! . . . the banquet-like table with its fruits, its nuts, its special breads, rogale, I think Mom called them, with raisin-dotted babka and sugar-coated chrusciki . . . a variety of fishes . . . a special kind of soup with mushrooms, or . . . bits of almonds floating in it."[10] Equally vivid are memories of Christmas, Easter, Passover, and other holidays. "Who can forget the rich poetry of church ritual from her childhood days? It is not to be forgotten, never to be forgotten; never can be," wrote a Slovenian who had marched in her church processional dressed as an angel. "The incense burning and swinging on its chains, the organ and choir shaking our souls with Easter music."[11]

Childhood in an ethnic community could also be parochial and limiting. "It took me a long time to get into gear, to realize that things can be done, because I was taught that they could not be done, that there was some kind of ominous threat 'out there,' " said an Italian-American woman, who also complained that as an Italian-American child in her neighborhood, "you had to obey everybody." Looking back, however, she saw advantages as well as disadvantages: "I grew up with a real sense of security; you were never afraid of anybody. I also grew up under a strong sense of rules. It's awful in a way, but it really did keep things out of your control, and if something's out of your control, you're not responsible. It let you be a child longer."[12]

Ambivalence was common even among the rebels. Some returned later to families and communities they had left; others incorporated some of the old values into their new life-styles. Even in their rebellion, daughters were deeply influenced by immigrant parents. A second-generation Jewish woman, for instance, left her comfortable American home and distraught parents to go to Israel, a foreign country where she did not even know the language. "I wanted to emulate the emigration of my parents," she acknowledged later.[13]

Finally, second-generation autobiographies and novels that stress rebellion may be misleading, as they are written by (and usually about) exceptional women. Recent oral histories provide insight into the lives of the vast numbers of women who remained geographically and emotionally close to their immigrant parents. In 1978 Corinne Azen Krause interviewed 225 immigrant, second-, and third-generation women of Jewish, Italian, and Slavic backgrounds in Pittsburgh.[14] Her study revealed close ties between elderly immigrant women and their middle-aged, American-born daughters. Two-thirds of the daughters saw their mothers at least once a week, and more than a third saw them daily. Daughters reported that they enjoyed spending time with their mothers and doing things for them, taking them shopping or to the doctor, cleaning their houses, washing their hair. They shared problems, and Krause noted "a great deal of trust and love" between the generations. "She always understood and never was judgmental," said one daughter about her immigrant mother.[15] Future research on mother-daughter relationships may show the warm ties documented by Krause to be more typical than conflict and rebellion.

Changing Life-styles

Many studies have demonstrated the survival of ethnic life-styles and values into the second and third generations and beyond. Jews remain concentrated in the northeast and people of Scandinavian descent in the midwest; southern Italians remain family-centered; Japanese-Americans are less likely than others to place elderly parents in old age homes; Slavic Americans remain loyal to ethnic parishes; and Americans of many backgrounds are still partial to traditional foods. Nevertheless, ethnic Americans generally tend to become more like mainstream Americans—and one another—with each succeeding generation. Two areas in which generational change can be seen most clearly in immigrant families are occupations and family life.

The Census of 1950 indicated that foreign-born Irish, German, and Scandinavian women were four or five times as likely to be domestic workers as their white American-born counterparts. This was not true of their daughters, who were heavily concentrated in clerical occupations, sales, and, to a lesser degree, women's professions such as teaching.[16] Some southern Italian, Jewish, and Polish daughters were "operatives," or factory workers, the favored occupation for their foreign-born mothers, but more were in clerical work, sales, or teaching.[17] A similar progression can be seen in the occupations of Japanese women. In 1970 the largest two occupations for foreign-born Japanese women were crafts and factory work (31%) and service occupations (33%). In the same year, the largest occupational categories for their American-born daughters were clerical and sales (47%) and professional, technical, and managerial (21%).[18]

The changing occupations of second- and third-generation ethnic women reflect their increasing levels of education and changes in the American economy, which have required more clerical and professional people as the twentieth century progressed. Nationality also influenced job mobility. In recent years Irish, Italian, Jewish, Chinese, Japanese, and some other groups have reached or exceeded national average family income, while the incomes of less advantaged groups such as Puerto Ricans and Mexican-Americans have remained low.

Various kinds of prejudice limit social mobility. Southern and eastern European women sometimes shortened their names and Jewish women sometimes wore crosses to improve their chances in a Protestant Anglo-Saxon job market, especially during the Great Depression of the 1930s. Color barriers are more severe, lasting, and difficult to avoid. California-born Alice Fong Yu was determined to be a teacher, but the admissions officer at San Francisco Teacher's College in the early 1920s let her in only after she explained (falsely) that she planned to teach in China, not California. Mexican-American high school graduates in California in the prosperous mid-1960s had trouble getting secretarial jobs: "Girls who looked 'almost white' got jobs first, but . . . some of the Mexican-looking girls never did find the kind of employment they sought."[19] Sexism poses an additional problem. In 1960 the median income for second-generation Mexican-American men was low—$2,489; but for women it was even lower—$1,095.[20]

Marriage was a common way for second- and third-generation women to achieve socioeconomic mobility.

Since I was an able student I was graduated from high school by the time I was fifteen. But for a girl of my generation and class, college was not perceived as an option. Instead, I went to work as a stenographer in a manufacturing firm and shared the family pride in a child who had taken a big step up the ladder. . . . If a girl wanted more, she married up. Four years later, at nineteen, I did just that. I married a college boy of 21 who was destined to be a professional and started the big climb into the middle class.[21]

Indeed, many parents educated their daughters in order to improve their chances in the marriage market, not the job market. For most second-generation women, success traditionally meant not having to work outside the home. Although for most racial minorities success continued to mean the luxury of staying home, for white women after the 1960s it increasingly meant a career. In Krause's three-generational study of Jewish, Italian, and Slavic women, none of the immigrant generation reported working at professional occupations. Yet 18 percent of their daughters were employed in professional occupations, and 46.7 percent of their granddaughters.

The second and third generations saw changes in personal life as well as occupation. Marriage outside the group, negligible among immigrants, increased among daughters and granddaughters. Outmarriage among Mexican-Americans in Los Angeles averaged about 10 percent between 1930 and 1950; by 1963 it had increased to 25 percent.[22] The outmarriage rate among Japanese-Americans of both sexes in 1924 was only 2 percent; by 1972 it was 49 percent and continuing to climb.[23] Marriage across ethnic and religious lines among Europeans also rose sharply.

In the first generation men were more likely than women to intermarry, but this was no longer true for many groups in the second and third generations. Among Mexican-Americans and Asian-Americans in the mid-twentieth century, women were more likely to intermarry than men. Intermarriage was most common among highly educated women in these groups, as there were relatively few potential partners of the same ethnicity with similar education. Among Puerto Rican women, outgroup marriage increased consistently as the occupational level of the husband rose, suggesting that women were "marrying out in order to marry up."[24] Increased intermarriage reflected increased contact among individuals of the various ethnic groups; it did not necessarily reflect alienation from the group.

Ethnic background continues to affect even third-generation women's attitudes toward family life. For example, Italian women in Krause's 1978 study were consistently less permissive in their attitude toward premarital sex and less favorable toward nontraditional sex roles within marriage than Slavic or Jewish women. Nevertheless, studies of American immigrant family life over two and three generations suggest a general progression, from traditional marriages in which the work and social life of the partners are segregated by sex toward mainstream middle-class patterns of companionate marriage and couple-oriented social life.[25]

Divorce, uncommon among first-generation Catholics and Jews, approached mainstream American norms among their daughters and granddaughters. In many ethnic groups birthrates fell dramatically. While Jewish, Italian, and Japanese immigrants had more children than mainstream American women, their daughters and granddaughters (by 1970) were having fewer. Puerto Rican and Mexican-American families, on the other hand, remained large; in 1972 one-half of all Mexican-Americans came from families of seven or more children.[26]

The fact that ethnic family life changed in succeeding generations does not necessarily mean that traditional cultures disappeared. The transition from traditional to companionate marriages, for example, may simply reflect higher levels of income and education, the passage from working class to middle-class life-styles. Similarly, the shrinking size of second- and third-generation Italian families probably indicated a reinterpretation rather than an abandonment of traditional Italian familialism. Numerous children strengthened the family in Italy, but in the United States the family was better served by providing more education to fewer children.

The continuing high birth rate among most Mexican-Americans may reflect continuity of ethnic values: "In our culture, raising kids is the most important thing you can do, not like among whites," said labor organizer Dolores Huerta, mother of ten.[27] On the other hand, M. L. Urdaneta's comparison of indigent and nonindigent Chicanas in a southwestern city suggests that large Mexican-American families are less the result of culture or ideology than of poverty and lack of communication between middle-class Anglo-American medical practitioners and working-class Chicana women.[28]

The Civil Rights Movement and the New Ethnicity

The social and political turmoil of the 1960s and 1970s accelerated change among ethnic women, as among other Americans. Polish-American activist Barbara Mikulski described how "the age of the two Johns—Kennedy and Pope John XXIII"—affected white working-class ethnic women:

> Our lives were changing faster than our self-image or basic values. The new social forces of civil rights, the Ecumenical Council, Watts, Washington, Selma, Viet Nam; issues like birth control and busing; new categories of people, like hippies, hard hats, and militants; new problems like drugs, inflation, crime, the urban

crisis—all frightened, confused and astounded us. Our world would never be the same.[29]

Some reacted to rapid change by holding more firmly than ever to traditional values and behaviors. Others took advantage of the new, more open social climate to reshape their lives, return to school, find new jobs, or end unsatisfactory marriages.

The impact of the African American civil rights movement was enormous. Following the example of African Americans, whose struggle against racism they understood and supported, Chicana, Puerto Rican, and Asian-American women stepped up their efforts to fight for civil rights, jobs, better education, and better living conditions for their own communities. They also organized to fight for recognition and respect for their ethnic language and heritage in the schools, the media, and the nation.

Working-class women from European ethnic backgrounds reacted to the African American civil rights movement with greater ambivalence. Some opposed racial integration of their neighborhoods and schools, blaming blacks for the crime and blight that threatened all urban Americans and fearing that their own interests were being ignored in the contest for the shrinking resources of the aging industrial cities. On the other hand, most supported the civil rights legislation and antipoverty programs of the 1960s and 1970s. Influenced by the example of blacks and by their own traditions of union and neighborhood activism, white ethnic women organized to improve local housing, education, and health care, to save cherished inner-city ethnic neighborhoods from the ravages of throughways and "urban renewal," and to promote respect for their history and life-style. As ethnic women picketed, demonstrated, lobbied, outmaneuvered local politicians, and ran for office themselves to bring about social change, they were unconsciously acquiring the self-confidence and skills to effect positive changes in their personal lives as well.

While working for the interests of their communities, many third-generation women rediscovered their ethnic backgrounds. They were now secure enough in their American identity to turn more openly to ethnicity; moreover, the "new ethnicity" was encouraged in the late 1960s and after by a national climate more favorable to individuality and diversity. The impact of the new ethnicity varied from individual to individual. Some women were virtually untouched. Others participated in ethnic heritage festivals, revived ethnic arts, crafts, dances, and foods, conducted ethnic holiday celebrations in their homes (perhaps for the first time), sent their children to ethnic schools and camps, and read—and sometimes wrote—about their ethnic backgrounds and immigrant ancestors. Some traveled to the ethnic homeland as tourists or students. Grandchildren sometimes made efforts to learn the language of their grandparents, efforts that helped bring the generations together.

From my granddaughter in New York
A letter in Japanese
As I read it
Tears of joy overflow[30]

The Women's Movement

The impact of the women's movement in the 1960s was equally significant and controversial. Middle-class, college-educated ethnic women found it easy to identify with feminist goals of legal and social equality for women, reproductive freedom, and the abolition of rigid sex roles in the family and the workplace. Indeed, many were among the leaders who had formulated these goals. White working-class women, however, were more likely to feel that the movement "doesn't speak for us," that it was "much too middle class," and that leaders who emphasized equality in the board room and the university "don't know how it is to be getting older with very little money and education.'[31]

Both white women and women of color were caught in apparent contradictions between the submissive sex roles dictated by many ethnic traditions and the assertive, egalitarian behavior advocated by the women's movement. Women of color had additional reasons to hesitate. Many were afraid that feminism would weaken the drive for civil and economic rights by dividing their communities into hostile male against female factions. Others did not want to join a movement dominated by whites unless white women made a commitment to fight racism as well as sexism. Prominent Chicana feminist Martha Cotera complained in 1976 that white feminists treated Chicana feminists with condescension, ignoring their long histories and the activism within their communities.[32]

The fourth, fifth, and sixth selections present the views of a Polish-American woman, a Chicana, and an Asian-American woman on feminism and its relation to their ethnic interests. As these selections suggest, the gap between ethnic women and the women's movement was narrowing. Inflation and divorce forced increasing numbers of ethnic women into the workforce, making them more sympathetic to feminist goals of economic and legal equality, better education, and public day care. Meanwhile, the women's movement broadened its appeal to the working-class women by emphasizing issues such as better health care, social security for homemakers, welfare rights, and the battle against involuntary sterilization as well as involuntary motherhood. Feminist organizations such as the National Organization for Women and the National Women's Studies Association developed ethnic caucuses for "women of color" and Jewish women and made efforts to address "diversity" in their programs.

Relegated to making coffee, typing reports, and serving as sex objects within ethnic rights organizations, Third World activists, like white activists, began to criticize the aspects of their respective cultures that were oppressive to women. By the 1980s many white women and women of color were working to end patriarchy in their own ethnic and religious communities, as well as in mainstream America. Asian women denounced imported feudal traditions that diminished their personhood, as well as the racism encountered by Asians in the United States. Chicanas denounced *machismo* as well as Anglo-American exploitation. Gloria Anzaldua wrote in 1987: "Though we 'understand' the root causes of male hatred and fear, and the subsequent wounding of women, we do not excuse, we do not condone, and we will no longer put up with it. It is imperative that mestizas support each other in changing the sexist elements in the Mexican-Indian culture."[33]

The women's movement gave second-, third-, and fourth-generation ethnic women a new appreciation of the strength and endurance of their immigrant predecessors. It also gave them new confidence that they could change and improve their lives. Women like the celebrated Japanese-American poet Janice Mirikitani (see the final selection) resolved the contradictions between feminism and the subordination of women in their ethnic culture by discovering and identifying with the strength of their immigrant foremothers. Some daughters and granddaughters, like Jewish poet Sally Ann Drucker, never realized that women were supposed to be weak:

Lineage

My grandmother and great-aunts
planted on their stoops like oaks
molded family and boarders
with strong hands practiced on
challah and gefilte fish.
Henche Silke, way back when
baked for the village
cared for the women
when the midwife left,
and fed five children
when her husband died
back in Poland
where the five left from.

In America, their men died young
of TB, heart, and Jewish angst
the garment district sewed their shrouds
but someone had to stay
to mind the store, the house, the kids.

A baby choking on a pit
turning blue
a fight between drunk boarders
they knew what to do
they knew what to do.

I never knew
women were weak
I never knew until
I read it in books
in school
in English.

Notes

1. Betty Lee Sung, *Mountain of Gold: The Story of the Chinese in America* (New York: Macmillan, 1967), p. 63.

2. Rose Mary Prosen, "Looking Back," in *Growing Up Slavic in America*, ed. Michael Novak (Bayville, N.Y.: EMPAC, 1976), p. 3.

3. Pat Lichty-Uribe, "I Had a Choice," in *Compañeras: Latina Lesbians (An Anthology)*, ed. Juanita Ramos (New York: Latina Lesbian History Porject, 1987), p. 32.

4. Joseph P. Fitzpatrick, *Puerto Rican Americans: The Meaning of Migration to the Mainland* (Englewood Cliffs, N.J.: Prentice-Hall, 1971), p. 155.

5. Lillian Breslow Rubin, *Worlds of Pain: Life in the Working Class Family* (New York: Basic Books, 1976), pp. 23, 58.

6. Gloria Evangelina Anzaldua, "Del Otro Lado," in *Compañeras*, pp. 2–3.

7. Amina Susan Ali, "Memories of Her," in *Cuentos: Stories by Latinas*, ed. Alma Gomez, Cherrie Maraga, and Manana Romo-Camona (New York: Kitchen Table: Women of Color Press, 1983), p. 76.

8. Ibid., p. 75.

9. Helen Epstein, *Children of the Holocaust* (New York: Bantam Books, 1979), pp. 181–84.

10. Sister M. Florence Tumasz, "Growing Up as a Polish American," as cited in *The Ethnic American Woman: Problems, Protests, Lifestyles*, ed. Edith Blicksilver (Dubuque: Kendall/Hunt, 1978), p. 255.

11. Prosen, "Looking Back," p. 1.

12. Elizabeth Stone, "It's Still Hard to Grow Up Italian," *The New York Times Magazine*, December 17, 1978, pp. 42–43.

13.   Epstein, *Children of the Holocaust*, p. 231.

14.   Corinne Azen Krause, *Grandmothers, Mothers, and Daughters: An Oral History Study of Ethnicity, Mental Health, and Continuity of Three Generations of Jewish, Italian, and Slavic-American Women* (New York: Institute on Pluralism and Group Identity of the American Jewish Committee, 1978), p. 156.

15.   Ibid.

16.   E. P. Hutchinson, *Immigrants and Their Children, 1850–1950* (New York: Wiley, 1956), table A-2b, pp. 354–64; see also pp. 266–67.

17.   Ibid., pp. 35–364, 266–67.

18.   Urban Associates, *A Study of Selected Socio-Economic Characteristics of Ethnic Minorities Based on the 1970 Census;* Prepared for Dept of Health, Education, and Welfare by Urban Associates, Inc. (Washington: Office of Special Concerns, Office of the Assistant Secretary for Planning and Evaluation, Department of Health, Education, and Welfare, 1974) p. 88.

19.   Ellwyn R. Stoddard, *Mexican Americans* (New York: Random House, 1973), p. 103.

20.   *U.S. Census of Population*, 1960 PC (2) 1 B, table 6, as cited in ibid., p. 159.

21.   Rubin, *Worlds of Pain*, p. 12.

22.   Stoddard, *Mexican Americans*, p. 103.

23.   Akemi Kikumura and Harry H. L. Kitano, "Interracial Marriage: A Picture of the Japanese Americans," *Journal of Social Issues* 29, no. 2 (1973): 69.

24.   Joseph P. Fitzpatrick, "Intermarriage of Puerto Ricans in New York City," in *The Blending Americans: Patterns of Intermarriage*, ed. Milton L. Barron (Chicago: Quadrangle, 1972), p. 160.

25.   Krause, *Grandmothers, Mothers, and Daughters*, p. 62; Stoddard, *Mexican Americans*, p. 104; Sung, *Mountain of Gold*, p. 162; and Lydio F. Tomasi, *The Italian American Family* (Staten Island: Center for Migration Studies, 1972), p. 23.

26.   Stoddard, *Mexican Americans*, pp. 104–5.

27.   Judith Coburn, "Dolores Huerta: La Fasionaria of the Farmworkers," *MS. Magazine* 5 (1976): 13.

28.   M. L. Urdaneta, "Fertility Regulation among Mexican American Women in an Urban Setting: A Comparison of Indigent vs. Non-indigent Chicanas in a Southwest City in the United States" (Ph.D. diss., Southern Methodist University, 1976).

29. Nancy Seifer, *Absent from the Majority: Working Class Women in America* (New York: National Project on Ethnic America, American Jewish Committee, 1973), p. ix.

30. Poem by Teiko Tomita, as quoted in Karen Blair, ed., *Women in Pacific Northwest History: An Anthology* (Seattle: University of Washington Press, 1988), p. 223.

31. Martha P. Cotera, "Issues That Divide Us: Racism and Classism," Feminism and Law Conference, Denver, Colo., 1976.

32. Martha Cotera, *The Chicana Feminist* (Austin, Tex.: Information Systems Development, 1977) *passim*.

33. Gloria Anzaldua, *Borderlands/La Frontera: The New Mestiza* (San Francisco: Spinsters/Aunt Lute Foundation, 1987), pp. 83–84.

1

------✦------

A Song for a Barbarian Reed Pipe

In the following selection from her autobiographical work, The Woman Warrior: Memoirs of a Girlhood among Ghosts *[whites], Maxine Hong Kingston describes her early years in a Chinese immigrant family in Stockton, California. Understanding neither the Chinese culture of her immigrant parents nor the American culture of the public school and the neighborhood, she was bewildered and intimidated by both. The tensions in her early life were so great that she found herself literally without a voice.*

Kingston overcame her childhood difficulties and learned to function in the world of the American "ghosts." Although her kindergarten teachers had declared her to have an IQ of zero, she graduated from the University of California at Berkeley in 1962 and has since taught high school and college English in California and Hawaii. She also came to understand her Chinese background and the behavior of her parents. The imaginative quality of her autobiography, which won the National Book Critics Circle award for nonfiction in 1976, suggests that, like many other second-generation ethnic Americans, she was ultimately more enriched than damaged by her double cultural heritage.

M y mother cut my tongue. She pushed my tongue up and sliced the frenum. Or maybe she snipped it with a pair of nail scissors. I don't remember her doing it, only her telling me about it. . . . Sometimes I felt very proud that my mother committed such a powerful act upon me. At other times I was terrified—the first thing my mother did when she saw me was to cut my tongue.

"Why did you do that to me, Mother?"

"I told you."

"Tell me again."

"I cut it so that you would not be tongue-tied. Your tongue would be able to move in any language. You'll be able to speak languages that are com-

Source: From THE WOMAN WARRIOR: MEMOIRS OF A GIRLHOOD AMONG GHOSTS, by Maxine Hong Kingston. Copyright © 1975, 1976 by Maxine Hong Kinston. Reprinted by permission of Alfred A. Knopt, Inc.

pletely different from one another. You'll be able to pronounce anything. Your frenum looked too tight to do those things, so I cut it. . ."

If my mother was not lying she should have cut more, scraped away the rest of the frenum skin, because I have a terrible time talking. Or she should not have cut at all, tampering with my speech. When I went to kindergarten and had to speak English for the first time, I became silent. A dumbness—a shame—still cracks my voice in two, even when I want to say "hello" casually, or ask an easy question in front of the check-out counter, or ask directions of a bus driver. I stand frozen, or I hold up the line with the complete, grammatical sentence that comes squeaking out at impossible length. "What did you say?" says the cab driver, or "Speak up," so I have to perform again, only weaker the second time. A telephone call makes my throat bleed and takes up that day's courage. . . .

My silence was thickest—total—during the three years that I covered my school paintings with black paint. I painted layers of black over houses and flowers and suns, and when I drew on the blackboard, I put a layer of chalk on top. I was making a stage curtain, and it was the moment before the curtain parted or rose. The teachers called my parents to school, and I saw they had been saving my pictures, curling and cracking, all alike and black. The teachers pointed to the pictures and looked serious, talked seriously too, but my parents did not understand English. ("The parents and teachers of criminals were executed," said my father.) My parents took the pictures home. I spread them out (so black and full of possibilities) and pretended the curtains were swinging open, flying up, one after another, sunlight underneath, mighty operas.

During the first silent year I spoke to no one at school, did not ask before going to the lavatory, and flunked kindergarten. My sister also said nothing for three years, silent in the playground and silent at lunch. There were other quiet Chinese girls not of our family, but most of them got over it sooner than we did. I enjoyed the silence. At first it did not occur to me I was supposed to talk or to pass kindergarten. I talked at home and to one or two of the Chinese kids in class. I made motions and even made some jokes. I drank out of a toy saucer when the water spilled out of the cup, and everybody laughed, pointing at me, so I did it some more. I didn't know that Americans don't drink out of saucers.

I liked the Negro students (Black Ghosts) best because they laughed the loudest and talked to me as if I were a daring talker too. One of the Negro girls had her mother coil braids over her ears Shanghai-style like mine; we were Shanghai twins except that she was covered with black like my paintings. Two Negro kids enrolled in Chinese school, and the teachers gave them Chinese names. Some Negro kids walked me to school and home, protecting me from the Japanese kids, who hit me and chased me and stuck gum in my ears. The Japanese kids were noisy and tough. They appeared one day in kindergarten, released from concentration camp, which was a tic-tac-toe mark, like barbed wire, on the map.

It was when I found out I had to talk that school became a misery, that the silence became a misery. I did not speak and felt bad each time that I did not speak. I read aloud in first grade, though, and heard the barest whisper with little squeaks come out of my throat. "Louder," said the teacher, who scared the voice away again. The other Chinese girls did not talk either, so I knew the silence had to do with being a Chinese girl.

Reading out loud was easier than speaking because we did not have to make up what to say, but I stopped often, and the teacher would think I'd gone quiet again. . . .

When my second grade class did a play, the whole class went to the auditorium except the Chinese girls. The teacher, lovely and Hawaiian, should have understood about us, but instead left us behind in the classroom. Our voices were too soft or nonexistent, and our parents never signed the permission slips anyway. They never signed anything unnecessary. We opened the door a crack and peeked out, but closed it again quickly. One of us (not me) won every spelling bee, though. . . .

After American school, we picked up our cigar boxes, in which we had arranged books, brushes, and an inkbox neatly, and went to Chinese school, from 5:00 to 7:30 P.M. There we chanted together, voices rising and falling, loud and soft, some boys shouting, everybody reading together, reciting together and not alone with one voice. When we had a memorization test, the teacher let each of us come to his desk and say the lesson to him privately, while the rest of the class practiced copying or tracing. Most of the teachers were men. The boys who were so well behaved in the American school played tricks on them and talked back to them. The girls were not mute. They screamed and yelled during recess, when there were no rules; they had fistfights. Nobody was afraid of children hurting themselves or of children hurting school property. The glass doors to the red and green balconies with the gold job symbols were left wide open so that we could run out and climb the fire escapes. We played capture-the-flag in the auditorium, where Sun Yat-sen and Chiang Kai-shek's pictures hung at the back of the stage, the Chinese flag on their left and the American flag on their right. We climbed the teak ceremonial chairs and made flying leaps off the stage. One flag headquarters was behind the glass door and the other on stage right. Our feet drummed on the hollow stage. During recess the teachers locked themselves up in their office with the shelves of books, copybooks, inks from China. They drank tea and warmed their hands at a stove. There was no play supervision. At recess we had the school to ourselves, and also we could roam as far as we could go—downtown, Chinatown stores, home—as long as we returned before the bell rang.

At exactly 7:30 the teacher again picked up the brass bell that sat on his desk and swung it over our heads, while we charged down the stairs, our cheering magnified in the stairwell. Nobody had to line up. . . .

You can't entrust your voice to the Chinese, either; they want to capture your voice for their own use. They want to fix up your tongue to speak for them. "How much less can you sell it for?" we have to say. Talk the Sales Ghosts down. Make them take a loss.

We were working at the laundry when a delivery boy came from the Rexall drug store around the corner. He had a pale blue box of pills, but nobody was sick. Reading the label we saw that it belonged to another Chinese family, Crazy Mary's family. "Not ours," said my father. He pointed out the name to the Delivery Ghost, who took the pills back. My mother muttered for an hour, and then her anger boiled over. "That ghost! That dead ghost! How dare he come to the wrong house?" She could not concentrate on her marking and pressing. "A mistake! Huh!" I was getting angry myself. She fumed. She made her press crash and hiss. "Revenge. We've got to avenge this wrong on our future, on our health, and on our lives. Nobody's going to sicken my children and get away with it." We brothers and sisters did not look at one another. She would do something awful, something embarrassing. She'd already been hinting that during the next eclipse we slam pot lids together to scare the frog from swallowing the moon. (The word for "eclipse" is *frog-swallowing-the-moon*.) When we had not banged lids at the last eclipse and the shadow kept receding anyway, she'd said, "The villagers must be banging and clanging very loudly back home in China."

("On the other side of the world, they aren't having an eclipse, Mama. That's just a shadow the earth makes when it comes between the moon and the sun."

"You're always believing what those Ghost Teachers tell you. Look at the size of the jaws!")

"Aha!" she yelled. "You! The biggest." She was pointing at me. "You go to the drugstore."

"What do you want me to buy, Mother?" I said.

"But nothing. Don't bring one cent. Go and make them stop the curse."

"I don't want to go. I don't know how to do that. There are no such things as curses. They'll think I'm crazy."

"If you don't go, I'm holding you responsible for bringing a plague on this family."

"What am I supposed to do when I get there?" I said, sullen, trapped. "Do I say, 'Your delivery boy made a wrong delivery'?"

"They know he made a wrong delivery. I want you to make them rectify their crime."

I felt sick already. She'd make me swing stinky censors around the counter, at the druggist, at the customers. Throw dog blood on the druggist. I couldn't stand her plans.

"You get reparation candy," she said. "You say, 'You have tainted my house with sick medicine and must remove the curse with sweetness.' He'll understand."

"He didn't do it on purpose. And no, he won't, Mother. They don't understand stuff like that. I won't be able to say it right. He'll call us beggars."

"You just translate." She searched me to make sure I wasn't hiding any money. I was sneaky and bad enough to buy the candy and come back pretending it was a free gift.

"Mymotherseztagimmesomecandy," I said to the druggist. Be cute and small. No one hurts the cute and small.

"What? Speak up. Speak English," he said, big in his white druggist coat.

"Tatatagimme somecandy."

The druggist leaned way over the counter and frowned. "Some free candy," I said. "Sample candy."

"We don't give sample candy, young lady," he said.

"My mother said you have to give us candy. She said that is the way the Chinese do it."

"What?"

"That is the way the Chinese do it."

"Do What?"

"Do things." I felt the weight and immensity of things impossible to explain to the druggist.

"Can I give you some money?" he asked.

"No, we want candy."

He reached into a jar and gave me a handful of lollipops. He gave us candy all year round, year after year, every time we went into the drugstore. When different druggists or clerks waited on us, they also gave us candy. They had talked us over. They gave us Halloween candy in December, Christmas candy around Valentine's day, candy hearts at Easter, and Easter eggs at Halloween. "See?" said my mother. "They understand. You kids just aren't very brave." But I knew they did not understand. They thought we were beggars without a home who lived in back of the laundry. They felt sorry for us. I did not eat their candy. I did not go inside the drugstore or walk past it unless my parents forced me to. Whenever we had a prescription filled, the druggist put candy in the medicine bag. This is what Chinese druggists normally do, except they give raisins. My mother thought she taught the Druggist Ghosts a lesson in good manners (which is the same word as "traditions"):

My mouth went permanently crooked with effort, turned down on the left side and straight on the right. How strange that the emigrant villagers are shouters, hollering face to face. My father asks, "Why is it I can hear Chinese from blocks away? Is it that I understand the language? Or is it they talk loud?" They turn the radio up full blast to hear the operas, which do not seem to hurt their ears. And they yell over the singers that wail over the drums, everybody talking at once, big arm gestures, spit flying. You can see the disgust on American faces looking at women like that. It isn't just the loudness. It is the way Chinese sounds, chingchong ugly, to American ears, not beautiful like Japanese sayonara words with the consonants and vowels as regular as Italian. We make guttural peasant noise and have Ton Duc Thang names you can't remember. And the Chinese can't hear Americans at all; the language is too soft and western music unhearable. I've watched a Chinese audience laugh, visit, talk-story, and holler during a piano recital, as if the musician could not hear them. A Chinese-American, somebody's son, was playing Chopin, which has no punctuation, no cymbals, no gongs. Chinese piano music is five black keys. Normal Chinese women's voices are strong and bossy. We American-Chinese girls had to whisper to make ourselves American-feminine. Apparently we whispered even more softly than the Americans. Once a year the teachers referred my sister and me to speech therapy, but our voices would straighten out, unpredicatably normal, for the therapists. Some of us gave up, shook our heads, and said nothing, not one word. Some of us could not even shake our heads. At times shaking my head no is more self-assertion than I can manage. Most of us eventually found some voice, however faltering. We invented an American-feminine speaking personality. . . .

We have so many secrets to hold in. Our sixth-grade teacher, who liked to explain things to children, let us read our files. My record shows that I flunked kindergarten and in first grade had no IQ—a zero IQ. I did remember the first grade teacher calling out during a test, while students marked X's on a girl or a boy or a dog, which I covered with black. First grade was when I discovered eye control; with my seeing I could shrink the teacher down to a height of one inch, gesticulating and mouthing on the horizon. I lost this power in sixth grade for lack of practice, the teacher a generous man. "Look at your family's old addresses and think about how you've moved," he said. I looked at my parents' aliases and their birthdays, which variants I knew. But when I saw Father's occupations I exclaimed. "Hey, he wasn't a farmer, he was a. . ." He had been a gambler. My throat cut off the word— silence in front of the most understanding teacher. There were secrets never to be said in front of the ghosts, immigration secrets whose telling could get us sent back to China.

Sometimes I hated the ghosts for not letting us talk; sometimes I hated the secrecy of the Chinese. "Don't tell," said my parents, though we couldn't tell if we wanted to because we didn't know. Are there really secret trials with our own judges and penalties? Are there really flags in Chinatown signaling what stowaways have arrived in San Francisco Bay, their names, and which ships they came on? "Mother, I heard some kids say there are flags like that. Are there? What colors are they? Which building do they fly from?"

"No. No, there aren't any flags like that. They're just talking-story. You're always believing talk-story."

"I won't tell anybody, Mother. I promise. Which buildings are the flags on? Who flies them? The benevolent associations?"

"I don't know. Maybe the San Francisco villagers do that; our villagers don't do that."

"What do our villagers do?"

They would not tell us children because we had been born among ghosts, were taught by ghosts, and were ourselves ghostlike. They called us a kind of ghost. Ghosts are noisy and full of air; they talk during meals. They talk about anything. . . .

Occasionally the rumor went about that the United States immigration authorities had set up headquarters in the San Francisco or Sacramento Chinatown to urge wetbacks and stowaways, anybody here on fake papers, to come to the city and get their files straightened out. The immigrants discussed whether or not to turn themselves in. "We might as well," somebody would say. "Then we'd have our citizenship for real."

"Don't be a fool," somebody else would say. "It's a trap. You go in there saying you want to straighten out your papers, they'll deport you."

"No, they won't. They're promising that nobody is going to go to jail or get deported. They'll give you citizenship as a reward for turning yourself in, for your honesty."

"Don't you believe it. So-and-so trusted them, and he was deported. They deported his children too."

"Where can they send us now? Hong Kong? Taiwan? I've never been to Hong Kong or Taiwan. The Big Six? Where?" We don't belong anywhere since the Revolution. The old China has disappeared while we've been away.

"Don't tell," advised my parents. "Don't go to San Francisco until they leave."

Lie to Americans. Tell them you were born during the San Francisco earthquake. Tell them your birth certificate and your parents were burned up in the fire. Don't report crimes; tell them we have no crimes and no poverty. Give a new name every time you get arrested; the ghosts won't recognize you. Pay the new immigrants twenty-five cents an hour and say we have no unemployment. And, of course, tell them we're against Communism. Ghosts have no memory anyway and poor eyesight. And the Han people won't be pinned down.

Even the good things are unspeakable, so how could I ask about deformities? From the configurations of food my mother set out, we kids had to infer the holidays. She did not whip us up with holiday anticipation or explain. You only remembered that perhaps a year ago you had eaten monk's food, or that there was meat, and it was a meat holiday; or you had eaten moon cakes or long noodles for long life (which is a pun). In front of the whole chicken with its slit throat toward the ceiling, she'd lay out just so many pairs of chopsticks alternating with wine cups, which were not for us because they were a different number from the number in our family, and they were set too close together for us to sit at. To sit at one of those place settings a being would have to be about two inches wide, a tall wisp of an invisibility. Mother would pour Seagram's 7 into the cups and after a while, pour it back into the bottle. Never explaining. How can Chinese keep any traditions at all? They don't even make you pay attention, slipping in a ceremony and clearing the table before the children notice specialness. The adults get mad, evasive, and shut you up if you ask. You get no warning that you shouldn't wear a white ribbon in your hair until they hit you and give you the sideways glare for the rest of the day. They hit you if you wave brooms around or drop chopsticks or drum them. They hit you if you wash your hair on certain days, or tap somebody with a ruler, or step over a brother whether it's during your menses or not. You figure out what you got hit for and don't do it again if you figured correctly. But I think that if you don't figure it out, it's all right. Then you can grow up bothered by "neither ghosts nor deities." "Gods you avoid won't hurt you." I don't see how they kept up a continuous culture for five thousand years. Maybe they didn't; maybe everyone makes it up as they go along. If we had to depend on being told, we'd have no religion, no babies, no menstruation (sex, of course, unspeakable), no death.

2

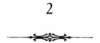

The Parish and the Hill

This selection, from Irish-American writer Mary Doyle Curran's novel, The Parish and the Hill, *describes the impact of social class on an Irish-American child, Mary O'Connor. Although Mary's parents began married life in the working-class Irish Catholic neighborhood known as "the parish," her father insisted on moving the family to "the hill," a prestigious middle-class Protestant neighborhood where*

Source: Mary Doyle Curran, *The Parish and the Hill* (Boston: Houghton Mifflin, 1948), pp. 15–99. Reprinted by permission of Russell and Vlokening as agents for the author. Copyright © 1948. Renewed 1976 by Mary Doyle Curran.

Mary's aunt already lived. Mary was less troubled by the Protestant "hill" people than by the snobbishness of her father, aunt, and cousin.

As this excerpt illustrates, there were class and status differences not only between ethnic and mainstream Americans, but also within ethnic communities. Differences were based partly on degrees of financial success in the United States, but also on overlapping criteria such as status and education in the country of origin (professionally educated Poles were "better" than uneducated "peasants"); geographic origin (northern Italians were "better" than southern Italians, and certain provinces, towns, and villages were "better" than others); religious affiliation (Reform Jews were "better" than Orthodox Jews); and time of immigration (earlier, more acculturated generations were "better" than "greenhorns"). A woman's social status generally followed that of her husband. Nevertheless, a woman from a lower-status family often had difficulty being accepted by the family and friends of a higher-status husband, whether he came from inside or outside her own ethnic community.

The struggle between my mother and father was at first a silent one, but it gradually became bitterly voluble. It was then that my grandfather came to live with us. He was my refuge, for a child cannot live "torn between," as my grandfather put it. My father had won the first great battle. He came home one night and announced that we would soon be moving to the Hill. Even my grandfather sided with my mother, as did all of Irish Parish. But we moved, and I grew up on the Hill, with my grandfather and then my mother protecting me as well as they could against the misery and shame of being shanty Irish on Money Hole Hill. All of us, for the first time, were introduced to an insecurity and isolation that has not lessened during the years. The cleavage we met first within our family spread to school, church, everything that our life consisted of. There was no escape from it and no hope that it would not leave its mark. We all bore it, the children of a shanty-Irish mother and a lace-curtain Irish father. . . .

After my grandfather's death, we were visited less and less by the people of Irish Parish and more and more by the people of the Hill. My father encouraged visits from the Yankees he worked with. They were all poor, but their names of Fuller and Parsons gave them social position. My mother, who did not like them, was nevertheless happy over the prospect of conversation.

I would slip shyly into the living room and sit quietly in a dark corner. The conversation, dull and dreary, was mostly shop talk. No one ever felt comfortable. My mother's wit flashed out occasionally into a shocked silence. At the end of the evening, my mother would go to the kitchen to prepare refreshments, homemade elderberry wine and cakes. After the "company" left, my mother would explode. "Not even good wine could loosen the knots in those tongues. Stiff as boards they are. I tell you, with their 'Yes, Mr. Parsons,' and 'No, Mrs. Parsons,' and their wooden respectability; pricing everything in the room." My father never answered these tirades, but the following Sunday we would have "company" again.

But my mother was too social a woman to remain completely isolated, and after a while she began to make friends among the Yankees, and even to maintain (to their detractors in Irish Parish) that they were good friends, but she seldom made friends with the members of her race on the Hill. Her scorn for the lace-curtain Irish was constant. She used to say, "Put an Irishman on a spit and you'll find a lace-curtain Irishman to turn him." My father paid no attention to her remarks. . . . Many of the things the lace-curtain Irish did he did not approve of, but out of a desire for respectability he joined ranks with them.

That desire for respectability drove my father into parental tyranny. We children were not allowed out of our own yard for fear we would disturb the neighbors. On the fourth of July the neighborhood exploded with fireworks, but we had none. I was required to play with children who disliked me and whom I disliked, to placate my father's sense of respectability. But all this play for a respectable position was in vain. Most of the Irish Parish visitors had been discouraged, but my father had not reckoned with the . . . [my mother's] brothers. Saturday nights the patrol wagon would deposit one or another of them on the back porch. When this first happened, my father, horrified, explained to the neighbors that it was all a mistake. But that explanation grew weak with the frequency of its repetition. "My God, what will the neighbors think?" grew to be a standard phrase in all our vocabularies.

My father did not dare to turn the brothers away. He knew where to draw the line, but he tried the impossible feat of getting them into the house as quickly and quietly as possible. This worked occasionally with all but my Uncle Smiley, who would come rolling up the street, singing at the top of his lungs the lewdest verses of "Mademoiselle from Armentières." . . .

The little Horrigan girl would say, sidling up to me the next day, "Does your uncle drink?" "Tell her it's a touch of sun," my mother would shout sarcastically from the kitchen window.

My father's tyranny never took the form of physical cruelty until one night when my brother Tabby came home in a state of drunkenness. My father, shaking with the indignity of it all, flew at him with a poker, shouting, screaming, "You're another one of the O'Sullivan bastards! It's all bad blood. Well, I won't put up with it, put up with it, put up with it!" As he repeated each phrase, he struck Tabby with the poker. My mother and the rest of us stood by helplessly. In the face of an animal fighting for the thing he had struggled so hard to secure, there is no defense. My father saw in Tabby the defeat of the values he had struggled to win. He was not responsible in the eyes of his world for the drunken uncles, but for the son, yes.

I, brought up by a grandfather and a mother to whom violence was anathema, flung myself on the floor, roaring out my despair and grief, beat ing and pounding the inanimate floor in my sorrow for the cruelty of the animate world. I had been "torn between" too long. . . .

My Aunt Josie looked and acted nothing like her sister, my mother. She was lace-curtain, and had a secure place among the Irish on Money Hole Hill. Tim and she, as she said in her tight-lipped way, were comfortable. They owned their own house and he was successfully established in the hardware business, which was the sole subject of his conversation. My father had a great respect for him. "A good solid businessman," he would say. My mother, taking advantage of Tim's deafness, would mutter when Josie was out of the room. "A good solid bore."

Aunt Josie had married Tim when she was thirty-two. The marriage had produced one child, a doll-like girl looking more china than human. They had bought a house on the Hill soon after their marriage, for "social reasons." "When you're in business," Tim would say, "you have to make contacts." Aunt Josie had worked very hard at respectability and achieved it in all its stuffiness. Everything in her house was exactly the same as in the other houses on Pearl Street. Her daughter acted and pleased exactly as the other little girls on Pearl Street. My Aunt Josie never visited Irish Parish, where she was born. She was loyal to her sister, but not to what she stood for. She was determined that she would make my mother lace-curtain. She was a strong woman and, in many ways, a cruel one. She was the only person my mother feared, for some reason that I felt unaccountable.

When Aunt Josie came to visit us, which was not very often, those visits were a source of terror to my mother. She would spend all day cleaning the house, trying to elevate her plain table by much polishing to the status of a marbletop. I used to sit on the bed and watch her desperate attempts to do her hair in a modish way. It would always end up in a fuzz of untidiness. Exasperated, she would slam the comb on the bureau, muttering. "Now what difference does it make at all, and why do I do it?" I knew exactly how she felt, though: if one could only walk into the room confident and sure that there was not a spot or speck showing.

Aunt Josie, always so confident and sure in her own "style," as she called it, characterized a hanging slip, a loose hair, a knot in the shoelace, as "shanty," and felt that when those lapses were remedied, the transformation from shanty to lace-curtain had begun. Consequently, she was always yanking or pulling at my hair ribbon, retying my bows, hauling at my frocks, commenting on my mother's lack of silk dresses, or staring at her hands that were roughened by dishwater. "Mame, how many times have I told you that you should wear rubber gloves when you wash dishes! Look at my hands. Dishwater never touches them." She would hold up soft, pudgy hands covered with rings. "Indeed," my mother would say after she had gone, "dishwater never touches them, and her with a hired girl."

Although we lived quite near my Aunt Josie, I rarely played with my Cousin Ann. The desire to was certainly not strong, for Ann was a refined little girl who never dirtied her dress. The times that I visited their house, she played primly under the shade tree in the back yard, giving a perfect imitation of her mother. I drank gallons of weak tea, talked myself tired about the state of her tidy children, her mythical husband, and his business. . . .

Once, with a great spurt of generosity, I had gone over to her house myself. My mother had given me all the equipment necessary for a lemonade stand. I looked forward with tremendous pleasure to the game which consisted of selling one glass of lemonade and drinking the rest of the cool, oversugared drink yourself. My brother Michael and I used to play this game all during the hot summer. Ann, surprisingly enough, was more than willing; but when everything was ready, she said it was not quite proper to set up a stand in front of the house, or to sell drinks. We settled down with all her little friends, exact replicas of herself, and played her game of tea with my lemonade. All the joy of being a grown-up entrepreneur was gone. I hated her doll-like charm which belied the strong will behind it. I felt exactly as helpless as my mother did before Aunt Josie.

Ann and I went to the same school. At school she never associated with me, moving gracefully among the other pretty, clean, lace-curtain children. During the Al Smith election, I wore his button to school and was fairly massacred by the Yankee children. One Yankee girl, the daughter of the bank president, knocked out my two front teeth. It was an epic battle. None of the lace-curtain children came to my rescue. They were horrified by my lack of refinement and discretion. As Aunt Josie said to my mother after Ann had reported the scene: "It's better, Mame, to keep politics to yourself. What if he's not elected?" That was the only time my mother flared up against Josie. "Let them keep it to themselves, then, pushing and shoving it into your face every chance they get! I tell you, Josie O'Sullivan, it is not your kind to be giving me lessons. My children will be honest if they do lose two front teeth for it. There comes a time when a man should fight, and not slink away for fear of losing business." Aunt Josie was not stopped by that, though. As long as she came, she corrected my mother's politics. My father always agreed with her. "It's not ladylike, Mame, for a woman to be attending political meetings." Aunt Josie would say. My mother never answered; she just went on attending them.

One Sunday, Aunt Josie and her family came to dinner. My mother sat at the table heaping generous helpings of food on our plates. I sat next to Ann, whom I could see surreptitiously wiping the silverware under the table.

After dinner, Tim and my father were smoking cigars in the living room; my mother was washing the dishes in the kitchen. I walked down the long hallway looking for Ann. One of the bedroom doors was closed and I could hear voices behind it. I was just about to go in when I heard, "But mother, she's so dirty and—" It was Ann's voice. "Yes, I know she is, but you must be generous, Ann. After all, she is your cousin." "I don't care. I won't play with her and I want to go home. I don't like any of them. The silverware was greasy." There was nothing Aunt Josie could do or say. She had produced this child.

I went to the end of the hallway and sat down. There was so much I could not understand. How could anyone not like my mother, and how could anyone speak against her? Was I dirty? I examined my hands. They were a little dirty. I went to the bathroom and started washing them; for an hour I soaped them and washed them over and over again, trying to change their brown to the milk-whiteness of Ann's. When my mother found me, I was crying over the hurt within me. When I told her, she said nothing; but I never played with Ann again.

3

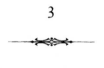

"This Is Selina"

Author Paule Marshall is the daughter of Barbadian immigrants who settled in New York City. She grew up in a West Indian neighborhood of Brooklyn, the setting of her first novel, Brown Girl, Brownstones.

Brown Girl, Brownstones *is the story of American-born Selina and her West Indian parents. Selina's mother, Silla, is a strong, hardworking woman, first a domestic, then a factory worker, and finally the owner of her own brownstone apartment building. Ambitious for her daughter, she pressures Selina into attending college and enrolling in a premedical program in which she has no interest. Selina rebels and decides to use scholarship money won from the local Barbadian Association (in which her mother is active) to run away with a dilettante artist of whom her mother disapproves.*

The initial passage describes Selina's joy in her superb performance at a college dance recital and her devastation at the racism she encounters immediately after. Like many minority women, Selina was shattered to find that others could not see beyond her color, then strengthened by a determination to "find a way for her real face to emerge." Shortly after the recital she ends her relationship with the artist, refuses to accept the scholarship money, and decides to leave home to find her own way. In the second excerpt, she tells her mother of her plans; there is a final confrontation—and reconciliation—between immigrant mother and daughter. Like many second-generation "rebels," Selina is ultimately her mother's daughter.

"You Don't Even Act Colored"

The following night at the recital, fear eddied, then heaved in a wave inside her as she waited—kneeling alone on the stage—for the lights and heard the restless, ominously breathing audience waiting for her in the darkness.

But as the light cascaded down and formed a protective ring around her, as the piano sounded and her body instinctively responded . . . her nervousness subsided, and she rose—sure, lithe, controlled, her head with its coarse hair lifting gracefully; the huge eyes in her dark face absorbed yet passionate. . . .

The music bore her up at each exuberant leap, spun her at each turn so that a wind sang past her ear; it responded softly whenever the sadness underscored her gestures—until at the climax, she was dancing, she imagined, in the audience, through the rows of seats, and giving each one there something of herself, just as the priest in Ina's church, she remembered, passed along the row of communicants, giving them the wafer and the transmuted blood. . . .

In the moment's stillness she knew that she had been good. And when the applause rushed her like a high wind, it was as if the audience was offering her something of itself in exchange for what she had given it. She bowed to that thunderous sound, exultant but a little shaken, and as she turned and leaped off-stage it was as if she was bearing something of them all away with her.

The other dancers awaited her in the wings and their extravagant praise was louder, headier, than the applause. They swarmed her and she lost all awareness of herself. The raw milk smell of their heated bodies and breath, the odor of grease paint and powder drowned out her mind like an intoxicant. Her happiness erupted in a wild hoot that cut through the din—and suddenly she wanted to remain with them always in the crowded wing, to shout and never get weary. . . . [A] thick-set blond girl was shouting from atop a chair, "Hey kids, let's celebrate at my house. I called and my mother says it's all right since my father's out. Come on, I live near here. I'll make some punch and we'll spike it with some of his you know what. . . ."

Their shrill acceptance echoed high in the wings and they lunged, one huge body with many legs and flailing arms, into the dressing rooms and there pulled on their coats over the costumes and then charged through the halls into the street. . . .

They trooped in bold formation down the street, spanning the entire sidewalk and spilling into the gutter. The wind snatched at the frothy costumes under their open coats and then scooted ahead, carrying their exhilaration in a warning to the other pedestrians. Selina, Rachel and the blond girl, Margaret Benton, were in the vanguard, and they made a startling trio—Selina, in the black leotard, her coat flaring wide, resembling somewhat a cavalier; Rachel a fabulous sprite and Margaret, her hair catching each passing light, a full-blown Wagnerian heroine.

They advanced through the East Side, bearing toward the river until Margaret led them into an old and ponderous greystone apartment house, whose grandeur had been eclipsed by a modern apartment house that was all lightness and glass beside it, and whose future was hinted in the decrepit row of tenements on its other side. They followed her through a tarnished gilt and marble lobby into the elevator cage, and when they spilled into the hall, Selina hardly noticed the smiling woman at the door, or how the smile stiffened as she entered. . . .

The woman quickly disappeared, and they sprawled on the livingroom rug, laughing and talking at a high pitch. They danced, Selina and Rachel doing a reckless lindy in their stockinged feet. Later, they flowed out into the kitchen to watch Margaret pour a long amber stream of bourbon into the punch. . . .

Gradually the noise died and they lay in an exhausted circle on the rug, talking softly and drinking. Selina and Rachel sat together. Rachel smoking and talking of Bobby and Selina halflistening and thinking of Clive. Later tonight, alone with him on the sofa under the bright lamp, the day would reach its fitting end. . . .

They were all dancing again—Selina and Rachel twirling each other dangerously—when Margaret hurried over and, taking Selina's arm, tried to pull her away. "Hey, come with me for a minute," she said, "my mother wants to meet you. . . ."

"Hello," she said and swung into the small sitting room behind Margaret.

The woman there must have carefully arranged her smile before Selina had entered. While she had been dancing down the hall perhaps or finishing her punch with Rachel, the woman's mouth, eyes, the muscles under her pale powdered skin must have been shaping that courteous, curious and appraising smile. Months, years later, Selina was to remember it, since it became the one vivid memory of the evening, and to wonder why it has not unsettled her even then. Whenever she remembered it—all down the long years to her death—she was to start helplessly, and every white face would be suspect for that moment. But now, with her mind reeling from the dance and slightly blurred from the punch she did not even notice it.

"This is Selina, Mother," Margaret said and the woman rose from a wing chair under a tall lamp and briskly crossed the room, her pale hand extended. Her figure in a modish dress was still shapely, her carefully applied make-up disguised her worn skin and the pull of the years at her nose and mouth. Under her graying blond hair her features were pure, her lackluster blue eyes almost colorless. Something fretful, disturbed, lay behind their surface and rove in a restless shadow over her face.

She took Selina's hand between hers, patting it, and Selina could *feel* her whiteness—it was in the very texture of her skin. A faint uneasiness stirred and was forgotten as the women led her to the wing chair and said effusively, "Well, my dear, how does it feel to be the star of the show?"

Selina fell back in the chair and, laughing, gestured upward. "A little like the real ones. Very high up. Out of this world almost. . . ."

The woman talked, but after a while the brightness left her eyes and from behind their pale screen she regarded Selina with an intense interest and irritation. Her lively voice became preoccupied. Other words loomed behind it and finally she could no longer resist them and asked abruptly, "Where do you live, dear, uptown?"

"No, Brooklyn."

"Oh? Have you lived there long?"

"I was born there."

"How nice," and her hair gleamed palely as she nodded. "Not your parents, I don't suppose."

"No." Despite the encouraging smile, Selina added nothing more. She was vaguely annoyed. It was all like an inquisition somehow, where she was the accused, imprisoned in the wing chair under the glaring lamp, the woman the inquisitor and Margaret the heavy, dull-faced guard at the door.

Suddenly the woman leaned forward and rested her hand on Selina's knee. "Are they from the South, dear?. . ."

She muttered evasively, "No, they're not."

The woman bent close, surprised, and the dry sting of her perfume was another indignity. "No . . . ? Where then?"

"The West Indies."

The woman sat back, triumphant. "Ah, I thought so. We once had a girl who did our cleaning who was from there. . . ." She caught herself and smiled apologetically. "Oh, she wasn't a girl, of course. We just call them that. It's a terrible habit. . . . Anyway, I always told my husband there was something different about her—about Negroes from the West Indies in general. . . . I don't know what, but I can always spot it. When you came in tonight, for instance. . ."

Her voice might have been a draft which had seeped under the closed windows and chilled the room. Frightened now, as well as annoyed, Selina gazed across to Margaret, who stood in a stolid heap at the door, her eyes lowered.

The woman's eyes followed Selina's and she called, "Can you remember Ettie, dear? She used to call you Princess Margaret because you looked so much like the real princess then."

"A little," the girl murmured. "She was very nice, Selina." Margaret gave Selina a fleeting glance.

"She was wonderful," her mother cried effusively. "I've never been able to get another girl as efficient or as reliable as Ettie. When she cleaned, the house was spotless. . . . We were all crazy about her. Margaret was always giving her things for her little girl. She was so ambitious for her son, I remember. She wanted him to be a dentist. He was very bright, it seems."

Her voice, flurrying like a cold wind, snuffed out the last small flame of Selina's happiness. She started to rise, and the woman's hand, like a swift, deadly, little animal, pounced on her knee, restraining her, and the brisk voice raced on, "We were heartbroken when she took ill. I even went to the hospital to see her. She was so honest too. I could leave my purse—anything—lying around and never worry. She was just that kind of person. You don't find help like that every day, you know. Some of them are . . . well. . ." And here she brought her powdered face with its aging skin close to Selina's, the hand fluttered apologetically, ". . . just impossible!" It was a confidential whisper. "Oh, it's not their fault, of course, poor things! You can't help your color. It's just a lack of the proper training and education. I have to keep telling some of my friends that. Oh, I'm a real fighter when I get started! I wish they were here tonight to meet you. You . . . well, dear . . . you don't even act colored. I mean, you speak so well and have such poise. And it's just wonderful how you've taken your race's natural talent for dancing and music and developed it. Your race needs more smart young people like you. Ettie used to say the same thing. We used to have these long discussions on the race problem and she always agreed with me. It was so amusing to hear her say things in that delightful West Indian accent. . ."

Held down by her hand, drowning in the deluge of her voice, Selina felt a coldness ring her heart. She tried to signal the woman that she had had enough, but her hand failed her. Why couldn't the woman *see*, she wondered—even as she drowned—that she was simply a girl of twenty with a slender body and slight breasts and no power with words, who loved spring and then the sere leaves falling and dim, old houses, who had tried, foolishly perhaps, to reach beyond herself? But when she looked up and saw her reflection in those pale eyes, she knew that the woman saw one thing above all else. Those eyes were a well-lighted mirror in which, for the first time, Selina truly saw—with a sharp and shattering clarity—the full meaning of her black skin.

And knowing was like dying—like being poised on the rim of time when the heart's simple rhythm is syncopated and then silenced and the blood chills and congeals, when a pall passes in a dark wind over the eyes. In that instant of death, false and fleeting though it was, she was beyond hurt. And then, as swiftly, terror flared behind her eyes, terror that somehow, in some way, this woman, the frightened girl at the door, those others dancing down the hall, even Rachel, all, everywhere, sought to rob her of her substance and her self. The thrust of hate at that moment was strong enough to sweep the world and consume them. What had brought her to this place? to this shattering knowledge? And obscurely she knew: the part of her which had long hated her for her blackness and thus begrudged her each small success like the one tonight . . .

"Oh, please say something in that delightful West Indian accent for us!" The woman was standing over her now, brightly smiling, insistent. As she gave Selina a playful shake the punch glass slid from her limp hands to the floor and broke, splintering the woman's brittle voice and its hold on Selina. Leaping up Selina savagely flung off the woman's hand. . . .

"Get out of my way!" She struck brutally at the soft white arms reaching for her. "Get out of my way!" She charged their circle, scattering them, and snatching up her coat, hurled from the apartment, down the long flights of echoing marble stairs, through the seedy lobby out of the building.

The woman's face, voice, touch, fragrance, pursued her as she careened through the maze of traffic and blurred white faces, past spiraling buildings ablaze with light. Car horns bayed behind her, the city's tumid voice mocked her flight. She ran until a stitch pierced her side and her leg cramped. Clutching her leg she limped—like an animal broken by a long hunt—into the deep entranceway of a vacant store and collapsed in the cold shadows there. . . .

Still groggy with pain, she raised her head after a time. The meager glow of a distant street light fell aslant the window and, suddenly curious, she held her face to the light. . . . She peered shyly at her reflection—the way a child looks at himself in the mirror. And, in a sense, it was a discovery for her also. She was seeing, clearly for the first time, the image which the woman—and the ones like the woman—saw when they looked at her. What Clive had said must be true. Her dark face must be confused in their minds with what they feared most: with the night, symbol of their ancient fears, which seethed with sin and harbored violence, which spawned the beast in its den; with the heart of darkness within them and all its horror and fascination. The woman, confronted by her brash face, had sensed the arid place within herself and had sought absolution in cruelty. Like the night, she was to be feared, spurned, purified—and always reminded of her darkness . . .

Above all, the horror was that she saw in that image—which had the shape and form of her face but was not really her face—her own dark depth. Her sins rose like a miasma from its fetid bottom: the furtive pleasures with Clive on the sofa, her planned betrayal of the Association, the mosaic of deceit and lies she had built to delude the mother. They took form in the shadows around her—small hideous shapes jeering her and touching her with cold and viscid hands. They were unbearable suddenly, monstrous. With a choked cry of disgust, her arm slashed out, her fist smashed that mouth, those eyes; her flat hand tried to blot it out. She struck the reflection until the entire glass wall trembled—and still it remained, gazing at her with her own enraged and tearful aspect.

It was no use. Exhausted, she fell against the glass, her feverish face striking the cold one there, crying suddenly because their idea of her was only an illusion, yet so powerful that it would stalk her down the years, confront her in each mirror and from the safe circle of their eyes, surprise her even in the gleaming surface of a table. It would intrude in every corner of her life, tainting her small triumphs—as it had tonight—and exulting at her defeats. She cried because, like all her kinsmen, she must somehow prevent it from destroying her inside and find a way for her real face to emerge.

"I'm Truly Your Child"

"Going 'way?" And before Silla [Selina's mother] could recover Selina added with finality, "Yes, even though I didn't take the money. I'll find a way. And I'll be going alone."

Silla—her body thrust forward as though it, as well as her mind, sought to understand this—stared at Selina's set face. Then, groping past her, Silla found a chair, and sat numb, silent, the life shattered in her eyes and the hanging coats gathered behind her like sympathetic spectators. Finally she said, but her eyes did not clear, "Going 'way. One call sheself getting married and the other going 'way. Gone so! They ain got no more uses for me and they gone. Oh God, is this what you does get for the nine months and pain and the long years putting bread in their mouth . . . ?"

And although Selina listened and felt all the mother's anguish she remained sure.

Silla was saying numbly, "Here it tis just when I start making plans to buy a house in Crown Heights she. . ."

"I'm not interested in houses!" Her scream burst the room and soared up to the main hall.

The mother nodded bitterly. "Yes, you did always scorn me for trying to get little property."

"I don't scorn you. Oh, I used to. But not any more. That's what I tried to say tonight. It's just not what I want."

"What it tis you want?"

"I don't know." Her reply was a frail lost sound and, strangely, it seemed to assuage Silla. She scrutinized Selina's pensive face, beginning dimly, it appeared, to understand. Her arms half lifted in a protective gesture, and her warning sounded. "Girl, do you know what it tis out there? How those white people does do yuh?"

At her solemn nod, at the sad knowing in her eyes, Silla's head slowly bowed.

Quickly Selina found her coat and, putting it on, stared at the mother's bowed face, seeing there the finely creased flesh around her eyes, the hair graying at her temples and, on her brow, the final frightening loneliness that was to be her penance. "Mother," she said gently, "I have to disappoint you. Maybe it's as you once said: that in making your way you always hurt someone. I don't know. . ." Then remembering something Clive had said, she added with a thin smile, "Everybody used to call me Deighton's [her father] Selina but they were wrong. Because you see I'm truly your child. Remember how you used to talk about how you left home and came here alone as a girl of eighteen and was your own woman? I used to love hearing that. And that's what I want. I want it!"

Silla's pained eyes searched her adamant face, and after a long time a wistfulness softened her mouth. It was as if she somehow glimpsed in Selina the girl she had once been. For that moment, as the softness pervaded her and her hands lay open like a girl's on her lap, she became the girl who had stood, alone and innocent, at the ship's rail, watching the city rise glittering with promise from the sea.

"G'long," she said finally with a brusque motion. "G'long! You was always too much woman for me anyway, soul. And my own mother did say two head-bulls can't reign in a flock. G'long!" Her hand sketched a sign that was both a dismissal and a benediction. "If I din dead yet, you and your foolishness can't kill muh now!"

4

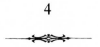

"We Can Begin to Move toward Sisterhood"

Polish-American activist and Congresswoman Barbara Mikulski has received wide recognition for her efforts in community organization and coalition building. She presented the following speech at a 1975 conference on "The Challenge of the

Source: Barbara Mikulski, "The White Ethnic Catholic Woman," in *Dialogue on Diversity: A New Agenda for American Women* ed. Barbara Peters and Victoria Samuels (New York: American Jewish Committee Institute on Pluralism and Group Identity, 1976), pp. 35–39. Reprinted by permission of Barbara Mikulski and American Jewish Committee.

Woman's Movement: American Diversity," a conference sponsored by the American Jewish Committee and attended by over seventy ethnically and economically diverse organizations and groups.

While many Third World women argue that liberation from sexism is meaningless unless all members of their community are also liberated from poverty and racism, the concerns of white ethnic women, as expressed here by Mikulski, are different. These women have fears—often promoted by the media—that the movement is inimical to the traditional family, their fortress against political oppression in the past and their main source of personal security in the present. Still as Mikulski points out, they share many of the movement's social and economic goals.

In the question and answer session that followed the formal speeches, Mikulski suggests that American business not only welcomes but promotes antifeminist "backlash" and divisiveness among women from different classes and ethnic backgrounds. Many corporations have a financial interest in keeping women either unemployed or employed as cheap labor. "We might not understand each other as well as we could, but we are not each others' enemy," coalition-builder Mikulski told the mixed gathering. "The enemy . . . is the two-martinis-for-lunch-bunch." *Efforts to build ethnic-feminist coalitions continued in the years that followed.

W e've heard a great deal of talk today about differences in the Women's Movement. I personally feel very much a part of a special constituency that is best represented by the phrase "European ethnic Catholic women." We are the people who represent a population of about 20 million women residing primarily in the urban areas of the North—from Boston to Baltimore, New York to Milwaukee—and other major industrial centers.

One of our problems is that many people don't understand us. We are stereotyped in the media as passive Edith Bunker types, even as reactionary. But if you know us, you will know this to be untrue. You'll find there are two themes that run through our public attitude. Number one, we are associated with the Democratic Party through the ideas of Franklin Delano Roosevelt and Jack Kennedy and programs like Social Security. But when you look at our cultural lives, which stem from both our ethnic traditions and our religious heritage, you'll find we are somewhat conservative in our outlook. So if you know us as politically and economically progressive but culturally moderate, then you will understand our attitudes in relationship to the Women's Movement. The women in our constituency have mixed feelings about the Women's Movement.

Peters and Samuels, ed., *Dialogue on Diversity*, p. 70.

Though we hate to categorize people, it seems there are two groups within the Movement. There are the women's rights activists and there are the women's liberation activists. The women's rights activists have been in the forefront of those programs dealing with concrete benefits for people in terms of child care, day care, educational opportunities, senior citizens programs, Social Security reform, changing the work place and fighting for the minimum wage to cover more people. We feel very much a part of this group.

Then there are the women's liberationists who perhaps have had the most publicity and have presented what we would regard as culturally provocative ideas. These are the people who have talked about role changes, changing life styles and changing orientations in the family. Many of the people in our communities find these ideas very threatening and very confusing.

A History of Involvement

When we look at the question of fighting for rights, the women in our community have been involved in this struggle for a long time. We go back to the early Trade Union Movement. We were "Rosie the Riveter." We're there now when it comes to reforming the work place. We see it in the working class communities around the country where women have organized. And it is interesting that this struggle is not necessarily for their own benefit, but is carried on in behalf of others, which has so often been the story of women.

The activities of the National Congress of Neighborhood Women in bringing increased educational opportunities to Brooklyn is an important part of this fight. . . .

Some people say that the older women in our communities don't feel a part of this. You're damn right they do, and let me give you an example. We have women in our community, which is comparable to neighborhoods in Brooklyn, who started a group called the Senior Citizens Activist Coalition— a working class version of the Grey Panthers. One of the things that they came to City Hall about was the whole issue of health services. What they were specifically addressing themselves to was that older women wanted to have PAP smears. Baltimore's health services provide PAP smears to women of child bearing age. But once you pass menopause you can't get the test, even though you are just as vulnerable to cancer.

The senior citizens came down with the women at the head and the men, normally associated with American Legion halls and Holy Name societies, stood beside them in meeting with the Mayor to bring this health service to our community. Now that's what we mean when we talk about organizing for women's rights in our community. And I think it's exciting.

The Way We Really Are

One of the problems we face—and we find it a major problem—is the orientation of our cultural and religious backgrounds. You have to understand that those of us of European ethnic backgrounds have always felt under the gun in this country. First for our ethnicity, then for our religion, both from the outside society and even within our own society. And now the confusion over something called women's liberation. The larger culture has always baffled us because they tell us to do one thing and 20 years later they ridicule us for doing it.

When we first came to America, we helped to build the railroads, we worked on the docks and in the coal mines, and we called ourselves Americans. But others were calling us Polack, Wop, Dago and Honky. We were ridiculed for our funny names and our funny foods. So we became "Americans." We became super-patriots, and as we became super-patriots we found ourselves harassed in the late 60's because we were proud to say we were Americans. We were proud to say we respected the flag and we were even proud of the fact that our men had gone to war.

While we faced this dilemma, many of us found solace and consolation in our Catholicism. We cherished our religion. There were certain nationality parishes and we had our own. In the Polish church there is a tremendous devotion to the Blessed Mother and that has always meant something to us. There's a Polish version of the Virgin Mary, which is the Madonna that guarded the capital of Poland from the time of Napoleon's invasion to the Nazi invasion. Her statue, her portrait, which is a charred face of the Madonna, has always been a symbol of freedom to the Polish people.

So as we continued to have our processions and our devotions in the 60's, along came the liberated Jesuits. They came in with their turtlenecks and their guitars and they said: "We're going to liberate you from the oppression of the Roman Catholic church. This is the Ecumenical Council. Throw out the statues. The Blessed Mother is out." We didn't know who was in! They didn't bring in Jane Addams or Rosie Schneiderman as a substitute. They just said: "She's out the window." And then we were told to go into folk masses.

Now, we didn't know how to sing *Go Tell It on the Mountain*. In my neighborhood, children learned to play the accordian. We didn't know what the hell a guitar was. We thought it was something Elvis Presley played. At the same time as they were telling us to get with it and be part of the 60's and the folk culture, our own folk culture was put down. We asked: "Couldn't we have a service and then afterwards have some other kind of music? Couldn't we have our traditional services?" They said no, and that was it.

It is within this context that in the past five years we began to be part of something else. It was called the Women's Movement. Again you have to understand how we feel. We and our mothers and grandmothers and great-grandmothers were the women of the sweatshops. The women who died in the Triangle Shirtwaist fire. And I can tell you something: when World War II was over, and McCall's magazine talked about family togetherness and get ting out of the factory, you're damn right my aunts and other relatives wanted to get out.

They wanted to be "ladies." They didn't find it especially gratifying to work in factories or to stand there trimming tomatoes so that at 70 years old all they've got out of their work is arthritis and very little Social Security. The title "lady" meant something, and they wanted their daughters to be "ladies." That's why many of them scrubbed floors and took other menial jobs to send their children to college. So when something came along that began to threaten that dream, it became a real problem.

The Threatening Issues Cause Ambivalence

One of the things that has always held us together—whether it was the 1,000 years of oppression in Czechoslovakia, in Poland, in Latvia or Estonia—is the concept of family. No matter what king, kaiser or czar marched through your country, somehow or other that family would hold you together. The family is not only a living arrangement. It has always been a symbol of survival. When that traditional family structure is challenged by views that some of our people consider as culturally provocative, we feel threatened.

On the one hand, we want equal pay for equal work. We want the benefits that are coming into our communities. We like being out on the barricades. We like bringing about change. But when threatening ideas come along, we have a tremendous feeling of ambivalence and hurt.

The women in our community are not hostile to the Women's Movement. But we're confused and we're searching. And we're looking to find ways that we can be together. Maybe one of the ways that we can begin to get together is to take a look at our cultural diversity and to respect the different feelings that we have. Respect the ambivalence, respect the reluctance, the shyness and inhibition to participate in some areas. . . .

Moving toward Sisterhood

We have always been taught that diversity has meant conflict in this country. We've always been taught that if we were different, that meant trouble. Yet, diversity—as you can see right here in this room and as you look at our coun try—is enrichment. If we begin to understand all of these cultural pulls and tugs, then I think we can begin to move toward sisterhood.

To me, women's liberation means that women should be free to be anything they want to be and that we should unite in a common front to remove all barriers that hamper that freedom. To me, that is what we are all about, and I am very glad we're all here today.

5

Join My Struggle: "A Poem for Marshall"

In this poem the "woman of color" finds herself torn between the woman's movement struggle for sexual equality and her ethnic community's struggle for racial equality. Advocates of each group claim priority for their cause and urge her to join them. In this imaginary and ironic dialogue, Chicana poet Anne Martinez expresses her frustration wih this tug-of-war for her loyalty.

"A Poem for Marshall" was published in 1991. At that time Martinez was a graduate student at the University of Michigan where she worked to make the university "more accepting of the needs, issues, and concerns of Latino students and other students of color." Students like Martinez have been working since the 1960s to make American campuses—and American society—more hospitable to minorities and to women. Martinez plans to continue her advocacy work after the completion of her degree.

A Poem for Marshall

(not because i love him
but because i laugh
whenever i think of him)
white women
and men of color
think
if i open my mind
and my heart

Source: Anne M. Martinez, "A Poem for Marshall," in *Inside Separate Worlds: Life Stories of Young Blacks, Jews, and Latinos,* ed. David Schoem (Ann Arbor: University of Michigan Press, 1991), pp. 233–34.

i can understand
what it is
        to be
a woman of color
(it's not that easy
        you don't see
                that because your mind
                        and heart
                are only ajar
                it is you
                that makes
        the woman of color
                        hurt sad cry)
you say
        join my struggle
        we want the same things
        we can work together
i say
        join my struggle
        we want the same things
        we can work together
you say
        no no you're missing the point
                (yeah i guess i am)
        we have to work together for the greater cause
                (which happens to be your cause)
        by fighting oppression we can free all of us
                (all of us but you first)
        once we free the people of color   [women]
        then we can free our women   [people of color]
i say
        so until then
        you'll just keep us in bondage
        —for the greater cause—
        of course
        you say
                now you understand
        yes now i understand
                either i laugh or i cry
                and i'm tired of crying
        so marshall
                i laugh whenever i think of you

6

Asian-American Women and Feminism:
"Gender Equality . . . Is Not the Exclusive Agenda

"Is feminism the agenda for women of color?" asked a plenary panel at the Na-
tional Women's Studies Association Meeting in June 1984. This meeting was one
of an increasing number at which "mainstream" feminist organizations have tried
to address the concerns of minorities. The passage that follows was the response of
panelist Lucie Cheng, director of the Asian American Studies Center at the Uni-
versity of California–Los Angeles.

Cheng reminds white feminists that white women, though oppressed them-
selves, have been oppressors of Asian women. She goes beyond this, however. She
asks the women's movement to recognize the strong identification Asian-American
women feel with Asians overseas, many of whom have also been the victims of
American racism. She urges that attention be paid to the needs of Asian women
immigrants in the United States. Finally, she argues that the women's movement
must address issues of class as well as issues of race and sex. A representative of
socialist rather than "liberal" feminism, Cheng believes that the lives of Asian and
other working-class women cannot be improved without a reorganization of the
American economy and a more equal distribution of resources.

As members of a male-oriented and male-dominated society, the answer
to the question for any women, white or colored, has to be a definite
"yes." The struggle for gender equality is a common agenda. But it should
not be the exclusive agenda, and for most Asian American women, it *is not*.

How do Asian American women activists relate to feminism and the
general organized women's movement? I quote from interviews gathered by
Susie Ling for a master's thesis on the Asian American women's movement.
To the question "As an Asian American woman, do you consider yourself a
feminist?" one woman answered:

People call me a feminist. I'm not sure what they mean by that. I
believe strongly in women's rights and equality for women, equal
pay for equal work, and those kinds of things. But there are dif-

Source: Reprinted by permission of *Sojourner: The Women's Forum* Vol. 10, No. 2 (October 1984). 42 Seavems Ave., Jamaica Plain, MA 02130.

ferent types of feminism. There is feminism where all the problems
of women in society are seen as caused by men. I don't believe in
that . . . I do believe that men and women have to work together to
solve the problems in society.

Another replied:

Essentially, I think I'm more Asian American than feminist. I basically support women's rights, but when it comes down to things,
I find myself analyzing things more from the basis of race. The passion comes from my being Asian, rather than a woman's angle.

In discussing the gap between Asian and white women, one woman
commented:

You have to look at the white women's movement along with
racism. I agree that white women are oppressed by this society. I
understand how they have to fight for their rights. But they also
belong to the group that oppresses minorities. That will always
make a difference. I cannot unite, but in many ways, the white
women's movement helps to move Asian women forward. Overall,
it's a help. But one has to be careful, because it can also serve to
oppress.

I do not believe that we need to choose between racism and sexism as the
target of our struggle, because both are oppressive, and one is related to the
other. It is important for white women to understand the profound impact of
racism on the experience of women of color, and the depth of identification
that we have with our people. For Asian American women, this identification
goes beyond national boundaries. When atomic bombs were dropped by the
U.S. over Hiroshima and Nagasaki; when the U.S. occupied the Philippines,
when American troops went to Korea and Vietnam, and when the U.S. government boycotted the People's Republic of China, both men and women in
these countries, our brothers and sisters across the Pacific, suffered. When
Japanese Americans were incarcerated in this country, no difference was
made between men and women. . . .

I believe women's studies has an obligation to teach the history of Asian
American women within the context of international relations and the context of Asian American history. I spent last night going over the program for
this conference, and I was greatly impressed by the sessions put together by
the NWSA Council and the Autonomous Institute. Many issues that I consider to be central to our joint struggle are being addressed by both white and
minority women. And here, I include discussions on anti-semitism in our
movement. I feel that what I've said so far may have been redundant. At the
same time, I am struck by the absence of discussions on an issue of deep

concern to me and to Asian American women and other women of color—the issue of immigrant women.

Since the passage of the 1965 immigration law and as a consequence of U.S. involvement in Asia, there has been a tremendous increase in Asian immigration. In the year the law passed, Asians comprised only seven percent of all immigrants. By 1977, however, over two-fifths of new immigrants to this country came from Asia. The major countries of origin are the Philippines, South Korea, China (Taiwan and Hong Kong), India, and Vietnam. The character of the new Asian immigration is remarkably different from the old. Most significantly, the number of female immigrants exceeds the number of males.

Who are these immigrant woman? How do they fare in America? What is their impact on the country? Their impact on the labor market? How are their needs addressed? Is the women's movement cognizant of their concerns? A recent study shows that more Asian immigrant women than white women participate in the labor force, and a larger proportion of these women are employed full-time. Yet the annual earnings of full-time, year-round Asian immigrant women workers are significantly lower than those of their white counterparts. For those Asian women who have four or more years of college education, it is significantly more difficult for Asian women to convert their education into high occupational status. Those large numbers of immigrant women with only a grade-school education are, on the other hand, trapped in economic ghettos and low-income jobs.

We must ask, what is the goal of feminist struggle? Is it simply to achieve parity with men? If the Reagan administration appoints an equal number of men and women to positions of power, do you think it would improve the lives of working-class people or, specifically, working-class women? Is it our goal to gain an equal opportunity to participate in the oppression of a segment of our population?

With each specific objective of the movement, we must ask, who will be the beneficiaries and who will suffer as a consequence? When, as professional women, we fight for equal employment, what should our position be on domestic work? Are we going to devote the same energies to fight for the industrialization of housework, the socialization of housework, and the redistribution of private wealth? Are we aware that we may be creating a new underclass occupied mainly by immigrant women of color and helping to trap them permanently in that position? As long as the family is the basic unit of consumption and identification, how can we expect Chinese immigrant women living in San Francisco's Chinatown, in sub-standard housing, with a median family income of $9,000, to identify with a women's movement that focuses on getting women into corporate positions that will boost their family income well over $100,000? Whatever the agenda of feminism is, it cannot be and *must not* be the perpetuation of the status quo.

I believe there are common causes among us. I believe that a rainbow coalition can be built and must be built to transform our society, to free it from sexism, antisemitism, and class exploitation.

7

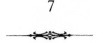

Generations of Women

The poems that follow, "Generations of Women" (an excerpt) and "Breaking Tradition," are by the celebrated Japanese-American poet Janice Mirikitani. They are from a collection titled, significantly, Shedding Silence. *Like many contemporary Japanese-American feminists, Mirikitani sees the immigrant generation through two lenses. In the first poem she admires the strength of women who endured, and helped their families endure, the hardships of immigration, the years of legalized discrimination, and the internment during World War II. She claims this strength as a legacy and builds upon it. In the second poem, however, she rejects the silence and passivity of the older generations, especially their acceptance of negative and limiting views of themselves as women.*

Mirikitani has broken with elements of her ethnic tradition by writing strong, often angry, poems about the experiences of Japanese women—by "shedding silence." She recognizes this. She also recognizes, in the second poem, that the cycle will not end here. Already her daughter looks at her critically, as she looked at her own mother. Her daughter, too, is breaking tradition.

"Mother, Grandmother / Speak in Me"

I claim
my place
in this line of
generations of women,
lean with work,
soft as tea,
open as the tunnels of the sea
driven as the heels of freedom's feet.
Taut fisted with reparations.

Source: From the poem "Breaking Tradition" and an except from "Generations of Women" © 1987 by Janice Mirikitani. Reprinted by permission of Celestial Arts, Berkeley, California.

Mother, grandmother
speak in me.
I claim their strong fingers
of patience, their knees
bruised with humiliation,
their hurt, longing,
the sinews of their survival.
Generations of yellow women
gather in me
to crush the white wall
not with the wearing of sorrow
not with the mildew of waiting,
not with brooding or bitterness or regret,
not with wilted flowers or red lipstick.
We crush
the white wall
with a word, a glance,
a garden new with nimosa bamboo,
juniper with barbed wire at their root,
splinters from barracks.
We will come like autumn shedding sleep
a sky about to open with rage,
thunder on high rocks.
I crush
the white wall
with my name.

> *Pronounce it correctly*
> *I say*
> *Curl it on their tongue*
> *Feel each and many*
> *syllable of it,*
> *like grains of warm rice*
> *and that will be pleasing.*

Generations of women
spilling each syllable
with a loud, yellow noise.

Breaking Tradition

For my daughter

My daughter denies she is like me,
her secretive eyes avoid mine.
    She reveals the hatreds of womanhood
    already veiled behind music and smoke and telephones.
I want to tell her about the empty room
    of myself.
This room we lock ourselves in
where whispers live like fungus,
giggles about small breasts and cellulite,
where we confine ourselves to jealousies,
bedridden by menstruation.
This waiting room where we feel our hands
are useless, dead speechless clamps
that need hospitals and forceps and kitchens
and plugs and ironing boards to make them useful.
I deny I am like my mother. I remember why:
She kept her room neat with silence,
defiance smothered in requirements to be otonashii,★
passion and loudness wrapped in an obi,★★
her steps confined to ceremony,
the weight of her sacrifice she carried like
a foetus. Guilt passed on in our bones.
I want to break tradition—unlock this room
where women dress in the dark.
Discover the lies my mother told me.
The lies that we are small and powerless
        that our possibilities must be compressed
        to the size of pearls, displayed only as
        passive chokers, charms around our neck.
    Break Tradition.
    I want to tell my daughter of this room
    of myself
    filled with tears of shakuhachi,★
    the light in my hands,
    poems about madness,

★otonashii—humble, unselfish, submissive
★★—a wide, heavy, constricting sash worn with a kimono.
★shakuhachi—a bamboo flute that makes a breathy, haunting sound.

the music of yellow guitars,
sounds shaken from barbed wire and
goodbyes and miracles of survival.

My daughter denies she is like me
her secretive eyes are walls of smoke
and music and telephones.
her pouting ruby lips, her skirts
swaying to salsa, Madonna and the Stones.
her thighs displayed in carnivals of color.
I do not know the contents of her room.
She mirrors my aging.

She is breaking tradition.

Bibliographical Essay

L iterature about immigrant women is extensive and growing rapidly. This bibliographical essay will introduce readers to this literature and provide starting points for further investigation.

General Works

Background on immigration history can be found in John Bodnar, *The Transplanted: A History of Immigrants in Urban America* (Bloomington: Indiana University Press, 1985), which emphasizes the transition from rural to urban life; and Thomas Archdeacon, *Becoming American: An Ethnic History* (New York: Free Press, 1983), which integrates native American and African-American history with European, Asian, and Hispanic immigration history. Unfortunately, these works give limited coverage to women. Maxine Schwartz Seller, *To Seek America: A History of Ethnic Life in the United States* (Englewood Cliffs, N.J.: Jerome S. Ozen, Publisher, Inc., 1977, 1988), which stresses ethnic cultural and community life, gives good coverage to women, as does Ronald Takaki, *Strangers from a Different Shore: A History of Asian Americans* (Boston: Little, Brown, 1989).

For background on women in American history, see Gerda Lerner, ed., *The Female Experience: An American Documentary* (Indianapolis: Bobbs-Merrill, 1977); Nancy Woloch, *Women and the American Experience* (New York: Alfred A. Knopf, 1984); and Sara Evans, *Born for Liberty* (New York: Free Press, 1989). For theoretical background, see Joan Scott, *Gender and the Politics of History* (New York: Columbia University Press, 1988); and Linda Kerber, "Separate Spheres, Female Worlds, Woman's Place: The Rhetoric of Women's History," *Journal of American History* 75, no. 1 (1988).

Although there is no comprehensive history of immigrant women in the United States, two useful general works are Cecyle Neidle, *America's Immigrant Women: Their Contributions to the Development of a Nation from 1609 to the Present* (New York: Hippocrene Books, 1975); and Doris Weatherford, *Foreign and Female: Immigrant Women in America, 1840–1930)* (New York: Schocken Books, 1986). Useful edited collections include George Pozzetta, ed., *Ethnicity and Gender: The Immigrant Woman* (New York: Garland, 1991); Edith Blicksilver, ed., *The Ethnic Woman: Problems, Protests, and Lifestyles* (Dubuque: Kendall/Hunt, 1990); Johnnetta B. Cole, ed., *All American*

Women: Lines That Divide, Ties That Bind (New York and London: Free Press and Collier Macmillan, 1986); Vicki Ruiz and Ellen C. DuBois, eds., *Unequal Sisters: A Multicultural Reader in U.S. Women's History* (New York: Routledge, Chapman and Hall, 1990). Donna Gabaccia, *Seeking Common Ground: Multidisciplinary Studies of Immigrant Women in the United States* (Westport, Conn.: Greenwood, 1992), includes original studies by historians, sociologists, anthropologists, psychologists, and literary scholars. Teresa Anott and Julie Matthaei, *Race, Gender, and Work: A Multicultural Economic History of Women in the United States* (Boston: South End Press, 1991), includes material on Asian-American, native American, Chicana, and Puerto Rican women. Among the journals featuring special issues on immigrant women are Jean Scarpaci, ed., *Immigrant Women and the City,* a special issue of the *Journal of Urban History* 4, no. 3 (May 1978); *International Migration Review* 18, no. 4 (Winter 1984); and Donna Gabaccia, ed., *Journal of American Ethnic History* 8 (Spring 1989).

For the historiography of immigrant women, including discussions of their marginality in immigration and ethnic studies, see Maxine S. Seller, "Beyond the Stereotype: A New Look at the Immigrant Woman, 1880–1924," *Journal of Ethnic Studies* 3 (Spring 1975): 59–70; Betty Bergland, "Immigration and the Gendered Subject: A Review Essay," *Ethnic Forum* 8, no. 2 (1988); Suzanne Simke, "A Historiography of Immigrant Women in the Nineteenth and Early Twentieth Centuries," *Ethnic Forum* 9, nos. 1–2 (1989): 122–45; Donna Gabaccia, "Immigrant Women: Nowhere at Home?" *Journal of American Ethnic History* 10 (Summer 1991): 61–87; and Sidney Stahl Weinberg, "The Treatment of Women in Immigration History: A Call for Change," *Journal of American Ethnic History* 11 (Summer 1992).

Ethnic Groups: European

The definitive book on Irish women is Hasia Diner, *Erin's Daughters in America: Irish Immigrant Women in the Nineteenth Century* (Baltimore and London: Johns Hopkins University Press, 1983); see also Janet A. Nolan, *Ourselves Alone: Women's Emigration from Ireland, 1885–1920* (Lexington: University of Kentucky Press, 1989). For Irish women's experience in the west, see Mary Murphy, "A Place of Greater Opportunity: Irish Women's Search for Home, Family, and Leisure in Butte, Montana," *Journal of the West* 31 (April 1992).

On Scandinavian women, see Theodore Blegen, "Immigrant Women and the American Frontier," *Norwegian-American Historical Association Studies and Records* 5 (1930): 26–29.

Betty Boyd Caroli, Robert F. Harney, and Lydio F. Tomasi, eds., *The Italian Immigrant Woman in North America* (Toronto: Multicultural History Society of Ontario, 1978), is a rich collection on Italian women including old world background, work, family life, cultural change, social services, and the arts. See also Virginia Yans-McLaughlin, *Family and Community: Italian Immigrants in Buffalo, 1880–1939* (Ithaca: Cornell University Press, 1977); and Donna Gabaccia, *From Sicily to Elizabeth Street: Housing and Social Change among Italian Immigrants* (Albany: State University of New York Press, 1985).

On Jewish women, see Charlotte Baum, Paula Hyman, and Sonya Michel, *The Jewish Woman in America* (New York: New American Library, 1978), a literary and cultural history; Jacob R. Marcus's survey *The American Jewish Woman, 1654–1980* and his source collection, *The American Jewish Woman: A Documentary History* (both New York: Ktav and the American Jewish Archives, 1980). See also Sydney Weinberg's perceptive *The World of Our Mothers: Lives of Jewish Immigrant Women* (Chapel Hill: North Carolina University Press, 1988), based on oral histories of immigrant mothers and their daughters. On the most recent Jewish immigration, see Rita J. Simon, et al., "The Social and Economic Adjustment of Soviet Jewish Women in the United States," in *International Migration: The Female Experience*, ed. Rita J. Simon and Caroline B. Bretell (Totowa, N.J.: Rowman and Allanheld, 1985), pp. 76–94.

On German women, see Linda Pickle, "Stereotypes and Reality: Nineteenth-Century German Women in Missouri," *Missouri Historical Review* 79 (April 1985); Klaus Hoffman, "Sewing Is for Women, Horses Are for Men: The Role of German Russian Women," in *Germans from Russia in Colorado*, ed. Sidney Heitman, (Ann Arbor: Western Social Science Association, 1978), pp. 131–44; and Walter D. Kamhoefner, et al., *News from the Land of Freedom: German Immigrants Write Home* (Ithaca: Cornell University Press, 1992).

Older studies that contain valuable material on eastern European women include Emily Balch, *Our Slavic Fellow Citizens* (Philadelphia: William F. Fell, 1910); and Bessie Pehotsky, *The Slavic Immigrant Women* (Cincinnati: Powell and White, 1925). John Bukowczyk, *And My Children Did Not Know Me: A History of the Polish Americans* (Bloomington: Indiana University Press, 1987), contains some information on women in the workplace, family, and community.

Other works containing substantial information about European immigrant women include Carl Ross and K. Marianne Wargelin Brown, eds., *Women Who Dared: The History of Finnish American Women* (St. Paul: Immigration History Research Center, 1986); Barton H. Arnold, "Scandinavian Immigrant Women's Encounter with America," *Swedish Pioneer Historical Quarterly* 25 (January 1974): 37–42; Grace Abbott, "A Study of Greeks in Chicago," *American Journal of Sociology* 15 (November 1909): 349–93; Charlotte Erickson, "English Women Immigrants in America in the Nineteenth Century: Expectations and Reality," *Fawcett Library Papers* 7 (London:

LLRS Publications, 1983): Kristian Hvidt, *Flight to America: The Social Characteristics of 300,000 Danish Emigrants* (New York: Academic Press, 1976); and Estelle M. Smith, "The Portuguese Female Immigrant: The 'Marginal Man,' " *International Migration Review* 14 (Spring 1980): 77–92.

Middle Eastern and East Asian

On Middle Eastern women, see Elaine C. Habopian and Ann Paden, eds., *The Arab Americans: Studies in Assimilation*, AAUUG Monograph Series no. 1 (Wilmette, Ill,: Medina University Press, 1969), and Alixa Naff, *Becoming American: The Early Arab Immigrant Experience* (Carbondale: Southern Illinois University Press, 1985); Parvin Abyaneh, "Post-Migration Economic Role of Females and Patriarchy in Immigrant Iranian Families" (Ph.D. diss., University of California–Riverside, 1986, order number DA 8706975); idem, "Immigrants and Patriarchy: The Case of Iranian Families," *Women's Studies* 17 (November 1989): 67–70; and Nira H. Lipner, "The Subjective Experience of Israeli Immigrant Women: An Interpretive Approach" (Ph.D. diss., George Washington University, 1987, order number DA 8708356).

There are as yet few general works on East Asian women. Social life among Indian and Sri Lankan women in American cities is described in Lorna Amara Singham, "Patterns of Friendship among South Asian Women," in *The Sourcebook on the New Immigration: Implications for the United States and the International Community*, ed. Roy S. Bryce-Laporte (New Brunswick, N.J.: Transaction Books, 1980). See also Shamita D. Casqupta, "Marching to a Different Drummer? Sex Roles of Asian Indian Women in the United States," *Women and Therapy* 5 (Summer 1986): 297–322; and Bruce La Brack, "Evolution of Sikh Family Form and Values in Rural California: Continuity and Change, 1904–1980," *Journal of Comparative Family Studies* 19, no. 2 (Summer 1988): 287–309. See also Marcelle Williams, "Ladies on the Line: Punjabi Cannery Workers in Central California," Rashmi Luthra, "Matchmaking in the Classifieds of the Immigrant Indian Press," and Jyotsna Vaid, "Seeking a Voice: South Asian Women's Groups in North America," all of which are in Asian Women United of California, ed. *Making Waves: An Anthology of Writings by and about Asian American Women* (Boston: Beacon Press, 1989).

Latina and Caribbean

Anthologies including material on Latinas along with other "women of color" include Gloria Anzaldua, ed., *Making Face, Making Soul: Creative and Critical Perspectives by Women of Color* (San Francisco: Aunt Lute Foundation, 1990); Cherrie Moraga and Gloria Anzaldua, eds., *This Bridge Called My Back: Writings by Radical Women of Color* (Lantham, N.Y.: Kitchen

Table/Women of Color Press, 1983); and Juanita Ramos, ed., *Compañeras; Latina Lesbians (An Anthology)* (New York: Lesbian History Project, 1987). Important books on Mexican-American women include Martha Cotera's early survey, *Diosa y Hembra: The History and Heritage of Chicanas in the United States* (Austin, Tex: Information Systems Development, 1976); Margarita B. Melville, ed., *Twice a Minority: The Mexican American Woman* (St. Louis: C. V. Mosby, 1980); Alfredo Mirande, *The Chicano Experience: An Alternative Perspective* (Notre Dame: University of Notre Dame Press, 1985); and Helen Deutch, *No Separate Refuge: Culture, Class, and Gender in an Anglo-Hispanic Frontier in the American Southwest, 1880–1940* (London: Oxford University Press, 1989). For material on Mexican-American lesbians, see Carla Trujillo's anthology of poetry, short stories, and articles, *Chicana Lesbians: The Girls Our Mothers Warned Us About* (Berkeley: Third Woman Press, 1991). On Puerto Ricans in Puerto Rico and on the mainland, see Blanca Vazquez, *Puerto Rican Women as Workers and Writers*, Centro de Estudios Puertoiquenos *Bulletin* 2, no. 7 (Winter 1989–1990); City University of New York and Edna Acosta-Belen, eds., *The Puerto Rican Woman: Perspectives on Culture, History, and Society* (New York: Praeger, 1979 and 1986). Ruth E. Zambrana, *Work, Family, and Health: Latina Women in Transition*, Monograph no. 7 (Hispanic Research Center, Fordham University, 1982), focuses primarily on Puerto Rican women and covers labor force participation, mental health, voluntary sterilization, and other issues.

On other Latinas, see Terry Doran, et al., *A Road Well Traveled: Three Generations of Cuban American Women* (Newton, Mass.: Education Development Center, Women's Educational Equity Act Publishing Center, 1988); Patricia R. Pessar, "The Linkage Between the Household and the Workplace in the Experience of Dominican Immigrant Women in the United States," *International Migration Review* 18, no. 4 (Winter 1984): 188–211, and Douglas T. Gurak and Mary M. Kritz, "Dominican and Colombian Women in New York City," *Migration Today* 10, nos. 3–4 (1982): 14–21. Multigroup studies of Latinas include Rina Alcalay, "Hispanic Women in the United States: Family and Work Relations," *Migration Today* 12, no. 3 (1984): 13–20, which contrasts family status of women among Mexican-Americans, Puerto Ricans, and Cubans; and the important collection edited by Delores Mortimer and Roy Bryce-Laporte, *Female Immigrants to the United States: Caribbean, Latin American and African Experiences* (Washington, D.C.: Research Institute on Immigration and Ethnic Studies, Smithsonian Institute, 1981).

On women from the Caribbean, see Nancy Foner, "Sex Roles and Sensibilities: Jamaican Women in New York and London," in *International Migration: The Female Experience*, ed. Rita J. Simon and Caroline B. Brettell, (Totowa, N.J.: Rowman and Allanheld, 1985); and Susan H. Buchanan, "Haitian Women in New York City," *Migration Today* 7 (September 1979): 19–25. Michael Laguerre, *American Odyssey: Haitians in New York City*

(Ithaca, N.Y.: Cornell University Press, 1984), also contains information on Haitian women. Insights into the social, economic, and personal lives of Japanese-American women are provided in an article on women's advice columnists in the Japanese-American press in the 1930s; see Valerie Matsumoto, "Desperately Seeking 'Dierdre': Gender Roles, Multicultural Relations, and Nisei Women Writers of the 1930s," *Frontiers* 12, no. 1 (1991): 19–32.

Pacific Asian

Works covering multiple ethnic groups include Nobuya Tsuchida, ed., *Asian and Pacific American Experiences: Women's Perspectives* (Minneapolis: University of Minnesota Press, 1982); Gail Miyasaki, *Montage: An Ethnic History of Women in Hawaii* (Honolulu: University of Hawaii Press, 1977); and the outstanding anthology *Making Waves: An Anthology of Writings by and about Asian American Women*, ed. Asian Women United of California (Boston: Beacon Press, 1989), containing poetry and memoirs as well as scholarly articles. See also Irene Fujitomi and Diane Wong, "The New Asian American Woman," in *Female Psychology: The Emerging Self*, ed. Su Cox (Chicago: Science Research Associates, 1976).

On Chinese women, see Ginger Chih, *The History of Chinese Immigrant Women, 1850–1940* (North Bergen, N.Y.: Author, 1977); Chinese Historical Society, *The Life, Influence, and Role of the Chinese in the U.S., 1776–1960*, especially the chapter titled "The Life, Influences, and Role of the Chinese Women in the United States" (San Francisco: Chinese Historical Society, 1975); and Judy Yung, *Chinese Women of America: A Pictorial History* (Seattle: University of Washington Press, 1986), which includes excellent narrative as well as pictures. Sylvia J. Yanigasako, *Transforming the Past: Tradition and Kinship among Japanese Americans* (Stanford: Stanford University Press, 1985), includes information on changing work and family roles. See also Yuji Ichioka, "Amerika Nadeshiko: Japanese Immigrant Women in the United States, 1900–1924," *Pacific Historical Review* 49 (1980): 339–57; Patsy S. Saiki, *Japanese Women in Hawaii: The First Hundred Years* (Honolulu: Kusaku 1985); and Valerie Matsumoto, "Japanese American Women during World War II," *Frontiers* 8 (1984): 6–14.

For material on other Pacific Asian women, see Eun Sik Yang, "Korean Women of America: From Subordination to Partnership, 1903–1930," *Amerasia* 11 (1984): 1–28, Eui-Young Yu and Earl H. Phillips, eds., *Korean Women in Transition: At Home and Abroad* (Los Angeles: Center for Korean-American and Korean Studies, California State University, 1987); and Keum-Young Chung Pang, *Korean Elderly Women in America: Everyday Life, Health, Illness* (New York: AMS Press, 1991). Gail P. Kelly, *From Vietnam to America: A Chronicle of the Vietnamese Immigration to the United States* (Boulder: Westview Press, 1977), includes considerable information on the social backgrounds and resettlement experiences of Vietnamese women. John Ten-hula, *Voices from Southeast Asia: The Refugee Experience in the United States* (New York: Holmes and Meier, 1991) contains interviews with many women. See also Florence S. Mitchell, "From Refugees to Rebuilder: Cambodian Women in America" (Ph.D. diss., Syracuse University, 1987, order number DA 8806696); Karen L. S. Muir, *The Strongest Part of the Family: A Study of Lao Refugee Women in Columbus, Ohio* (New York: AMS Press, 1988): and Belinda Aquino, "The History of Filipino Women in Hawaii," *Bridge* 7 (Spring 1979): 17–21.

Immigration

Two important collections that explore women's immigration to the United States in the context of global economic and social changes are Rita J. Simon and Caroline B. Brettell, eds., *International Migration: The Female Experience* (Totowa, N.J.: Rowman and Allanheld, 1985), and Delores M. Mortimer and Roy S. Bryce-Laporte, *Female Immigrants to the United States* (Washington, D.C.: Smithsonian Institution, Research on Immigration and Ethnic Studies, 1981). See also Marion Houstoun, et al., "Female Predominance of Immigration to the United States since 1930: A First Look," *International Migration Review* 18 (Winter 1984): 908–65; and, on women who returned to their homelands, Mirjana Morokvasic, "Birds of Passage Are Also Women . . . ," *International Migration Review* 18 (Winter 1984): 886–907. Saskia Sassen Koob, "Notes on the Incorporation of Third World Women into Wage-Labor Through Immigration and Off-Shore Production," *International Migration Review* 18 (Winter 1984): 1144–67, argues that the massive increase in Third World women's immigration to the United States after 1965 was related to a worldwide feminization of wage labor. The difficulties women encountered during the immigration process in the early twentieth century are described in Francis A. Kellor, "The Protection of Immigrant Women," *Atlantic* 101 (February 1908): 246–55; and Judy Yung, " 'A Bowl-ful of Tears': Chinese Women Immigrants on Angel Island," *Frontiers* 2 (Summer 1977): 52–55.

Adjustment and Americanization

Some of the best accounts of adjustment problems and Americanization among European women in the late nineteenth and early twentieth centuries were written by the social reformers (mostly women) of that era. See, for example, Grace Abbott, *The Immigrant and the Community* (New York: Century, 1917); Jane Addams, *The Spirit of Youth and the City Streets* (New York: Macmillan, 1909); idem, *Twenty Years at Hull House* (New York: Macmillan 1919); and idem, *Democracy and Social Ethics* (New York: Century, 1917), all of which provide information on urban life, intergenerational conflict, and the problems of cultural change. Sophonisba P. Breckinridge, *New Homes for Old* (New York: Harper Brothers, 1921) is a unique source on homemaking, consumer patterns, and childrearing. Mary K. Sinkhovitch, *The City Worker's World in America* (New York: Macmillan, 1917), includes a broad range of information on family life, education, work, recreation, health, politics, and religion, with attention to women throughout. Italian and Slavic women are described in Margaret Byington, *Homestead: The Households of a Mill Town* (New York: Russell Sage Foundation, Charities Publication Committee, 1910). John Daniels, *America via the Neighborhood* (New York: Harper and Brothers, 1920), describes the activities of settlement houses and ethnic organizations, including women's clubs. Insight into the lives of some of the poorest immigrant women is provided by Mary Bogue, *Administration of Mothers Aid in Ten Localities: With Special Reference to Health, Housing, Education, and Recreation*, United States Department of Labor Children's Bureau Publication no. 184 (Washington, D.C.: U.S. Government Printing Office, 1928).

More recent studies of the lives of nineteenth- and early twentieth-century immigrants and their daughters include Elizabeth Ewen, *Immigrant Women in the Land of Dollars: Life and Culture on the Lower East Side, 1890–1925* (New York: Monthly Review Press, 1985), which focuses on Jewish and Italian women; Dorothy Schneider, "For Whom Are All the Good Things in Life? German American Housewives Discuss Their Budgets," in *German Workers in Industrial Chicago, 1850–1910*, ed. Hartmut Keil and John B. Jentz (Dekalb: Northern Illinois University Press, 1983), pp. 145–62; and Harriet Bloch, "Changing Domestic Roles among Polish Immigrant Women," *Anthropological Quarterly* 49 (January 1976): 3–10. Excellent material on the acculturation of second-generation women, including education, health, sexual mores, and methods of childcare can be found in Neil M. Cowan and Ruth Schwartz Cowan, *Our Parents' Lives: The Americanization of Eastern European Jews* (New York: Basic Books, 1989). Women, mainly eastern European, were the subjects of one-third of the interviews for John Bodnar's study *Workers' World: Kinship, Community, and Protest in an Industrial Society, 1900–1940* (Baltimore and London: John Hopkins University Press, 1982). Kathy Peiss, *Cheap Amusements: Working Women and Leisure in Turn of the Century New York* (Philadelphia: Temple University Press, 1986); and Christine Stansell, *City of Women: Sex and Class in New York, 1789–1860* (New York: Alfred A. Knopf, 1986), do not deal with ethnicity explicitly, but both explore the changing life-styles of young women who were primarily immigrants or the daughters of immigrants. Elizabeth Ewen describes the impact of popular culture on the American-born daughter of European immigrants in "City Lights: Immigrant Women and the Rise of the Movies,"

Signs 5 (1980): 545–65. See also George Eisen, "Sport, Recreation, and Gender: Jewish Immigrant Women in Turn-of-the-Century America (1880–1920)," *Journal of Sport History* 18, no. 1 (1991): 103–20.

Examples of the vast literature on the impact of cultural change on more recent immigrants are Vicki L. Ruiz and Susan Tiano, eds., *Women on the U.S.-Mexican Border: Responses to Change* (Boston: Allen and Unwin, 1987); I. Walter, "One Year after Arrival: The Adjustment of Indochinese Women in the United States, 1979–1980, *International Migration Review* 19 (1981): 129–52; Lani Davidson, "Women Refugees: Special Needs and Programs," *Journal of Refugee Resettlement* 1 (1981): 16–26, which focuses on sexual abuse, health, and education among the Vietnamese, Hmong, and Indochinese; and Beverly Sewell-Coker, et al., "Social Work Practice with West Indian Immigrants," *Social Casework* 66 (November 1985): 563–68, which describes the problems of young West Indian women denied the social freedom of their American-born friends. Margarita B. Melville, "Mexican Women Adapt to Migration," *International Migration Review* 12 (Summer 1978), emphasizes the special stress experienced by illegal immigrants. Breda Murphy Bova, "Hispanic Women at Midlife," *Journal of Adult Education* 18, no. 1 (Fall 1989): 9–15, uses oral histories of women in the southwest to explore critical life events and areas of cultural conflict. Karen L. S. Muir, *The Strongest Part of the Family: A Study of Lao Refugee Women in Columbus, Ohio* (New York: AMA Press, 1988), uses interviews and participant observation.

Studies emphasizing success as well as difficulty, continuity as well as change include Corinne A. Krause, *Grandmothers, Mothers, and Daughters: An Oral History Study of Ethnicity, Mental Health, and Continuity of Three Generations of Jewish, Italian, and Slavic American Women* (New York: American Jewish Committee Institute on Pluralism and Group Identity, (1978); Donna Gabaccia, *From Sicily to Elizabeth Street: Housing and Social Change among Italian Immigrants* (Albany: State University of New York Press, 1984); Margaret S. Boone, "The Uses of Traditional Concepts in the Development of New Urban Roles: Cuban Women in the United States," in *World of Women: Anthropological Studies of Women in the Societies of the World*, ed. Erika Bourguignon, et al. (New York: Praeger, 1980); and John Connor, "Acculturation and Family Continuities in Three Generations of Japanese Americans," *Journal of Marriage and Family* 36, no. 1 (1974): 159–68. Cultural change among immigrant nuns is described in Susan Peterson, "Religious Communities of Women in the West: The Presentation Sisters' Adaptation to the Northern Plains Frontier," *Journal of the West* 21 (April 1982): 65–70. On cultural survival, see Raymond Sanchez Mayers, "Use of Folk Medicine by Elderly Mexican-American Women," *Journal of Drug Issues* 19, no. 2 (Spring 1989): 283–95.

Family

For additional information on changing patterns of family life, see Charles
H. Mindel, *Ethnic Families in America: Patterns and Variations* (New York:
Elsevier, 1988), which includes chapters on Polish, Irish, Italian, Mexican,
Cuban, Korean, Chinese, Japanese, Vietnamese, Jewish, and Arab families;
and Elizabeth H. Pleck, "Challenges to Traditional Authority in Immigrant
Families," in *The American Family in Social-Historical Perspective*, 3d. ed.,
ed. Michael Gordon (New York: St. Martin's Press, 1983). On intermarriage, see Richard Bernard, *The Meltingpot and the Altar* (Minneapolis: University of Minnesota Press, 1980); Harry H. Kitano, et al., "Asian American
Interracial Marriage," *Journal of Marriage and the Family* 46 (February
1984): 179–90; and Juliana Haeyun Kim, "Voices from the Shadows: The
Lives of Korean War Brides," *Asian American Journal* 17, no. 1 (1991): 15–
30. On changing family life within a single community, see Richard Griswold
del Castillo, *La Familia: Chicano Families in the Urban Southwest, 1848 to the
Present* (Notre Dame: Notre Dame University Press, 1985); Coleen L.
Johnson, *Growing up and Growing Old in Italian-American Families* (New
Brunswick: Rutgers University Press, 1985); William M. Meredith and
George Roue, "Changes in Lao Hmong Marital Attitudes after Immigrating
to the United States," *Journal of Comparative Family Studies* 17 (Spring
1986): 117–26; and Louise Lamphers, et al., "Kin Networks and Strategies
of Working-Class Portuguese Families in a New England Town," in *The Ver-
satility of Kinship*, ed. Linda Cordell and Stephen Beckerman (New York:
Academic Press, 1980), pp. 219–49.

Changing patterns of fertility and changing traditions about childbirth
are discussed in Michael Davis, *Immigrant Health and the Community* (New
York: Harper and Brothers, 1920); Eugene Declercq and Richard Lacroix,
"The Immigrant Midwives of Lawrence: The Conflict Between Law and
Culture in Early Twentieth-Century Massachusetts," *Bulletin of the History of
Medicine* 59 (1985): 232–46; Kathleen Ford, "Declining Fertility Rates of
Immigrants to the United States (with Some Exceptions)" *Sociology and So-
cial Research* 70, no. 1 (1985): 68–70; and Georges Sabagh and Dorothy S.
Thomas, "Changing Patterns of Fertility and Survival among the Japanese
on the West Coast," *American Sociological Review* 10 (October 1945): 651–85,
which shows fertility declining by generation. On changing views of sexuality, see Ruby B. Rich and Arguelles Lourdes, "Homosexuality, Homophobia
and Revolution: Notes toward an Understanding of the Cuban Lesbian and
Gay Male Experience, part II," *Signs* 11 (Autumn 1985): 120–36, which argues that lesbians and gay men were more likely to "come out" after immigration because of greater tolerance in the United States; and Oliva Espin,
"Cultural and Historical Influences on Sexuality in Hispanic/Latin
Women," in *All American Women: Lines That Divide, Ties That Bind*, ed.

Johnnetta B. Cole (New York and London: Free Press and Collier Macmillan, 1986), pp. 272–84.

An important discussion of "dysfunctional" families that victimize women is Nilda Romone, "Domestic Violence among Pacific Asians," in *Making Waves: An Anthology of Writings by and about Asian American Women*, ed. Asian Women United of California (Boston: Beacon Press, 1989), pp. 327–37. Deeana Jang, Debbie Lee, and Rachel Morello-Frosch analyze domestic violence in relation to immigration law and American court procedures in "Domestic Violence in the Immigrant and Refugee Community: Responding to the Needs of the Immigrant Woman," *Response-to-the Victimization-of-Women-and-Children* 13, no. 4 (Winter 1990): 22–27.

Work

Information on European immigrant women as domestic workers is included in Faye Dudden, *Serving Women: Household Service in Nineteenth Century America* (Middletown, Conn.: Wesleyan University Press, 1983); and David M. Katzman, *Seven Days a Week: Women and Domestic Service in Industrializing America* (New York: Oxford University Press, 1978). See also Evelyn Glenn, *Issei, Nisei, Warbride: Three Generations of Japanese American Women in Domestic Service* (Philadelphia: Temple University Press, 1986). Excellent material on immigrant women and their daughters in industrial work is in Rosalyn Baxandall, Linda Gordon, and Susan Reverby, *America's Working Women: A Documentary History* (New York: Random House, 1976), which contains songs, excerpts from diaries, and other primary sources. See also Barbara M. Wertheimer, *We Were There: The Story of Working Women* (New York: Pantheon Books, 1977); and an older but very useful work, Elizabeth B. Butler, *Women and the Trades: Pittsburgh, 1907–1908* (New York: Russell Sage Foundation, Charities Publication Committee, 1909). On farm work, see Barbara Levorson, "Our Bread and Meat," *Norwegian American Studies* 22 (1965): 178–97. Studies of the impact of work on women's status in the family include Florence T. Bloom, "Struggling and Surviving—the Life Style of European Immigrant Breadwinning Mothers in American Industrial Cities, 1900–1930," *Women's Studies International Forum* 8, no. 6 (1985): 609–20; Myra M. Feree, "Employment Without Liberation: Cuban Women in the United States," *Social Science Quarterly* 60 (1978): 35–50; and Vilma Ortiz and Rosemary Cooney, "Sex-Role Attitudes and Labor Force Participation among Young Hispanic and Non-Hispanic White Females," *Social Science Quarterly* 65 (June 1985): 392–400. On prostitution, see Lucie Cheng, "Free, Indentured, Enslaved: Chinese Prostitutes in Nineteenth-Century America," in *Labor Immigration under Capitalism: Asian Workers in the United States before World War II*, ed. Lucie Cheng and Edna Bonacich (Berkeley: University of California Press, 1984), pp. 423–34.

On Progressive Era immigrant workers, see Barbara Klaczynska, "Why Women Work: A Comparison of Various Groups in Philadelphia, 1910–1930," *Labor History* 17 (Winter 1976): 73–87; Louise Lamphere, *From Working Daughters to Working Mothers: Immigrant Women in a New England Industrial Community* (Ithaca: Cornell University Press, 1987); and Thomas Kessner and Betty B. Caroli, "New Immigrant Women at Work: Italians and Jews in New York City," *Journal of Ethnic Studies* 5 (Winter 1978): 19–32. On the work status of post-1965 immigrants, see Geoffrey Carliner, "Female Labor Force Participation Rates for Nine Ethnic Groups," *Journal of Human Resources* 16 (Spring 1981): 286–93; A. M. Hughey, "The Incomes of Recent Female Immigrants to the United States," *Social Science Quarterly* 71 (June 1990): 383–91. On Asian immigrants, see Mary Sheridan and Janet W. Salaf, eds., *Lives: Chinese Working Women* (Bloomington: University of Indiana Press, 1984); Elaine H. Kim, *With Silk Wings: Asian American Women at Work*, which highlights the experience of successful career women; Haya Stier, "Immigrant Women Go to Work: Analysis of Immigrant Wives' Labor Supply for Six Asian Groups," *Social Science Quarterly* 72, no. 1 (1991): 67–82; and Deborah Woo, "The Socioeconomic Status of Asian American Women: An Alternative View," *Sociological Perspectives* 28 (July 1985): 307–38. For an analysis of Hispanic women's disadvantageous position in the labor force and the role government might take to help, see Marta Escutia and Margarita Prieto, *Hispanics in the Work Force. Part II: Hispanic Women* (Washington, D.C.: National Council of La Raza, 1986). See also Sheldon L. Maram, *Hispanic Workers in the Garment and Restaurant Industries in Los Angeles County: A Social and Economic Profile* (La Jolla, Calif.: University of California–San Diego, 1980); and Denise A. Segura, "Labor Market Stratification: The Chicana Experience," *Berkeley Journal of Sociology* 29 (1984): 57–89.

Political and Social Activities

For information on naturalization, citizenship, and suffrage of early twentieth-century immigrant women, see Charles Hartshorn Maxson, *Citizenship* (New York: Oxford University Press, 1930), chap. 9; and John Palmer Gavit, *Americans by Choice* (New York: Harper and Brothers, 1922), chap. 10. The assimilation of West Indian women into African-American political life is described by Henry Keith in "The Black Political Tradition in New York: A Conjunction of Political Cultures," *Journal of Black Studies* 7, no. 4 (June 1977): 455–84. The motivation, problems, and achievements of immigrant and second-generation Asian women in American politics in the 1980s is described in Judy Chu, "Asian Pacific Women in Mainstream Politics," in *Making Waves: An Anthology of Writings by and about Asian American Women*, ed. Asian Women United of California (Boston: Beacon Press,

1989). For Latinas in politics in the 1980s, see Carol Hardy-Fanta, "Latina Women, Latino Men, and Political Participation in Boston: *La Chispa que Prende*" (Ph.D. diss., Brandeis University, 1991).

Information on immigrant women as labor activists is found in Carolyn D. McCreesh, *Women in the Campaign to Organize Garment Workers, 1880–1917* (New York: Garland, 1985); Nancy S. Dye, *As Equals and as Sisters: Feminism, Unionism, and the Women's Trade Union League of New York* (Columbia: University of Missouri Press, 1980); Vicki L. Ruiz, *Cannery Women, Cannery Lives: Mexican Women, Unionization, and the California Food Processing Industry, 1930–1950* (Albuquerque: University of New Mexico Press, 1987); and Mari Jo Buhle, *Women and American Socialism, 1870–1920* (Urbana: University of Illinois Press, 1980). See also Alice Henry, *Women and the Labor Movement* (New York: George H. Doran, 1923); Rosemary Gallick, *Workers and Allies: Female Participation in the American Trade Union Movement, 1824–1976* (Washington, D.C.: Smithsonian Institution Press, 1975); and Joyce Maupin, *Labor Heroines, Ten Women Who Led the Struggle* (Berkeley, Calif.: Union W.A.G.E. Educational Committee, 1974), with biographical sketches of Clara Lemlish, Rose Schneiderman, Leonora Barry, Elizabeth Gurley Flynn, Dolores Huerta, and other immigrant and ethnic labor activists.

On religious activism, see Herman L. Fritschel, *A Story of One Hundred Years of Deaconess Service* (Milwaukee: Lutheran Deaconess Motherhouse, 1949); Mary Ewens, *The Role of the Nun in 19th Century America, Variations on the International Theme* (New York: Arno Press, 1978); Ellen Sue Elwell, "The Founding and Early Programs of the National Council of Jewish Women: Study and Practice as Jewish Women's Religious Expression" (Ph.D. diss., University of Indiana, 1982), order number DA 8301060); and Rosemary R. Ruether and Rosemary S. Keller, eds., *Women and Religion in American Life* (New York: Harper and Row, 1981). The impact of religion is described in Ada Isasi-Diaz and Yolanda Tarango, *Hispanic Women: Prophetic Voice in the Church* (San Francisco: Harper and Row, 1988), in which Mexican and Cuban women discuss their faith; and Alice Chai, "Korean Women in Hawaii, 1903–1945: The Role of Methodism in Their Liberation and Their Participation in the Korean Independence Movement," in *Women in New Worlds: Historical Perspectives on the Wesleyan Tradition*, ed. Hilah F. Thomas and Rosemary S. Keller (Nashville: Abingdon, 1981).

On secular community activism, see Rebecca Kohut, "Jewish Women's Organizations," *American Jewish Yearbook* 33 (1931–1932): 165–201; Ronald Lawson, *The Tenant Movement in New York City, 1904–1984* (New Brunswick: Rutgers University Press, 1986); Carl Ross, "Servant Girls: Community Leaders, Finnish American Women in Transition," in *Women Who Dared: The History of Finnish American Women*, ed. Carl Ross and K. Marianne Wargelin Brown (St. Paul: Immigration History Research Center,

1986), pp. 41–54; Lucia Birnbaum, "Earthmothers, Godmothers, and Radicals: The Inheritance of Sicilian American Women," *Marxist Perspectives* 3 (Spring 1980): 128–41; Mall Jurma, et al., *Baltic Women's Council: 25 Years of Friendship and Cooperation, 1947–1972* (New York: Baltic Women's Council, 1972); and Eui-Young Yu, "The Activities of Women in South California Korean Community Organizations," in *Korean Women in Transition: At Home and Abroad*, ed. Eui-Young Yu and Earl H. Phillips (Los Angeles: Center for Korean Studies, California State University, 1987), pp. 249–99. Neighborhood, political, and union activism of black and Hispanic as well as white ethnic women are described in the oral histories in Nancy Seifer, *Nobody Speaks for Me: Self-Portraits of American Working Class Women* (New York: Simon and Schuster, 1976).

On immigrant women and feminism, see Carl Ross, "The Feminist Dilemma in the Finnish Immigrant Community," *Finnish Americans* 1 (1978): 71–83; Elinor Lerner, "Jewish Involvement in the New York City Woman Suffrage Movement," *American Jewish History* 70 (June 1981): 442–61; Esther N. Chow, "The Development of Feminist Consciousness among Asian American Women," *Gender and Society* 1 (September 1987): 284–99; Marta P. Cotera, *The Chicana Feminist* (Austin, Tex.: Information Systems Development, 1977); Rabbi Sally Priesand, *Judaism and the New Woman* (New York: Behrman House, 1975); and Anne L. Lerner, " 'Who Hast Not Made Me a Man': The Movement for Equal Rights for Women in American Jewry," *American Jewish Yearbook 1977* (Philadelphia: Jewish Publication Society of America, 1976). See also Mirta Vidal, *Chicanas Speak Out: Women, New Voices of La Raza* (New York: Path Press, 1971; and Patsy G. Fulcher, Aileen C. Hernandez, and Eleanor R. Spikes, *Report of the Task Force on Minority Women and Women's Rights* (Washington, D.C.: National Organization for Women, May 1974).

Education

Maxine S. Seller, "The Education of the Immigrant Woman, 1900–1935," *Journal of Urban History* 4 (1978): 307–30, provides an overview of informal as well as formal education for early twentieth-century immigrants. For the same period, see Education Committee for Non-English-Speaking Women, *A New Country and Women from the Old World* (New York: Education Committee for Non-English-Speaking Women, 1925), which includes pictures of home classes for immigrant mothers; John McClymer, "Gender and the 'American Way of Life': Women in the Americanization Movement," *Journal of American Ethnic History* 10 (Spring 1991): 3–21; and Miriam Cohen, "Changing Education Strategies among Immigrant Generations: New York Italians in Comparative Perspective," *Journal of Social History* 15 (1982): 433–66. For a summary of the role of Irish women religious as educators, see

Grace Donovan, "Immigrant Nuns: Their Participation in the Process of Americanization: Massachusetts and Rhode Island, 1880–1920," *Catholic Historical Review* 77, no. 2 (1991): 194–208. Leonard Covello's classic study, *The Social Background of the Italo-American School Child* (Leiden: E. J. Brill, 1968), provides material on the family life as well as the schooling of the southern Italian immigrant child. Sydney Stahl Weinberg, "Longing to Learn: The Education of Jewish Immigrant Women in New York City, 1900–1934," *Journal of American Ethnic History* 8 (Spring 1989): 108–27, uses oral histories to describe the educational ambitions, usually unrealized, of her subjects. Information about attitudes toward education, compulsory school laws, juvenile courts, and truancy among Progressive Era immigrant girls is provided in Edith Abbott and Sophonisba Breckinridge, *Truancy and Non-Attendance in the Chicago Schools* (Chicago: University of Chicago Press, 1917). The use of home economics classes to impose behavior acceptable to the middle-class Anglo-Americans on Mexican-American girls is described in Pearl Idelia Ellis, *Americanization Through Homemaking* (Los Angeles: Wetzel, 1929).

On the education of adults, see the chapter on women in William Sharlip and Albert Owens, *Adult Immigration Education: Its Scope, Content, and Methods* (New York: Macmillan, 1928); Mary Van Kleeck, *Working Girls in Evening Schools: A Statistical Study* (New York: Russell Sage Foundation, 1914); and Florence H. Schneider, *Patterns of Workers Education: The Story of the Bryn Mawr Summer School* (Washington, D.C.: American Council on Public Affairs, 1941), which summarizes the educational activities provided by unions in the early decades of the century. Mexican immigrant women's resistance to Americanization while using the services of missionary agencies is documented in Vicki Ruiz, "Dead Ends or Gold Mines: Using Missionary Records in Mexican-American Women's History," *Frontiers* 12, no. 1 (1991): 33–56.

Thaddeus C. Radzialowski, "Reflections on the History of the Felicians in America," *Polish American Studies* 23, no. 1 (Spring 1975): 19–28, describes a Polish sisterhood, one of many immigrant teaching orders that pioneered in bilingual/bicultural education while offering immigrant daughters higher education and careers in religious life. A negative view of an ethnic parochial school is presented in Robert Hill, "Ethnic Status, Culture, and Community: The Polish-American Underclass in the Roman Catholic School System" (paper presented at the Ethnicity and Education Symposium in the Department of Anthropology, University of Pittsburgh, 1971, ERIC document ED U58 372), which suggests that the German and Irish staff of the high school studied worked with the Polish immigrant home to discourage lower-class girls from the pursuit of higher education.

For perspectives on the education of post-1965 immigrants, see Maxine B. Zinn, "Employment and Education of Mexican-American Women: The

Interplay of Modernity and Ethnicity in Eight Families," *Harvard Educational Review* 50, no. 1 (1980): 47–62; and Donna Gray, "The Impact of Higher Education and Feminism on Women in the Brain Drain," in *The Brain Drain from the West Indies and Africa*, ed. Norma Niles and Trevor G. Gordon (East Lansing: Michigan State University West Indian Students Association, 1977). Elvira Valenzuela Crocker, *The Report Card on Educating Hispanic Women* (Washington, D.C.: NOW Legal Defense and Education Fund, 1982), demonstrates that Hispanic women have the lowest educational attainment of any U.S. minority, which contributes to their low earning power. Ambivalence of a group of Hispanic immigrant women in Los Angeles toward becoming literate in English is explored in Kathleen Rockhill, "Literacy as Threat/Desire: Longing to be SOMEBODY," *TESL-Talk* 10, no. 1 (1990): 89–110. Material on the education of girls is included in Betty Lee Sung, *Chinese Immigrant Children in New York City: The Experience of Adjustment* (Washington, D.C.: Center for Immigration Studies, 1987); Joan McCarty and John Willshire Carrera, *New Voices: Immigrant Students in the U.S. Public Schools* (Boston: Coalition of Advocates for Students, 1988). Reasons for the relatively small presence of Chicanas in positions of educational leadership in the public schools are provided in Regina Cortina, "Women as Leaders in Mexican Education," *Comparative Education Review* 33, no. 3 (August 1989): 357–76.

Memoirs and Autobiographies—European

For first first-hand accounts of their lives of Scandinavian women, see David Nelson, trans. and ed., *The Diary of Elizabeth Koren, 1853–1855* (Northfield, Minn.: Norwegian American Historical Association, 1955); Pauline Farseth and Theodore Blegen, trans. and ed., *Frontier Mother: The Letters of Gro Svendsen* (Northfield, Minn.: Norwegian American Historical Association, 1950); and the story of Swedish-born labor activist and first director of the Women's Bureau, *Woman at Work: The Autobiography of Mary Anderson* as told to Mary N. Winslow (Minneapolis: University of Minnesota Press, 1951). See also Karen Schwencke Millberg, a Danish immigrant, *Fight Against the Wind* (New York: Odyssey Press, 1947); and Ingeborg Sonland, *My Reasonable Service* (Minneapolis: Augsberg, 1938), by a Norwegian Lutheran nurse and deaconess.

A German-American childhood in the American west is described by Clara Hilderman Ehrlich, *My Prairie Childhood* (Fort Collins: Colorado State University, 1977). See also Adolph Schroeder and Carla Schultz-Geisberg, eds., *Hold Dear, As Always: Jette, A German Immigrant Life in Letters* (Columbia, Mo.: University of Missouri Press, 1988), a collection of letters to Germany from 1836 to 1897. For the lives of other central and east

European immigrants, see Helen Helsenrad, *Brown Was the Danube* (New York: Yoseloff, 1966); Wanda Gag (a Bohemian-American artist), *Growing Pains* (New York: Coward McGann, 1940); Olga Petrova, (a Russian-born actress), *Butter with My Bread* (Indianapolis: Bobbs-Merrill, 1942); and World War II refugee Eva Lips, *Savage Symphony: A Personal Record of the Third Reich*, trans. Dorothy Thompson (New York: Random House, 1938).

The wide range of life-styles among Irish immigrant women is suggested by two roughly contemporary life stories: Mary Field Parton, ed., *The Autobiography of Mother Jones* (Chicago: Charles H. Kerr, 1925), the intrepid labor organizer, and Sisters of Reparation of the Congregation of Mary, *Blessed Are the Merciful: The Life of Mother Mary Zita, 1844–1917* (New York; n.p., 1953), about a woman who was a factory worker, a nurse on Blackwell's Island, and the founder of St. Zita's Home for Friendless Women. *Rosa: The Life of an Italian Immigrant*, as told to Marie Hall Ets (Minneapolis: University of Minnesota Press, 1970), is the story of an uneducated early twentieth-century immigrant. In contrast, Laura Fermi, *Atoms in the Family: My Life with Enrico Fermi* (Chicago: University of Chicago Press, 1954), describes highly educated mid-twentieth-century immigrants.

On east european Jewish women, see Mary Antin's classic success story *The Promised Land* (Boston: Houghton Mifflin, 1912); Rose Cohen, *Out of the Shadows* (Garden City, N.Y.: Doubleday/Doran, 1918); and Kate Simon, *Bronx Primitive: Portraits of a Childhood* (New York: Harper and Row, 1982) and *A Wider World: Portrait of an Adolescence* (New York: Harper and Row, 1986). Autobiographies of labor activists include Rose Pesotta, *Bread upon the Waters* (New York: Dodd, Mead, 1945); Rose Schneiderman, *All for One* (New York: Paul S. Eriksson, 1967); and Elizabeth Hasanovitz, *One of Them: Chapters from a Passionate Autobiography* (Boston: Houghton Mifflin, 1918). Memoirs by concentration camp survivors include Sala Kaminska Pawlowicz, *I Will Survive* (New York: Norton, 1962); and Gerda Klein, *All but My Life* (New York: Hill and Wang, 1957). Oral histories of Holocaust survivors who immigrated to the United States, including many women, are recorded in Dorothy Rabinowitz, *New Lives: Survivors of the Holocaust Living in America* (New York: Alfred A. Knopf, 1976).

Alfreda Post Carhart, *It Happened in Syria* (New York: Revell, 1940), describes an immigrant's girlhood in the Middle East. A more recent Middle Eastern memoir is Elmaz Abinader, *Children of the Roomje* (New York: W. W. Norton, 1991), by the daughter of a Lebanese Christian immigrant family. See also Arsha L. Armaghanian, *Arsha's World and Yours* (New York: Vantage Press, 1977), the diary of an Armenian immigrant, and Arlene Avakian, *Lion Woman's Legacy: An Armenian Legacy* (New York: Praeger, 1991). Helen P. Jannopoulo tells her story as a Greek immigrant in *And Across Big Seas* (Caldwell, Idaho: Caxton, 1949).

Memoirs and Autobiographies—Asian, Latina, and Caribbean

Memoirs of Chinese immigrants and their daughters include Jeanne Joe, *Ying-Ying: Autobiography of a Chinese Girl* (Boston: Pandora Press, 1986); Chuang Hua, *Crossings* (Boston: Northeast University Press, 1988); Jade Snow Wong, *Fifth Chinese Daughter* (New York: Harper and Row, 1965); Etsu Inagaki Sugimoto, *A Daughter of the Samurai* (Garden City, N.Y.: Doubleday/Page, 1925); and Maxine Hong Kingston, *The Woman Warrior: Memoirs of a Girlhood among Ghosts* (New York: Random House, 1976). Memoirs of Japanese immigrants include Akemi Kikumura, *Through Harsh Winters: The Life of a Japanese Immigrant Woman* (Novato, Calif.: Chandler and Sharp, 1981); Monica Itoi Sone, *Nisei Daughter* (Boston: Little, Brown, 1953); and Etsu Inagaki Sugimoto, *A Daughter of the Samurai* (New York: Doubleday, 1925). For memoirs of the internment of the Japanese during World War II, see Jean Wakatsuki Houston and James D. Houston, *Farewell to Manzanar* (Boston: Houghton Mifflin, 1973); and Yoshika Uchida, *Journey to Topaz* (Berkeley: Creative Arts Press, 1985). See also Mary Paik Lee, *Quiet Odyssey: A Pioneer Korean Woman in America*, with an introduction by Sucheng Chan (Seattle: University of Washington Press, 1990).

For a Mexican-American story of acculturation, education, and social mobility, see Elizabeth Loza Newby, *A Migrant with Hope* (Nashville: Broadman Press, 1977). A different Mexican-American memoir is the oral history of second-generation labor activist Jessie Lopez de la Cruz in Ellen Cantarow, *Moving the Mountain: Women Working for Social Change* (Old Westbury, N.Y.: Feminist Press, 1980), pp. 94–151. See also Mercedes Goday, *When I Was a Girl in Mexico* (Boston: Lathrop, Lee, and Shepherd, 1919), in which a diplomat's daughter describes growing up in Mexico, Cuba, and the United States; Nan Elsassaer, Kyle MacKenzie, and Yvonne Tixier y Vigil, eds., *La Mujeres: Conversations from a Hispanic Community* (Old Westbury, N.Y.: Feminist Press and McGraw Hill, 1980), a collection of oral histories; and the unique essay/memoir of lesbian poet Gloria Anzaldua, *Borderlands/ La Frontera: The New Mestiza* (Spinsters Aunt Lute Foundation, 1987).

For a delightful memoir of childhood in Puerto Rico and New York punctuated by the author's poetry, see Judith Ortiz Cofer, *Silent Dancing: A Partial Remembrance of a Puerto Rican Childhood* (Houston: Arte Publico Press, 1990). Congresswoman Shirley Chisholm's two volumes, *Unbought and Unbossed* (Boston: Houghton Mifflin, 1970) and *The Good Fight* (New York: Harper and Row, 1973) tell the story of her childhood in Barbados, her election to Congress, and her run for the presidency. Two memoirs of Cuban revolutionaries who came to the United States in the nineteenth century are Evangelina Cisneros, *The Story of Evangelina Ciseros* (Continental, 1898); and the unique Loreta J. Velasquez, *The Woman in Battle: A Narrative of the Exploits, Adventures and Travels of Madame Loreta Janeta Velazquez, Other-*

wise Known as Lietenant Harry T. Buford, Confederate States Army (Hartford: T. Belknap, 1876).

Fiction—European

Two novels describing Irish women in the slums of New York at the turn of the century are Zoe Beckley, *A Chance to Live* (New York: Macmillan, 1918); and Betty Smith, *A Tree Grows in Brooklyn* (New York: Harper and Row, 1947). See also Margaret Marchand, *Pilgrims in the Earth* (New York: Crowell, 1940), about conflict in a Pennsylvania steel town; Elizabeth Cullinan, *House of Gold* (Boston: Houghton Mifflin, 1970); and Susan Sheehan, *Kate Quinton's Days* Boston: Houghton Mifflin, 1984). The life of a Swedish immigrant woman, Kristina Nilsson, is sensitively portrayed in Vilhelm Moberg's superb trilogy *The Emigrants, Unto a Good Land,* and *The Last Letter Home* (New York: Simon and Schuster, 1951, 1954, and 1961). See also Lillian Budd, *April Snow* (Philadelphia: J. B. Lippincott, 1951) and *April Harvest* (New York: Duell, Sloan, and Pearce, 1959). For the story of Beret, a Norwegian woman whose adjustment to America is slow and painful, see O. E. Rolvaag's *Giants in the Earth* (New York: Harper and Brothers, 1927) and *Peder Victorious* (New York: Harper and Brothers, 1929). Norwegian-American novelist Martha Ostenso has written many novels about ethnic life in Minnesota, including *Wild Geese* (Toronto: McClelland and Stewart, 1925) and *O River Remember* (New York: Dodd, Mead, 1943). See also Kathryn Forbes, *Mama's Bank Account* (New York: Coward, 1947). Parent-daughter conflict in the Finnish community is the theme of Helen Miller, *Kirsti* (New York: Doubleday, 1965).

For fictional accounts of German women on the Iowa frontier, see Ruth Sockow, *Country People* and *Cora* (New York: Alfred A. Knopf, 1924 and 1929). Family sagas focusing on German women include Antoinette Spitzer, *These Are My Children* (New York: MacCauley, 1935); and Hester Fine, *The Waltz Is Over* (New York: Farrar and Rinehart, 1943). See also Hortense Lion, *The Grass Grows Green* (New York: Houghton Mifflin, 1935), which follows a Bavarian immigrant woman from her coming to the United States in the mid-nineteenth century to avoid war to the ironic and sad conclusion in which the United States enters World War I. Novels about German-Russian women include Mela Meisner Lindsay, *The White Lamb* (Lincoln: American Historical Society of Germans from Russia, 1976), which stresses life in the homeland; and Hope Williams Sykes' moving novels of rural life in the American West, *The Second Hoeing* (New York: G. P. Putnam's Sons, 1935) and *The Joppa Door* (New York: G. P. Putnam's Sons, 1937).

For the story of an Italian immigrant and her granddaughter, see Helen Barolini, *Umbertina* (New York: Seaview Books, 1979). See also Elizabeth Christian, *A Nice Italian Girl* (New York: Dodd, 1976), for the story of a second-generation unwed mother. Family sagas that focus on Italian women include Mario Puzo, *The Fortunate Pilgrim* (New York: Lancer Books, 1964); Pietro Di Donato, *This Woman* (New York: Ballantine, 1948); and Mary Fenollosa, *Sunshine Beggars* (Boston: Little, Brown, 1918). For Greek women's stories, see Mary Vardoulakis, *Gold in the Street* (New York: Dodd, Mead, 1945); and Harry Mark Petrakis, *The Odyssey of Xostas Volakis* (New York: David McKay, 1963). Armenian-American Marjorie Housepian writes humorously about life in her community in *A Houseful of Love* (New York: Random House, 1957).

For novels about working-class Polish life, see Stella Rybacki's autobiographical *Thrills, Chills, and Sorrows* (New York: Exposition, 1954); and Jean Karsavoma, *Tree by the Waters* (New York: International Publishers, 1948). See also John Alexander Abucewicz, *Fool's White* (New York: Carlton Press, 1969), about a Polish-American woman who becomes a nun; Wanda Luzenska Kubiac, *Polonaise Nevermore* (New York: Vantage Press, 1962), about Poles in Wisconsin; Helen O. Bristol, *Let the Blackbird Sing: A Novel in Verse* (New York: Exposition, 1952); and Monica Krawczyk, *If the Branch Blossoms and Other Stories* (Minneapolis: Polanie, 1950).

On Jewish women, English language fiction written by immigrants includes Abraham Cahan, *Yekl: A Tale of the New York Ghetto* (1896; reprint, New York: Dover, 1970); and the many superb novels and short stories of Anzia Yezierska, such as *Hungry Hearts* (Boston: Houghton Mifflin, 1920), *Children of Loneliness* (New York: Funk and Wagnalls, 1923), *Salome of the Tenements* (New York: Boni and Liveright, 1924); *Bread Givers* (Garden City, N.Y.: Doubleday, 1925); *Arrogant Beggar* (Garden City, N.Y.: Doubleday, 1927), and the semiautobiographical *All I Could Never Be* (N.Y.: Brewer, Warren, and Putnam, 1932). A fictional interpretation of the "uprising of the 20,000," the 1909 dressmakers' strike in New York, can be found in Florence Converse, *The Children of Light* (Boston: Houghton Mifflin, 1912). See also Edna Ferber, *Fanny Herself* (New York: A. Stokes, 1917); Meredith Tax, *Rivington Street* (New York: William Morrow, 1982); and anthologies such as Julia W. Mazow, ed., *The Woman Who Lost Her Names* (San Francisco: Harper and Row, 1980); Joyce Antler, ed., *America and I: Short Stories by American Jewish Women Writers* (Boston: Beacon Press, 1990); and Melanie Kay Kantrowitz and Irena Klepfisz, eds., *The Tribe of Dinah: A Jewish Woman's Anthology* (Montpelier, Vt: Sinister Wisdom Books, 1986).

Fiction—Asian, Latina, and Caribbean

Although Asian women did not immigrate in large numbers until after 1965, these women and their daughters have produced an impressive body of fiction in the United States. For unique insights into Chinese women who rejected assimilation, see a collection of stories by Sui Sin Far (pseud. for

Edith Maud Eaton), *Mrs. Spring Fragrance* (Chicago: A. C. McClurg, 1912). For other fiction by and about Chinese-American women, see Diana Chang, *A Woman of Thirty* (New York: Random House, 1959) and *A Perfect Love* (New York: Jove Books, 1978); Hazel Aia Chun Lin, *The Moon Vow* (New York: Pageant, 1958) and *House of Orchids* (New York: Citadel Press, 1960); and Tai-yi Lin (Anor Lin), *The Golden Coin* (New York: John Day, 1946). Each of these authors published other novels. More recent novels focusing on women include Shirley Lim, *Another Country* (Singapore: Times Books International, 1982); Hualing Nieh, *Mulberry and Peach: Two Women of China* (Boston: Beacon Press, 1988); and the bestselling works of Amy Tan, *The Joy Luck Club* (New York: Putnam, 1989) and *The Kitchen God's Wife* (New York: Putnam, 1992).

Recent Chinese-American poetry includes Diana Chang, *The Horizon Is Definitely Speaking* (Port Jefferson, N.Y.: Backstreet Editions, 1982); Fay Chiang, *In the City of Contradictions* (New York: Sunbury Press, 1979); Shirley Geok-Lin Lim, *Crossing the Peninsula* (Singapore/Hong Kong: Heineman Educational Books, 1980); Kitty Tsui, *The Words of a Woman Who Breathes Fire* (San Francisco: Spinsters Ink, 1983); and Nellie Wong, *Dreams in Harrison Railroad Park* (Berkeley: Kelsey St. Press, 1977) and *The Death of Long Steam Lady* (Los Angeles: West End Press, 1986).

For novels portraying Japanese-American women's lives, see Etsu Inagaki Sugimoto, *A Daughter of the Narikin* (Garden City, N.Y.: Doubleday, 1932), *A Daughter of the Nohfu* (Garden City, N.Y.: Doubleday, 1935), and *Grandmother O Kyo* (Garden City, N.Y.: Doubleday, 1940). Karo Ishiguro describes the life of a Japanese war bride in *A Pale View of Hills* (New York: Penguin Books, 1983). See also Yoshiko Uchida, *The Best Bad Thing* (New York: Atheneum, 1983) and *Picture Bride: A Novel* (Flagstaff, Northland Press, 1987); Joy Kogawa, *Obesan* (Boston: David Godine, 1982); Cynthia Kadohata, *The Floating World* (New York: Ballantine Books, 1989); and by the poet Janice Mirikitani, *Awake in the River* (San Francisco: Isthmus, 1978). For short stories, see Suniti Namjoshi, *Feminist Fables* (Exeter, N.H.: Wheeler, 1984); and Hisaye Yamamoto, *Seven Syllables and Other Stories* (Latham, N.Y.: Kitchen Table/Women of Color Press, 1988).

Japanese-American women's poetry includes older works such as Yone Noguchi, *From the Eastern Sea* (New York: Kenerley, 1910); and June Fujita, *Poems in Exile* (Chicago: Covic, 1923); and new work, such as Janice Mirikitani, *Awake in the River* (San Francisco: Isthmus, 1978) and *Shedding Silence* (Berkeley: Celestial Arts, 1987); Mitsuye Yamada, *Desert Run: Poems and Stories* (Latham. N.Y.: Kitchen Table/Women of Color Press, 1988); and Margaret Tsuda, *Urban River* (Newark: Discovery Books, 1976).

An outstanding novel about Korean immigrant life from a woman's perspective is Kim Ronyoung, *Clay Walls* (Seattle: University of Washington Press, 1987). Korean-American poetry includes Alison Kim, *Mirror Mirror*

(*Woman, Woman*) (Santa Cruz: Dancing Bird Press, 1986); and Chungmi Kim, *Selected Poems* (Anaheim, Calif.: Korean Pioneer Press, 1982). For other Asian-American poetry, see the work of Filipino-American Myrna Peña-Reyes, *The River Singing Stone* (Oreg.: Pacific House, 1983); and Indian-American Angela Lobo-Cobb, *Roots and Restlessness: Poems of Indian History, Change, and Migratory Experience* (Calcutta: Writers Workshop, 1983). Filipino women are portrayed in Linda Ty-Casper, *The Peninsulas* (Manilla: Bookmark, 1964) and *The Secret Runner and Other Stories* (Manilla: Florentino, 1974). Two anthologies of Asian-American women's writing are Shirley Geok-lin Lim, *The Forbidden Stitch* (Corvallis, Oreg.: Calyx Books, 1988); and Unbound Feet (A Chinese American Women Writers' Collective), *Unbound Feet* (San Francisco: Isthmus Press, 1981). For creative writing by Asian-American and Latina women, see Gloria Anzaldua, ed., *Making Face, Making Soul, Haciendo Caras: Creative and Critical Perspectives by Women of Color* (San Francisco: Aunt Lute Foundation, 1990). See also Dexter Fisher, *The Third Woman: Minority Women Writers of the United States* (Boston: Houghton Mifflin, 1980).

There has been an explosion of writing by Chicanas in the past two decades, much of it exploring the intersection of gender and ethnicity. Acclaimed Chicana novels of recent years include the autobiographical work by Gina Valdes, *There Are No Madmen Here* (San Diego: Maize Press, 1981); Estela Portillo Trembley, *Trini* (Binghamton, N.Y.: Bilingual Press, 1986), about a woman who immigrates from Mexico illegally to give birth in the United States; Ana Castillo, *The Mexquiahuala Letters* (Binghamton, N.Y.: Bilingual Press, 1986), an innovative novel in the form of letters between two women, a poet and an artist; and Roberta Fernandez, *Intaglio: A Novel in Six Stories* (Houston: Arte Publico Press, 1990). Short story collections include Sandra Cisneros, *The House on Mango Street* (Houston: Arte Publico Press, 1983) and *Woman Hollering Creek* (New York: Random House, 1991); and Helena Maria Viramontes, *The Moths and Other Stories* (Houston: Arte Publico Press, 1985). An anthology of short stories by Chicanas, Puerto Ricans, and other Latinas is Alma Gomez, Cherrie Moraga, and Mariana Romo-Carmona, *Cuertos: Stories by Latinas* (New York: Kitchen Table/Women of Color Press, 1983). See also Evangelina Vigil, ed., *Woman of Her Word: Hispanic Women Write* (Houston: Arte Publico Press, 1983).

Poets who write in English about gender and ethnic issues and the often harsh realities of Chicanas' lives include Lorna Cervantes, *Emplumada* (Pittsburgh, University of Pittsburgh Press, 1981); Ama Villanueva, *Bloodroot* (Austin: Place of Herons Press, 1977) and *Mother, May I* (Pittsburgh: Motheroot Publications, 1978); and Bernice Zamora, *Restless Serpents* (Menlo Park, Calif.: Diseños Literarios, 1976).

Literature by first- and second-generation women from the Caribbean includes Jamaican-born Opal Palmer Adisa, *Bake Face and Other Guava Sto-*

ries (Kelsey St. Press, 1986); Julia Alvarez, *How the Garcia Girls Lost Their Accents* (Chapel Hill, N.C.: Algonquin Books of Chapel Hill, 1991); and *Getting Home Alive*, a unique combination of prose and poetry written jointly by a mother and daughter of Jewish and Puerto Rican background, Aurora Levins Morales and Rosario Morales (Ithaca, N.Y.: Firebrand Books, 1986). Perhaps the most widely acclaimed works by a second-generation Caribbean woman are Paule Marshall's novels *Brown Girl, Brownstones* (New York: Random House, 1959) and *Daughters* (New York: Atheneum, 1991). See also her short story collection, *Reena and Other Stories* (City University of New York, Feminist Press, 1983).

Critical works dealing wholly or in part with ethnic women's writings include Elain H. Kim, *Asian American Literature: An Introduction to the Writings and Their Social Context* (Philadelphia: Temple University Press, 1982); Mary V. Dearborn, *Pocahontas's Daughters: Gender and Ethnicity in American Culture* (New York and Oxford: Oxford University Press, 1986), which includes material on European-American, African-American, and native American writers; Annette Atkins, "Women on the Farming Frontier: The View from Fiction," *The Midwest Review*, 2nd series, 3 (Spring 1981): 1–10; Daniel J. Casey and Robert Rhoades, eds., *Irish-American Fiction, Essays in Criticism* (New York: AMS Press, 1979); J. R. Christianson, "Literary Traditions of Norwegian-American Women," in *Makers of an American Immigrant Legacy,* ed. Odd S. Lovell (Northfield, Minn,; Norwegian-American Historical Association, 1980); Norma F. Pratt, "Culture and Radical Politics: Yiddish Women Writers in America, 1890–1940," *American Jewish History* (September 1980): 68–90; Sonya Michel, "Mothers and Daughters in American Jewish Literature: The Rotted Cord," in *The Jewish Woman: New Perspectives,* ed. Elizabeth Koltun (New York: Schocken Books, 1976), pp. 272–82; and Mariolina Salvatori, "Women's Work in Novels of Immigrant Life," *Melus* 9 (Winter 1982): 39–58.

For Further Research: Bibliographies

There are two comprehensive bibliographies: Francesco Cordasco, *The Immigrant Woman in North America: An Annotated Bibliography of Selected References* (Metuchen, N.J.: Scarecrow Press, 1985); and more recent and more comprehensive, Donna Gabaccia, *Immigrant Women in the United States: A Selectively Annotated Multidisciplinary Bibliography* (Westport, Conn.: Greenwood, 1989).

Bibliographies on women of specific ethnic backgrounds include Betty Boyd Caroli, "Italian Women in America: Sources for Study," *Italian Americana* 2 (1976): 242–54; Aviva Cantor, *The Jewish Woman, 1900–1980: A Bibliography* (Fresh Meadows, N.Y.: Biblio Press, 1981); Ellen S. Ellwell and Edward R. Levenson, eds., *The Jewish Women's Studies Guide* (Fresh Meadows, N.Y.: Biblio Press, 1982); Catherine Loeb, "La Chicana: A Biblio-graphic Survey," *Frontiers* 5 (Summer 1980): 59–64; Martha Cotera, *Latina Sourcebook: Bibliography of Mexican American, Cuban, Puerto Rican and Other Hispanic Women Materials in the U.S.* (Austin, Tex.: Information Systems Development, 1982), which lists unpublished and pamphlet materials; Lyn K. Stoner, *Latinas of the Americas: A Source Book* (New York: Garland, 1988); Mary L. Doi, et al., *Pacific/Asian American Research: An Annotated Bibliography*, Bibliographical Series no. 1 (Chicago: Pacific/Asian American Mental Health Research Center, 1981); Alice Y Chai, "Toward a Holistic Paradigm for Asian American Women's Studies," *Women's Studies International Forum* 8, no. 1 (1985): 59–66; and Elizabeth Jameson, "Toward a Multicultural History of Women in the Western United States," *Signs* 13 (Summer 1988): 761–91, which reviews the literature on Mexican-American, Chinese-American, and Japanese-American women.

Many bibliographies that do not deal directly with immigrant women contain much valuable material about them. Especially useful are Rosemary Brana-Shute and Rosemarijn Hoefte, *A Bibliography of Caribbean Migration and Caribbean Immigrant Communities* (Gainesville: University of Florida Libraries in cooperation with the Center for Latin American Studies, 1983); Carol Fairbanks and Sara B. Sundberg, *Farm Women on the Prairie Frontier: A Sourcebook for Canada and the United States* (Metuchen, N.J., and London: Scarecrow Press, 1983); Susan Kennedy, *America's White Working Class Women: A Historical Bibliography* (New York and London: Garland, 1981); Martha J. Soltow, et al., *Women in American Labor History, 1825–1935: An Annotated Bibliography*, (Lansing, Mich.: Michigan State University, School of Labor and Industrial Relations, 1973); Evangline Thomas, *Women Religious History Sources: A Guide to Repositories in the United States* (New York and London: R. R. Bowker, 1983); Catherine H. Kerst, *Ethnic Folklife Dissertations from the United States and Canada, 1960–1980: A Selected and Annotated Bibliography* (Washington, D.C.: American Folklife Center, Library of Congress, 1985); James C. Holte, *The Ethnic I: A Sourcebook for Ethnic-American Autobiography* (New York: Greenwood, 1988); Babette Inglehart and Anthony Mangione, *The Image of Pluralism in American Literature: The American Experience of European Ethnic Groups* (New York: American Jewish Committee Institute on Pluralism and Group Identity, 1974); and Maryann Oshana, *Women of Color: Filmography of Minority and Third World Women* (New York: Garland, 1985).

As this essay demonstrates, material about immigrant women can be found in past and current periodical literature of many disciplines—history, women's studies, American studies, ethnic studies, education, sociology, psychology, anthropology, literature, and others. Statistical data can be found in the reports of the Commissioner of Immigration (annual since 1820) and the Census (every ten years). Especially useful are Census reports such as E. P. Hutchinson, *Immigrants and Their Children, 1850–1950* (New York: Wiley, 1956), with data on employment and social mobility. Also useful are the reports of state and national commissions on immigration, including the forty-two volume *Report of the Immigration Commission, 1909–1911*. Though biased against southern and eastern European immigrants, this voluminous study contains a wealth of data on education, employment, crime, prostitution, charity, housing, and other subjects, much of which is categorized by gender as well as ethnic group. Finally, much information awaits the resourceful investigator in local and regional archives; in the ethnic press; in the papers of charities, unions, churches, hospitals, and ethnic and women's organizations, and in the recollections of immigrant women themselves.

Index

Abbott, Grace, 141, 219
Abolitionism, 30, 257, 270
Abortion, 132, 305, 260
Acculturation: of Jewish women, 190;
and marriage, 129–131; of Mexican
women, 240–241; in Pittsburgh, 65–69;
of Polish women, 62–67; of second
and third generations, 297–307, of
Syrian women, 145–149. *See also*
Americanization
Addams, Jane, 259
Adult education, 206–210, 220–222, 225.
See also Americanization
African Americans. *See* black immigrants
Agriculture, women in, 16, 17, 57, 87–88,
95–98
Aid to Dependent Children, 179, 298
Alessandro, Antonietta Pisanelli, 177
Amalgamated Clothing Workers of
America, 287
Americanization: and community agencies,
178–181, 191, 196–199, 206–210; of
Koreans, 206–210; in night schools,
220–222; in public schools, 5–6, 217–218;
of Vietnamese, 248–251. *See also*
Acculturation
Anarchism, 255, 258
Anderson, Mary, 19
Andrade, Flores de, 19
Angel Island, 18
Anthony, Susan B., 192, 257
Antin, Mary, 220
Antisemitism, 16, 35–39, 338. *See also* Dis-
crimination; Prejudice
Anzaldua, Gloria Evangelina, 162, 198
Arab immigrants, 145–149, 175. *See also*
Syrian immigrants
Argentinian immigrants, 223
Armenians, 16
Asian immigrants 3, 9, 85, 122, 208, 223,
260, 337–340. *See also* Cambodian;

Chinese; Japanese; Korean; Mien; Paki-
stani; Southeast Asian; South Asian;
Vietnamese
Asian Indian Women's Network of Los An-
geles, 176
Austrian immigrants, 143–144
At the End of the Sante Fe Trail, 267

Baca, Judy, 180, 181
Barbados, 14, 174, 260
Barry, Leonora Kearney, 262
Beard, Mary, 284
Beautiful Senoritas, 124
Beauvoir, Simone de, 8
Beggars' Soap Opera, The, 124
Berger, Meta, 258
Berkman, Alexander (Sasha), 273
Biculturalism, 243
Bilingualism, 223, 243
Birth control, 132, 154, 258, 273–275
Birthrate, 132–133, 303
Black immigrants, 14, 86, 162–163, 214. *See
also* Barbados; Caribbean immigrants;
Haitian immigrants; Jamaican immigrants;
West Indian immigrants
Black nationalism, 261, 285–287
Blackwell, Elizabeth, 99, 100
Blackwell, Emily, 99, 100
Blast, The, 277
Blegen, Theodore, 87
Boat people, 18, 41–43
Boarders, 89, 107, 118, 129, 141
Bohemian (Czech) immigrants: family life,
109, 142; work, 86, 89; social activists,
259, 262
Boltanica, 124
Booth, Mary L., 99
Boston Society for the Prevention of Pauper-
ism, 5
Bread Givers, 2, 173
Breckinridge, Sophonisba P., 103

371